First among Abbots

First among Abbots

THE CAREER OF
ABBO OF FLEURY

Elizabeth Dachowski

The Catholic University of America Press
WASHINGTON, D.C.

Copyright © 2008
The Catholic University of America Press
All rights reserved
Printed in the United States of America

The paper used in this publication meets the minimum requirements
of American National Standards for Information Science—
Permanence of Paper for Printed Library Materials, ANSI Z39.48-1984.
∞

LIBRARY OF CONGRESS CATALOGING-IN-PUBLICATION DATA
Dachowski, Elizabeth.
First among abbots : the career of Abbo of Fleury
/ by Elizabeth Dachowski.
p. cm.
Includes bibliographical references and index.
ISBN 978-0-8132-1510-5 (cloth : alk. paper)
ISBN 978-0-8132-2617-0 (pbk. : alk. paper)
1. Abbo, of Fleury, Saint, ca. 945–1004.   I. Title.
BX4700.A23D33 2008
271′.102—dc22   2007015490
[B]

CONTENTS

Acknowledgments	vii
Abbreviations	xi
Map of Abbo's World	xiii
1. Introduction	1
2. The Making of a Monk	23
3. The Making of an Abbot	57
4. Regional Politics	82
5. Royal Politics	125
6. Papal Politics	151
7. Monastic Politics	189
8. The Making of a Martyr	232
9. Conclusion	253
Chronology of Abbo's Life and Times	269
Bibliography	273
Index	287

ACKNOWLEDGMENTS

My interest in Abbo of Fleury began in Bernard S. Bachrach's graduate course at the University of Minnesota on medieval Latin historians, when he handed me a photocopy of the *Vita sancti Abbonis* from the edition in the *Patrologia Latina*. As a result, I have been living and working with Abbo of Fleury for more than twenty years. My first thanks go to Bernie for setting me on the road to "Abbo studies" and supporting me with his suggestions and comments along the way. Since this is my first book, however, I wish to go back further and acknowledge all the people and institutions that contributed to making me a medievalist.

My parents, Meg and Larry Dachowski, brought me up in a house full of books and encouraged my childhood obsession with all things medieval, never dreaming that I would not outgrow it. I would also like to thank the New Orleans Public School System. While there was and is much that needs improvement in public education in New Orleans, even before the devastation of Hurricane Katrina, there were some excellent schools within the system, including the three I attended, Robert M. Lusher Elementary School, Eleanor McMain Middle School, and Benjamin Franklin Senior High School. Among all the good teachers I had over the years, a few stand out as extraordinary. My sixth-grade teacher, Miss Houston, whose first name I never knew, ran a wonderful classroom where children learned to work at their own pace and where she helped them explore the world of literature. In high school I learned my first Latin with Dr. Amelia Clarke, studied French with Rosemary Eddy and Julia Schueler, and picked up some Italian and Russian with Anthony Parisi. My English teacher, Fleur Simmons, instilled in me the desire for exactitude in speaking and writing, and my history teacher, Diego Gonzalez-Grande, introduced me to the concept of changing historiography through his lecture on Reconstruction.

As an undergraduate at Indiana University, I benefited from the Center for Medieval Studies, ably run by Emanuel Mickel, and particularly remember classes and advice from Barbara A. Hanawalt and C. Clifford Flanigan. At the University of Minnesota, the following professors were of great help in forming me as a medieval historian in general and in my work on Abbo of Fleury: Bernard S. Bachrach, Barbara A. Hanawalt, James D. Tracy, and Oliver P. Nicholson.

Over the years, I have received much support from the interlibrary loan departments of libraries at the University of Minnesota, Lock Haven University in Pennsylvania, Auburn University, and most recently Tennessee State University, under the auspices of Barbara Vanhooser. I am grateful to the National Endowment for the Humanities for allowing me to participate in a summer seminar at the British Library, "Anglo-Saxon Manuscripts and Texts," taught by Paul Szarmach and Timothy Graham, and to the Newberry Library for the opportunity to participate in a summer institute, "French Archival Sciences and the *Ancien Régime.*" Fordham University graciously awarded me a postdoctoral fellowship in medieval studies, which allowed me use of their wonderful library of printed texts as well as contacts within a supportive community of faculty and students. The University of Minnesota has aided me at every step of my journey, beginning with a university fellowship at the beginning of my graduate career, followed by a grant from the Graduate School and the Minneapolis Foundation–Frances E. Andrews–Hunt Fund for research abroad, and finally a Department of History Endowed Fellowship. While abroad, I received a kind welcome and ready assistance at the fol-

Acknowledgments

lowing libraries and archives: the British Library in London, the Bibliothèque nationale in Paris, the Bibliothèque municipale of Orléans, the Archives départemantales of the Loiret, the Bibliothèque municipale of Dijon, and the library of the Faculté de médecine at Montpellier.

Several people have helped me greatly by reading and commenting on early versions of this work. Amy Livingstone and Steven Fanning provided helpful substantive comments on the text of the manuscript. Members of the Friends of the Saints in New York City and the English department's Medieval Subgroup at the University of Minnesota have given me encouragement and feedback on oral presentations of my research into Abbo's career. My graduate school colleagues Jill Keen, Pat Price, Shari Horner, Gloria Betcher, and Steve Alvin gave constant reassurances that my work on Abbo did indeed have a future as well as useful suggestions about how to shape my narrative.

I would like to thank David McGonagle, Theresa Walker, Elizabeth Benvenides, and Robin DuBlanc at the Catholic University of America Press. Between them, they have made the process of taking my work from typescript to published book as smooth and painless (for the author at least) as possible.

This work would not have been possible without friends and family who encouraged and supported me along the way. I would like to thank my high school friends Anne and Mary Poole, Sally Peyrefitte Firestone, and Laurie Blum as well as my New Orleans neighbors Betty and Manny Alessandra for their encouragement. Of my Bloomington, Indiana, friends, special notice should go to Carol Ormond, Ian Andrew Engle, Celeste Land, and Polly Lin. I was blessed in Pennsylvania with remarkable friends and colleagues, including Karen and Paul Harvey, Janet Irons, Al Thurman, Chris and Carol Hill, John Washburn, and Laird and Svitlana Jones. I regret that two of my Pennsylvania colleagues, Frank Perna and Alan Golden, did not live to share my joy in publishing Abbo. Among my friends in Nashville, I want to thank Joel Dark, Lynetta Alexander, Erik Schmeller, and Jenny Frampton for their support during the final phases of this project. A special thanks goes to the Paraléjo family of Orléans, Joséph, Maria, Soraya, and Sébastien, who made me feel at home in the heart of their family while I was doing my research in French archives.

Most especially, I want to thank my husband, John Miglietta, who always believed in me and never tried to dissuade me from buying a book that I really wanted. John and I both want to thank our dog, Flash, for reminding us that sometimes we just need to get up from our desks and go for a walk.

ABBREVIATIONS

AASS Bolland, Jean, Jean Carnandet, et al., eds. *Acta Sanctorum quotquot toto orbe coluntur.* Paris/Rome, 1643–.

Abbo, *Apologeticus* Abbo of Fleury. *Liber apologeticus.* London, BL 10972, ff. 15v–22v. Most readily available edition of text is *PL* 139:461–72.

Abbo, *Collectio canonum* Abbo of Fleury. *Collectio canonum.* Paris BN lat. 2400, ff. 154–163r, 172v–173r, 183r. Most readily available edition of text is *PL* 139:473–508.

Abbo, letters 1–14 Abbo of Fleury. *Epistolae.* London, BL 10972, ff. 1r–15r, 23r–33v. Numbers of letters in text correspond to numbers in *PL* 139:419–61.

Aimoinus, *VsA* Aimoinus of Fleury. *Vita sancti Abbonis.* Ed. and trans. Robert-Henri Bautier and Gillette Labory. In *L'Abbaye de Fleury en l'an mil.* Source d'histoire médiévale. Paris: Centre national de la recherche scientifique, 2004.

BL British Library

BN Bibliothèque nationale

GC Gallia Christiana in provincias ecclesiasticas distributa. Paris, 1715–1865.

Lattin Gerbert of Aurillac. *The Letters of Gerbert with his Papal Privileges as Sylvester II.* Ed. and trans. Harriet Pratt Lattin. New York: Columbia University Press, 1961.

MGH Monumenta Germaniae historica

Abbreviations

MGH SS   Monumenta Germaniae historica. Scriptores. Ed. Georg Heinrich Pertz et al. 1826–.

MsB   Eugène de Certain, ed. *Les miracles de Saint Benoît écrits par Adrevald, Aimoin, André, Raoul Tortaire et Hugues de Sainte Marie, moines de Fleury.* Paris: Mme. Ve. Jules Renouard, 1858.

PL   Migne, J.-P., ed. *Patrologiae cursus completus . . . series Latina.* 221 vols. Paris, 1841–1864.

Weigle   Gerbert of Aurillac. *Die Briefsammlung Gerberts von Reims.* Ed. Fritz Weigle. MGH Die Briefe der Deutschen Kaiserzeit 2. [Berlin: Weidmannsche Verlagsbuchhandlung, 1966].

MAP OF ABBO'S WORLD

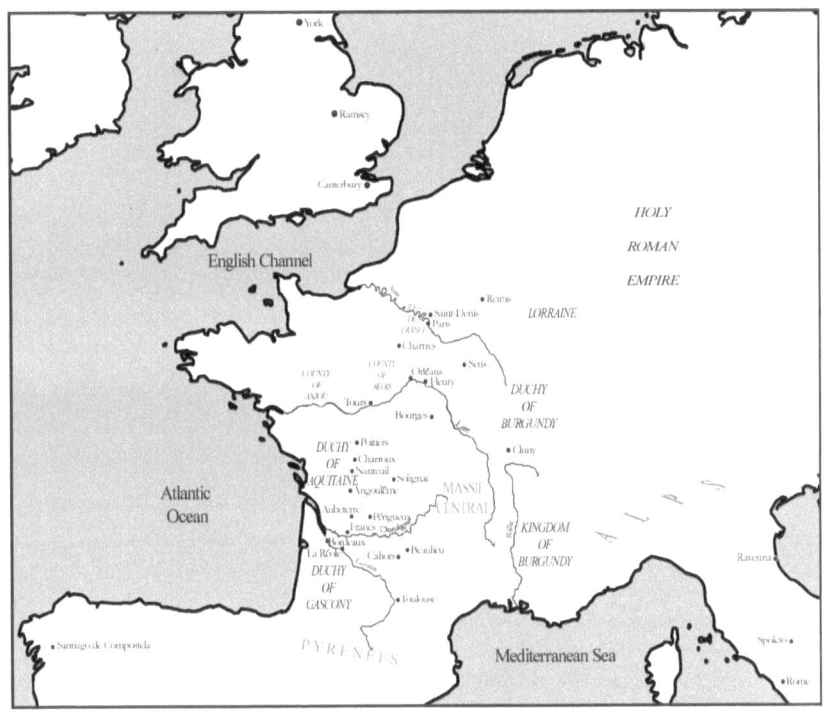

First among Abbots

I

INTRODUCTION

AT THE BEGINNING of December 1004, monks from all over France began to arrive at the monastery of Fleury on the banks of the Loire River in anticipation of an important festival in the monastic calendar.¹ On 4 December the monks of Fleury would celebrate the anniversary of the translation of the relics of St. Benedict of Nursia to their present location in the monastery's church of Notre Dame. The ceremony was to begin with a vigil on 3 December, the eve of Benedict's translation, followed by a procession on 4 December. This would be an opportunity to be near the bones of the holy man, which the monks of Fleury claimed to have rescued from obscurity at the ruined monastery of Monte Cassino more than a century earlier. The festival would also be a time for visiting, hearing the news of far-off monasteries, and renewing acquaintances between abbots, teachers, and students. The host of this event, Abbot Abbo of Fleury, was well known to all, if only by reputation. Abbo had become abbot of Fleury at a difficult time, amid controversy within Fleury and po-

---

1. The problem of what to call the place where Abbo lived and died is a thorny one. Here the term *France* refers to the area that roughly corresponds to the modern country of France. Whenever possible, however, I will use the term *Francia* to refer to the former kingdom of Charlemagne (heirs of Charles the Bald) and *West Francia* to refer to the political entity ruled by the later Carolingians and the first Capetians.

litical change outside of the monastery. In the sixteen years of his abbacy he had made a name for himself in the monastic world. He had spoken out at Church councils, stood up to kings, bishops, and popes when monastic rights were threatened, written letters of advice (sometimes friendly but often admonitory) to his fellow abbots, administered Fleury's far-flung priories and landholdings, and overseen the flourishing school of Fleury, while still finding time for his own scholarly pursuits. Even those who had never met Abbo knew him by reputation as a graying but still robust man who took his duties seriously but was also notable for his ready wit and substantial girth. Of those who knew him personally, some had not seen Abbo since the previous year, while others had perhaps taken leave of him as recently as the preceding October. Abbo's fellow abbot Odilo of Cluny may have just recently received a letter written by Abbo at Poitiers on 1 November. Their surprise and dismay must have been great when they found the monks of Fleury not in a mood of joyful celebration but in mourning for their abbot. Probably no more than a day or two before the feast, a handful of Fleurisian monks had returned from Fleury's Gascon priory of La Réole with devastating news for the congregation. Abbo had been killed in a riot while trying to enforce the monastic rule at La Réole.[2]

The news of his dramatic death marked the beginning of the retelling of Abbo's life. Almost immediately, Abbo's former associates began trying to make sense of his life and death. Hervé, the treasurer of Saint-Martin of Tours and a former student at Fleury, lost no time in commissioning a biography of Abbo. His choice for biographer was Aimoinus, a monk of Fleury and noted writer of historical and hagiographical texts as well as one of Abbo's companions on his final journey. The task facing Aimoinus as well as Abbo's subsequent chroniclers was how to integrate the various

---

2. Aimoinus, *VsA*, c. 21, states that the monks remained at Abbo's tomb for four days, then stayed two days with a member of the local nobility before heading north. Since on their southward journey they had taken a week to travel from Poitiers to La Réole and probably another week from Fleury to Poitiers, they probably needed two weeks to return to Fleury, arriving between 2 December and 4 December.

Introduction 3

aspects of Abbo's career into a coherent whole. For Aimoinus the task was made easier by the circumstances of Abbo's death. The Fleurisian monks were quick to proclaim him a martyr, and as such subsequent generations would remember him primarily for his heroic death, although proofs of a worthy life would also be necessary to include in a work of hagiography. Although Aimoinus discussed almost all of Abbo's major accomplishments, whether administrative, political, or scholarly, his primary focus was Abbo's death, and he avoided the most controversial moments in his subject's life. A thousand years later Aimoinus of Fleury's *Vita sancti Abbonis*, though problematic, shapes our understanding of Abbo's life, providing a framework within which to understand the relatively sparse remains of his life, as preserved in letters, charters, and Abbo's own literary and scientific works. While providing a picture of Abbo as he might have wished to be remembered, at the peak of his influence on behalf of Fleury, Aimoinus leaves it to the modern historian to trace his evolution from the uncertainty of his abbacy's first years through numerous confrontations with secular authorities on Fleury's behalf to his eventual elevation of Fleury to the position of leading monastery of Gaul.

Aimoinus's credentials as Abbo's biographer are impeccable. As a monk of Fleury and former pupil of Abbo, he was an eyewitness to many of the most important events of Abbo's life, including Abbo's last journey. Additionally, Aimoinus had ready access to oral and written sources of information for those events that he did not witness himself. Aimoinus had a critical mind and had been quick to point out discrepancies between diplomatic sources and oral tradition in his contributions to the *Miracula sancti Benedicti*.[3] He was also a scholar and an elegant, if somewhat affected, writer.[4] Although not without biases, his work is, because of his position as

3. Robert-Henri Bautier, "La place de Fleury dans l'historiographie française du IXe au XIIe siècle," in *Etudes ligériennes d'histoire et d'archéologie médiévales*, mémoires et exposées présentés à la Semaine d'études médiévales de Saint-Benoît-sur-Loire, 3–10 July 1969, ed. René Louis, publication de la Société de fouilles archéologiques et des monuments historiques de l'Yonne (Paris: Clavreuil, 1975), 28.
4. See Christine Le Stum, "L'*Historia Francorum* d'Aimoinus de Fleury: Etude et

friend and student, a valuable source for Abbo's life. Aimoinus did not outlive his abbot by more than about five years, and so must have written the *Vita sancti Abbonis* while Abbo's memory was still fresh in his mind and that of the other monks of Fleury.[5]

Although modern historians are tempted to regard Aimoinus primarily as Abbo's historian or biographer, his writing actually falls into the medieval genre of hagiography. Hervé, treasurer of the important monastery of Saint-Martin of Tours and former pupil of Abbo, had commissioned the life, which was to be a work for posterity and for the praise of God as well as a tribute to the saintly Abbo from those who knew and loved him.[6] As a hagiographer, Aimoinus's main task was to present evidence for Abbo's saintly character and put his life in a familiar and understandable framework. Abbo's monastic career and Aimoinus's own monastic profession meant that this work would emphasize the monastic virtues of chastity and humble obedience in Abbo's life. Aimoinus did not, however, hide Abbo's more militant side, his strident defense of monastic rights in the face of challenges from kings, bishops, and unruly monks, such as his assassins at La Réole. In fact, his *Vita* of Abbo is almost as much a martyrology, an account of a martyrdom, as a hagiography, an account of a saintly life. Aimoinus began his work with a justification for considering Abbo a martyr, even though his death was in the cause of monastic reform rather than missionary activity.[7] Nearly one-third of his *Vita sancti Abbonis* concerns the weeks leading up to Abbo's death, with an emphasis on both Abbo's understanding of the danger he faced and his calmness and faith in the face of that danger.

édition critique," positions des thèses (Paris: Ecole de Chartes, 1976), 91, for a critique of his language in his *Historia Francorum*.

5. Alexandre Vidier, *L'historiographie à Saint-Benoît-sur-Loire et les miracles de saint Benoît* (Paris: A. et J. Picard, 1965), 93–94, gives the date of Aimoinus's death as after 1008, but Joseph L. Strayer. ed., *Dictionary of the Middle Ages* (New York: Scribner, 1982–1989), gives it as after 1010.

6. See "Epistola Aimoini Floriacensis monachi ad Herveum s. Martini thesaurarium," preface to Aimoinus, *VsA*.

7. Pierre Riché, *Abbon de Fleury: Un moine savant et combatif (vers 950–1004)* (Turnhout, Belgium: Brepols, 2004), 266–68, discusses Abbo's claim to martyrdom.

Medieval hagiographers, and Aimoinus was no exception, used their works to do more than simply present a portrait of a holy man or woman. As a monk of Fleury, someone intimately involved in the monastery's political and economic struggles, Aimoinus had a partisan agenda. His overriding goal was the glorification of Fleury, whose reputation would grow with the addition of each saint to the ranks of its monks and abbots. Aimoinus portrayed Abbo as learned, patient, and calm in the face of death, but Abbo's saintly qualities were not, apparently, obvious to everyone. In many passages, Aimoinus went to great lengths to defend Abbo (frequently using Abbo's own words) from criticisms, potential or actual, ranging from insinuations of gluttony to charges of heresy. In addition to stressing Abbo's sanctity, Aimoinus lost no opportunity to remind his readers that Fleury was also blessed with the earthly remains of St. Benedict. Aimoinus also had the narrower goal of bringing La Réole (the priory in Gascony where Abbo died) firmly under Fleurisian control and justifying the activities of Fleury at La Réole. The structure of the *Vita* makes this clear. Out of twenty-one chapters, six are devoted to Abbo's final journey to La Réole and his death there (a period of a few weeks out of an abbacy of at least sixteen years). This emphasis was essential to claiming Abbo as a martyr. Aimoinus's tone in these chapters places the guilt for Abbo's death on the recalcitrant, even barbarous monks of La Réole. By promoting Abbo's tomb as a local shrine, Aimoinus could hope to bring the formerly rebellious Gascon monks and townspeople more firmly within Fleury's orbit. If the cult had achieved local popularity, Abbo's glory would cast his murderers in the role of offenders against God as well as man and possibly discourage similar revolts. Aimoinus appended an account of several miracles that occurred after Abbo's death, which suggests an organized effort to establish the abbot's cult at La Réole.[8] If a larger cult of Abbo were to arise in Europe,

---

8. The only miracles recorded are the five appended to the *Vita sancti Abbonis* by Aimoinus himself. Since Aimoinus died, at the latest, in 1010 (just six years after Abbo's death), the cult, if it existed, was short lived. Anselme Davril finds limited evi-

La Réole could have reaped the economic advantages of being a pilgrimage site and thus would have tied itself more closely still to Fleury as Abbo's center of activity.[9] By arguing for Abbo's sanctity, Aimoinus, by implication, justified the actions of Fleury with respect to La Réole while promising benefits to the La Réolais from the success of the cult.

Aimoinus's dual goals of glorifying Abbo and Fleury and encouraging peace between Fleury and its neighbors and dependents meant that he minimized conflict in Abbo's all too contentious life. Aimoinus glossed over, as much as possible, the internal dissensions at Fleury, though events were too recent for him to omit the most notorious clashes completely. He contradicted rumors of dissension between Abbo and his predecessor, Oylbold, and muted the significance of opposition to Abbo's election.[10] He completely omitted any reference to the monastic disputes chronicled in Abbo's letters, including the terrible Frederick whom Abbo expelled from Fleury and regarded as a fomenter of heresy.[11] Gerbert of Aurillac, later Pope Sylvester II, received no mention at all in the *Vita,* despite Gerbert's clash with Abbo at the Council of Saint-Basle. Political tensions also disappear in Aimoinus's account of Abbo's life. Abbo's successor as abbot, Gauzlin, had close ties to King Robert the Pious, and was even rumored to be Robert's illegitimate brother. Under this new regime, Fleury had become a major center for royal propaganda, so it is not surprising that Abbo's early conflict with the newly

---

dence for the persistence of a liturgical cult as late as the time of Mabillon (Davril, "Le culte de saint Abbon au Moyen Age," in *Actes du Colloque du millénaire de la fondation du prieuré de La Réole,* La Réole, 11–12 November 1978 [Bordeaux: Société des bibliophiles de Guyenne, 1980], 143–58).

9. The cult of Abbo does not appear to have ever had a wide following. It was not incorporated into the liturgy at Fleury until the twelfth century, and even then only in a minor way. A seventeenth-century work describes a lost liturgical document from La Réole but does not mention Abbo. A liturgical cult of Abbo at La Réole is dubious, although a popular cult is possible and more in keeping with the character of the miracles described by Aimoinus, which do not, for the most part, involve monks (Davril, "Le culte de saint Abbon").

10. Aimoinus, *VsAs,* c. 6.

11. Abbo, letter 8.

founded Capetian dynasty is only hinted at. Dissension between bishops and abbots also had become less important by the early eleventh century than it had been in the 980s. After describing the murderous attack on Abbo by the retainers of the bishop of Orléans, Aimoinus very evenhandedly added that apart from this one incident the bishop always behaved very honorably.[12] Instead, Aimoinus emphasized the subsequent development of more cordial relations between Abbo and Robert the Pious. Aimoinus's vilification of Abbo's Gascon murderers also supports the Capetian political agenda, as he portrays the Gascons as being wild and ungovernable and in need of strong royal leadership.

Though the peculiarities of the *Vita sancti Abbonis* require the historian to exercise care in its use, it is still the single most valuable source for Abbo's life. Since the author was a monk of Fleury with access to the monastery's records and one of Abbo's former pupils, he had available more information on Abbo's life and character than any historian since. As an eyewitness to Abbo's final weeks, Aimoinus comes closer to his subject's thought and actions than most biographers and hagiographers. Even when he paints too rosy a picture of Abbo and his monastery, this picture represents at least in part the face that Abbo would have wished to present to the world. Omissions or outright falsifications in the *Vita sancti Abbonis* are themselves indicative of the state of the monastery and the political agenda of one of its most learned and influential monks at Abbo's death. The real danger in relying too heavily on Aimoinus's account lies not in his depiction of the details of Abbo's life but in the temptation to adopt his broader organization, which preserves a discreet silence on the early tumultuous years of Abbo's abbacy and which creates a false distinction between his scholarly, administrative, and political agendas.

Aimoinus's propaganda effort was stunningly effective in shaping later narratives of Abbo's life. Apart from Aimoinus, few have attempted a comprehensive overview of Abbo's life, and they have

---

12. Aimoinus, *VsA*, c. 8: "cum in reliquis actibus suis, honestis semper se demonstraret pollere moribus."

relied heavily on Aimoinus for both organization and interpretation. The cult of Abbo was largely neglected until the seventeenth century, though his writings began to attract study by humanists in the later sixteenth century.[13] In the nineteenth century, however, the retelling of Abbo's life took on a new vigor. The Abbé Pardiac wrote a detailed, but largely hagiographical, biography of Abbo, and the *Month* (a Catholic periodical) published an anonymous study of Abbo's life that relied heavily on Pardiac's work.[14] Pardiac's study was part of a larger effort on the part of the archbishop of Bordeaux, Cardinal Donnet (1836–1882), to revive the cults of indigenous saints in his archdiocese. The cult of Abbo had survived at Fleury and at La Réole into the eighteenth century but barely withstood the destruction of his shrine during the French Wars of Religion and finally disappeared in the face of the anticlericalism of the French Revolution. Cardinal Donnet entrusted the resurrection of the cult to Pardiac.[15] The anonymous article in the *Month* was a defense of the Catholic Church against charges of harboring superstition and fomenting panic at the approach of the millennium. Abbo appears in this account as a rational and pious figure who used his extensive learning to repress foolish superstitions, namely, the fear of the millennium, among the ignorant masses. Both Pardiac and the anonymous writer for the *Month* had religious motives for writing, which did not preclude a full critical analysis of the sources, but neither did their agenda encourage a detailed evaluation of the exact chronology of Abbo's life, something made difficult by the nature and survival of the tenth-century sources, nor an examination of his political evolution.

The twentieth century saw the restoration of the monastic

13. Riché, *Abbon de Fleury*, 270–272.
14. Jean-Baptiste Pardiac, *Histoire de saint Abbon, abbé de Fleury-sur-Loire, martyr à La Réole en 1004* (Paris, 1872); "Studies in Biography II: An Abbot of the Tenth Century," *Month and Catholic Review* (January–April 1874), 163–77 and (May–August 1874), 28–42. Near the end of the article, the author acknowledges that Pardiac is "the writer of whose work we have made continual use" (41).
15. Charles Teisseyre, "Le renouveau du culte de saint Abbon à La Réole au XIXe siècle," in *Actes du Colloque du millénaire de la fondation du prieuré de La Réole*, La Réole, 11–12 November 1978 (Bordeaux: Société des bibliophiles de Guyenne, 1980), 231.

Introduction 9

community at Saint-Benoît-sur-Loire, the site of Abbo's monastery at Fleury, and with it another biography of Abbo. Patrice Cousin justified his replacement of Pardiac's work as follows: "The length of the work [Pardiac's biography], the style—pseudo-classical, pompous, and vague—the lack of critical faculty, and its long unavailability from the publisher make it dull reading and its replacement desirable."[16] Cousin's work rectified some of these problems, but his study still leaves much to be desired. His work is shorter, more clearly written, less digressive, and less overtly hagiographical than Pardiac's, but is still insufficiently critical of the sources, and, like Pardiac's, has fallen out of print. Close examination of his text indicates that his narrative is almost entirely a point-by-point summary (and often a word-for-word translation) of the published sources for Abbo's life. The result is that he is too apt to take the statements of the sources at face value and seldom considers the wider implications of their assertions in the context of medieval French history. Cousin's method of composition results in a topical, rather than a strictly chronological, treatment of Abbo's life. This, in turn, has led him to portray Abbo as a static figure, one who did not learn from experience or mature as a person or as a monk. Furthermore, this approach prevents an appreciation of how the various aspects of Abbo's life were related to each other. Finally, since Cousin's main purpose in writing a biography of Abbo was to celebrate the newly restored monastery of Saint-Benoît-sur-Loire, the work is parochial in scope and adds little to our understanding of Abbo's contributions to French political and ecclesiastical history as opposed to a narrowly defined Fleurisian history.

Most recently Abbo's life has been retold in commemoration of the millennium of his death. In 2004 Brepols published a critical examination of Abbo's life by the renowned French historian

16. My translation. Patrice Cousin, *Abbon de Fleury-sur-Loire: Un savant, un pasteur, un martyr à la fin du Xe siècle* (Paris: P. Letielleux, 1954), 30–31: "Cependant la longueur de l'ouvrage, le style faux classique, pompeux et général, l'insufisance de la critique et son épuisement ancien en librairie enrendaient la lecture laborieuse et le remplacement désirable."

Pierre Riché. Riché has relied much less heavily on Aimoinus's structure in his organization of the life. Instead, he has followed his own interests in literate culture, placing a greater emphasis on Abbo's scholarly writings than had other modern biographers. When discussing Abbo's political activities, for example, Riché has given a detailed summary of his canonical works as a means of explaining the context of those works as well as giving insight into the history of ideas. He is less interested in Abbo's forming or reforming of political alliances than in the intellectual precursors of his ideas. He has, however, dated the evolution of Abbo's political involvement from defensive during the first few years of his abbacy to offensive, after 994, when he began composing texts on the Church hierarchy and the social order. Another turning point came in 997 when Abbo received a privilege from Pope Gregory V granting Fleury immunity from episcopal oversight and naming it the "first monastery of Gaul," a title that gave Abbo the authority to intervene in the internal conflicts of neighboring monasteries. Riché's work has provided a broader context and better periodization for Abbo's life than previous works, but ultimately this work is mainly a popular history, designed to appeal to a well-read but not necessarily scholarly French audience and perhaps to students wishing to begin work with the primary sources. Those wishing a more detailed treatment of the texts may refer to Riché's numerous articles, in which Abbo often appears as a supporting figure, usually alongside the better-documented and better-known figure of Gerbert of Aurillac. In any case Riché himself suggests that this, like all scholarship, should be considered provisional in light of the new information that is likely to come to light as a result of the commemoration of the millennium of Abbo's death.[17] The result is that Riché has kept historiographical discussion to a minimum and has given a greater space to narrative and translated quotations (often extensive) from primary source documents.

Apart from these full biographies, other authors have given

---

17. Riché, *Abbon de Fleury*, 7–8.

Introduction 11

Abbo a scholarly treatment but often at the expense of the comprehensiveness that would enable them to see the development of his thought and policies over time and the relationship between his different areas of endeavor. With the close of the second millennium, scholarly interest in apocalyptic and millenarian movements of the Middle Ages increased. Abbo's refutation of apocalyptic preachers, mentioned only in passing in the primary sources, has been seen as evidence either for the relatively limited role of apocalypticism around the year 1000 or for a massive repression and cover-up of millenarian expectations.[18] Most historians of the last century, however, have focused on his political and institutional role. Ferdinand Lot noted his role as a mediator in relations between the Capetians and the papacy and the value of his advice to Hugh Capet and Robert the Pious.[19] Christian Pfister, in his study of Robert the Pious, likewise recognized Abbo's importance as one of the most learned men of his day and an important adviser to the king.[20] Jean-François Lemarignier took a contrary view of Abbo's activities when he wrote that the disintegration of the previous cooperation between the Carolingian monarchs and the monasteries "began at Fleury, or rather it was begun by Abbo of Fleury; for at the beginning it was one man's action that did all." For him, Abbo's accomplishment was his assertion of monastic independence from both kings and bishops, in favor of exclusive obligation to the pope.[21] This undermining of previous mo-

---

18. Richard Landes, "Introduction: The *terribles espoirs de 1000* and the Tacit Fears of 2000," in *The Apocalyptic Year 1000: Religious Expectation and Social Change, 950–1050*, ed. Richard Landes, Andrew Gow, and David C. Van Meter (Oxford: Oxford University Press, 2003), 3–15, especially 10.

19. Ferdinand Lot, *Etudes sur le règne de Hugues Capet et la fin du Xe siècle*, Bibliothèque de l'Ecole des hautes études, sciences historiques et philologiques, fasc. 147 (Paris: Emile Bouillon, Editeur, 1903), for example, 107, 115, 124–27.

20. Christian Pfister, *Etudes sur le règne de Robert le Pieux (996–1031)* (Paris, 1885), for example, 11–15, 33, 54–55.

21. Jean-François Lemarignier, "Political and Monastic Structures in France at the End of the Tenth and the Beginning of the Eleventh Century," trans. Frederic Cheyette, in *Lordship and Community in Medieval Europe: Selected Readings* (New York: Holt, Reinhart, and Winston, 1968 [revised translation of "Structures monastiques et structures politiques dans la France de la fin du Xe et des débuts du XIe siècle," in *Il*

narchical-monastic relations, according to Lemarignier, came at a time when the monarchy was particularly vulnerable, as ties of loyalty and traditions of royal prerogatives were disintegrating.[22] Nevertheless, Lemarignier acknowledged Abbo's role in simultaneously reaffirming and reshaping ideas of royal power in the later tenth century.[23] More recent authors have found Abbo's writings on kingship important evidence for tenth-century attitudes as well as important sources for the Church councils and other public events in which he participated.[24] Even general studies of the entire Capetian monarchy do not completely neglect Abbo's contribution to the establishment of the Capetian dynasty.[25] What these very different treatments have in common, however, is that they do not acknowledge that over the course of his abbacy Abbo reshaped his own approach to the Capetian monarchy and in the process helped form Capetian policies toward the monastic movement within the kingdom.

Abbo's political thought has received much more thorough study than his political activity, albeit outside of the narrow context of his intellectual and political development throughout his career. Georges Duby has argued that Abbo's *Apologeticus* reflected a popular perception of governmental instability.[26] Jacques LeGoff considered the *Apologeticus* an important early example of the me-

---

monachisimo nell'alto medioevo: Settimane di Studio del Centro italiano di studi sull'alto medioevo 4 (Spoleto, Italy, 1957), 112}.

22. Jean-François Lemarignier, *Gouvernement royal aux premiers temps capétiens (987–1108)* (Paris: Editions A. et J. Picard, 1965), 37–65.

23. Ibid., 25–27.

24. Andrew W. Lewis, *Royal Succession in Capetian France: Studies on Familial Order and the State* (Cambridge, Mass.: Harvard University Press, 1981), 19–20, 33; Geoffrey Koziol, *Begging Pardon and Favor: Ritual and Political Order in Early Medieval France* (Ithaca, N.Y.: Cornell University Press, 1992), 122, 167, 220–21; Jean-Pierre Poly and Eric Bournazel, *The Feudal Transformation, 900–1200*, trans. Caroline Higgitt, Europe Past and Present Series (New York: Holmes and Meier, 1991), 16–17, 146–47, 175.

25. Elizabeth Hallam, *Capetian France, 987–1328* (London: Longman, 1980), 65. 94; Jean Dunbabin, *France in the Making, 843–1180* (Oxford.: Oxford University Press, 1985), 167, 177, 134.

26. Georges Duby, *The Three Orders: Feudal Society Imagined*, trans. Arthur Goldhammer with a foreword by Thomas N. Bisson (Chicago: University of Chicago Press, 1980), 87–92.

dieval theory of a tripartite society.[27] Marco Mostert's study of Abbo's political thought includes not only Abbo's theory of a tripartite society but also consideration of kingship and the place of the Church in society.[28] Mostert's study is the only one to address systematically the relationship between Abbo's public activities and his theoretical writings. Jean Batany has rightly criticized Mostert for often being content to summarize Abbo's work rather than provide a detailed commentary on it. Batany identified four areas in which further work on Abbo's political thought is still needed: examination of the exegetical works used by Abbo, comparison with English intellectual developments, consideration of Abbo's ideas in light of biographical works on kings and princes, and fuller consideration of Abbo's treatment of heresy.[29] Nevertheless, Mostert's work has, lacking more detailed study, made Abbo's ideas readily accessible, in a historical context, to a wider scholarly audience. Unfortunately, although Mostert has done a better job than most in putting Abbo's works in a historical context, he concentrated more on the literary antecedents of Abbo's work than on a systematic consideration of Abbo's political and intellectual development within a chronological framework.

Abbo's wide range of scholarly interests is well represented in recent scholarly editions and commentaries. A. Van de Vyver couples his edition of Abbo's philosophical works with a detailed analysis of the sources of his logical forms.[30] Abbo's astronomical work has also received detailed attention, most recently from Ron Thomson.[31] Anita Guerreau-Jalabert's introduction to his

27. Jacques LeGoff, *Time, Work, and Culture in the Middle Ages,* trans. Arthur Goldhammer (Chicago: Chicago University Press, 1980), 53–57.
28. Marco Mostert, *The Political Theology of Abbo of Fleury* (Hilversum, Netherlands: Verloren, 1987).
29. Jean Batany, Review of *The Political Theology of Abbo of Fleury,* by Marco Mostert, *Cahiers de la civilisation médiévale* 33.4 (1990): 402–3.
30. Abbo of Fleury, *Syllogismorum categoricorum et hypotheticorum enodatio,* in *Abbonis Floriacensis opera inedita I,* ed. A. Van de Vyver, in *Rijksuniversiteit te Gent: Werken Uitgegeven foor de Faculteit van de Letteren en Wijsbegeerte* 140 (Bruges, Belgium: De Tempel, 1966).
31. Abbo of Fleury, "Two Astronomical Tractates of Abbo of Fleury," ed. Ron B. Thomson, in *The Light of Nature: Essays in the History and Philosophy of Science Presented*

Quaestiones grammaticales is a small treatise in itself and includes detailed discussion of previous analyses of Abbo's work.[32] Michael Winterbottom's introduction to Abbo's *Life of St. Edmund* is limited to a brief discussion of the manuscripts and the date of composition, but several other scholars have considered the work in more detail as an element in the development of the legend of St. Edmund.[33] A study of Abbo's entire career, however, is beyond the scope of any of these works.

Abbo's letters, the other major source for the events of the abbot's career, present a similar problem in their selection. Most of Abbo's surviving letters exist in a single manuscript (London BL Add 10972), written shortly after Abbo's death and emanating from the library of Fleury.[34] The purpose of this letter collection is not clear. It contains such diverse items as letters to and from Pope Gregory V, accounts of Abbo's intervention in the disputes of several monasteries of the Loire valley, and several long letters that are essentially short treatises on such diverse subjects as reading canon tables and the importance of celibacy in the secular clergy. A theme common to many of the letters is the protection of monastic rights and the regulation of monastic behavior, but this is not obviously present in all the letters.[35] This collection also con-

---

to *A. C. Crombie*, ed. J. D. North and J. J. Roche (Dordrecht, Netherlands: Martinus Nijhof, 1985), 113–33.

32. Abbo of Fleury, *Abbo Floriacensis, Quaestiones grammaticales / Abbon de Fleury, Questions grammaticales*, ed. and trans. Anita Guerreau-Jalabert, Auteurs Latins du Moyen Age (Paris: Société d'édition "les Belles lettres," 1982).

33. See Winterbottom's introduction to Abbo of Fleury, *Vita s. Edmundi*, in *Three Lives of English Saints*, ed. Michael Winterbottom, Toronto Medieval Latin Texts (Toronto: Pontifical Institute of Medieval Studies for the Centre for Medieval Studies, 1972).

34. Marco Mostert, *The Library of Fleury: A Provisional List of Manuscripts*, Middeleeuwse Studies en Bronnen 3 (Hilversum, Netherlands: Verloren, 1989), 105–6. See also Elisabeth Pellégrin, *Bibliothèques retrouvées: Manuscrits, bibliothèques et bibliophiles du Moyen Age et de la Renaissance, recueil d'études publiées de 1938 à 1985* (Paris: Editions du Centre national de la recherche scientifique, 1988).

35. In London BL Add 10972, letters 1–4 are to or from Pope Gregory V; letters 5, 8, 9, 11, and 12 contain either advice or warnings to other monasteries; letter 6 is an introduction to Abbo's *Apologeticus* addressed to Hugh Capet and Robert the Pious (the *Apologeticus* appears later in the manuscript but does not immediately follow this let-

tains a letter from Albert of Micy to Pope John XVIII on the subject of certain rights granted to Micy. The reasons for the inclusion of this letter in the collection are not immediately obvious. Micy is not dependent on Fleury, and neither Abbo nor Fleury are mentioned. The subject, however, is consonant with Abbo's other letters: the preservation of monastic prerogatives, frequently with the aid of the papacy. Abbo may have aided Albert in drafting the letter or the collector may have included it because the theme fit his agenda in collecting the letters. At least five letters from Abbo survive outside of this collection: a letter written to Abbot Oylbold of Fleury before Abbo became abbot, two on astronomy, and two more giving advice to a former pupil.[36] These letters clearly do not form a representative sample of Abbo's correspondence. As with Aimoinus's *Vita*, these letters provide a wealth of detail for reconstructing Abbo's career. Like the *Vita*, however, they emphasize developments of the latter half of his abbacy and mask important changes in his policies over the course of his entire career.

The surviving sources overemphasize the consistency of Abbo's policies, but a closer examination of the chronological context of his life demonstrates that he shifted his political strategy in the second half of his abbacy. Abbo became abbot at a tumultuous time in French history. The last French king of Charlemagne's line, Louis V, died in 987 in a riding accident after only a year on the throne. Hugh Capet took advantage of the situation to have him-

---

ter); letter 7 is a response to some young monks of Cluny who had asked them about reading canon tables; letter 10 is to an unnamed bishop on oaths; letter 14 is a long letter of advice to "G," who is probably a monk and possibly an abbot. (The letters in the manuscript are not numbered, but the edition in *PL* 139 assigns numbers following the order of the manuscript. The numbering of the letters has been followed by subsequent historians. Although the *Apologeticus* was divided into unnumbered paragraphs in the manuscript, subsequent editors have followed their own editing principles in paragraphing. Thus, the only divisions practicable in citing this lengthy text are folio numbers from the manuscript or page or column numbers in the printed edition.)

36. Abbo's letter to Oylbold is edited by Marco Mostert in "Le séjour d'Abbon de Fleury á Ramsey," *Bibliothèque de l'Ecole de chartes* 144 (1986): 199–208. Abbo's letters on science are edited by Van de Vyver, *Abbonis Floriacensis opera inedita I*. Two letters to Bernard of Beaulieu are excerpted in Aimoinus, VsA, c. 10 but are found in full in Paris, BN lat 4568, f. 182r.

self elected king by the nobility. Hugh's family had long been the leading noble clan of the Ile-de-France region; in the early tenth century it had even taken the throne briefly when the Carolingian claimant was too young and inexperienced to meet the challenges of the Viking raids.[37] Hugh was determined to make this a permanent change of dynasty, however. He had himself crowned in June 987 and crowned his son Robert as coruler in December of the same year. Meanwhile, he had to repulse the claims of Charles of Lorraine, the Carolingian claimant to the throne. Abbo's monastery of Fleury played a key role in the transition from Carolingian to Capetian rule. Although Fleury depended on the patronage of the Carolingians, it lay in the heart of the Capetian lands and had often benefited from the support of Hugh Capet and his ancestors.[38] The wealth and learning of Fleury could easily be used to bolster or undermine the claims of the new dynasty. When Abbo became abbot less than a year after Hugh Capet's accession, he found himself at the heart of a political maelstrom. The first half of his abbacy was marked by continual conflict and negotiation with the secular rulers of West Francia. Only in the second half of his abbacy was he able to press for the adoption of a more cooperative political philosophy, one in which kings and bishops supported the peaceful interests of monks.

When viewed as a whole, Abbo's life demonstrates his devotion to the cause of pressing for monastic prerogatives in a climate of political change. This is the most important unifying force in the disparate activities of his career as monk and abbot. Abbo's participation in life outside of the cloister complemented his duties as monk and abbot: only by participating in this wider community could he promote the good of the monastery and help

37. For the early history of Hugh Capet's family, see Constance Bouchard, "The Origins of the French Nobility: A Reassessment," *American Historical Review* 86.3 (1981): 512–14.

38. See Maurice Prou and Alexandre Vidier, eds., *Recueil des chartes de l'abbaye de Saint-Benoît-sur-Loire,* Documents: Société historique et archéologique du Gâtinais 5 and 6 (Paris: A. Picard et fils, 1900–1907), nos. 44 (9 January 938), 61 (8 September 975), and 69 (987).

it fulfill its mission as a Christian institution. Abbo strengthened Fleury's ties to the reformed monasteries of western Francia and did not hesitate to admonish his fellow monks and abbots if they seemed to fall away from the monastic ideal. Through his correspondence with the kings of the new Capetian dynasty, he furthered the cause of reformed monasticism as well as articulating a view of Christian kingship in which the king's interests and the Church's were closely aligned. He steered his monastery toward prosperity as well as spiritual and intellectual distinction at a time when central authority was weak and secular princes plundered monasteries for their worldly rather than their spiritual treasures.

In no area has Abbo left a more significant mark than in the realm of relations between the secular clergy, the regular clergy, and the monarchy. Abbo used the incredible influence of Fleury to reshape Capetian policy toward monasticism. Fleury occupied a unique place in the history of monastic relations with the monarchy and the episcopate. Although Fleury does not today have the name recognition of Cluny, one could argue that in the tenth century it played a far more decisive role in the shaping of relations between the monarchy and the monastic movement in West Francia. Fleury was a Merovingian foundation, which had subsequently come under the jurisdiction of the Carolingians. By the tenth century, it was also heavily patronized by the "dukes of the Franks," who were none other than the Robertian ancestors of the Capetians. Politically these antecedents made the wealthy monastery of Fleury and its learned congregation pivotal in the struggles between the first Capetian kings and the Carolingian pretender to the throne, Charles of Lorraine.

Fleury, however, had a significance beyond its political affiliation. The old view of Cluny as the administrative center from which all tenth-century monastic reforms emanated has long since been displaced by a landscape of independent, but cooperative, centers of reform.[39] Although reformed by Cluny in 930,

---

39. Constance Bouchard, "Merovingian, Carolingian, and Cluniac Monasticism: Reform and Renewal in Burgundy," *Journal of Ecclesiastical History* 41.3 (1990): 364–88.

Fleury was not its priory, nor dependent on it in any way. On the contrary, Fleury had from long before the tenth century enjoyed an exalted status among its fellow monasteries because of its possession of the relics of St. Benedict. Furthermore, during Abbo's abbacy, the house received papal confirmation of its status as the leading monastic house in "Gaul": Fleury's abbot would have precedence at any general meeting of French abbots. Given Fleury's enormous influence in the region, the monastery's change of policy toward the monarchy and the episcopacy is a major development in the history of Capetian consolidation of power.

The benefit of hindsight has caused many historians to see Abbo's political activities as a continual process of helping the Capetian dynasty establish itself. A close examination of Abbo's career reveals, however, that, far from being one of the earliest and strongest of the Capetians' supporters, he found himself opposing Kings Hugh Capet and Robert the Pious on many of the major issues of their joint reign (987–996). Although Hugh Capet did, in fact, support Abbo's election as abbot of Fleury against internal opposition, the new abbot showed early signs of being unwilling to support the king's political agenda in its entirety. The clearest and most public division between the abbot and the king came at the Council of Saint-Basle in 991, when Abbo led the opposition to the deposition of Archbishop Arnulf of Reims, who had betrayed Reims to Hugh's Carolingian rival, Charles of Lorraine. Although unsuccessful, Abbo's arguments at the council could hardly be considered those of a royal propagandist. The monastery of Fleury, furthermore, had a long-standing series of disputes with Arnulf, the bishop of Orléans and one of the Capetians' most important supporters. Some of the tensions between the two probably stemmed from questions of episcopal jurisdiction over Fleury, while others clearly arose from local disputes over lands and revenues. The most dramatic confrontation between the two factions occurred when some retainers of the bishop made a murderous attack on the abbot and his retinue, in late 993 or early 994. Shortly thereafter, at the Council of Saint-Denis, just outside of

Paris, in 994, Abbo led a group of monks who opposed an episcopal plan to limit the collection of tithes by monks and laymen and was accused by Bishop Arnulf of Orléans of inciting the riot that ended the council. The riot at Saint-Denis appears to have convinced Abbo of the need for a rapprochement between Fleury and the Capetians, if only to preserve the peace and stability necessary for the observance of the monastic rule in the Loire valley. Only then, when he saw the needs of reformed monasticism and Capetian stability converging, did he attempt to redefine his initially contentious relationship with the monarchy.

Abbo's attempt to defend himself from charges stemming from the disturbance at Saint-Denis represents the first clear shift in his political strategy toward conscious accommodation to Capetian political needs. He composed his *Apologeticus,* addressed to both King Hugh and King Robert, shortly after the events at Saint-Denis. In this work, he presented a tripartite view of society, in which laymen, secular clergy, and regular clergy cooperated for the good of Christendom. Within this framework, he argued for the moral superiority of monks over other members of society and rehearsed his own complaints of mistreatment by his bishop. Characteristically, Abbo did not mention Arnulf by name. This omission was of a piece with his tendency to view the respect and responsibilities associated with an office as more important than the individual holding it. Although Abbo and Arnulf would never be close allies, Abbo presented a scenario in which the bishop of Orléans and the abbot of Fleury would learn to behave appropriately toward each other, despite the misbehavior of the current bishop. The *Apologeticus* inaugurated a period of greater cooperation between Abbo and the monarchy. Marco Mostert commented cynically, "The kings were taken in by Abbo's arguments."[40] In the next three years, Abbo's influence within the French Church increased tremendously, due to his friendship with the new pope, Gregory V (996–999), from whom he received a charter granting Fleury premier status among French monasteries.

---

40. Mostert, *Political Theology,* 51.

Even after his decision to cooperate with the Capetians, the Fleurisian abbot did not completely adhere to the wishes of the kings. Abbo had agreed to present several requests of King Robert (sole ruler after his father's death in 996) to the pope, but Gregory V—almost certainly at Abbo's behest—had refused the most important: recognition of Robert's marriage to his cousin, Bertha of Blois. On the other hand, Abbo had likewise urged the refusal of a request by Robert's adversary, Count Fulk Nerra of Anjou. The abbot's strategy, then, lay not in promoting one side in French politics above the other but in maintaining the current balance of power between the opposing sides within West Francia while promoting the authority of the papacy. Only within a stable political structure could Abbo hope to realize the social order delineated in his *Apologeticus*, which depended on the peaceful and independent survival of reformed monasteries.

The historiography of this period in French political history has, however, painted a very different picture of Abbo's career. Historians usually depict the tenth century as the age of principalities, in which regional magnates exercised power independently of the king, whether Carolingian or Capetian. Such was the fragmented nature of power in the tenth century that "the king was only as effective as the lands he controlled in person and as the men he could dominate."[41] Under the last Carolingians and the first Capetians, the royal domain, described by Jean Dunbabin as "that bundle of rights and lands which provided income, devoted followers, and patronage for its royal owner," had been considerably reduced and was often indistinguishable from the family lands of the ruling dynasty.[42] According to traditional interpretations, the Capetians met the challenge of the region-

41. Hallam, *Capetian France*, 80. See also Olivier Guillot, "Formes, fondements et limites de l'organisation politiques en France au Xe siècle," in *Il secolo di ferro: Mito e realità del secolo X*, 17–19 April 1990, Settimane di Studio del Centro italiano di studi sull'alto medioevo 38 (Spoleto, Italy: Presso la sede del centro, 1991), 1:57–58; Lot, *Hugues Capet*, 187–90, 216.

42. Dunbabin, *France in the Making*, 31, 129–34; William Mendel Newman, *Le domaine royal sous les premiers Capétiens* (Paris: Recueil Sirey, 1937), 3–4; Lot, *Hugues Capet*, 3.

al principalities through a conscious strategy of extending their royal authority outward from their domain lands through their control of episcopal appointments and monastic houses.[43] Bishoprics provided kings with vehicles through which they could extend their influence and authority beyond the boundaries of their secular domain.[44] Furthermore, both monasteries and bishoprics had been, from Carolingian times, "a source of revenues and extra power, a reservoir of lands to be drawn on for benefices for loyal followers and also in many cases providers of military contingents."[45] Robert Fawtier stressed that control of bishoprics was the most important element in the Capetians' consolidation of power, but he introduced his discussion of other Church institutions by saying, "What was true of the bishoprics was partly true also of the parish churches and monasteries."[46] In addition, the Capetians relied on "a new source of image-making—the monastic reform movement."[47]

Within this context, the monastery of Fleury and its abbot, Abbo (987 or 988–1004), have appeared among the Capetians' most valuable monastic allies from the inception of their rule. Dunbabin has singled out Abbo's *Collectio canonum*, "compiled soon after the change of dynasty and dedicated to the new kings," as an example of a work of monastic propaganda that used Carolingian writings to bolster the claims of the Capetians to succeed to the rights and lands of the previous dynasty.[48] Others have also cited Abbo's works as early vehicles of royal propaganda.[49] A striking exception was Jean-François Lemarignier, who saw Abbo as a

43. Lot, *Hugues Capet*, 216, 225.
44. Karl Ferdinand Werner, "Hugues Capet, duc puissant—roi faible, un essai d'explication," in *Xème siècle: Recherches nouvelles*, ed. Pierre Riché, Carol Heitz, and François Heber-Suffrin, Contribution au Colloque Hugues Capet 987–1987, cahier IV, Centre de recherches sur l'antiquité tardive et le Haut Moyen Age (Paris: Centre national de la recherche scientifique, 1987), 10; Dunbabin, *France in the Making*, 129–30.
45. Hallam, *Capetian France*, 18.
46. Robert Fawtier, *The Capetian Kings of France: Monarchy and Nation (987–1328)*, trans. Lionel Butler and R. J. Adam (London: Macmillan, 1960), 72.
47. Dunbabin, *France in the Making*, 134.
48. Ibid.
49. Hallam, *Capetian France*, 65; Geoffrey Koziol, "Political Culture," in *France in*

consistent champion of papal rights against royal, episcopal, and noble claims.[50] Although most of Abbo's writings have not been definitively dated, historians have cited these works in a context that suggests that Abbo's support came in the critical early years of the Capetian dynasty, rather than at a point later in his career when the most important resistance to Capetian rule had been answered.[51]

The challenge facing the modern chronicler of Abbo's career is to represent the changing focus of his political thought and activity as well as to integrate his administrative responsibilities and myriad intellectual pursuits into the narrative. In addition, Abbo's career must first be considered not in the framework of later monastic and political developments—namely, the growth of French monarchical power or the spread of papal exemptions for monasteries—but as the outgrowth of the political and religious situation that Abbo inherited upon his accession to the abbacy in 987 or 988. To these ends, this study takes a chronological approach to Abbo's life, including the almost undocumented years of his youth. The result is by its very nature uneven, but any other form of presentation risks obscuring, as so many earlier studies have done, the major evolution in Abbo's ideas following the increasingly violent incidents of the first half of his abbacy and the continuing importance of his intellectual life in shaping his political agenda. Nevertheless, this study should make clear that Abbo's loyalties throughout his life lay not with specific individuals but with his devotion to the promotion of Benedictine monasticism, as understood by tenth-century French reformers, within European religious and political culture.

---

the *Central Middle Ages, 900–1200*, ed. Marcus Bull, the Short Oxford History of France (Oxford: Oxford University Press, 2002), 51; Dunbabin, *France in the Making*, 134.

50. Lemarignier, "Political and Monastic Structures" and "L'exemption monastique."

51. See Lewis, *Royal Succession*, 19; Bernd Schneidmüller, *Karolingische Tradition und frühes französisches Königtum: Untersuchungen zur Herrschaftslegitimation der westfränkisch-französischen Monarchie im 10. Jahrhundert* (Wiesbaden, Germany: Franz Steiner, 1979), 71–72; Poly and Bournazel, *Feudal Transformation*, 16–17; Karl Ferdinand Werner, *Histoire de France*, vol. 1, *Les origines (avant l'an mil)*, gen. ed. Jean Favier ([Paris]: Fayard, 1984), 31.

2

THE MAKING OF A MONK

A BBO'S FAMILY MEMBERS ensured his early exposure to the values of reformed monasticism when they enrolled him in the monastic school of Fleury. Their choice reflected the options available to people of their social standing and geographical location. In the tenth and eleventh centuries, family had a tremendous impact on the opportunities open to a young man or woman. Social class in the tenth century was more flexible than in either the preceding or following century, but family, wealth, and class still determined a person's opportunities for education and advancement. Free birth was a prerequisite for most opportunities. A freeborn child could exercise a broader range of choices, but these were often limited by wealth and family connections.[1] Inheritance of land secured a person's place in an agricultural community, while most other professions required an apprenticeship, either with a family member or upon a financial agreement. The Church was no

---

1. For social mobility during the tenth century, see Bouchard, "Origins of the French Nobility," 501–32, which concludes that the post-Carolingian nobility was neither entirely "new" nor entirely "old" but a mixture. See also David Herlihy, "Three Patterns of Social Mobility in Medieval History," *Journal of Interdisciplinary History* (1973): 623–47, which indicates that the categories of freedom and servility were somewhat fluid, as economic pressures might drive a freeman to become a serf, while an unfree man might take advantage of this blurring of the classes to become free (632–33).

different. Monastic schools usually required a donation before a child could be entered into the school, and monasteries expected an endowment before accepting a youth into the chapter. Women's choices were restricted to a decreasing number of nunneries, but men in the tenth century had a wider range of opportunities in both the regular and secular clergy.[2] Those wishing to enter the secular clergy needed a monastic education but also patronage in order to secure a benefice. Which schools and monasteries were open to a child depended in large part on family connections. A relative in the monastery or on the list of previous donors would smooth the way for admission. Advancement within the Church depended equally on ability and influence. Although young men from modest backgrounds, such as Abbo and his contemporary Gerbert of Aurillac, could advance within the Church, they often found their paths less smooth and clearly marked than those who came from families of great wealth or noble status.[3]

Abbo was born in the 940s or 950s into a free but not noble family in the region around Orléans, which lay just thirty-five kilometers (about twenty-two miles) from Fleury. Aimoinus described his birthplace as the *pagus* of Orléans, that is, the area around the city of Orléans, not the city proper.[4] The use of the term *pagus,* rather than *civis* or *urbs,* points to a rural origin for

---

2. Herlihy, "Social Mobility in Medieval History," 624, lists several churchmen who rose from relative obscurity to high offices, including that of pope, within the Church. He linked this mobility with restrictions on the marriage of clergy, which ensured the periodic introduction of "new men" into the priesthood through the creation of barriers to father-son inheritance.

3. Jane Martindale, "The French Aristocracy in the Early Middle Ages: A Reappraisal," *Past and Present* 75 (May 1977): 34–37.

4. Aimoinus, *VsA,* c. 1: "Venerabilis igitur Abbo Aurelianensi natus est in pago"; *VsA,* c. 1 (Dijon 1118: "Aurelianensi ortus est in pago"). The published editions of the *VsA,* in contrast to the manuscript versions, identify Abbo in the chapter headings or the margins as a *civis* (citizen) of Orléans, clearly an erroneous assumption, as Cousin, *Abbon de Fleury-sur-Loire,* 48n, recognized. Barbara Rosenwein, *To Be the Neighbor of St. Peter* (Ithaca, N.Y.: Cornell University Press, 1989), 27, gives a brief discussion of the meaning of the term *pagus.* In this context, the first two definitions under "pagus" in J. F. Niermeyer, *Mediae Latinitatis lexicon minus* (Leiden: E. J. Brill, 1984), "territory of a 'civitas'" and "the countryside of a 'civitas' as contradistinguished from the city" (based on sixth-century usage), are most sensible.

the family. According to Aimoinus, Abbo's parents, Laetus and Ermengard, were of "proud blood, not swollen from empty nobility," but "the liberty derived from grandsires and great-grandsires adorned them."[5] Abbo's family had enjoyed this freedom (*libertas*) for at least three generations (as far back as Abbo's great-grandfather), possibly longer since the phrase "grandsires and great-grandsires" (*avi attavique*) may be formulaic, merely indicating several generations of ancestors.[6] The exact nature of this freedom is likewise ambiguous. Georges Duby found only hints of a middle stratum between lords and their tenants, of "peasants who farmed their own *manses*" and "who succeeded in preserving at least some of their economic independence."[7] The Carolingian notion of a *liberus* as "a free man not bound to the soil but subject to heavy obligations of military service" did not, however, preclude descent to the level of a tenant farmer.[8] Since they had held this status for several generations, as Aimoinus pointed out, the implication is that they were not among the upwardly mobile classes often found in villages.

5. Aimoinus, *VsA*, c. 1: "Quos quidem non vana tumens de nobilitate superbus alebat sanguis, sed tamen avis attavisque derivata eos honestabat libertas."
6. In a charter to Fleury from the Frankish king Lothar (954–986), Louis the Pious (Lothar's great-great-great-grandfather) is called Lothar's *avus* (Prou and Vidier, *Recueil de chartes de Saint-Benoît-sur-Loire*, no. 55 [5 June 967]). David Herlihy, *Medieval Households* (Cambridge, Mass.: Harvard University Press, 1985), 47, indicated that the early Germanic tribes forbade intermarriage within seven degrees of consanguinity; that is, cousins who had only a great-grandparent in common would be forbidden to marry, but more distant relations would not. The maximum number of generations he found in genealogies of the early charters of Amalfi was seven, but the most common numbers were three or four.
7. Georges Duby, *Rural Economy and Country Life in the Medieval West*, trans. Cynthia Postan (Columbia: University of South Carolina Press, 1968), 33–34. Duby suspected that this "middle class" was more numerous than documents indicate, since most polyptychs and other lists were compiled for the purpose of administering a lord's domain. Duby cited the example of one family that, though apparently free for many generations, appeared in documents only when it presented its land to a monastery. The concept of liberty in the Middle Ages was a matter of great complexity and varied from place to place. See Robert Fossier, *Enfance de l'Europe, Xe–XIIe siècle, aspects économiques et sociaux*, vol. 1: *L'homme et son espace*, 2nd ed. (Paris: Presses universitaires de France, 1982), 516–17.
8. Herlihy, "Social Mobility in Medieval History," 634–35.

Although not noble, Abbo's family was not necessarily composed of farmers. A generation later, one could be a vassal or knight, that is, a member of a nobleman's military retinue, without partaking of nobility. One of the disqualifications of Charles of Lorraine for the kingship of West Francia was his marriage to a woman of the military class (*uxorem de militari ordine sibi imparem duxerit*).[9] Since Aimoinus several times commented favorably on the noble status of important figures in Abbo's life, including Aimoinus's own relatives Rosemberga and Girald, he would hardly have minimized the status of Abbo's family.[10] Writers of Abbo's day clearly knew what it meant to be noble, so much so that they never thought it worthwhile to define the term. Wealth and power were necessary attributes of a nobleman, but nobility also carried with it a necessary concept of heritability, extending to both men and women.[11] Aimoinus must also have been aware, however, that a small but significant number of free families in each generation managed to rise from the status of free commoners into the nobility through military service or marriage—more usually both. The most significant instance were the Capetians, whose ancestor Robert the Strong began as a common soldier, but similar stories held true for others, most notably the dukes of Burgundy. Thus, most of the noble families of the later tenth century, though "new" in the sense of having a recent nonnoble male ancestor, were "old" in that they had married into well-established noble families and had held their titles for several generations.[12]

9. Richer, *Histoire de France*, ed. and trans. Robert Latouche, les Classiques de l'histoire de France au Moyen Age 17 (Paris: Société d'édition "les Belles lettres," 1937), bk. 4, c. 11 (2:160–61).

10. See Aimoinus, *V&A:* Archbishop Oswald of York: "vir magnae apud eos nobilitatis" (a man of great nobility among them) (c. 4); Abbot Oylbold of Fleury: "vir secundum seculi dignitatem genere ac moribus clarus" (a man distinguished in family and behavior, according to the value of the world) (c. 4); Bernard of Beaulieu: son of a *procer* [prince] of Aquitaine (c. 10); Pope Gregory V: "nobilitate generis . . . clarus" (distinguished by nobility of family) (c. 11); Girald: *dominus* [lord] of Aubeterre (c. 18); Rosemberga: wife of *vicecomes* [viscount] Amalguin (c. 21).

11. Martindale, "French Aristocracy," 20–32.

12. Bouchard, "Origins of the French Nobility," especially 502–3, 525–26.

The Making of a Monk

Whatever the exact meaning of the term, free status even without nobility was becoming increasingly important in medieval society, as families took advantage of economic opportunities as well as opportunities for social advancement, and Abbo's family must have valued its place in society both for its position in the village and for the possibilities that free status would open for Abbo in the Church.

Abbo's family had a strong commitment to the monastic life. We know the names of four relatives of Abbo, apart from his parents, three who had entered the service of God and another who gave generously to the Church. Gombaudus and Christianus, relatives on his mother's side, had already entered Fleury, the first as a monk, the second as a cleric, but both ordained as priests.[13] A third relative, Gislebert, had also entered the Church and had become the abbot of Saint-Cyprien of Poitiers.[14] Aimoinus did not specify their exact relationship with Abbo, but both uncles and cousins frequently played important roles in shaping a young man's career. Before entering the monastery himself, Abbo probably saw his relations at Fleury at least occasionally, probably on important feast days, when the monks would have held processions through the village surrounding the monastery.

The evidence of Abbo's other relations bear out this picture of a religiously inclined free family, but one without claims to prominence in the Orléanais. In his correspondence as abbot, Abbo mentioned a fourth relative, a woman named Ildegard, who had requested that Abbo write to Pope Gregory V (996–999) on her behalf concerning the endowment of a pair of monastic houses (*monasteria*), one of canons and one of nuns.[15] Ildegard, at least, if

---

13. Aimoinus, *VsA*, c. 1: "carnis affinitas matri eius propinquos effecerat. Unus dicibatur Gunboldus, qui ... habitum monastici susceperat ordinis. alter vocatus est Christianus, qui sub clericali veste Christo studebat deservire.... Ambo in ordine presbiteratus."

14. Ibid., c. 17, did not specify the nature of the relationship. It is perhaps significant that an "Abbot Abbo" appears in a witness list for a charter of Saint-Cyprien of about 995 (Paris, BN Coll. Moreau 16, ff. 19r–20r).

15. Abbo of Fleury, *Epistolae*. London, BL 10972, ff. 1r–15r, 23r–33v, letter 3 (num-

no one else in the family, enjoyed substantial discretionary wealth. Apart from Ildegard, however, Abbo's other relatives do not appear to have made substantial donations to monastic communities. The charters of Fleury do not mention any of Abbo's family members as patrons of the monastery, despite their conspicuous presence at Fleury. The names Abbo, Christianus, Hildegard, and Laetus do not appear in the charters of Fleury either before or after Abbo's abbacy. The name Ermengard appears in only one charter, a donation by Teotard and his wife, Ermengard, written sometime between 923 and 930.[16] While it is tempting to imagine a relationship between the Ermengard of the charter and Ermengard, wife of Laetus and mother of Abbo, the name Ermengard is too common to establish such a link. Likewise, the occurrence of names with the first element *Ermen-* and *Hilde-* in the charters of Fleury cannot reveal much about family connections, given the frequency of both elements in tenth- and eleventh-century France and Germany. The name Gombaudus (and variations) is less common, and only one other person with that name appears in the cartulary of Fleury, Bishop Gumbald of Bordeaux, who, with his brother, Guillaume Sanche, duke of the Gascons, gave the priory of La Réole to Fleury.[17] Since Aimoinus explicitly denied Abbo's noble parentage,

---

bers of letters in text correspond to numbers in PL 139:419–61). Abbo did not specify the nature of the relationship, only that she asked him to intervene by "right of kinship" (*jure propinquitatis*). The name "Ildegardis" or "Hildegardis," though common, does not appear in the *indices* of *Gallia Christiana in provincias ecclesiasticas distributa* (Paris, 1715–1865) in association with the foundation of monasteries or cells during the pontificate of Gregory V (996–999). Cyr Ulysse Chevalier, *Repertoire des sources historique du Moyen Age bio-bibliographique* (Paris, 1903–1907), lists several people named "Hildegarde," including a wife of Charles Martel, a wife of William IX, duke of Aquitaine (repudiated c. 1116), and a viscountess of Châteaudun, but none seems connected to Abbo or Fleury.

16. Prou and Vidier, *Recueil des chartes de Saint-Benoît-sur-Loire*, no. 39 (c. 923–930).

17. Chevalier, *Bio-bibliographique*, lists only one person with this name for this time period, Gombaud, bishop of Agen (977–982), who also appears in the cartulary of Fleury. Prou and Vidier, *Recueil des chartes de Saint-Benoît-sur-Loire*, nos. 42 (January 933) and 43 (March 936). On Bishop Gombaud's exact titles and the dates at which he held them, see Robert-André Sénac, "L'évêché de Gascogne et ses évêque (977–1059)," in *Actes du 104e Congrès national des sociétés savantes*, Section de philologie et d'histoire jusqu'à 1610, vol. 2, Bordeaux, 1979 (Paris: CTHS, 1981), especially 135–38.

The Making of a Monk   29

the correspondence of the two names cannot denote a family connection. On the other hand, Abbo's relative Gislebert had become the abbot of a monastery in Aquitaine, which suggests family ties to that region. Since the name Abbo occurs most frequently in the southwest of France, the family may have had ties outside of the Orléanais. Thus, Abbo's relative Gombaud may well have had ties to southwestern France. In fact, the preceding analysis of the charters of Fleury does not contradict Aimoinus's suggestion that the family was not particularly well connected.[18]

Despite the fragmentary nature of these data, modern prosopographical techniques permit some elucidation of Abbo's family background.[19] Ermengard, Gombaud, and Ildegard are all Latin forms of Germanic names. Ermengard and Ildegard are particularly common names, and the repetition of the final element, *-gardis,* would suggest that Ildegard came from Ermengard's side of the family, rather than Abbo's father's, if both names were not so widespread.[20] Christianus is a Christian name of no particular ethnic

---

18. Joachim Wollasch, "Exkurs I: Zur Verbreitung des Namens Abbo in Aquitanien (bis zum Ende des 10. Jahrhunderts)," in *Neue Forschungen über Cluny und die Cluniacenser,* ed. Gerd Tellenbach (Freiburg, Germany: Herder, 1959), 153–55. This is not to say that Abbo's family had never made donations to Fleury, only that the donations were not recorded. Since donations were frequently a prerequisite for acceptance into the monastic community, it seems more likely that written records of small, uncontested donations were not preserved for any length of time. The overall low survival rate for charters of Fleury may be partially accounted for by fires at Fleury in the late tenth and early eleventh centuries, several in Abbo's lifetime.

19. See, for example, Karl Ferdinand Werner, "Important Noble Families in the Kingdom of Charlemagne—A Prosopographical Study of the Relationship between King and Nobility in the Early Middle Ages," trans. Timothy Reuter, in *The Medieval Nobility: Studies on the Ruling Classes of France and Germany from the Sixth to the Twelfth Century,* ed. Timothy Reuter, Europe in the Middle Ages, Selected Studies 14 (Amsterdam: North-Holland, 1979), 137–202 [originally published as "Bedeutende Adelsfamilien im Reich Karls des Grossen: Ein personengeschichtlicher Beitrag zum Verhältnis von Königtum und Adel im frühen Mittelalter," in, *Karl der Große, Lebenswerk und Nachleben 1: Persönlicheit und Geschichte,* ed. H. Beumann (Düsseldorf: Schwann, 1965), 83–142; appendices omitted in translation]; and Steven Fanning, *A Bishop and His World Before the Gregorian Reform: Hubert of Angers (1006–1047),* Transactions of the American Philosophical Society 78.1 (Philadelphia: American Philosophical Society, 1988), 22–43.

20. Chevalier, *Bio-bibliographique,* lists nearly a dozen women named "Ermengarde," including a wife of Louis the Pious, and several named "Hildegarde" as well (see above, note 15).

background but fairly common in the Middle Ages, and one that appears several times in Fleury's lists of the dead for whom the monks said prayers.[21] Another Abbo appears in the list for Saint-Martial of Limoges, further identified simply as a "monk," as well as a commemoration of Abbo of Fleury under commemorations for 10 November (though Abbo died on 13 November).[22] Laetus is somewhat less common, though it has strong local ties; it was the name of a monk of Saint-Mesmin of Micy in the sixth century.[23] The name does not appear, however, among the dead commemorated at Fleury.[24] Though in the early Middle Ages most noble families named their children of both sexes for the father's side of the family, naming for the mother's side was not unheard of, particularly in the Germanic tradition, and, in fact, the pattern had begun to change by the end of the tenth century, as members of the nobility sought to give their children the benefit of both maternal and paternal family connections. Beginning with the Capetians, naming children for relatives on the mother's side of the family had become much more common among the nobility.[25] Presum-

---

21. Vidier, L'historiographie, 127, 131, 132. Chevalier, Bio-bibliographique, lists several people named "Chrétien," many of them, such as Chrétien de Troyes, from the later Middle Ages, but one contemporary with Abbo, a monk of Corbie and abbot of Saint-Pantaléon of Cologne (964–1001).

22. Léopold Delisle, ed., Rouleaux des morts du IXe au XVe siècle, Libraire de la Société de l'histoire de France (Paris: Mme Ve Jules Renouard, 1866), 14–16.

23. Chevalier, Bio-bibliographique, under "Lié."

24. Vidier, L'historiographie, 113–34 (with "Index onomastique des obituaires," 257–64).

25. Werner, "Important Noble Families," 151–52; Constance Bouchard, "Patterns of Women's Names in Royal Lineages, Ninth–Eleventh Centuries," Medieval Prosopography 9.1 (1988): 16–19. Here and elsewhere (Bouchard, "The Migration of Women's Names in the Upper Nobility, Ninth–Twelfth Centuries," Medieval Prosopography 9.2 [1988]: 1–2), Bouchard noted that though noble and royal men rarely named their children for their wives, they frequently named them for their mothers. Unfortunately, no studies on naming practices of the free peasantry have appeared, so arguments about this social class carry considerably less weight than for the upper echelons of society. As noted above, the tenth century was a period of transition in naming practices, thus rendering consideration of Abbo's family relations even more tentative. Alexander C. Murray, Germanic Kinship Structure, Studies in Law and Society in Antiquity and the Early Middle Ages (Toronto: Pontifical Institute of Medieval Studies, 1983), 60, noted "a relatively close bond between an individual and his mother's family."

The Making of a Monk 31

ably the free nonnobles, particularly if upwardly mobile, would have followed this pattern as well, but the evidence is scarce. They may equally well, however, have purposely taken names from the powerful nobility to whom they looked for advancement and protection.[26] Again, the sources bear out Aimoinus's contention that Abbo came from a relatively modest background.

Several names in Abbo's family point to an origin outside the Orléanais. The name Abbo, though common in Poitou, the Aunis, and the Saintonge, is rare elsewhere.[27] Like the name Abbo, the name Gombaud is not common in the Orléanais, though it appears a couple of times in Fleury's lists of the dead.[28] It occurs more frequently in southwestern France and in Poitou.[29] The frequent occurrence of the names Abbo and Gombaud in Poitou, to the southwest of the Orléanais, suggests a family connection in that area. Since Gombaud was a maternal relation and Abbo's father had a name, Laetus, with close ties to the Orléanais, the most likely conclusion is that his mother's family had come originally from Poitou. Abbo's kinship with the abbot of Saint-Cyprien of Poitiers reinforces this conclusion. Since two of Ermengard's relatives, Gombaud and Christianus, were at Fleury, Abbo's mother

---

26. Bouchard, "Origins of the French Nobility," 506–7.

27. Joachim Wollasch, "Abbo in Aquitanien," in *Neue Forschungen über Cluny und die Cluniacenser,* ed. Gerd Tellenbach (Freiburg: Herder, 1959), 153. For an example of the occurrence of the name outside of Aquitaine, see Patrick J. Geary, *Aristocracy in Provence: The Rhône Basin at the Dawn of the Carolingian Age* (Philadelphia: University of Pennsylvania Press, 1985), which examines a will of someone named Abbo from Provence.

28. Vidier, *L'historiographie,* 126, 128.

29. For example, Bishop Gumbald of Gascony entrusted the reform of La Réole to Fleury (Prou and Vidier, *Recueil des chartes de Saint-Benoît-sur-Loire,* nos. 62 [977] and 63 [978]). Witnesses and participants named Gombaudus (or variations) appear in the tenth-century charters of Saint-Cyprien of Poitiers ("Cartulaire de l'abbaye de Saint-Cyprien de Poitiers," *Archives historiques de Poitou* 3 [1874]: nos. 5, 7, 50, 60, 210, 308, 310, 369, 472, 476, 539, 556), in the charters of Saint-Jean of Angély ("Cartulaire de Saint-Jean d'Angély," *Archives historiques de la Saintonge et de l'Aunis* 30 [1901] and 33 [1903]): nos. 61, 68, 189, 200, 242), in the charters of Saint-Maixent ("Chartes de l'abbaye de Saint-Maixent," *Archives historiques de Poitou* 16 [1886] and 18 [1888]: nos. 14, 17, 42), and in the charters of Saint-Hilaire of Poitiers ("Documents pour l'histoire de l'église de Saint-Hilaire de Poitiers," *Mémoires de la Société des antiquaires de l'Ouest* 14 [1847]: nos. 15, 18, 21).

was probably not the first generation of that family in the Orléanais. If Ermengard's family did indeed come from Poitou, then Abbo was probably named for a relative on his mother's side of the family.

Abbo's family was resident in the Orléanais and clearly had close ties to Fleury, as demonstrated by the presence of Christianus and Gombaud in the monastery. Families frequently patronized a monastery through donations before a member of the family actually entered the house. Though the evidence is more extensive for wealthy and socially prominent families, this was certainly true for all levels of society except the poorest families, as recent studies have shown for Burgundy and Anjou in the tenth and eleventh centuries.[30] At Fleury itself, though few charters survive from the ninth through eleventh centuries, the same pattern emerges. For example, a certain Elisiernus, as an old man, gave land to Fleury upon his entry into the monastery in 941.[31] During Abbo's abbacy (987/8–1004), Aimoinus wrote that a monk named Elisiernus—probably the same man, by now very old indeed, or possibly a relative—witnessed Abbo's healing of a leper.[32] In the mid-eleventh century, yet another monk named Elisiernus, perhaps a relative of the first, became the *custos* of the monastery of Saint-Benoît-du-Sault.[33] Abbo's family was not the only one with multigenerational ties to the monastery.

---

30. For Burgundy, see Rosenwein, *Neighbor of St. Peter*, 49–77; Constance Bouchard, *Sword, Miter, and Cloister: Nobility and the Church in Burgundy, 980–1198* (Ithaca, N.Y.: Cornell University Press), 46–64; for Anjou, see Penelope D. Johnson, *Prayer, Patronage, and Power: The Abbey of La Trinité, Vendôme (1032–1187)* (New York: New York University Press, 1981), 85–98.

31. Prou and Vidier, *Recueil des chartes de Saint-Benoît-sur-Loire*, no. 47 (November 941).

32. Aimoinus, *VsA*, c. 14. The possibility that this is the same Elisiernus is only just within the range of chronological possibility. If he were around forty when he entered the monastery (he had two grown children) in 941, then he would have been just over a hundred years old when Aimoinus heard the story after Abbo's death, probably in 1005. The Elisiernus who witnessed the miracle died within a year of relating the story to Aimoinus. Although this could have been the same man, it is more likely that two monks named Elisiernus, probably closely related, lived at Fleury in the tenth century.

33. André de Fleury, *Vita Gauzlini, Vie de Gauzlin*, ed. and trans. Robert-Henri

The Making of a Monk 33

While historians can trace the influence of prominent family members on the career of a young churchman, for those of obscure background, such as Abbo, such an evaluation of the influence of his relatives is difficult if not impossible. History has left us numerous examples of how powerful and influential relatives paved the way for advancement within the Church. One need look no further than the careers of such figures as Abbot Maiolus of Cluny (who "glittered with double nobility from both his parents") and his equally noble successors Odilo and Hugh.[34] Likewise, appointing bishops from noble families was considered normal if not praiseworthy. In contrast, one seldom encounters the promotion within the Church of men from relatively humble background, such as Abbo, who would eventually become the most important abbot in northern France, and his contemporary Gerbert of Aurillac, who held several important positions before becoming pope.[35] While his cousins may have provided important role models and smoothed the way for his acceptance within the monastic community, no evidence suggests that Abbo benefited from their influence in his eventual rise to power.

Following family tradition, Abbo's parents enrolled him in the school of Fleury in order to learn letters under the clerics of the Church of Saint-Pierre of Fleury. Upon arrival the young boy probably found himself in a friendly community, one in which he was already known because of his kinsmen, and in a school welcoming to any boy or young man of intellectual and spiritual merit, but also one highly conscious of social status.[36] His relatives in the Church were undoubtedly instrumental in securing him a position in the school of Fleury and helping him pursue his studies

---

Bautier and Gillette Labory (Paris: Centre national de la recherche scientifique, 1969), bk. 1, c. 25a; Eugène de Certain, ed., *Les miracles de saint Benoît écrits par Adrevald, Aimoin, André, Raoul Tortaire, et Hugues de Sainte Marie, moines de Fleury* (Paris: Mme. Ve. Jules Renouard, 1858), bk. 4, c. 6.

34. Odilo, *Vita Sancti Maioli,* quoted in Martindale, "French Aristocracy," 35.

35. Martindale, "French Aristocracy," 34–37.

36. Aimoinus, *VsA,* c. 1: "scholae clericorum aecclesiae sancti PETRI obsequentium traditur litteris imbuendus."

at other schools. On the other hand, Abbo's lack of noble connections may have played a role in some of the opposition within the Fleurisian community to his extended studies and his eventual election as abbot. Although the meek might inherit the earth, the Church tended to choose its leaders from among the ruling classes of society. In tenth- and eleventh-century Burgundy, for example, Church leaders, both bishops and abbots, frequently came from the nobility. Though some may have deplored the rich trappings of wealthy churchmen, others saw servile status as a definite impediment to participation in the Church, and even free but nonnoble status had its disadvantages for a churchman trying to assert authority over recalcitrant nobles among his monks or parishioners.[37] Even Aimoinus's largely laudatory account of Abbo's career contains references to problems caused by jealousy, which may mask social snobbery. Although the Rule of St. Benedict could not completely eradicate social distinctions within a monastery, its ideology created a climate in which someone of modest background could excel on the basis of merit. A boy of respectable, if not illustrious, background would certainly receive every opportunity to succeed, both spiritually and intellectually.

Abbo's formal education began when he was about seven years old with his entry into the school of Fleury, the monastery he was

37. Bouchard, *Sword, Miter, and Cloister,* 65–78, cites Ivo of Chartres (letter 59, *PL* 162:70) as an example of a churchman who mentioned nobility of birth as one of the points in favor of an archbishop of Sens and notes that even the abbots of Cluny came from the families of castellans and knights. According to her study, even after reforms designed to diminish the power of particular families, the composition of the Church hierarchy merely shifted from upper nobility to lower nobility. In addition to Ivo, she cites as authorities Candidus ("Vita Eigilis abbatis Fuldensis"), Bernard of Segni ("Commentaria in Matthaeum"), and Guigo of Chartreuse ("Vita S. Hugonis Gatianopolitani"). Alexander Murray, *Reason and Society in the Middle Ages* (Oxford: Clarendon, 1978), 406–15, has noted the social origins of a select group of saints and ecclesiastical reformers for the High Middle Ages (including Abbo); nonnobles are clearly in the minority, though they form a large enough group to indicate that social class was not an absolute impediment to advancement in the Church. Patrick Wormald, "Æthelwold and His Continental Counterparts: Contact, Comparison, Contrast," in *Bishop Æthelwold: His Career and Influence,* ed. Barbara Yorke (Woodbridge, England: Boydell, 1988), 22, observed that Abbo was "one of the few major early medieval churchmen specifically said *not* to have been an aristocrat."

The Making of a Monk 35

to serve for the rest of his life. According to Aimoinus, this school was run by clerics of the church of Saint-Pierre at Fleury, and it was by the ordering of divine providence that Abbo received his education at the same place where he was later to teach.[38] Evidently, Aimoinus did not consider it a foregone conclusion that a child trained at the school of Saint-Pierre would continue in his association with Fleury, nor that the monks of Fleury had necessarily received their initial education at that school. Although Abbo's parents may have intended a monastic, or at least ecclesiastical, career for him, they may also have wished merely to give him an opportunity to succeed in northern Europe's increasingly literate culture.[39] External schools for children were common at many monasteries, though the nature and existence of such a school at Fleury is not certain.[40] In either an internal or an external school, Abbo probably fell under the protection of a monk who supervised the education and general behavior of his young charges.[41] The *Consuetudines* of Fleury called for a *custos infantum*, who was to oversee the children in the monastery and who was to have help-

38. Aimoinus, *VsA*, c. 1: "Divina procerto ut credimus id preordinante providentia. ut inde primordia sumeret litterarum. ubi postmodum plenissime fluenta doctrine mentibus erat propinaturus sapientiam sitientium; Redderetque illis seu [et] eorum posteris. duplicatum suscepti fenoris fructum a quibus simplicia tantum acceperat rudimenta elementorum." Aimoinus did not state Abbo's age at entry into the school, but seven was a common age at which to begin such studies.

39. Other reasons for entering a child in a monastery included fulfillment of a vow or a desire to provide a living for several children, not all of whom could be accommodated on the family lands. For a somewhat earlier period, Pierre Riché, *Education and Culture in the Barbarian West from the Sixth through Eighth Century*, trans. John J. Contreni, foreword by Richard E. Sullivan (Columbia: University of South Carolina Press, 1976) [original French edition, 1962], 450, gives examples of all of these reasons for sending children to monasteries. In contrast, however, Bouchard, *Sword, Miter, and Cloister*, 59–62, notes that by the eleventh century, at least among the upper nobility, the decision to send a child into a monastery was not necessarily an economically advantageous one. In fact, she stressed that religious vocation occasionally led families to pursue dynastically suicidal courses in which all children of a generation (along with their land) entered the Church.

40. Guerreau-Jalabert, in her notes to Abbo, *Quaestiones grammaticales*, 18, argues against the existence of such a school at Fleury.

41. Riché, *Education and Culture*, 451–52, described this as the typical arrangement at monasteries. Abbo apparently fulfilled a similar role for Bernard of Beaulieu, whose father sent him to be educated at Fleury (Aimoinus, *VsA*, c. 10).

ers, depending on the number of children and their educational needs. The custos infantum and his aides provided both parental kindness and stern discipline, including beatings where necessary, to the boys under their care.[42] The boys in the monastic school, regardless of their ultimate destinations, probably formed strong bonds with each other and their teachers in these early years. By the time Abbo had completed his early education he had come to know intimately many of the boys who would become the leading churchmen of his generation.

Sometime before Abbo reached the age of fourteen, during Wulfald's abbacy (948–963), he took the monastic habit and became a monk of Fleury.[43] *The Monastic Ritual of Fleury* required from each candidate a thorough knowledge of the monastic rule and acceptance by the abbot and the entire congregation. Before entering the chapter house, each boy underwent an examination on the monastic rule. Then the prospective monks went with their master (*magister*) before the entire chapter, where each one of them in turn prostrated himself before the abbot and requested admittance to the monastic life from the entire congregation. When admission had been granted, the novice kissed the abbot's feet and wrote his profession. Interestingly enough, despite the strong emphasis on knowledge of the monastic rule, the novice did not have to be able to write. If he were unable to write for himself, the ritual allowed him to have someone else write for him. The new monk promised his stability, profession, and obedience according to the Benedictine Rule. Finally, after many prayers,

---

42. Thierry of Fleury [Thierry of Amorbach], *Consuetudines Floriacenses antiquiores*, ed. Anselme Davril and Lin Donnat, Corpus consuetudinorum monasticarum 7.3 (Sieburg, Germany: Schmitt, 1984), c. 18. Davril elsewhere makes the case that this set of customs was probably descriptive rather than prescriptive, designed to give the monks of a German monastery insight into the practices at Fleury. See Anselme Davril and Eric Palazzo, *La vie des moines au temps des grands abbayes Xe–XIIIe siècles* (Paris: Hachettes, Litératures, 2000), 34.

43. Aimoinus, *VsA*, c. 2, referred to Abbo as a *puer*. For common usage in such a context, see Pierre Riché, *Les écoles et l'enseignement dans l'Occident chrétien de la fin du Ve siècle au milieu du XIe siècle*, Collection historique (Paris: Aubier Montaigne, 1979), 200; Riché, *Education and Culture*, 447–48.

the abbot brought the monastic habit for each young man.[44] Abbot Wulfald seems to have asked each entrant his name. When he came to Abbo, Aimoinus tells us, Wulfald punned on the name, noting that the name Abbo differed in only one letter from the Greek (actually Aramaic) for "father" (*abba*), the root of the Latin *abbas*, meaning "abbot," and admonished the boy to live up to the promise of the name.[45]

The abbot of Fleury must have been a distant and awesome figure to the pupils and young monks. Wulfald had needed to ask the postulants their names, even though they had been studying in the monastic school for at least a year, probably longer. Wulfald was probably seldom, if ever, at Fleury during the last year of his abbacy. Once he had been appointed bishop of Chartres in 962, his episcopal duties undoubtedly kept him away from the cloister for long periods of time. After Wulfald's death in 963, business must have taken Richard, his successor, away from Fleury for long periods as well. June of 967 found Abbot Richard presenting a petition for confirmation of Fleury's privileges to King Lothar at Verberie. On a similar mission in 974 Richard met Lothar at Compiègne. In both instances Richard was over 200 kilometers (about 125 miles) from home.[46] If one assumes a rate of travel of no more than 30 kilometers a day for a well-staffed retinue, then the abbot spent at least two weeks on the road in each instance, but his absence would have been much longer if he made any side trips or stayed any length of time with the royal court or at friendly priories, monasteries, or episcopal schools along the way. These cannot have been the only times, however, that the abbot trav-

---

44. Anselme Davril, ed., *The Monastic Ritual of Fleury (Orléans, Bibliothèque Municipale, MS 123 [101])* (London: Henry Bradshaw Society, 1990), 122–26 (ritual for making a monk) and 31–33 (Davril's explication of the ritual): "stabilitatem meam et conversionem morum meorum et obedientiam secundam reguli sancti BENEDICTI."

45. Aimoinus, *VsA*, c. 2. Aimoinus did not indicate the source for this story. He cannot have witnessed the incident himself since he did not enter the monastery until Amalbert's abbacy (978–985), at least fifteen years later. Other members of Abbo's "class" may have remembered the incident or Abbo may have recounted it himself.

46. Prou and Vidier, *Recueil des chartes de Saint-Benoît-sur-Loire*, nos. 55 (5 June 967), 56 (5 June 967), and 60 (974, before 12 November).

eled abroad, to inspect distant priories, to resolve minor disputes, which never found their way into Fleury's cartulary, or merely to remind kings, counts, bishops, and other abbots of Fleury's interests in the region and its claims to prominence within the religious community of the Loire valley.

These excursions into the world outside of the cloister bore fruit in Fleury's wealth and reputation, which were factors attracting young men of Abbo's caliber to the monastery. Fleury's prestige was great enough that early in Wulfald's abbacy Bishop Mabbo of Pol-de-Léon, fleeing unrest in Brittany, brought the relics of St. Paul Aurelian to Fleury. Soon afterward, in what must have been one of the most impressive ceremonies of Wulfald's abbacy, the monks transferred the relics of St. Benedict from the crypt to the upper church at Fleury where they shared a repository with the newly acquired relics of St. Paul Aurelian.[47] Fleurisian monks had previously participated in the reforms of Saint-Evre of Toul and Saint-Vincent of Laon, and in about 950, impressed by Fleury's reputation, Bishop Ragenfred of Chartres invited Wulfald to carry out the spiritual and intellectual reform of Saint-Père of Chartres.[48]

Fleury's reputation for monastic purity had by this time spread beyond the Loire River valley and even across the Channel to the British Isles. Ironically, this English connection may well have begun when Continental monks fled to England to avoid reforms such as those at Fleury and Saint-Bertin.[49] When the English were ready to embrace reform, however, Fleury, the possessor of

---

47. Thomas Head, *Hagiography and the Cult of the Saints: The Diocese of Orléans, 800–1200* (Cambridge: Cambridge University Press, 1990), 56, 158. *MsB* 3.11, 7.16. For the earlier history of the relics of St. Benedict at Fleury, see Benedicta Ward, *Miracles and the Medieval Mind* (Philadelphia: University of Pennsylvania Press, 1982), 46–56; Patrick J. Geary, *Furta Sacra: Thefts of Relics in the Central Middle Ages* (Princeton, N.J.: Princeton University Press, 1978), 145–49.

48. Riché, *Abbon de Fleury*, 14; James Westfall Thompson, *The Medieval Library* (New York: Hafner, 1965), 229, 231.

49. John Nightingale, "Oswald, Fleury, and Continental Reform," in *Saint Oswald of Worcester: Life and Influence*, ed. Nicholas Brooks and Catherine Cubitt (London: Leicester University Press, 1996), 25–33.

St. Benedict's relics, became a magnet for reformers. Shortly before Abbo's time, in the early 940s, the Scottish monk St. Cathroé (Cadroe) studied with his Scottish companions at Fleury before becoming abbot of Waulsort on the Meuse, whence he went on to found a monastery near Metz.[50] Although Cathroé began in Ireland, where he had studied at Armagh, his journey to Fleury apparently encompassed the royal courts of Scotland and England before taking him to France.[51] He had probably heard of the suitability of Fleury for monastic profession while still in England from Archbishop Oda of Canterbury, who had studied there earlier in the century.[52] Bishop Æthelwold sent another English monk, Osgar, to Fleury so that he could bring back reformed ways to England.[53] The English connection continued in the next generation. Several English monks came to Fleury seeking a more rigorous form of monastic life than they could find at home. The most famous of these, Oswald, returned to England in 958, where he subsequently became bishop of Worcester and then archbishop of York, but several other English monks remained at Fleury, including Germanus, whom Oswald recalled to England in 961 to become abbot of Westbury-on-Trym.[54] At about the same time the bishop of Laon called on a dozen monks of Fleury, under the leadership of an Irish monk, to reform the monastery of Saint-Vincent of Laon.[55] Abbo was much younger than any of these monks, but he would have remembered their devotion to the monastic life when, a quarter of a century later, he agreed to teach in England.[56]

The year after Germanus returned to England, Wulfald be-

50. Riché, *Abbon de Fleury*, 14. David N. Dumville, "St. Cathroé of Metz and the Hagiography of Exoticism," in *Studies in Irish Hagiography: Saints and Scholars,* ed. John Carey, Máire Herbert, and Padráig O Riain (Dublin: Four Courts, 2001), 173.
51. Dumville, "St. Cathroé," 174–77.
52. Ibid., 184.
53. Nightingale, "Oswald, Fleury, and Continental Reform," 24.
54. David Knowles, *The Monastic Order in England: A History of Its Development from the Times of St. Dunstan to the Fourth Lateran Council, 943–1216* (Cambridge: Cambridge University Press, 1949), 40.
55. Dumville, "St. Cathroé," 186–87.
56. Aimoinus, *VsA,* c. 4. For Abbo's stay in England, see chapter 3.

came bishop of Chartres, an office he held for only one year before his death in 963. Upon his death, the monks of Fleury buried him in the church of Notre Dame at Fleury, before the altar of John the Evangelist. His epitaph briefly recorded his term as bishop and his devotion to St. Benedict.[57] Wulfald's successor, Richard, left a more extensive record of his administrative activities than either his predecessor or his successor. Over the course of his abbacy Richard secured royal protection for Fleury's rights and holdings. In 967 he successfully petitioned King Lothar of West Francia (954–986) for confirmation of Fleury's immunities and possessions in northern Francia. Although he did not mention specific holdings, Lothar promised protection for widespread holdings, including "churches or fields, villas or other possessions." At the same time, Lothar confirmed possessions in "the *pagus* of Orléans and in the *pagus* of Blois and in the *pagus* of the Gâtinais and in the *pagus* of Autun."[58] In 974 Lothar reconfirmed the immunity of Fleury with the added provision that the monks of Fleury could freely elect their abbots.[59] Between 963 and 975, Richard accepted for Fleury generous donations of land, *servi,* and, in one case, a silver cross.[60] Gifts continued under Richard's successor, Amalbert (978–986), though the record is not as extensive; in addition to the confirmation of Fleury's privileges by the king, only one charter survives from Amalbert's eight-year abbacy.[61]

Challenges to Fleury's prerogatives occupied the abbot's time as well. Richard had granted Herbert, lord of Sully (thirteen kilometers or eight miles from Fleury), some rights or land in benefice, but Herbert took over as well what had been set aside for the use of the monastery. Richard's efforts to force Herbert to relent

---

57. *MsB* 3.11. Hermannus Hagenus, ed., *Carmina nedii aevi maximam partem inedita* (1877; repr., Berne: Georgius Frobenius et soc., 1961), 136–37 (no. 81).
58. Prou and Vidier, *Recueil des chartes de Saint-Benoît-sur-Loire,* nos. 55 (5 June 967) and 56 (5 June 967).
59. Ibid., no. 60 (974, before 12 November).
60. Ibid., nos. 53 (July 963), 54 (October 964), 57 (November 968), 59 (June 970), and 61 (8 September 975), the last at Paris.
61. Ibid., nos. 64 (979), 67 (March 981), and 68 (16 October 982).

The Making of a Monk   41

were unavailing, and only the intervention of St. Benedict himself secured Herbert's deathbed repentance and the restoration of the property.[62] In another case in the 970s a dispute arose between the monks and a certain Romald over division of foraging land for pigs. Even the intervention of Bishop Arnulf of Orléans (972–1003) could not persuade Romald to mend his ways and come to an agreement with the monastery.[63] As with Herbert, the monks regained their rights only with the death of Romald, hastened a bit by St. Benedict.[64] Despite these adversities, Richard enjoyed a reputation as a holy and able administrator, and Aimoinus attributed to his reputation the decision by the lay protectors of La Réole in Gascony to turn the monastery over to Fleury for reform in 977 (a year before Richard's death). As it turned out, the monks of La Réole were an incorrigible lot who, according to Aimoinus, caused not only Richard but his successors, Amalbert and Oylbold, much trouble; many years later Abbo met his death trying to quell disturbances in the southern priory.[65]

Fleury's nearly ideal setting on the Loire River contributed to its overall prosperity and accounted for the covetousness of certain of the monks' neighbors for the monastery's lands and revenues. The monastery lay near the banks of the Loire, on the fertile floodplain. Although serious flooding occasionally threatened the monks and their livelihood, as was the case in 1003, the gains in soil fertility and access to water transport more than outweighed the risks of rising waters in most years.

A far more serious threat to a monastery in the Middle Ages was fire. The descriptions of the fires in the *Miracula sancti Benedicti* provide a wealth of detail on the buildings of the monastery.

---

62. *MsB* 2.7.
63. For the dating of Arnulf's episcopate, see Eugène de Certain, "Arnoul, évêque d'Orléans," *Bibliothèque de l'Ecole des chartes,* ser. 3, vol. 4 (1853): 425–32.
64. *MsB* 2.8.
65. Aimoinus, *VsA,* c. 16. Despite earlier contentions that the charter granting La Réole to Fleury was a forgery, Prou and Vidier consider the charter authentic but the appended donation of lands to La Réole a forgery (*Recueil des chartes de Saint-Benoît-sur-Loire,* no. 62 [977], including discussion by Prou and Vidier, pp. 159–65).

The monastic complex was enclosed by a wall and included two churches: Notre Dame, which held the relics of St. Benedict, and Saint-Pierre. Buildings serving the needs of the monks crowded together within the enclosure: a dormitory, a kitchen, a bake house, a guesthouse, and several granaries. Other passages in the *Miracula* mention a sacristy, a library, a treasury, an infirmary, and various other buildings.[66] The cramped layout of the monastic enclosure made it particularly vulnerable to fire, always difficult to fight due to the preponderance of flammable building materials and the difficulty of transporting water.[67] Abbo undoubtedly retained clear memories of the fires of Richard's abbacy. Sometime before 974 the church of Saint-Pierre and an adjoining granary caught fire. Miraculously, Fleury's other church, dedicated to the Virgin and housing the relics of St. Benedict, as well as the other monastic buildings escaped entirely. Not long afterward, in 974, some workmen who had been casting a new bell for the church left a candle burning on the lintel before they retired for the night. The candle burned down and set fire to the straw beds. The flames threatened the other buildings, and the brothers feared that the church of St. Benedict would catch fire as well. They rushed in to save the relics of St. Benedict, which they

---

66. Robert-Henri Bautier, "Le monastère et les églises de Fleury-sur-Loire sous les abbatiats d'Abbon, de Gauzlin et d'Arnaud (988–1032)," *Mémoires de la Société nationale des antiquaires de France,* ser. 9, vol. 4 (1968): 87–88.

67. For other examples of fires (real and imagined), see Gregory the Great, *Dialogues, Book II: St. Benedict,* trans. Myra L. Uhlfelder, Library of Liberal Arts (Indianapolis: Bobbs-Merrill Educational, 1967), 19 (c. 10); Gregory of Tours, *The History of the Franks,* trans. Lewis Thorpe (1974, repr., New York: Penguin, 1982), 465–67 (VIII.33); Bede, *The Life of St. Cuthbert,* ed. and trans. Bertram Colgrave, in *Two Lives of St. Cuthbert* (1940; repr., Cambridge: Cambridge University Press, 1985), 198–203 (chaps. 13–14); Bede, *Ecclesiastical History,* ed. and trans. J. E. King, Loeb Classical Library (Cambridge, Mass.: Harvard University Press and London: William Heinemann, 1963), bk. 3, c. 17, and bk. 4, c. 25; Rudolf of Fulda, *The Life of St. Leoba,* ed. and trans. C. H. Talbot, in *The Anglo-Saxon Missionaries in Germany,* The Makers of Christendom, ed. Christopher Dawson (London and New York: Sheed and Ward, 1954), 218–19. These examples make clear the immense destruction wreaked by fires and the difficulty of putting them out. In these examples, as at Fleury, even buildings built primarily of fire-resistant materials, such as stone, had enough flammable materials in the superstructure to allow considerable damage from fire.

The Making of a Monk 43

wrapped in the altar cloth. Once again the community avoided complete disaster. The wind, which had been threatening the granaries, died down, and the fire left the church of St. Benedict, along with the guesthouse, kitchen, and bake house, untouched. Within three years Abbot Richard and the monks had restored the burned church to its original glory.[68] When Abbo became abbot himself, he took steps to protect the monastery's most precious possessions from fire; Aimoinus records that Abbo's treasurer, Gauzfred, had a fireproof chamber built to house the monastery's valuables.[69] The precaution was worthwhile. A major fire threatened Fleury in 1002, two years before Abbo's death, and fire struck twice more under the abbacy of Abbo's successor, Gauzlin, in 1005 and in 1026.[70]

Despite the disruptions caused by fire, Abbo had almost certainly completed his basic education by the end of Richard's abbacy. Basic education in the early Middle Ages consisted of reading and writing Latin, chanting the Psalms, and figuring simple sums. The monastery could not, of course, spare the relatively expensive parchment for these lessons, so the young students practiced on wax tablets.[71] When they had completed this basic instruction, the boys could then enter the monastery and make use of Fleury's library. Here Abbo and his peers would have studied the works of the grammarians Priscian and Donatus, but they would also have had access to the works of writers such as Alcuin.[72] Now they were under the charge of the librarian and schoolmaster (*armarius*), a stern figure who "had great honor among the brothers" and was considered "equal to an apostle." When he corrected the students, they were to tremble at his voice, "as if at thunder."[73] Per-

---

68. *MsB* 2.9; "Annales Floriacenses," 974, in Vidier, *L'historiographie*, 219. Although the primary dedication of Fleury's second church is to the Virgin, after that church received the relics of St. Benedict, it was usually referred to as the church of St. Benedict.
69. Aimoinus, *VsA*, c. 15.
70. Bautier, "Fleury-sur-Loire," 87–89.
71. Riché, *Education and Culture*, 461–68.
72. Riché, *Abbon de Fleury*, 23–25.
73. Thierry of Fleury [Thierry of Amorbach], "Le coutumier de Fleury," ed. and

haps as important as their formal lessons, the young boys also acquired a sense of the rhythms of monastic life and the importance of the physical layout of the monastery in the life of a monk. Each day was divided into periods of work, study, eating, rest, and most important, worship. Monks arose in the early hours of the morning, well before dawn, to chant the Psalms together. From then until they went to bed at night, the monks and the boys under their care followed the schedule of work and prayer laid out in the Rule of Saint Benedict, modified to suit local circumstances. A text referred to as the *Horologium stellare monasticum* told the monks which stars would appear at which windows throughout the night, so that the monk in charge of waking the others could gauge the passage of time. The description of the monastery strongly suggests that this work was written specifically for Fleury, but the basic method must have been part of the oral (and possibly written) culture of many monasteries of the day.[74]

When he had mastered the most basic material, Abbo received the responsibility of teaching reading and chant to younger pupils. He was probably the brother (or one of two) assigned to help the custos infantum according to the *Consuetudines* of Fleury. Aimoinus did not describe Abbo's teaching duties in detail, and the *Consuetudines* of Fleury are vague on this point, but Abbo probably oversaw the education and also the leisure hours of a small group of youths.[75] When Hugh, an Aquitainian magnate, sent Bernard, one of his many sons, to be educated at Fleury, Abbot Richard put Bernard under Abbo's care.[76] Bernard was evidently a great favorite of Abbo, who later had the pleasure of teaching Bernard the liberal arts — probably some years later, after he had completed

---

trans. Anselme Davril and Lin Donnat, c. 9, in *L'abbaye de Fleury en l'an mil,* Sources d'histoire médiévale 32 (Paris: Centre national de la recherche scientifique, 2004), 182–85.

74. Davril and Palazzo, *Vie des moines,* 74–77, 208–9.

75. Riché, *Education and Culture,* 451–52, describes a *formarius, senior,* or *decanus* as fulfilling this function in Carolingian monasteries. In the tenth-century *Consuetudines Floriacenses antiquiores,* Thierry of Fleury assigned these functions to the *custos infantum* and his aides (cc. 18, 30).

76. Aimoinus, *V&A,* c. 10.

The Making of a Monk 45

advanced studies at the great schools of Paris and Reims. Abbo's pupil did not long remain with him, however. Soon after his education was completed, Bernard's father called him back to Aquitaine to be abbot of Solignac and later of Beaulieu-sur-Dordogne.[77] Abbo's other students included Gauzlin, who succeeded Abbo as abbot, and probably his biographer, Aimoinus, who entered Fleury under Richard's successor, Amalbert, as well as the monks Gerald and Vitalis, to whom he addressed a treatise on the Dionysian era.[78] Pierre Riché would add to this list Bern of Reichenau, Thierry of Fleury (later of Amorbach), Letald of Micy, Odolric of Saint-Martial of Limoges, and the Fleurisian monks Lantfred, Milanus, and Constantine, though their inclusion in the list is not as certain.[79] A poem by Adso of Montier-en-Der mentions both a brother named Richer and a teacher named Abbo, but whether these are Abbo of Fleury and his contemporary, the monk and historian Richer of Reims, is uncertain. Jason Glenn, however, notes that if Richer knew Adso, then "Adso's poem would suggest that Richer and Adso also knew Abbo of Fleury" when he studied there in the 960s.[80] While this identification is anything but certain, it opens the possibility that we are looking into the associations formed by the intellectual community at Reims.

After he had taught for several years, Abbo began intensive study of the seven liberal arts. The schools of Abbo's day do not appear to have followed the progression that characterized the later Middle Ages, from the basic skills of the trivium (grammar, rhetoric, and dialectic) to the more advanced skills of the quadriv-

---

77. Ibid. Bernard became bishop of Cahors in about 1005. See Pius Bonifacius Gams, *Series episcoporum ecclesiae Catholicae* (1873–1886; repr., Graz, Austria: Akademische Druck-u. Verlagsanstalt, 1957), 525.

78. For Gauzlin, see Helgaud de Fleury, *Vie de Robert le Pieux [Epitoma Vitae Regis Botherti Pii]*, ed. and trans. Robert-Henri Bautier and Gillette Labory (Paris: Centre national de la recherche scientifique, 1965), 120–21 (sec. 25); for Aimoinus, see *MsB* 2.18 (121); for Gerald and Vitalis, see A. Van de Vyver in Abbo of Fleury, "Les oeuvres inédits d'Abbon de Fleury," ed. A. Van de Vyver, *Revue bénédictine* 47 (1935): 154.

79. Riché, *Abbon de Fleury*, 74–76.

80. Jason Glenn, *Politics and History in the Tenth Century: The World and Works of Richer of Reims* (New York: Cambridge University Press, 2004), 274–75.

ium (arithmetic, geometry, music, astronomy). While still at Fleury, Abbo gained some knowledge of grammar, arithmetic, and dialectic, but when he wished to pursue the study of the remaining liberal arts, he had to leave Fleury for another school. He went to Paris and Reims for astronomy, though Aimoinus said that he did not learn as much from the masters at either school as he wished. Gerbert of Aurillac, the famous teacher who later became Pope Sylvester II, taught at the cathedral school of Reims for about ten years beginning in the early 970s, but Aimoinus did not mention him or any other master in his discussion of Abbo's education. Abbo seems to have left Reims before Gerbert arrived. He may have studied logic under Gerbert's master Gerranus, though Aimioinus stated that Abbo had already mastered logic before seeking Reims.[81] Even early in his education, Abbo had a strong interest in astronomy. His surviving works indicate that he had an impressive command of the techniques of *computus,* the science of determining the dates of movable feasts, such as Easter, and a strong interest in the movements of the planets.[82] After studying at Paris and Reims, Abbo returned to the neighborhood of Fleury to learn music from a cleric at Orléans. Apparently there were monks at Fleury who opposed spending monastic resources on his education. Aimoinus stated that Abbo had to learn music in secret, and at considerable cost, because of certain "jealous persons." Even with this outside education Abbo was not able to master all seven of the liberal arts; he had to learn rhetoric and geometry on his own.[83] Abbo's problems in achieving his educational goals indicate the shortcomings of the educational system in

---

81. Richer did not mention Abbo in his account of Gerbert's teaching career (*Histoire,* 3.43–65 [2:50–81]), nor did Adémar de Chabannes, *Chronique,* ed. Jules Chavanon (Paris: Alphonse Picard et fils, 1897), bk. 3, c. 39 (161), mention details of Abbo's education in his brief note on Abbo's death. For Gerannus, see Riché, *Abbon de Fleury,* 27–28. For Abbo's education, see Aimionus, *VsA,* c. 3.

82. For Abbo's work, see below, this chapter.

83. Aimoinus, *VsA,* c. 3. If Gerbert had been at Reims when Abbo arrived, Abbo could have learned geometry there, since Gerbert was one of the few experts on geometry in tenth-century Francia. For Gerbert's preeminence in mathematics, see Murray, *Reason,* 157–59.

The Making of a Monk   47

the West Frankish kingdom in the tenth century, even at Fleury.

Though the details of Abbo's experiences as a student have not been fully chronicled, the academic peregrinations of his contemporary, Gerbert of Aurillac, provide a fuller picture of the problems inherent in attempting to complete a well-rounded education in tenth-century Europe. Like Abbo, Gerbert came from a modest background and rose to be one of the leading scholars of his day as well as a major political figure. Many modern researchers name Abbo and Gerbert as the two most learned men and influential teachers of their day, though Gerbert's learning is usually ranked above Abbo's.[84] A comparison of Gerbert's educational quest with Abbo's indicates that Abbo's peregrinations were far from exceptional. As with Abbo, our main source for Gerbert's early career is one of his students, in Gerbert's case Richer, who included several chapters on his old teacher in his history of France.[85] Gerbert was Aquitanian by birth and spent his youth in the monastery of Saint-Gérald of Aurillac, where he learned grammar. As was the case with Abbo at Fleury, the abbot of Saint-Gérald recognized that the resources of his monastery were not adequate for the education of so promising a student as Gerbert. So Gerbert's abbot arranged for a pilgrim from Spain to take the young man back with him to the Iberian Peninsula to receive a fuller education, probably in 967.[86] Spain was one of the few areas of Europe in the tenth century where any scholars pursued serious mathematical studies, and Gerbert, along with many other Christians from western Europe, found the unfamiliar subject exceedingly difficult.[87] Gerbert's knowledge of mathematics (which apparently included

---

84. See, for example, Cora Elizabeth Lutz, *Schoolmasters of the Tenth Century* (Hamden, Conn.: Archon, 1977), 18,153; Pierre Riché, "L'enseignement de Gerbert de Reims dans le contexte européen," in *Gerberto: Scienza, storia e mito,* Atti del Gerberti Symposium, Bobbio 25–27 July 1983 (Bobbio, Italy: A. S. B. publicazione annuale, Studio II, 1985), 52; Riché, *Abbon de Fleury,* 5.

85. Richer, *Histoire,* 3:43–65 (2:50–81).

86. For the date see Lutz, *Schoolmasters of the Tenth Century,* 127; Latouche's notes on Richer, *Histoire* (2:51 n. 3).

87. Murray, *Reason,* 157–61.

arithmetic, music, and astronomy) made him, later in life, much sought after as a teacher.[88] He accompanied his teacher, Bishop Hatto, to Rome in 971, and, on the bishop's death there, the Emperor Otto I (936–973) invited Gerbert to return to Germany with him. Although this was an invitation that was difficult to refuse, Gerbert declined Otto's offer, and instead went to Reims, where he traded his knowledge of mathematics for instruction in logic from Gerannus of Reims, who was still at Reims when Abbo arrived to study astronomy.[89]

Gerbert, like Abbo, took up teaching after completing his studies at Reims. Gerbert's learning greatly impressed Archbishop Adalbero of Reims, who invited Gerbert to teach in the cathedral school of that city. Gerbert accepted and put his students through a rigorous program including Porphyry, Victorinus, and Boethius for logic and a thorough grounding in the classical Latin poets for rhetoric. Finally, he instructed his students in arithmetic, astronomy, and music. Since many students found astronomy particularly difficult, Gerbert constructed charts and three-dimensional models of the universe to facilitate their learning.[90] During his tenure at Reims, probably from about 972 to about 982 and again from the mid-980s until 989, Gerbert also functioned as a secretary to the archbishop of Reims, Adalbero.[91] Although

---

88. Richer, *Histoire*, 3:44 (2:52–53), mentions that when Gerbert arrived in Italy, a person skilled in astronomy and music was considered a great rarity, and in c. 49 that arithmetic was the most basic element of mathematics (*mathesis*). Richer did not specifically mention the study of geometry, but his description of Gerbert's astronomical studies (3:50–53 [2:58–63]) implies a thorough understanding of the principles of three-dimensional geometry.

89. Glenn, *Politics and History*, 62–63.

90. Lutz, *Schoolmasters of the Tenth Century*, 153, noted that the most respected teachers of the tenth century (Gerbert, Abbo, and Byrhtferth) frequently prepared charts and models to illustrate the more difficult of their subjects.

91. The exact dating of events in Gerbert's life is highly speculative. Our best sources for the period before he became pope are Richer, *Histoire*, and Gerbert's own letters (*Die Briefsammlung Gerberts von Reims*, ed. Fritz Weigle, MGH Die Briefe der Deutschen Kaiserzeit 2 [Berlin: 1966]). Most scholars agree that Gerbert arrived in Reims between about 970 and 972: Riché, "Enseignement de Gerbert," 55; Lutz *Schoolmasters of the Tenth Century*, 129; Harriet Pratt Lattin, introduction to *The Letters of Gerbert with his Papal Privileges as Sylvester II*, ed. and trans. Harriet Pratt Lattin

The Making of a Monk 49

Abbo probably studied at Reims before Gerbert's time, another monk of Fleury, Constantine, did study with Gerbert, and the two continued to correspond for several years afterward.[92]

Only much later, in the bitterly contested ecclesiastical debates of Abbo's early abbacy, do we have any record of contact between Abbo and Gerbert, often linked in modern scholarship as the two most learned men of the tenth century.[93] Gerbert and Abbo frequently came down on opposite sides of political questions in Church councils (such as monastic tithes at the Council of Saint-Denis and the deposition of Archbishop Arnulf of Reims at the Council of Saint-Basle of Verzy). Curiously enough, however, Aimoinus never mentioned Gerbert, either positively or negatively, in the entire *Vita sancti Abbonis*. Aimoinus may have been covering up a personal animosity between the two men (though the few times they mention each other in their letters they are coolly respectful) or may have been avoiding discussion of a Gerbertian faction at Fleury that threatened to disrupt monastic tranquility during the early years of Abbo's abbacy. Abbo much later wished to count Gerbert among his friends, but did not mention him as a teacher.[94]

Like Gerbert, Abbo began to produce specialized works, for his own use and that of his students. According to Aimoinus, Abbo's early works consisted of several discussions of astronomy, a work on computus (the reckoning of dates), and another on syllogisms.[95] In all of his works, like those of his student Byrhtferth

---

(New York: Columbia University Press, 1961), 4. In the early 980s Gerbert became abbot of Bobbio, but internal opposition to his rule forced him to vacate that post and return to Reims after only a short stay. For a discussion of Gerbert's relationship with Bobbio, see Michele Tosi, "Il governo abbaziale de Gerberto a Bobbio," in *Gerberto: Scienza, storia, e mito,* Atti del Gerbert Symposium, Bobbio, 25–27 July 1983 (Bobbio, Italy: A. S. B. publicazione annuale, Studio II, 1985), 71–234, particularly 74, which contains a helpful chart outlining the various dates suggested for Gerbert's abbacy.

92. See letters of Gerbert (Lattin, letters 2–7, 92, 148, 151, 204; Weigle, letters 86, 142, 143, 191).

93. See Lutz, *Schoolmasters of the Tenth Century*, 18.

94. Abbo, letter 1: "amicum colo et colui."

95. Aimoinus, *VsA,* c. 3. Modern scholars have made reasonably certain identifica-

and his contemporary Gerbert, Abbo tried to clarify the subject by the use of diagrams and charts.[96] Abbo illustrated his work on astronomy with diagrams showing planetary latitudes and the phases of the moon.[97] Likewise, Abbo's computistical work showed a preference for spatial representations of complex concepts and contained many mnemonic devices.[98] Abbo probably intended his syllogisms for students as well. He dedicated his work to "B," whom Van de Vyver tentatively identified as Abbo's student Bernard of Beaulieu,[99] and his syllogisms relied heavily on the writings of Boethius, whose work also appeared prominently in Gerbert's curriculum for the cathedral school of Reims.[100]

Despite his learning Abbo appears not to have held any position higher than a teacher under supervision of the schoolmaster (*armarius*) after becoming an aide to the *custos infantum*, the teacher of the children. Marco Mostert described Abbo as "the renowned schoolmaster of the school of Fleury," but the evidence does not indicate that Abbo actually headed the school of Fleury, although we cannot definitively rule out this possibility.[101] Since

---

tions of all of these works. For the manuscripts, see Van de Vyver in Abbo, "Les oeuvres inédits," 125–69. For an edition of Abbo's syllogisms, see Van de Vyver's edition of Abbo's works, *Abbonis Floriacensis opera inedita*. For an edition of two of Abbo's astronomical treatises, see "Two Astronomical Tractates," 113–33.

96. Lutz, *Schoolmasters of the Tenth Century*, 153.

97. Abbo, "Two Astronomical Tractates," 124, 128. Thomson noted that Abbo's astronomical works are almost universally regarded as "highly derivative" and suggested that most of the material (including the chart of planetary latitudes) ultimately derived from Pliny's *Natural History* (115).

98. Faith Wallis, "Abbo of Fleury and the Reckoning of Time," paper presented at the Twenty-fifth International Congress on Medieval Studies, Western Michigan University, Kalamazoo, Mich., 10–13 May 1990.

99. Van de Vyver, in Abbo, *Abbonis Floriacensis opera inedita*, 27. Given that we know the names of very few of Abbo's students and that names beginning with B were common in tenth-century Francia, the identification is tenuous at best. Another candidate is Byrhtferth, whom Abbo taught in England, though Aimoinus indicated that Abbo composed his work on syllogisms before going to England (Aimoinus, *V&A*, c. 3).

100. Richer, *Histoire*, 3.46 (2:54–57); Van de Vyver, in Abbo, *Abbonis Floriacensis opera inedita*, 21.

101. Marco Mostert, "The Political Ideas of Abbo of Fleury," *Francia* 16.1 (1989): 85. Elsewhere (*Political Theology*, 30), Mostert states that Abbo held the office of *armarius* (schoolmaster, librarian) of Fleury, though he gives no source for this information,

The Making of a Monk 51

the *Consuetudines,* composed in 1010, only shortly after Aimoinus wrote his *Vita* of Abbo, give specific titles to the officials of the monastery, probably using titles long traditional at Fleury, it is highly unlikely that Aimoinus would have omitted this information. Someone more senior may have been schoolmaster, or "jealousy," such as that which forced him to learn music in secret, may have kept Abbo from holding that post. The only monk suspected of rivaling Abbo in learning or monastic preferment at Fleury is Constantine; however, other monks, equally learned, may have resided at Fleury. Regardless of his specific position, it is probably about this time that Abbo received the rank of deacon (*levita*).[102] In the early Middle Ages deacons had served mainly as assistants to priests, but in the context of tenth- and eleventh-century ecclesiastical bureaucracy, this title often carried with it the duty of serving as a teacher or a scribe.[103]

Though in the 960s Fleury had not been able to provide for Abbo's educational needs, by the time Abbo had completed his studies the standard of learning at Fleury may have increased through the efforts of his contemporaries, few of whom have left a record of their work. Constantine, whose learning is unquestioned, is known chiefly through his correspondence with Gerbert of Reims and his fleeting career as abbot of Micy, one of Fleury's neighbors.[104] An account of Abbo's own education and early career survives only in the *Vita sancti Abbonis,* which owed its composition to Abbo's abbacy and martyrdom, rather than to his learning. Abbo's memory would have survived, of course, through his own works, but his early education, the context for many of

---

and the term *armarius* does not occur in Fleurisian documents from this era. Cousin made a similar assertion when he described Abbo as the *écolâtre* of Fleury (*Abbon de Fleury-sur-Loire,* 56), though he admitted that he was extrapolating from the sources.

102. Aimoinus, *VsA,* c. 4, which indicates that Abbo had attained this office before leaving for England in about 985.

103. Fanning, *A Bishop and His World,* 71–72.

104. For Constantine's career, see F. M. Warren, "Constantine of Fleury, 985–1014," *Transactions of the Connecticut Academy of Arts and Sciences* 15 (July 1909): especially 286–90, for his rivalry with Abbo.

those works, and the overall shape of his career, other than his elevation to the abbacy, would have been all but impossible without the help of Aimoinus's *Vita*. Fleury may thus have housed several monks capable of directing the school, perhaps somewhat less learned than either Abbo or Constantine but better suited by temperament and age to the oversight of a large and important school.[105]

Abbo's training in the liberal arts received an early practical test in refuting beliefs that the end of the world was at hand. Abbo's first contact with apocalyptic beliefs came in his student days at Paris. Many years later, Abbo recalled that when he was a young man or perhaps a teenager (*adolescentulus*) studying at Paris,[106] he heard a preacher in a church claiming that when one thousand years from the birth of Christ had been fulfilled the Antichrist would come and Judgment Day would not be far behind. Such apocalyptic expectations had appeared periodically throughout the early Middle Ages, and the ecclesiastical authorities regarded them as threatening to political stability and established institutions.[107] Abbo quickly saw that the best way to refute this argument was through the traditional references to biblical accounts of the end of the world from the Gospels, the Apocalypse

---

105. André, *Vita Gauzlini*, bk. 1, c. 2, listed several learned monks of Fleury, some of whom were active during Abbo's abbacy and a few of whom may have completed their education before Abbo took office in 987 or 988. For more on scholarly activity at Fleury, see chapter 6.

106. The term *adolescentulus*, like most other terms indicating age, had no fixed meaning. Riché, *Education and Culture*, 448, notes that several late antique writers applied the term *adolescens* to youths over the age of fourteen, but he also cites writers of the same period who applied the term to children as young as eight and men as old as thirty-six. Charlton T. Lewis and Charles Short, *A Latin Dictionary* (1879, repr., Oxford: Clarendon, 1966), note a similar ambiguity for the classical period (under *adulescens* and *adulescentulus*). Since Abbo was sufficiently mature to leave the monastery and even, given provocation, to argue in public, he must have been over fourteen and probably close to twenty, or possibly even older.

107. Richard Landes, "Lest the Millennium Be Fulfilled: Apocalyptic Expectations and the Pattern of Western Chronography, 100–800 C.E.," in, *The Use and Abuse of Eschatology in the Middle Ages*, ed. Werner Verbeke, Daniel Verhelst, and Andres Welkenhuysen (Louvain, Belgium: Leuven University Press, 1988), 207–8.

The Making of a Monk   53

of John, and the book of Daniel.[108] One might suppose that he also drew on the commentaries of Augustine and Jerome, both of whom wrote against the possibility that a person could easily predict the end of the world. Was this apocalyptic preacher an isolated individual or part of a widespread movement? Abbo's recollections suggest the former, but the ecclesiastical authorities would hardly have felt it worthwhile to refute him unless he at the very least had touched a responsive chord among his hearers. Giving the task of refutation to a young man, even if a promising student, however, suggests that Abbo's teachers perhaps regarded the preacher more as a convenient target for an academic exercise than as a serious threat. Others have seen this preacher not as a herald of the imminent apocalypse but someone using an old Carolingian method of quieting apocalyptic expectations by postponing the end times until the millennium of Christ's birth — a tactic that was more soothing in 800 than in 970.[109]

Sometime later, probably in the late 960s, Abbot Richard received a letter from Lotharingia describing another heresy involving the end of the world. Unlike the preacher Abbo refuted in Paris, the proponents of this heresy clearly had a widespread following, and "the rumor [of their teachings] filled almost the whole world."[110] The followers of the heresy believed that when the Annunciation (25 March) and Good Friday fell on the same day the world was going to end. This was hardly a new belief. Just over a century earlier, in 865, Christian of Stavelot had suggested the apocalypse would come when Easter and the Annunciation (25 March) coincided. Christian left a degree of uncertainty as to the year, however, as he posited merely that each conjunction of dates indicated the possibility of the apocalypse, not that any one year

---

108. Abbo, *Apologeticus,* London, BL Add 10972, f. 22v (= *PL* 139:471). Abbo did not mention exactly what passages he cited, only the names of the books of the Bible.
109. Richard Landes, "The Fear of the Apocalyptic Year 1000: Augustinian Historiography, Medieval and Modern," in *The Apocalyptic Year 1000: Religious Expectation and Social Change, 950–1050,* ed. Richard Landes, Andrew Gow, and David C. Van Meter (Oxford: Oxford University Press, 2003), 250–51.
110. Abbo, *Apologeticus,* London, BL Add 10972, f. 22v (= *PL* 139:471–72).

could be singled out with certainty.[111] It is probable, however, that this belief had a much longer history, as indirect evidence suggests that a woman preaching the apocalypse in Mainz in the 840s may have also taken the conjunction of the Annunciation and the Passion of Christ on Good Friday as the basis for her predictions.[112] In the tenth century Easter fell on 27 March (and hence Good Friday on 25 March) in 908, 970, 981, and 992.[113] Since Richard was abbot from 963 to 978, however, it is possible that the heretics were looking ahead to 981. The cluster of potentially apocalyptic dates all within a few years of each other may well have heightened expectation that the apocalypse was approaching rapidly.[114] On the other hand, it seems probable that the sixty-two-year gap between 908 and 970 had fostered a renewed fear of the conjunction, as an unusual thing (not remembered by many still alive).

Abbot Richard delegated the task of refuting this belief to Abbo.[115] Richard may have chosen Abbo because of his activities in Paris as well as other interests that prepared him particularly well for this task. Unfortunately, Abbo's work on the subject is lost, but we can nevertheless speculate on the points he must have raised. Abbo, like most religious scholars of his day, had an excellent command of scriptural references, as he had already demonstrated in Paris, but his work on computus would have given his arguments a basis in "scientific" as well as scriptural authority. Whether Abbo undertook the refutation of these apocalyptic claims because of his background in computus or whether he studied computus in order to be armed against these heresies can-

---

111. David C. Van Meter, "Christian of Stavelot on Matthew 24:42 and the Tradition that the World Will End on March 25th," *Recherches de théologie ancienne et médiévale* 63 (1996): 68–70.

112. Ibid., 86–87.

113. According to Cousin, *Abbon de Fleury-sur-Loire*, 55 and n22, Good Friday fell on the day of the Annunciation only once during Richard's abbacy, in 970; the last previous coincidence of these holy days was in 908. The chronological table in Arthur Giry, *Manuel de diplomatique* (Paris, 1894), indicates that in the tenth century Easter fell on 27 March (and hence Good Friday on 25 March) in 908, 970, 981, and 992.

114. Van Meter, "Christian of Stavelot," 88.

115. Abbo, *Apologeticus*, f. 22v (= PL 139:471–72).

The Making of a Monk

not be known. He turned his computistical work to good purpose shortly after 981, when he produced a correction of the Dionysian era. According to Abbo, Christ was actually born twenty-one years earlier than suggested by the Dionysian calendar. Thus, the millennium of Christ's birth had already passed in 979, thereby rendering the year 1000 harmless.[116]

Scholars have hotly debated how widespread these beliefs in the impending apocalypse were in the tenth century.[117] While some see the relatively meager references to apocalypticism in the sources as an indication of the minor role played by these ideas, others have seen the very paucity of references as an indication of how deeply troubled "establishment" writers were by these potentially disruptive movements, to the point that they referred to them as little as possible in their own writings. For Abbo's immediate milieu of Fleury, expectation of final times seems to have been relatively muted. Both of the incidents recorded above occurred outside of Fleury, in the big city of Paris and in the west Frankish borderlands of Lotharingia. Closer to home, those making gifts to Fleury in the 960s and 970s mentioned "fear of the Last Judgment" in the preambles to their charters, but only in 974 did King Lothar specifically mention the "end of time" (*sub fine saeculi*) in a confirmation made to Fleury, a formula used by his successor, Louis V, in 979 and copied verbatim along with the rest of the preamble by Hugh Capet in his confirmation of 987.[118] This suggests that Lothar did have the imminent end of the world in mind in 974, but that his successors, who merely copied his formula, and the other donors to Fleury did not see this as a strong enough motivation to emphasize it in their bequests. While apocalypticism may have formed a backdrop for much of Abbo's life

---

116. Landes, "Fear of the Apocalyptic Year 1000," 252–53.

117. For the pro-apocalyptic side of the debate, see Landes, "Introduction: The *terribles espoirs* de 1000," 3–15. This volume, unfortunately, does not include any essays on anti-apocalyptic interpretations, but Landes does discuss the French historiography in detail in his introductory essay.

118. Prou and Vidier, *Recueil des chartes de Saint-Benoît-sur-Loire*, nos. 60 (974, before 12 November) and 64 (979).

and impinged on his career at several key points, his later life contained enough immediate problems, from disputed abbatial elections to murderous bishops, to keep him otherwise occupied.

Abbo's educational career and the respect accorded him by his abbot and peers indicate that though social class continued to play a role in monastic preferment, an intelligent monk of respectable but nonnoble background could gain the esteem of the monastic community through his intellectual prowess. His contact with the English monks, who migrated to Fleury in search of a purer form of monasticism, must undoubtedly have impressed upon him his good fortune in living in one of the great monastic centers of Europe. Conversely, Abbo also learned much of the pettiness of monastic life. The "jealous" monks who would have prevented him from learning music give a hint of the sort of trivial conflicts that can be an irritation in any closed community. Even Fleury, however, could not provide a complete education, and his travels in search of knowledge gave him a strong academic background but also insights into the problems facing religious and lay communities throughout northern Francia. By the time he reached adulthood Abbo had received training at the most important schools of the region and had experienced monastic life both at its best and in its least attractive aspects.

3

THE MAKING OF AN ABBOT

By the 980s Abbo had left his student days long behind and was now an active participant in the life of his monastery. He was by now one of the most learned monks of Fleury and was naturally drawn into the politics of the abbey. The monastic life under the Benedictine Rule promised the ideal of a harmonious society in which the monks left behind worldly possessions and status. All monks would be equal in humility and obedience, like children under the fatherly care of the abbot, being given offices according to their monastic merits rather than according to previous status or wealth. In practice this ideal was no more often perfectly realized than most others. Monastic literature is filled stories of monks and nuns who tried to retain their worldly status and privileges within the confines of the cloister. One of the earliest stories of St. Benedict, the sixth-century author of the Benedictine Rule, tells of how Benedict reproved a well-born monk for rebellious thoughts while serving those he considered beneath him. At the famous Benedictine establishment of Wearmouth-Jarrow overcoming social class was a major challenge facing the abbots.[1] Class distinctions were not the only forces, however, that could divide a monastic com-

---

1. Henry Mayr-Harting, *The Venerable Bede, the Rule of Saint Benedict, and Social Class,* Jarrow Lecture (Jarrow, England: Rector of Jarrow, 1976) includes a summary of

munity. Politics, monastic ideology, and jealousy among the monks might also disturb the internal tranquility of the monastery. A good abbot will smooth over these differences, and bestow honors based on seniority or merit in humility and obedience.[2] An abbatial election, however, can bring out the worst in the congregation, as factions form around one or another candidate. Abbo received his introduction to the full ferocity of internal monastic politics when he was in his late thirties.

The death of Abbot Amalbert in 985 precipitated three years of internal conflict at Fleury that ended only after Abbo's establishment as abbot early in 988. Abbo's eventual succession to the abbacy was anything but a certainty. Although one of the most learned monks at Fleury, Abbo did not have significant administrative experience at this time nor the political connections necessary to protect Fleury's interests. Later events show that Abbo would have been an excellent choice, but none of the sources mention his candidacy.[3] Instead, the monks made a controversial decision and elected Oylbold as abbot, a move approved by King Lothar.[4] Aimoinus described Oylbold as "distinguished in birth and habits, according to the values of the world."[5] This emphasis on the secular nature of Oylbold's qualifications to the exclusion of his monastic background suggests that Oylbold's spiritual accomplishments were less well developed than some monks would have preferred. The general impression left by the meager documents relating to his abbacy is that he may have been a good man, but not a notable one, for either learning or piety, in the monastic world.[6]

Opposition to Oylbold's abbacy arose almost immediately.

---

the anecdote from Gregory the Great's *Dialogues* (2–3), followed by a discussion of social class in the Benedictine Rule and other rules (3–8), before entering into a detailed discussion of social class in the works of Bede (8–18).

2. Benedict of Nursia, *RB 1980: The Rule of Benedict in Latin and English, with Notes*, ed. Timothy Fry et al. (Collegeville, Minn.: Liturgical Press, 1981), c. 2.16–22 (174–75).

3. Aimoinus, *VsA*, c. 4–7; *MsB* 2.18, 3.1.

4. *MsB* 2.18.

5. Aimoinus, *VsA*, c. 4: "secundum seculi dignitatem genere ac moribus clarus."

6. The major chronicles of the day do not mention Oylbold. See Rodulfus Glaber, *Historiarum libri quinque/The Five Books of the Histories*, ed. Neithard Bulst, trans.

The Making of an Abbot   59

Gerbert, the head of the cathedral school of Reims, and Archbishop Adalbero of Reims denounced the new abbot of Fleury as a "usurper" and conducted an intense letter-writing campaign against him. Gerbert wrote letters in Adalbero's name urging Ebrard, abbot of Saint-Julien of Tours, and Maiolus, abbot of Cluny, to oppose the usurper publicly and to refuse to correspond with him. Maiolus, though condemning the usurper, hesitated to interfere directly in the internal affairs of another monastery. He continued contact with the usurper, perhaps in hopes of persuading him to step down. Gerbert wrote back that Maiolus must match his actions to his words and cut off the intruder completely, lest the abbot inadvertently lend legitimacy to the usurper's rule. Ebrard apparently responded more favorably; he wrote back concurring with Gerbert's opinion of the usurper. For his part, Gerbert replied that Ebrard and Maiolus had convinced him of the need for action. In other words, after lobbying Ebrard and Maiolus to condemn the newly elected abbot, he deferentially suggested that their arguments had persuaded him to oppose the usurper. As a result of Gerbert's efforts, the abbots of Reims rallied behind Gerbert and issued a letter to the monks of Fleury in which they condemned the usurper and urged his expulsion.[7]

John France and Paul Reynolds (Oxford: Clarendon, 1989); Adémar, *Chronique;* Richer, *Histoire*. The *MsB* describes events that occurred under Oylbold's abbacy in only two chapters (2.18–2.19) and mentions him in passing in two others (3.1 and 7.13).

7. Lattin, letters 76, 87, 93, 94, 97; Weigle, letters 69, 80, 87, 88, 95. Lattin, in her notes to the letters, identifies the usurper with Oylbold. Weigle summarizes the literature on the question in the notes; his dating of the letters suggests that he agreed with this identification. Unfortunately, these letters do not name the usurper, are not dated, and survive only in copies. Scholars have dated the letters approximately using internal references and the relative position of the letters in the register. Lattin and Weigle differ slightly on the dating of the letters but never by more than a month or two (see Lattin's introduction, 20–24, 29–31). None of these letters mentions Oylbold by name. In four of the letters directly concerned with this affair, Gerbert described the abbot as a *pervasor* (usurper) (Lattin, letters 76, 92, 93, 151; Weigle, letters 69, 86, 87, 142). In the remaining letters Gerbert and his correspondents called him *perfides* (Lattin, letter 94; Weigle, letter 88), or mentioned his crime (*crimen*) (Lattin, letter 87; Weigle, letter 80), or referred to him simply as *persona* (Lattin, letter 97; Weigle, letter 95). For simplicity's sake I have followed Gerbert's preferred usage and refer to him as the usurper throughout.

Gerbert's intense interest in the abbacy of Fleury requires some explanation. He was a close adviser to Archbishop Adalbero of Reims (c. 969–989), in whose name he wrote several letters concerning the situation at Fleury. But Fleury was not in the archdiocese of Reims; it fell under the jurisdiction of the archbishop of Sens, Seguin (977–999), whom Gerbert never mentioned in his correspondence on Fleury. Gerbert and Adalbero's interest in Fleury stemmed in part from its preeminence among French monasteries. Fleury boasted a Carolingian foundation and had received the support of several generations of kings of Francia. Its reputation for monastic discipline and learning stretched across the Channel to England, and it was the proud possessor of the relics of St. Benedict, though it did not reach the height of its fame and influence until Abbo's abbacy. Nevertheless, Adalbero had relied on the assistance of monks from Fleury and Brogne as well as Saint-Remi in his reform of the monasteries of Mouzon and Saint-Thierry in 971 and 972,[8] and he may well have retained an interest in Fleury as a center of monastic reform. Furthermore, Fleury and Reims maintained contact through the latter's cathedral school. Before becoming a teacher at Fleury, Abbo had studied briefly at Reims,[9] as had other Fleurisians of his generation, including Constantine of Fleury, one of Gerbert's students at Reims. After returning to Fleury from Reims, Constantine maintained a correspondence with his old teacher and kept Gerbert informed of affairs at Fleury. Before the affair of the usurper, Gerbert had written several letters to Constantine on astronomy, arithmetic,

---

8. Michel Bur, ed. and trans., *Chronique ou livre de fondation du monastère de Mouzon / Chronicon Mosomense seu liber fundationis monasterii sanctae Mariae O.S.B. apud Mosomum in diocesi Remensi* (Paris: Centre national de la recherche scientifique, 1989), 135.

9. Aimoinus, *VsA*, c. 3. Gerbert had begun teaching at Reims in the 970s, when Abbo would have been in his twenties or thirties. Though it is not improbable that the two men knew each other at Reims, no surviving sources connect the two. Aimoinus never mentioned Gerbert in the *VsA* or in the *MsB;* Abbo referred to Gerbert in a letter (letter 1) but did not mention having known Gerbert as a student. For the dates of Gerbert's teaching, see Lutz, *Schoolmasters of the Tenth Century,* 129; Riché, "Enseignement de Gerbert," 55.

The Making of an Abbot   61

music, and the use of the abacus.[10] Once the usurper took control, Gerbert urged Constantine to come to Reims rather than give legitimacy to the new abbot by remaining at Fleury.[11] Constantine apparently did not avail himself of this invitation, but at the death of the usurper Gerbert wrote again, urging both Constantine and the new abbot (if elected in time) to come celebrate the feast of St. Remigius (1 October) at Reims.[12]

Constantine's role in the election and subsequent opposition to Oylbold is ambiguous. Gerbert, in a letter congratulating Constantine on the death of the usurper, held his former student partly responsible for cooled feelings between Gerbert and the Fleurisians over the disputed election.[13] Constantine soon after asked Gerbert's aid in a small problem, the theft of monastic property, which would be easier to solve than the important affair in which Gerbert had been unsuccessful. The important affair was, presumably, the matter of the usurper at Fleury. The tone of the letter suggests that Constantine had been convinced by Gerbert's thinking on this matter.[14] If Constantine, one of the leading scholars

---

10. Lattin, letters 2–7. Weigle does not include these letters in his collection.
11. Lattin, letter 92; Weigle, letter 86.
12. Lattin, letter 151; Weigle, letter 142. Lattin dates the letter 5 December 988, before letter 151 in her collection (142 in Weigle). Weigle, following the order of the manuscript, places it immediately after letter 142 (Lattin, 151), and dates the two letters September 988 and September–October 988 respectively.
13. Lattin, letter 151; Weigle, letter 142: "affectus noster a Floriacensibus te faciente paululum abalienatus, te faciente sit plurimum reconciliatus." Lattin translates this as "our affection, alienated somewhat from the monks of Fleury in spite of your efforts, may be fully regained through your efforts." Cousin, *Abbon de Fleury-sur-Loire*, 91–92n2, however, interprets *te faciente* in the first clause as meaning that Constantine was influential in alienating Gerbert's affection, not that Constantine tried unsuccessfully to prevent the loss of affection. Cousin's reading seems more probable in light of the Latin and the overall tone of the letter.
14. Lattin, letter 148; Weigle, letter 143. Constantine referred to Gerbert's attempts to liberate Fleury from the enemy (*hoste*), though his advice was rejected (*contempti estis*). Both editors agree that the affair in question was the usurpation of Fleury's abbacy. This letter is problematic. Lattin translates the passage, "Modo quia liberavit nos Dominus" as "Now that the Lord has delivered us." The reading "Just as the Lord delivered us" is equally likely, though, and would indicate that Constantine is referring to the small matter rather than to the large one of the usurper. Cousin, *Abbon*

of Fleury, had sided with the usurper, however briefly, the usurper cannot have been as thoroughly unworthy as Gerbert portrayed him, and his support at Fleury must have been fairly broad. In any case, Constantine was now turning to his mentor Gerbert for help with a problem that was rightly the concern of the new abbot, though its outcome would affect the entire abbey. This situation does not appear to have been a case of an outside power, such as the West Frankish king, imposing a candidate upon an unwilling congregation.[15]

Although Abbo's name does not appear in these discussions, he must have played an important part in this dispute. As a former student at Reims, he undoubtedly had personal contacts with several teachers at the cathedral school, though not, apparently, with Gerbert himself. He also had a reputation for eloquence, which he had exercised in writing a rebuttal to certain heretical doctrines at the request of Abbot Richard.[16] Even if he had desired to be neutral in this matter, both sides would have exerted pressure on the young man to use his rhetorical skill on their behalf, and the opposition may even have suggested his name as a potential rival, with or without his consent. Since Oylbold clearly had at least grudging support from Constantine, who probably equaled Abbo in erudition and connections, the opposition would have exerted even greater pressure on Abbo to come over to its

---

de Fleury-sur-Loire, 91–92n2, apparently followed Lattin's reading, since he cited this passage to characterize the usurper.

The identification of the "lord and lady" with whom Gerbert is to use his influence is unclear. Lattin identifies them as Hugh Capet and Queen Adelaide and Weigle prefers this but notes that others have suggested Otto III and Theophanu. Gerbert and Adalbero had close ties with both couples, but Hugh Capet undoubtedly had more influence in the Loire valley than did the German emperor.

15. Warren, "Constantine," 285–92, interpreted Constantine's subsequent moves to Micy and Nouaillé as motivated by the unsympathetic atmosphere in the Orléanais under Oylbold (whom Warren identified as the usurper) and Abbo. According to this analysis, Oylbold and Abbo opposed the open-minded "proto-scholasticism" (my term) of Gerbert and Constantine with their own rigid monastic-patristic thought. This analysis provides insights into the factionalism at Fleury but is anachronistic in its portrayal of monastic-scholastic divisions.

16. Abbo, *Apologeticus,* f. 22v (= *PL* 139:471–72).

The Making of an Abbot　　　　　　　63

side. The dispute over the abbacy pointed up, once more, the potential rifts within the monastic community as well as the intense external political pressure that a monastery of Fleury's reputation had to endure. Abbo cannot be blamed if he wished to escape to a more spiritual and intellectual existence.

His opportunity came from an unexpected quarter. At about this time, early in Oylbold's abbacy, legates from Oswald, archbishop of York, came to Fleury to request a teacher who could help restore advanced learning to the English monasteries. Oswald's connection with Fleury went back many years. His uncle, Oda, archbishop of Canterbury (d. 958), had spent a brief period at Fleury shortly after the monastery's reform in 930.[17] Oda greatly admired the monastic practice of Fleury and took the monastic habit there, though he did not reside at Fleury and continued as archbishop. In about 950 he sent Oswald, the future archbishop of York, there to become a monk. Several English monks followed Oswald to Fleury, including Germanus, who eventually became abbot of Ramsey Abbey in England. Oswald stayed at Fleury until called home by his uncle in 958. Upon becoming bishop of Worcester in 961, Oswald sent for his compatriot Germanus, who had remained at Fleury, and entrusted him with a new monastic settlement at Westbury-on-Trym. Oswald continued seeking a more suitable site for the monastery, eventually accepting the offer of the estate of Ramsey from the ealdorman Æthelwine in about 971.[18] By the 980s Oswald evidently felt that the intellectual basis for monastic reform in England needed strengthening, and asked Fleury to send a teacher to Ramsey Abbey.[19]

Oylbold persuaded Abbo to undertake this task, though whether through gentle persuasion, without threats, as Aimoinus insisted, is problematic. That Aimoinus would even have mentioned

---

17. On the dating of Oda's reign as archbishop, see Knowles, *Monastic Order,* 35, 39. Oda became archbishop before visiting Fleury (reformed c. 930) but (Knowles implies) after 927, at which time he was bishop of Ramsbury.

18. Ibid., 35, 40, 51.

19. Aimoinus, *VsA,* c. 4.

the possibility of coercion suggests a highly charged atmosphere at Fleury in the mid-980s. In any event, Abbo and Aimoinus both considered removal to England a hardship equivalent to exile, though a worthwhile sacrifice, given Fleury's long friendship with the English monks and the needs of St. Benedict. Several monks tried to dissuade Abbo from going. According to Aimoinus, these "jealous" persons (*invidi*) contended that Oylbold was sending Abbo away only in hopes that he would never return. Aimoinus dismissed this rumor by noting that Oylbold showed the greatest respect for Abbo and sent him off with a magnificent train.[20]

For Aimoinus even to mention these jealous whisperings suggests that rumors of tensions between Abbo and Oylbold were widespread, whatever their factual basis, and time had still not entirely erased their memory two decades later when Aimoinus sat down to write Abbo's life. Abbo may have doubted his abbot's intentions, for Oylbold took care when asking Abbo to return from England to quell his fears that he was unwelcome at Fleury.[21] Modern scholars have found it probable that Abbo was a candidate for the abbacy and left because in his disappointment he did not care to serve under his successful rival.[22] This interpretation explains both Abbo's willingness to leave Fleury and Oylbold's willingness to give up one of his most learned scholars to the English monastic reform. Even if Abbo bore no ill will toward Oylbold, he may have found it politic to absent himself for a brief period to avoid becoming the center of a disaffected faction.

The extent of Abbo's sacrifice in agreeing to aid the English monastic reform is clear when we consider the difficulty of the journey. After a journey of over 400 kilometers (about 250 miles), or at least two weeks under ideal conditions, Abbo and Riculf, the head of the English delegation, arrived at their port of embarkation, possibly Wissant, near Calais, on the French coast.[23] The

20. Ibid.: "apparatus itineris . . . magnificus."
21. Edition in Mostert, "Le séjour," 208.
22. Head, *Hagiography*, 238; Mostert, "Le séjour," 203.
23. Aimoinus, *VsA*, c. 4, states that they embarked in the region of Morini, where

The Making of an Abbot 65

Channel crossing in the Middle Ages could be perilous and often involved long delays. Some of our most detailed records of the hazards of crossing the Channel in the Middle Ages come from accounts of the Norman Conquest of England in 1066. When King Harold of England disbanded his fleet of ships, which had guarded the southeastern coast of England against the Norman threat, in early September, many ships went down before they could make it back to London. Likewise, the troops of Duke William of Normandy, while he was moving his ships up the Norman coast a few days later, suffered casualties due to the waves. Stormy weather prevented William from crossing the Channel for just over two weeks, though when the conditions improved, his fleet was able to cross overnight.[24] Less well known are the problems often encountered by Irish monks crossing in the other direction. St. Cathroé, who had been at Fleury before Abbo's time, was not unusual in having his first attempt at crossing thwarted by a storm. Following the pattern of other Celtic saints' lives, Cathroé was able to cross only when he had sent back all but the apostolic number of twelve followers.[25] Despite these dangers, travel in the Channel and in the North Sea was common in the Anglo-Saxon period and continued after the Norman Conquest.[26]

Abbo's Channel crossing was certainly not unusual. Adverse

---

the crossing was shortest. Cousin, *Abbon de Fleury-sur-Loire,* 66n, suggests that Wissant was the port of embarkation. He supports this suggestion by reference to a contemporary itinerary in which the crossing point was near Wissant. (See William Stubbs, ed., *Memorials of Saint Dunstan,* Rolls Series 63 [London, 1874], 395.) Pierre Riché, *Daily Life in the World of Charlemagne,* trans. and intro. by JoAnn McNamara (1978; repr., with expanded footnotes, Philadelphia: University of Pennsylvania Press, 1988), 22–23, estimated that travelers in the Carolingian period could cover between thirty and forty kilometers in a day—but that must have been at a brisk pace indeed. Since northern Francia experienced disruptions in trade due to Viking incursions and local warfare in the two centuries between Charlemagne's time and Abbo's, travel probably did not become any easier, and may have deteriorated.

24. J. Neumann, "Hydrographic and Ship-Hydrodynamic Aspects of the Norman Invasion, AD 1066," *Anglo-Norman Studies* 11 (1988): 222–23.

25. Dumville, "St. Cathroé," 178.

26. Archibald R. Lewis and Timothy J. Runyan, *European Naval and Maritime History, 300–1500* (Bloomington: Indiana University Press, 1985), 86–110 (before 1066) and 111–43 (1066–1377). John Le Patourel, *The Norman Empire* (Oxford: Clarendon, 1976),

winds prevented Abbo and his party from crossing the Channel immediately. When they had spent nearly a month waiting at the shore, Abbo was ready to turn back.[27] He asked when a crossing was likely, and the shipmaster replied that conditions were unpredictable but that the wind seemed to be shifting. Abbo and his companions spent the night in prayer: if the turbulent seas continued, he would take it as a sign that God did not intend for him to go to England. In the morning the seas were calm, and nine ships set sail. They must have been fairly large ships, perhaps cargo vessels similar to the Scandinavian ships that had come into use by the end of the tenth century.[28] When they had left the harbor, Abbo was able to climb up on the deck and see porpoises and dolphins playing wildly around the boats, a sure sign, according to the sailors, of an approaching storm. Abbo instantly began to pray for their safe passage, apparently with some effect; his ship and two others made it safely across. The other six ships went down, along with their crew and passengers.[29]

Upon landing in England, probably at Dover, Abbo immediately set out for Ramsey Abbey, a distance of a little over 200 kilometers (about 125 miles), or at least a week of travel. When he finally arrived at Ramsey after two months' travel or more, his new home must have made a bleak contrast with Fleury. While Fleury overlooked a busy commercial river and was less than a day's travel by either land or water from Orléans, which had been a cultural and administrative center since Gallo-Roman times, Ramsey was an island in the East Anglian fenlands.[30] This was a land of

---

164–65, argues that the Anglo-Norman kings crossed the Channel "frequently" (once every eighteen months or so) with their retinues.

27. For the factors, including wind and tides, likely to affect the Channel crossing, see Neumann, "Hydrographic," 227–29, 233–34.

28. For a description of this type of boat, see Richard W. Unger, *The Ship and the Medieval Economy, 600–1600* (Montreal: McGill-Queen's University Press, 1980), 77.

29. Aimoinus, *VsA*, c. 4. Aimoinus's vivid account of Abbo's journey has a firsthand quality. Aimoinus may have heard directly from Abbo after his return to Fleury, or Abbo may have written a letter of his adventures after his arrival at Ramsey.

30. Pauline Stafford, *The East Anglian Midlands in the Early Middle Ages* (Leicester, England: Leicester University Press, 1985), 5, 19 (fig. 8), 25 (fig. 9). H. C. Darby,

The Making of an Abbot 67

swamps and marshy pools, mists and fogs. The agricultural communities just outside the fen country regarded the fens with suspicion, as the "paths of exile," populated by fantastic monsters such as Grendel and his dam from the epic poem *Beowulf*.[31] Though many villages lay in the uplands of the region, the Domesday Book (compiled nearly a century later) lists no villages in the fenlands, and in fact, the peat fens near Ramsey, unlike the silt fens to the east, offered no stable ground for settlements except for small islands of firmer ground.[32] The abbey and its buildings lay on a narrow peninsula in the swamp, accessible only by boat until the construction of a causeway in the twelfth century. Getting between the monastic buildings was not much easier. The monks of Ramsey had to travel between the abbey and the church using either a boat or a small bridge, though the exact layout of the earliest monastic buildings and the routes taken are lost to the archaeological record.[33] Fifteen miles south of Ramsey as the crow flies lay the nearest town, Huntingdon. Huntingdon minted coins, though by the end of the tenth century its output was minimal, and it had begun minting coins bearing the king's head only with the accession of Edgar in 973. Its population was also small, not exceeding three thousand, roughly half the size of Lincoln.[34] The contrast with Orléans, the bustling commercial, administrative, and educational center where Abbo had studied music, must have been great.

Despite their inhospitableness to grain production, the fens could sustain certain economic activities. They provided profitable fisheries, including Whittlesey Mere, where Ramsey and oth-

---

The Domesday Geography of Eastern England, 3rd ed. (Cambridge: Cambridge University Press, 1971), 333, confirms the low population density for the eleventh century as well.

31. Stafford, *Midlands,* 16.

32. Darby, *Domesday Geography,* 321; H. C. Darby, *The Changing Fenland* (Cambridge: Cambridge University Press, 1983), 10–31.

33. Anne Reiber Dewindt and Edwin Brezette Dewindt, *Ramsey: The Lives of an English Fenland Town, 1200–1600* (Washington, D.C.: The Catholic University of America Press, 2006), 13, 15.

34. Stafford, *Midlands,* 44–45, 53.

er abbeys of the region owned valuable rights, as well as excellent eeling grounds and a good supply of fowl. At its foundation neighboring Thorney Abbey received several boats and nets, bean seed, swine, and mill oxen, as well as servants such as a swineherd and a dairymaid. This foundation implies limited grain farming but a varied production of other foodstuff. In addition, the income to Thorney included significant rents paid in eels.[35] The vegetation of the fens included reeds, rushes, and sedges, all useful as building material and occasionally as bedding for livestock. The peat itself was an important source of fuel for those living near the fens. Finally, in the drier summer months, the peat land provided rich pastures for the villages bordering the fens.[36]

Though often uninviting and frightening to farmers, the eerie and thinly populated fenlands attracted monks seeking escape from the world; Thorney, Peterborough, and Crowland abbeys all lay within a fifty-kilometer radius of Ramsey.[37] Since Ramsey did not lie directly on a major road nor on the River Nene (though it was situated on a minor waterway), communication with neighboring towns and religious houses was far more difficult than mere distance suggests.[38] Oswald, searching for a site removed from the cares and temptations of the world, found its isolation all he could wish for and accepted the ealdorman Æthelwine's offer of Ramsey after failing to act on other offers.[39] Once Oswald had established the abbey at Ramsey, the monks flourished. Ramsey held valuable fishing rights, disputed a stone quarry with Peterborough, and by the eleventh century ranked among the ten

---

35. "Assignments of Property to Thorney Abbey," in A. J. Robertson, ed. and trans., *Anglo-Saxon Charters* (Cambridge: Cambridge University Press, 1956), 252–57 (Old English with facing modern English translation), notes 502–5.

36. Darby, *Fenland*, 22–24, 26–28; Darby, *Domesday Geography*, 342–43.

37. Stafford, *Midlands*, 130; Darby, *Fenland*, 6.

38. Stafford, *Midlands*, 7 (fig. 2), 10 (fig. 3); David Hill, *An Atlas of Anglo-Saxon England* (Toronto: University of Toronto Press, 1981), 139 (fig. 231); Darby, *Fenland*, 33 (fig. 24).

39. Eadmar, *Vita sancti Oswaldi*, in *The Historians of the Church of York and Its Archbishops*, ed. James Rayne, Rolls Series 71 (London, 1886), 2:19, noted Æthelwine's description of the place as an island in the swamps and Oswald's visit to Ramsey.

The Making of an Abbot   69

richest religious houses in England due to its extensive landholdings.[40] Abbo was undoubtedly more struck on arrival at Ramsey with its desolation than with the potential fertility of terrain so different from that of the Orléanais, though he later learned to appreciate the fenlands' riches.

The monks of Ramsey gave Abbo a warm welcome. Abbo may have already met Germanus, the abbot of Ramsey, at Fleury in the late 950s, though Abbo had been very young at the time. He soon gained the affection and respect of the other monks at Ramsey, though their friendly reception did not entirely reconcile him to his life far from his home on the Loire. After returning to Fleury, Abbo wrote fondly of his students at Ramsey, hinting that only their pleasant company and his own studies had alleviated the sadness of his exile across the vast sea.[41] He described the land in his *Vita sancti Edmundi* as harsh, but also fertile and rich in fish, and noted that the swamps attracted monks seeking hermetic isolation.[42] Likewise, though Abbo found the English diet strange at first, he must eventually have come to appreciate its richness. Aimoinus later described Abbo as fat and attributed this weight gain to foreign cooking and fermented beverages (probably beer or mead), not to the sin of gluttony.[43] Abbo must have been in his thirties or older by 985, when he arrived in England; his increase in girth at this time may have been due to "middle-age spread" rather than the direct result of English cooking. Abbo was apparently heavy enough to cause comment or else Aimoinus would hardly have felt compelled to mention the topic at all. It is an interesting note on culinary history that the effects of English cooking (possibly suggested by Abbo himself) seemed the most persuasive means available to defend Abbo from charges of gluttony. Apart from the

---

40. Stafford, *Midlands*, 27, 55, 35–36.
41. Abbo, *Quaestiones grammaticales*, 210–11 (c. 3). Abbo did not mention any of his students by name in this letter, but Byrhtferth of Ramsey must surely have been among them.
42. Abbo, *Vita s. Edmundi*, 69–70 (cc. 2–3).
43. Aimoinus, *VsA*, c. 11: "nam in transmarinis regionibus peregrinorum ciborum inusitata qualitas decocteque potionis haustus corpus eius pingue reddiderat."

dubious pleasures of the table, Abbo relieved his feelings of homesickness by writing letters to his former companions at Fleury. Although none of Abbo's correspondence in exile survives, a passage in Oylbold's letter to Abbo indicates that the exiled monk wrote at least once, probably more often, to his Fleurisian brothers. Oylbold clearly recognized the hardship of Abbo's situation; in his letter calling Abbo home he compared Abbo's stay in England to the Babylonian captivity, though he also feared that Abbo would forget his old friends at Fleury.[44]

Abbo acquired in England a view of reformed monasticism very different from that of northern Francia. Both England and the Continent in the tenth century embraced the ideal of monastic reform along the lines laid out by St. Benedict of Nursia in his sixth-century rule. This rule provided for monks taking vows of poverty, chastity, and obedience and living under the rule of an abbot, a father figure elected by the congregation of monks. While Benedict and his rule had always enjoyed a degree of favor in western Europe, strict adherence to the Benedictine Rule for all monasteries was a relatively new innovation. Although in the ninth century Benedict of Aniane, the adviser of Emperor Louis the Pious, had promoted Benedictine monasticism in Francia, most houses retained their own rules, and many different varieties of monastic experience remained acceptable. By the tenth century reformers sought to drive out those religious who had taken wives or were living lives of luxury or who simply did not have the strong abbot-centered form of governance outlined by St. Benedict. In both Francia and England the initial impetus for monastic reform had originated with the nobility. Unlike in Francia, however, English monastic reform was sustained by a combination of strong royal power and a generation of monastic bishops who oversaw the monasteries in their dioceses with paternal care. Both monks and kings gained from this alliance. The king provided the monks with protection from local magnates, and the

---

44. Edition in Mostert, "Le séjour," 207–8.

The Making of an Abbot   71

monks provided the king with respectable supporters and educated propagandists within the Church.[45] The most important of the monastic bishops were Æthelwold (d. 984), Dunstan (d. 988), and Oswald (d. 992), all of noble stock, all educated as monks, in contrast to the French bishops with whom Abbo found himself at odds through most of his later career. These monk-bishops founded the network of reformed monasteries that laid the basis for subsequent English monastic development. Under their auspices, in 971, the English monasteries agreed on a single rule for monastic life, the *Regularis concordia*.[46]

By the later 980s the English monastic revival had finished its first rapid growth and was entering a period of gradually increasing importance in English religious and political life. Of the three great reforming bishops only Dunstan and Oswald were still alive.[47] While in England, Abbo met Oswald and Dunstan, with whom he corresponded after his return to Fleury.[48] Both bishops were already old men and would not long survive Abbo's departure, but the trend toward appointing monks, especially abbots, as bishops was firmly established. From the time of King Edgar (959–975) until that of Canute (1016–1035), English bishops regularly came from monasteries.[49] Despite the close ties between English bishops and monks, royal support of monasteries was unpredictable. King Edgar had supported reformed monasticism as a vehicle for extending centralized royal control over England, by expelling clerks from old houses and introducing monks living under a reformed rule. But Edgar had died in 975. Some nobles, such as Æthelwine, continued to support the monasteries, but many

45. Eric John, *Orbis Britanniae and Other Studies* (Leicester, England: Leicester University Press, 1966), 177–80.
46. Knowles, *Monastic Order*, 42. Knowles suggested that Abbo had visited England in about 970 and may have attended the synod of Winchester where the *Regularis concordia* was drawn up (46n), but this seems unlikely.
47. Ibid., 53–55.
48. This correspondence is printed in Stubbs, *Memorials of St. Dunstan*, 378–480, 410–12.
49. Knowles, *Monastic Order*, 65. Of eight monks from Glastonbury who became bishops, six were first abbots.

took advantage of the weak monarchy and attempted to expel the monks and reintroduce clerks in an effort to regain some of the power they had lost during Edgar's reign.[50]

Abbo's primary contribution to the English reform movement was his teaching at Ramsey. Perhaps the best known of his students there was Byrhtferth, who later wrote a manual that enjoyed widespread circulation in England for teaching computus, rhetoric, and number symbolism to monks and priests. In his manual he referred several times to Abbo and his teaching methods, for which he had great respect.[51] Abbo's teaching duties at Ramsey also included grammar, and after returning to Fleury he wrote a short treatise answering the questions of his former students in England.[52] As one of the only men "in the tenth century . . . known to have mastered all seven of the liberal arts," Abbo's duties would have been much more extensive, though he was probably able to delegate the most basic instruction to others, certainly after his first year if not immediately.[53]

During Abbo's absence from Fleury, Oylbold had worked diligently to uphold Fleury's integrity and his own. In addition to defending his right to govern Fleury from the machinations of Gerbert, Oylbold continued to fulfill normal abbatial functions and to secure the rights of his monastery. Arnulf, the bishop of Orléans (d. 1003), who later became one of Hugh Capet's strongest supporters, frequently disputed rights over lands and customary payments with the monks of Fleury. Sometime during Oylbold's abbacy, Arnulf had allowed his retainers to overrun a vineyard just outside of Orléans belonging to Fleury, preventing the monks from harvesting the grapes. When appeals to the bishop failed to produce satisfactory results, Oylbold and the monks brought the

---

50. Ibid., 53.
51. Byrhtferth, *Byrhtferth's Manual*, ed. and trans. S. J. Crawford, Early English Text Society, o.s. 177 (London: Oxford University Press, 1929), 56–57, 232–35, 246. Byrhtferth does not refer to Abbo by name on 56–57, but Crawford identifies "Prudens, a wise scholar" (*Prudens, án snotor wita*) as Abbo.
52. Abbo, *Questiones grammaticales*.
53. Lutz, *Schoolmasters of the Tenth Century*, 18.

The Making of an Abbot 73

relics of the Saints Maurus and Frotgerius to protect Fleury's interests. Bishop Arnulf's men withdrew rather than challenge the relics, while at least one of the local peasants took advantage of the procession to petition (successfully, of course) for a miraculous cure.[54]

The death of Louis V and the election of Hugh Capet in 987 may also have given Oylbold cause for concern. Louis's father, Lothar, had confirmed Oylbold as abbot, possibly with the consent of Hugh Capet, duke of the Franks and lord of the Orléanais. Nevertheless, the acceptance of Oylbold by Hugh Capet, who relied heavily on the counsel of the abbot's old enemy Gerbert, was anything but certain. Hugh, on the other hand, may not have had the power or the inclination, upon his accession, to remove an abbot from Fleury when the outrage of the ecclesiastical community had proved useless, especially since he faced many more urgent problems. Although Hugh's control of his ecclesiastical domain was stronger than that of his secular domain, he still depended largely on the support of the bishops for his power. Bishop Arnulf of Orléans (970–1003), in whose diocese Fleury lay, was one of the Capetians' strongest supporters.[55] If Arnulf had not opposed the usurper in 985, two years before Hugh's election, the selection must have been agreeable to the bishop. The Capetians would not have risked alienating Arnulf by trying in 987 to oust the abbot who had enjoyed the bishop's support for the preceding two years. Gerbert apparently did not succeed in inciting the king against Oylbold. Hugh probably realized that Gerbert's patron Archbishop Adalbero of Reims was less easily alienated than the bishop of Orléans: Adalbero had been the target of "a campaign of accusations and threats" from Hugh's rival Charles of Lorraine, while Arnulf's archbishop, Seguin of Sens, continued to oppose Hugh's accession.[56] In September of 987, therefore, Oyl-

---

54. *MsB* 2.19; Head, *Hagiography*, 238–39. For the years of Arnulf's episcopate, see Head, *Hagiography*, 58n,1 245–51.
55. See Hallam, *Capetian France*, 78–91, for the power of the Capetians.
56. Lewis, *Royal Succession*, 17–18.

bold secured confirmation of the privileges of Fleury from Hugh and thus recognition of his legitimacy as abbot.[57]

By the time Abbo had spent two years in England, Oylbold felt comfortable enough to recall him to Fleury. Aimoinus quoted extensively from Oylbold's letter in the *Vita sancti Abbonis* to illustrate the abbot's high regard for Abbo.[58] Mostert's edition of the complete text of the letter confirms Aimoinus's transcription but also indicates that Aimoinus omitted allusions to differences between Abbo and Oylbold.[59] Oylbold may by this time have genuinely regretted their previous disagreements or he may have been softened by advances from Abbo himself, who appears to have maintained a correspondence with the monks of Fleury. Mostert believes that Oylbold called Abbo back largely because of pressure from his congregation at Fleury.[60] Although internal pressure may have been a motive, it is unlikely that Oylbold would have recalled Abbo if he had still been a serious threat to his authority.[61]

Abbo's life in England had included much besides teaching. He had become acquainted with Dunstan, archbishop of Canterbury, from whom he heard the story of St. Edmund, which he

---

57. Prou and Vidier, *Recueil des chartes de Saint-Benoît-sur-Loire*, no. 69 (987). The introductory and closing formulae of this charter are identical to those of an earlier confirmation of immunity granted Fleury by Louis V in 979 (no. 64). This intentional imitation of the early wording would have had the effect of legitimizing the authority of both king and abbot. Lewis, *Royal Succession*, 16–24, chronicles another manifestation of the early Capetian quest for legitimacy; two of Robert's three wives (Rozola Suzanna of Flanders and Constance of Arles) were selected at least in part for their royal antecedents; the third (Bertha of Blois), though not royal in lineage, would have connected Robert with the most important families of northern Francia. For the role of Robert's marriages to Bertha and Constance in relations with the counts of Anjou and the counts of Blois, see Bernard S. Bachrach, *Fulk Nerra, A Neo-Roman Consul in the Eleventh Century* (Berkeley and Los Angeles: University of California Press, 1993), especially 62–141.

58. Aimoinus, *VsA*, c. 6.   59. Mostert, "Le séjour," 203–5.

60. Ibid., 205.

61. Mostert, *Political Theology*, 40, believes that Oylbold intended to resign his office in favor of Abbo. This is an ingenious conjecture, but the evidence does not indicate Oylbold's intentions one way or another when he recalled Abbo. Since Abbo became abbot only upon Oylbold's death, and then against substantial opposition, this hypothesis is untenable.

The Making of an Abbot

later recorded in the *Vita sancti Edmundi*.[62] Though Dunstan may have traveled to Ramsey, it seems more likely that Abbo met him at the archiepiscopal court in Canterbury, perhaps on his way to or from the coast.[63] Abbo later addressed three acrostic poems to Dunstan.[64] Abbo also met with King Æthelred and with Oswald, who visited Ramsey annually with the ealdorman Æthelwine, Ramsey's lay founder.[65] When Abbo returned to Fleury, he carried gifts to the monastery from both archbishops.[66] The most tangible indication of his increased maturity and authority was his advance in ecclesiastical rank. When Abbo left for England he had held only the position of deacon (levita), but before returning to Fleury, he had been consecrated as a priest, someone able to perform the central sacrament of medieval Christianity.[67]

Oylbold did not live long after Abbo's return, and indeed may have been motivated to recall him by his own ill health. He died some time between the summer of 987, when a charter from Hugh Capet identified him as abbot, and early 988, when Abbo had al-

---

62. Abbo, *Vita s. Edmundi*, 67.

63. Mostert, *Political Theology*, 45, suggests that Abbo composed this work after his return to England but before the death of Dunstan (19 May 988). He argues that Abbo incorporated many of his concerns with the relationship of the last Carolingians to the Church into his account of ideal kingship, and thus probably wrote the *Vita* while in France. Winterbottom, in Abbo, *Vita s. Edmundi*, however, interprets a passage in Abbo's prologue as indicating that Abbo embarked on the work immediately after returning to Ramsey from seeing Dunstan (5): "digressus sum cum multa alacritate cordis et ad monasterium quod nosti festinu redii, coeperunt me obnixe hi cum quibus, fraterne karitate detentus, hospitando hactenus degui pulsare manu sancti desiderii ut mirabilius patratoris Eadmundi regis et martyris passionem litteris digererem." (67). Given the unstable situation at Fleury upon Abbo's return (see below), he is unlikely to have had time to compose this work between his return to Fleury and Dunstan's death.

64. Stubbs, *Memorials of St. Dunstan*, 410–412.

65. Knowles, *Monastic Order*, 55; Aimoinus, *VsA*, c. 5.

66. Aimoinus, *VsA*, c. 6.

67. Aimoinus, *VsA*, cc. 4 and 6; he noted Abbo's promotion from *levita* to *presbyter*. This suggests that Abbo passed the canonical age for being ordained as a priest while in England (985–987). If so, this would make him younger than most estimates, as he could not have been born much before 950 (as the canonical age was between thirty and thirty-five, depending on the time and place). Abbo might not have been ordained at the earliest possible age, however.

ready succeeded him.[68] Oylbold had been abbot for at most three years, probably closer to two and a half. Internal support for Oylbold must have been fairly strong for him to weather Gerbert's well-orchestrated and persistent campaign to oust him. His abbacy was not long enough, however, to allow the controversy surrounding his election to die down before his death made a new election necessary.

Abbo's election, although lacking the drama of Oylbold's, was anything but trouble free. Aimoinus, who had strong motives for understating the conflict within Fleury, wrote in the *Vita sancti Abbonis* that a faction at Fleury opposed Abbo's election. Abbo's supporters eventually overcame this faction, partly through the triumph of sounder judgment and partly through the aid of a certain Hugh, "at that time prince of the royal court of the Franks"— undoubtedly Hugh Capet.[69] The reference to sounder judgment is a direct echo of the provision in the Rule of St. Benedict providing for the election of an abbot: an abbot should "be selected either by the whole community acting unanimously in the fear of God or by some part of the community, no matter how small, which possesses sounder judgment."[70] The "more wise part" of the community may have been a special group chosen by the bishop, or perhaps a small minority, the "senior monks" and the officials known as *decani*, elected the abbot, while the majority merely ratified their choice, or the phrase may not refer to a formal procedure at all.[71] Whatever the exact meaning of the Rule, the impli-

---

68. Prou and Vidier, *Recueil des chartes de Saint-Benoît-sur-Loire*, no. 69 (987). Ferdinand Lot, *Les derniers Carolingiens: Lothaire, Louis V, Charles de Lorraine, 954–991*, Bibliothèque de l'Ecole des hautes études, Sciences philologiques et historiques 24 (Paris: Emile Bouillon, 1891), 405–06, reproduced a charter to Micy dated at Orléans, 25 August 987. The charter to Fleury was probably made at about the same time.

69. Aimoinus, *VsA*, c. 7: "per idem tempus regiae Francorum aulae princeps." This identification is supported by the statement in the *MsB* 2.1.3, that Hugh Capet confirmed the election.

70. Benedict, *RB 1980*, c. 64.1 (280–81): "quem sive omnis concors congregatio secundum timorem Dei, sive etiam pars quamvis parva congregationis saniore consilio elegerit."

71. Ibid., 370–78, contains a lengthy discussion of this question by the editors.

cation of this allusion is that a majority of the monks did not select Abbo, though Aimoinus implied that those supporting Abbo were the best qualified to choose. Aimoinus did not mention the opposition to Abbo's election in the *Miracula sancti Benedicti* but did note that Hugh Capet confirmed him in office.[72]

The opposition to Abbo does not appear to have prevailed for long, though Ferdinand Lot at one time believed that an anonymous monk controlled the abbey for several months following the death of Oylbold. This, in his view, was the opposition mentioned by Aimoinus in his discussion of Abbo's election and the anonymous usurper of Gerbert's letters. Lot disagreed with suggestions that Oylbold was the usurper in question; Aimoinus described Oylbold as a good, upright, and moral person, whereas Gerbert described the usurper in unflattering terms. Lot later revised this view, noting that, then as now, eminent persons have differed in their opinions.[73] The length of Oylbold's abbacy (assuming him to be the usurper) is somewhat surprising, although those most vocal in their opposition had no direct jurisdiction over Fleury, and Oylbold had at least some internal support, not to mention support at the royal court in Laon.[74]

Since Hugh did confirm Fleury's privileges under Oylbold, he was clearly trying to cultivate support at the monastery. This would have several political advantages for the new dynasty. First, by associating himself with the established powers at Fleury, an important royal monastery, Hugh gave his own kingship an aura of legitimacy. The Capetians were canny in their use of the Church to establish their power base in West Francia, and Fleury was a powerful monastery with widespread holdings. Furthermore, Fleury lay at the heart of the Capetian power base. The monastery was

---

72. *MsB* 3.1. Hugh is styled *rex* in this account.
73. Lot, *Derniers Carolingiens*, 188n4. Cousin, *Abbon de Fleury-sur-Loire*, followed Lot's initial impression (91–92n2). Lot, *Hugues Capet*, 13n5. Cousin, *Abbon de Fleury-sur-Loire*, 91–92n2, argued vehemently for the presence of an unnamed usurper between Oylbold and Abbo, but his arguments are not convincing when given careful scrutiny.
74. Lattin's note to letter 97. The abbot of Cluny, Maiolus, was apparently less ready to condemn than Gerbert (Lattin, letters 92 and 93; Weigle, letters 86 and 87).

only thirty-five kilometers (about twenty-two miles) up the Loire from Orléans, already an important Capetian stronghold, and had had a close relationship with Hugh's father, Hugh the Great.[75] Hugh Capet had probably influenced the selection of abbots, even under the last Carolingians, and continued good relations with Fleury would have been essential to maintaining his power in the region. Fleury's support would also have been helpful in counterbalancing the reluctance of Seguin, the archbishop of Sens (977–999), in whose province Fleury lay, to support Capetian rule.[76] Finally, Hugh Capet was not averse to aligning himself with former partisans of the Carolingians, as shown by his later selection of Arnulf as archbishop of Reims. Unless Oylbold were actively hostile to Hugh's accession, Hugh would have been unwilling to risk the loyalty of Fleury for the sake of appeasing Gerbert.

The unstated assumption of those scholars who have argued for an anonymous usurper between Oylbold and Abbo is that the monks of Fleury agreed with Gerbert's assessment of him and therefore did not include him in lists of abbots or even mention his name in histories of the abbey. In the *Miracula sancti Benedicti* Aimoinus noted that upon Oylbold's death Abbo was elected by the brothers with the assent of King Hugh. He did not mention a gap in the succession or any internal opposition to the election.[77] Aimoinus certainly knew of the opposition to Abbo's abbacy since it occurred while he was at Fleury and, in fact, he recorded it in passing in the *Vita sancti Abbonis*.[78]

If Aimoinus had omitted reference to this disagreement in the *Miracula sancti Benedicti* in order to present Fleury as immune from

---

75. See Prou and Vidier, *Recueil des chartes de Saint-Benoît-sur-Loire*, no. 44 (9 January 938). Lewis, *Royal Succession,* 8, noted that between the time of Robert the Strong (d. 866) and Hugh the Great (c. 898–956), Hugh Capet's father, the center of the family's strength had shifted from the Tourraine to the Paris-Orléans region.

76. Gerbert wrote a letter in Hugh's name urging the archbishop to pledge fidelity (*fidem*) to the king as others had already done (Lattin, letter 114; Weigle, letter 107).

77. *MsB* 2.1.3.

78. Aimoinus, *VsA* 7. Aimoinus mentioned that he entered Fleury under Amalbert (*MsB* 1.18.32).

The Making of an Abbot 79

internal dissension, he would hardly have referred to the affair in the *Vita sancti Abbonis*. It is more likely that he did not see the affair as relevant to an account of St. Benedict's miracles at Fleury but recognized that, given contemporary memory, he could not omit it from his *Vita* of Abbo, though even there he dismissed it in a summary fashion. Such considerations do not adequately explain his failure to mention a usurper in either the *Miracula sancti Benedicti* or the *Vita sancti Abbonis*. Gerbert's usurper must have remained in office for at least two years.[79] Aimoinus could not simply omit an abbacy, however illegitimate, of two years without arousing comment among his contemporaries and calling into question the reliability of his account. Since the usurper apparently died after only two years in office, if Aimoinus had wished to revile him, he could have attributed his (presumably) untimely demise to divine retribution.[80] In Aimoinus's view and that of many of his contemporaries, there was no usurper abbot at Fleury in the later tenth century.

Acceptance of Abbo's election was not immediate. By Aimoinus's testimony, Hugh Capet approved the election, but Aimoinus did not state that Hugh's approval was decisive in overcoming internal opposition, though one of Abbo's supporters would hardly be likely to admit so much.[81] Aimoinus noted that Hugh Capet quickly granted his assent to Abbo's election, but only af-

---

79. Lattin dates the first of Gerbert's letters dealing with the usurper at Fleury February 986 and the last 11 December 988 (letters 76 and 151). Weigle puts the letters between January–February 986 and September–October 988 (letters 69 and 143). Their dating, however, is based on the assumption that Oylbold was the usurper; the internal evidence of the manuscript suggests the relative order of the letters, not their exact dates. Between the letters about Fleury are several concerning other matters, including one, dated 2 March (VI Non. Martias) that mentioned the funeral of Lothar, who died 2 March 986 (Lattin, 78; Weigle, letter 71) and another, written in the name of King Hugh, who was crowned in July 987 (Lattin, letter 114; Weigle, letter 107). These letters support Weigle's and Lattin's dating of the letters regarding the usurper.

80. Aimoinus frequently recounted the punishments, including death, inflicted upon other opponents of Fleury. See *MsB* 2.2, 2.5–8, 2.14, 2.15, 3.5, 3.8, 3.10, 3.13. Unfortunately, Aimoinus's history of the abbots of Fleury, potentially the most valuable source for these events, is lost.

81. Aimoinus, *VsA*, c. 7; *MsB* 2.1.3.

ter considerable debate did the entire congregation of Fleury accept Abbo as abbot. Hugh appears to have assented to the choice of a minority of monks, those among whom "sounder judgment" prevailed.[82] The gap between Abbo's election and his acceptance as abbot may account for the contradictory dating of the sources. The "Annales Floriacenses" recorded the beginning of Abbo's abbacy under the year 987.[83] When Aimoinus wrote in the *Vita sancti Abbonis* that Abbo had filled the office of abbot for "sixteen continuous years" before leaving on his first journey to La Réole, he may have been counting from Abbo's final acceptance by the entire congregation of Fleury.[84]

The succession of abbots from Amalbert's death through Abbo's accession gave Abbo a clear lesson in the role of internal and external politics of monastic governance. By the time Abbo re-

82. Aimoinus, *VsA*, c. 6. See above for the implications of this statement in light of the Rule of St. Benedict.

83. Paris, BN, lat 5543, f. 21v: "Abbo abbas Floriacensis monasterii" ("Abbo, abbot of the monastery of Fleury." The interpretation of the tironian notes is Pertz's). The entry is a marginal addition in tironian notes to a calendar showing the nineteen-year cycles used in calculating the date of Easter. The printed editions of the "Annales Floriacenses" place this entry in 988 (in conformity with Aimoinus's statement that Abbo had been abbot for sixteen years), though it was clearly written on the line with 987. The death of Louis V and the accession of Hugh Capet are accurate in the calendar (987), as is the death of Abbo (1004), though the death of Hugh Capet is off by one year (997 instead of 996). If Fleury began the year on 25 March, then it could, in fact, refer to an event in early 988. The printed editions are "Annales Floriacenses" in *Scriptores rerum Ingallensium: Annales, chronica et historiae aevi Carolini*, ed. Georgius Heinricus Pertz, MGH SS, vol. 2 (Hanover, 1829), 254–55; *PL* 139:581–84; Vidier, *L'historiographie*, appendix 3, 215–20 (posthumous, appendices added by monks of Saint-Benoît-sur-Loire who edited the book). For the beginning of the year at Fleury, see Reginald L. Poole, *Studies in Chronology and History*, ed. A. L. Poole (Oxford: Clarendon, 1934), 15–20 [originally published as "The Beginning of the Year in the Middle Ages," *Proceedings of the British Academy* 10 (1921)]. Interestingly enough, though modern writers are almost unanimous in placing the beginning of Abbo's abbacy in 988, Rosamund McKitterick, *The Frankish Kingdoms under the Carolingians, 751–987* (London: Longman, 1983), 297, parenthetically indicated that Abbo's abbacy began in 987.

84. Aimoinus, *VsA*, c. 16: "sexdecim annos continuos." Most scholars read this as indicating that Abbo became abbot very late in 988, November or December. Aimoinus, however, indicated that Abbo had been abbot for sixteen years not when he died on 13 November 1004 on his second journey to La Réole but when he started for La Réole on his first journey. The "Annales Floriacenses" noted Abbo's accession in 987.

turned from England, he had acquired a much broader perspective on monastic politics as well as valuable contacts with the Archbishops Dunstan of Canterbury and Oswald of York, and had gained at least one royal audience. Despite his clear spiritual and scholarly qualifications, something that Oylbold had perhaps lacked, Abbo faced opposition to his abbacy only slightly less well organized than that which had threatened Oylbold two years earlier. Only with the help of the new kings, Hugh Capet and Robert, and probably episcopal support from Archbishop Seguin of Sens, did Abbo begin the arduous task of protecting and extending Fleury's position in the politically volatile climate of late-tenth-century Francia.

4

REGIONAL POLITICS

HINDSIGHT has allowed historians to view the support of Abbo and his monastery as an essential element of the Capetian dynastic strategies almost from the beginning of their reign. In fact, however, Abbo's immediate concerns were initially far more local in character, and often hostile to the Capetians' well-documented reliance on support from the episcopate. This misapprehension arises from overreliance on later records, which describe the more cordial relationship that developed between Fleury and the Capetian kings in the years immediately after Abbo's death in the early eleventh century. The preponderance of evidence for Abbo's early abbacy was written under Abbo's successor, Gauzlin, whose rule firmly established Fleury as a strong supporter of the Capetians. The only narrative sources to treat Abbo's early abbacy in any detail are the *Vita sancti Abbonis* and the *Miracula sancti Benedicti,* both written by Aimoinus of Fleury shortly after Abbo's death. Gauzlin was of noble birth, with close ties to the Capetians, and one writer, albeit implausibly, claimed he was the illegitimate son of Hugh Capet.[1] Aimoinus, writing

---

1. André, *Vita Gauzlini,* bk. 1, c. 1. For Gauzlin's parentage, see Adémar, *Chronique,* bk. 3, c. 39 (p. 161). For a discussion of Adémar's claims, see the editors' introduction to André, *Vita Gauzlini,* 18–19.

while Gauzlin was abbot and nearly twenty years after the Capetian accession, had strong motives for portraying Abbo, as Fleury's most learned abbot and most recent martyr, as a close associate of the Capetians. Because Abbo had secured an important privilege for Fleury and later became an important mediator between the Capetians and their adversaries, it was politically useful for the monks of Fleury to minimize his early conflicts with the monarchy.[2] Careful consideration of the sources for the early years of Abbo's abbacy nevertheless indicates that he had more difficulty establishing his authority at Fleury than a casual reading of either the *Vita* or the *Miracula* suggests, and furthermore that his relationship with the Capetian kings was not initially as amicable as later sources indicated.

Abbo became abbot in 988 in the wake of political upheaval. The year 987 saw the end of the Carolingian dynasty, which had ruled Francia since the eighth century. and the accession of the Capetian dynasty, which was to rule until the fourteenth century. This change of dynasty did not necessarily represent a violent break with the past for many of the king's subjects. The Carolingian dynasty had seen its power being eroded for the past century. The ancestors of the Capetians, known as the Robertians, had meanwhile been consolidating their position in the realm. First Odo (888–898) and later his brother Robert I (922–923), followed by Robert's son-in-law Radulf (923–936), had temporarily filled the kingship during the unsettled period of Viking raids. In both 923 and 936, however, a Carolingian had reclaimed the throne, without opposition from the Robertians and arguably with their connivance. Meanwhile, Hugh the Great, the son of Robert I, became a more important political power in the Ile-de-France region and took the title of duke of the Franks. In spring 987 the newly crowned Carolingian king, Louis V, died suddenly in a riding accident. Hugh Capet, the son of Hugh the Great and grand-

---

2. For the papal privilege that Abbo secured, see chapters 5 and 6. For Abbo's rapprochement with the Capetians, see chapter 5.

son of Robert I, quickly took advantage of the situation. The northern Frankish lords elected him king, and the archbishop of Reims crowned and anointed him before the Carolingian claimant, the unpopular Charles of Lorraine, could make his move. Hugh Capet did not intend to be an interim ruler. In December 987 he had his son Robert II crowned as his coruler. The Carolingian Charles of Lorraine did not acquiesce, however, so the first two Capetian kings soon found themselves having to defend their kingdom.[3] As both the Robertians and the Carolingians had been strong patrons of Fleury, the monks could only hope that they would be able to maintain their favored position without having the monastery become a pawn of either of the contenders for the throne.

In early 988 Abbo's first and most formidable task as the newly elected abbot of Fleury was to bring harmony to a monastic community that had been riven by two divisive elections in three years. He had only recently returned from England and could not possibly have kept up with developments in the factions of Fleury during his two-year absence, as would have been the case had he remained at the monastery. The acquiescence of Hugh Capet in his election had created the implied support of Fleury for the Capetians in their struggle to repulse Charles of Lorraine and build up their own political power. This involvement in secular politics could only have added to any factions or divisions within the monastery, though our sources are mute on this point. Furthermore, Abbo was no longer a young man by medieval standards. When he became abbot in early 988, Abbo was at least in his midthirties and possibly a decade or more older. His colleagues noted that he had gained a substantial amount of weight in England, enough to make the arduous travel required of the abbot of Fleury difficult.[4] By the tenth century, Fleury's holdings in the Loire

---

3. For a more detailed account, see Jean Dunbabin, "West Francia: The Kingdom," in *The New Cambridge Medieval History*, vol. 3 (c. 900–c. 1024), ed. Timothy Reuter (Cambridge: Cambridge University Press, 1999), 372–90.

4. Aimoinus, *VsA*, c. 11.

River valley and elsewhere were substantial, so Abbo, as part of his normal administrative routine, would have had to travel extensively. The charters of Fleury indicate that Abbo's predecessors were frequently away from Fleury, and Abbo probably visited many of the priories of Fleury within the first few years of his abbacy. Fleury's landholdings were dispersed in the Orléanais, the Gâtinais, the Blésois, and the Autunois,[5] though not all of these holdings would necessarily have been associated with a priory. We know that by the time of his death in 1004, Abbo had visited Cluny at least once, La Réole in Gascony at least twice, Rome twice or three times, as well as Paris, Reims, Poitiers, and Tours.[6] From a purely physical point of view, the government of the abbey must have been difficult for him.

The surviving evidence for Fleury gives the impression of a wealthy house with vast holdings and rights. Fleury was home to several dozen monks in the tenth century,[7] but the monastery also held extensive possessions along the Loire River. The earliest recorded donation to the monastery appears in the *Testamentum Leodebodi* of A.D. 651. Leodebodus, the abbot of Saint-Aignan of Orléans, gave Fleury six *villae*, several smaller pieces of land, revenues from the *fiscus* of Fleury, and vineyards in the *oppidum* of Orléans.[8] In the Middle Ages Fleury held more priories in the diocese of Orléans than any other monastery,[9] though it is not certain that all of these houses belonged to Fleury at Abbo's accession. By the tenth century Fleury possessed at least four priories in the diocese of Orléans: Saint-Benoît-de-Retour, within the walls of Orlé-

---

5. Prou and Vidier, *Recueil des chartes de Saint-Benoît-sur-Loire*, no. 56 (5 June 967).

6. See Abbo, letter 7; Aimoinus, *VsA*, cc. 8, 9, 11, 16; Prou and Vidier, *Receuil des chartes de Saint-Benoît-sur-Loire*, no. 70 (993, after 1 June); Gerbert of Aurillac, "Acta Consilii Remensis ad Sanctum Basolum," in *Annales, chronica et historiae aevi Saxonici*, ed. Georgius Heinricus Pertz, MGH SS, vol. 3 (Hanover, 1839), 658–86; Paris, BN, Coll. Moreau 16, ff. 19r–20r.

7. Riché, *Abbon de Fleury*, 56.

8. Prou and Vidier, *Recueil des chartes de Saint-Benoît-sur-Loire*, no. 1 (27 June 651), with an extensive commentary on the text by the editors (pp. 11–19).

9. Jean-Marie Berland, "La présence bénédictine dans le diocèse d'Orléans," *Bulletin de la Société historique, archéologique et artistique du Giennois* 29 (1981): 24.

ans, as well as Bonnée, Châtillon-sur-Loire, and Gien-le-Vieil.[10] In addition to land rights, Fleury had possessed valuable fishing and transport rights along the Loire River since Carolingian times.[11] Fleury's influence extended beyond the diocese of Orléans. In 876 Heccard, count of the Burgundians, gave Fleury the priory of Perrecy-les-Forges in the pagus of Autun.[12] Fleury also received the priory of La Réole on the Garonne River in 977 during Richard's abbacy.[13] Abbo could have delegated the administration of these widely dispersed holdings to reliable monks, but an abbot frequently had to oversee his representatives in person. In 1004, for example, when the monks whom he had sent to the priory of La Réole encountered difficulties, Abbo felt compelled to visit the monastery in person—as, he noted, had his predecessors Amalbert and Oylbold.[14] Given these demands on his time and attention, it is not surprising that Abbo seldom appears in accounts of royal politics.

The support Hugh Capet enjoyed from the bishops may also partially explain Abbo's nonappearance among the kings' supporters in the early years of the Capetian dynasty. Bishops and abbots have historically had tense relations, but the tenth century, the period of the rise of reformed monasticism, was a period of heightened conflicts between their competing interests.[15] Because the bishops, often nobly born, represented an outside power with

10. Ibid., 4–5, 12, 14–17.
11. Prou and Vidier, *Recueil des chartes de Saint-Benoît-sur-Loire*, no. 15 (27 July 818).
12. Ibid., no. 25 (c. January 876), and *MsB* 33.15 (161).
13. Prou and Vidier, *Recueil des chartes de Saint-Benoît-sur-Loire*, no. 62 (977). Prou and Vidier recognize that the act is inauthentic but add that the fact of the donation is not necessarily false: "In our opinion it is an act which has been reworked, but not fabricated in every respect" (p. 165: "Pour nous c'est un acte remanié, mais non fabriqué de toutes pièces"). In any case, Fleury certainly possessed La Réole before Abbo's abbacy (see Aimoinus, *VsA*, c. 16).
14. Aimoinus, *VsA*, c. 16.
15. Adrian H. Bredero, "Cluny et le monachisme carolingien: Continuité et descontinuité," in *Benedictine Culture*, ed. W. Lourdaux and D. Verhelst, Medievalia lovaniensia, ser. 1, studia 9 (Louvain, Belgium: Leuven University Press, 1983), 50–51, for example, sees the spread of the Cluniac reform in the tenth century as presaging the Gregorian reforms and the investiture conflict.

Regional Politics

strong secular interests, reformed monasteries often saw freedom from outside interference as the cornerstone of their attempts to implement Benedictine ideals in their monastic practice. Unfortunately for Hugh, Abbo appears to have been unwilling to put aside Fleury's quarrels with local bishops for the sake of smoothing the way of the Capetian dynasty. A number of these quarrels were recurring problems that had their roots in long-standing local rivalries, but several arose from the emerging philosophy of reformed monasticism. When Cluny reformed Fleury in the early part of the century, Fleury entered into the circle of abbeys that followed Cluny's lead in stressing the importance of freedom from direct control by bishops. Unlike Cluny, however, which tolerated little control from local rulers, Fleury accepted confirmation of abbots by the king, though the monks maintained their right to select their own abbots.[16] The monks of Fleury did not, however, accept the interference of bishops in their affairs.

The bishops of Orléans were the natural adversaries of Fleury. Like most bishops of his day, Arnulf of Orléans came from the local nobility.[17] Therefore, his family had direct interests in many of the lands to which Fleury also had claims. Arnulf of Orléans had never liked the monks of Fleury, according to the *Miracula sancti Benedicti,* since they owed their allegiance to the king rather than the bishop.[18] Aimoinus specifically claimed that Bishop Arnulf "clearly

---

16. Prou and Vidier, *Recueil des chartes de Saint-Benoît-sur-Loire,* no. 14 (27 July 818). In this charter, Louis the Pious confirmed the right of the monks of Fleury to elect their own abbots, as granted by his father Charlemagne and his grandfather Pepin. Other evidence indicates that kings continued to approve the choice of abbot (Aimoinus, *VsA,* c. 7; *MsB* 2.18, 121; *MsB* 3.1, 127).

17. Constance B. Bouchard, "The Geographical, Social, and Ecclesiastical Origins of the Bishops of Auxerre and Sens in the Central Middle Ages," *Church History* 46 (1977): 282. Of the thirty-five bishops surveyed, Bouchard identified all but five as definitely noble.

18. *MsB* 2.19, 123–24: "Arnulfus, Aurelianorum episcopus . . . nunquam ad purum praelatos hujus Floriacensis loci dilexit, ideo quam maxime quod illi ditioni solummodo parentes regiae, subjectionem, qua ipse ultra modum delectabatur, nequaquam ei ad ipsius voluntatis dependerent nutum." This argument is self-serving since it freed the monks from acknowledging the possible legitimacy of any of Arnulf's claims, but it is valuable since it indicates a pattern of tensions between the two parties.

showed himself to be his [Abbo's] enemy," though Aimoinus admitted that Arnulf was generally honorable.[19] Under Abbo's predecessor as abbot, Arnulf had sent his retainers to take possession of a vineyard belonging to Fleury.[20] The monks of Fleury did not record any conflicts between the abbey and the bishop in the first few years of Abbo's abbacy, but in 993 a nephew of Arnulf, also named Arnulf, improperly laid claim to payments from the *castrum* of Yèvre.[21] Although these episodes were resolved to the satisfaction of the monks, they present a picture of continuing conflict between the abbot of Fleury and the bishop of Orléans.

Fleury was not alone in its problems with its neighbors. Such recurring disputes between monks, bishops, and the nobility were a frequent feature of monastic life in the tenth century. Bernard S. Bachrach found comparable patterns in Anjou. Abbo himself complained of Fulk Nerra's exploitation of churches, and Bachrach suggests that Fulk was systematically expropriating the goods of the Church for the general good of the state.[22] Sharon Farmer's study of the religious establishments of Tours demonstrates that disputes between religious houses and their neighbors (including other religious houses) could indicate a significant ideological rift between the disputants. The canons of Saint-Martin of Tours, for example, separated their interests from those of the archbishops of Tours, even though the canons of Saint-Martin never embraced the principles of monastic reform found at Saint-Julien of Tours or at Marmoutier, but instead exhibited a "tendency to blend in

---

19. Aimoinus, *VsA*, c. 8: "Unde idem pontifex ARNULFUS nomine ... manifestum se ei ostendit inimicum," but "in reliquis actibus suis, honestis semper se demonstravaret pollere."

20. *MsB* 2.19, 124.

21. Prou and Vidier, *Recueil des chartes de Saint-Benoît-sur-Loire*, no. 70 (993, after 1 June). This charter is a rarity among the charters of Fleury; Prou and Vidier had access to the original diploma.

22. Bernard S. Bachrach, "Fulk Nerra's Exploitation of the *Facultates Monachorum* ca. 1000," in *Law, Custom and the Social Fabric in Medieval Europe: Essays in Honor of Bryce Lyon*, ed. with an Appreciation by Bernard S. Bachrach and David Nicholas, Studies in Medieval Culture 28, Medieval Institute Publications (Kalamazoo: Western Michigan University Press, 1990), 32, 41–42. Abbo, letter 1.

with their secular surroundings."[23] In contrast, Saint-Julien, despite the influence of Cluniac reforms, remained closely tied to the cathedral.[24] Secular politics also intruded on the lives of the religious of Tours. The Capetians were historically lay abbots of Saint-Martin, while Marmoutier, in contrast, was allied with the counts of Blois.[25] On the other hand, bishops often provided the impetus for reform, as was the case of Bishop Bruno of Langres, Archbishop Teotilo of Tours, and Bishop Herbert of Auxerre, who asked Cluny to reform Saint-Bénigne of Dijon, the deserted monastery of Saint-Julien of Tours, and Saint-Germaine of Auxerre respectively.[26] Successive archbishops of Reims sponsored the reform of Saint-Remi of Reims with the help of Abbot Gerard of Brogne in Ghent and then with monks from Fleury. The archbishops sent the monks of Saint-Remi in turn to help reform other monasteries in the archdiocese.[27] As these examples indicate, monasteries in the Touraine, Anjou, the Orléanais, and the Rémois encountered significant challenges to their rights and possessions in the tenth and eleventh centuries from both secular and episcopal authorities, but cooperation between secular, episcopal, and monastic interests could be fruitful if political conditions were right.

Although disputes between Fleury and the bishop of Orléans could not have surprised any contemporary observer, such disagreements must have sorely vexed Hugh Capet. In the first years of Abbo's abbacy and Hugh's reign, Hugh relied heavily on the support of local bishops and abbots to maintain his hold on power.[28] With Fleury and the bishopric of Orléans on opposite

23. Sharon Farmer, *Communities of Saint Martin: Legend and Ritual in Medieval Tours* (Ithaca, N.Y.: Cornell University Press, 1991), 189. Farmer's work treats the tenth century in a cursory manner, so some of her conclusions may indicate an anachronistic reading back of later disputes into the tenth century, though I am convinced by her general picture of a religious community permeated by political divisions.
24. Ibid., 30.
25. Ibid., 34–35, 65. See also Lewis, *Royal Succession,* 8n7.
26. Barbara Rosenwein, *Rhinoceros Bound: Cluny in the Tenth Century* (Philadelphia: University of Pennsylvania Press, 1982), 48, 54–55.
27. Glenn, *Politics and History,* 70–74.
28. For the enfeeblement of the monarchy and Hugh Capet's reliance on abbots and bishops, see, for example, Lot, *Hugues Capet,* 215–16.

sides in the center of his heartland, Hugh must have found himself caught in between the conflicting claims.

Unlike many other monasteries, Fleury had a traditional alliance not only with the Carolingian kings but with the Robertian ancestors of Hugh Capet. Long before the Capetians became kings of West Francia, Hugh Capet's father, Hugh the Great, under the title duke of the Franks, had exercised significant influence in the Orléanais.[29] Hugh Capet's son and coruler, Robert the Pious, was born in Orléans.[30] Fleury, in particular, had a long-standing friendly relationship with the Robertians. Although Fleury was a royal monastery, the duke of the Franks figured prominently along with the kings of West Francia in its charters from the early tenth century.[31] For example, Hugh Capet's father, Hugh the Great, aided Odo of Cluny in reforming Fleury and in 938 joined Odo in asking Pope Leo VII to confirm the holdings of Fleury. Another charter of Fleury is dated "in the time of Hugh the Great." Nearly twenty years later, in 975, Hugh Capet confirmed the gift of lands by his vassal and himself confirmed the immunity of Fleury upon his becoming king in 987.[32] Fleury's background seems to have made it a logical ally of the Capetians.

From a monastery such as Fleury, the Capetians could rea-

29. Hallam, *Capetian France*, 88–89; Werner, *Les origines*, 463, 473; Dunbabin, *France in the Making*, 67; Lewis, *Royal Succession*, 8; Edward James, *The Origins of France: From Clovis to the Capetians, 500–1000*, New Studies in Medieval History, ed. Maurice Keen (London: Macmillan, 1982), 183; Schneidmüller, *Karolingische Tradition*, 173–74n21.
30. Pfister, *Robert le Pieux*, 1.
31. Hallam, *Capetian France*, 87, specifically mentions Fleury as a royal monastery, one that was "formerly under the domination of the Carolingian kings," in contrast to monasteries that were "foundations or refoundations of the Capetians themselves" and monasteries that came under Capetian control through other means. Hallam does not discuss the specific historic precedence for royal control of Fleury, but consultation of the early charters of Fleury reveals royal interests in Fleury from Merovingian times (Prou and Vidier, *Recueil des chartes de Saint-Benoît-sur-Loire*, nos. 1–3 [27 June 651, 657–73, 675–76]) and the significant royal interest in Fleury in Carolingian times (see especially nos. 14 [27 July 818] and 15 [27 July 818]. which supply the only surviving references to earlier Carolingian charters). Hallam fails to mention the Robertian interests in reforming Fleury in the early tenth century.
32. Prou and Vidier, *Recueil des chartes de Saint-Benoît-sur-Loire*, nos. 44 (9 January 938), 51 (8 April–17 June 956), 61 (8 September 975), and 69 (987).

Regional Politics 91

sonably have expected propaganda in favor of their claim to the throne. Hugh the Great had patronized Fleury in the past, as had the Carolingian kings. As Hugh's son and the elected and crowned king, Hugh Capet might have expected a degree of support on both counts. Later, by the early eleventh century, the kings attempted to exercise patronage in the appointment of abbots or possibly in the appropriation of monastic lands.[33] From Fleury, however, the Capetians apparently received little immediate support beyond recognition of their claim to the throne. From a center of learning such as Fleury, a monarch might have expected sympathetic writings, such as a biography, a collection or canons, or some supportive letters,[34] but not until several years after Abbo's death did the monks of Fleury compose a highly laudatory life of Hugh Capet's son, King Robert the Pious.[35] Nor is there evidence that the Capetians heavily exploited Fleury's landholdings.[36] Fleury's support of Hugh seems to have been entirely passive in the early years of Abbo's abbacy.

Though Abbo's apparent aloofness from royal politics may have disappointed Hugh Capet, the king was partially compensated by the more substantial support of the bishops of the region. If anything, Hugh Capet relied even more heavily on bishops than on abbots for consolidation of royal power and prestige. Among the signatories to royal diplomas during his reign are the archbishops of Reims, Sens, and Bourges, and the bishops of Soissons, Châlons, Paris, Amiens, Laon, and Beauvais.[37] The king claimed the right to appoint bishops in several dioceses in northwestern

---

33. Hallam, *Capetian France*, 87–88.
34. Abbo, for his own purposes, later put together a collection of canons on Church-State relations (*Collectio canonum*) and frequently wrote letters to other abbots advising them on how to govern their monasteries.
35. Helgaud, *Vie de Robert le Pieux*.
36. The charters of Fleury contain no mention of any disputes during this period (Prou and Vidier, *Recueil des chartes de Saint-Benoît-sur-Loire*). The *MsB* do not mention specifically Capetians depredations under Abbo's abbacy, though they do mention Fleury's disputes with Arnulf of Orléans.
37. Lemarignier, *Gouvernement royal*, table 2a and pp. 46–47, 51.

Francia.[38] Bishops could support the king through propaganda and through the material resources at their disposal. Archbishop Adalbero of Reims and Bishop Arnulf of Orléans were among the strongest of Hugh's early supporters. Adalbero, in particular, with his secretary Gerbert, waged a letter-writing campaign to try to convince Archbishop Seguin of Sens to recognize Hugh's coronation.[39] Since bishoprics were sources of material wealth as well as spiritual prestige and influence, the king could use appointments as leverage among the local nobility. Within the first two years of his reign, Hugh had the opportunity to appoint the archbishops of Bourges and Reims, the bishop of Noyon, and possibly the bishops of Senlis and Beauvais.[40] Given Hugh Capet's need for both episcopal and abbatial support, any disputes between abbots and bishops in the region would have cut into his power base and put him in the awkward position of having to take sides among divided allies.

The most dramatic confrontation between Abbo and Hugh came over the deposition of Archbishop Arnulf of Reims in 991. When Abbo assumed the abbacy of Fleury in 987, Adalbero, Arnulf's predecessor, had already been archbishop of Reims for many years. Abbo probably knew Adalbero slightly, and he certainly understood the importance of the archiepiscopal see of Reims to Fleury. Past archbishops of Reims had actively supported monastic reform both within the archdiocese of Reims and farther afield. Abbo had himself studied at the cathedral school of Reims in his youth, and the connection between Fleury and Reims continued into his abbacy. Indirect evidence suggests that Adalbero's protégé Gerbert had taught the monk Constantine of Fleury at the cathedral school of Reims, and Gerbert certainly continued to correspond with Constantine about affairs at Fleu-

---

38. Hallam, *Capetian France*, 86; Bouchard, *Sword, Miter, and Cloister*, 67.
39. Lattin, letter 114; Weigle, letter 107. See also Lot, *Hugues Capet*, 41–42, 141.
40. For Dagobert of Bourges, see *GC* 2, col. 36–37; Bachrach, *Fulk Nerra*, 28; for Ratbold of Noyon, see *GC* 9, cols. 992–93. The exact dates of the appointment of Odo as bishop of Senlis (*GC* 10, cols. 1388–89) and Hervé as bishop of Beauvais (*GC* 9, col. 704) are not known. For the appointment of Archbishop Arnulf of Reims, see below.

ry and Reims. Constantine's correspondence with Gerbert is a major source of our knowledge of opposition to Oylbold's abbacy, and Gerbert seemed intent on using his influence with Archbishop Adalbero of Reims to find Constantine an intellectual and spiritual haven outside of Fleury.[41] Unlike Constantine, Abbo had probably never studied under Gerbert or corresponded extensively with him, though the two shared academic interests in astronomy and poetics. He certainly recognized Gerbert as Adalbero's protégé, who had drafted many important letters in Adalbero's name, and as one of the most learned men of their generation.[42] Though the archbishop of Reims did not have direct jurisdiction over Fleury, Reims was an important see, and Abbo had already seen the potential reach of Reims in Gerbert's letter-writing campaign against his predecessor, Oylbold.

By the time Adalbero died in January of 989, Abbo had held office for about a year, and his need to stabilize his own position as abbot undoubtedly overshadowed affairs outside of his own immediate neighborhood. Even so, the death of Adalbero must have been an interesting piece of news at Fleury. Adalbero was an old man, known to be seriously ill with a fever, so news of his death was probably not a complete surprise.[43] The monks of Fleury, along with most ecclesiastics in northern Francia, probably considered Gerbert Adalbero's certain successor. Gerbert had wanted an episcopal appointment for some time. While Adalbero was still alive, he and Gerbert had written several letters hinting that such a position would be appreciated. By coincidence, at about the time that the bishop of Verdun was ill, Adalbero had written to the German empress Theophanu asking her to keep Gerbert in mind if a bishopric should happen to fall vacant. The next letter in Gerbert's collection, which may never have been sent, is a ge-

---

41. Oylbold's death may not have entirely remedied Constantine's discontent with Fleury, and Constantine certainly took advantage of the opportunity to move to the monastery of Micy a few years later (Warren, "Constantine," 289).

42. For Gerbert's fame, see Lutz, *Schoolmasters of the Tenth Century*, 18; for his letter writing on behalf of Adalbero of Reims, see Weigle, letters 68, 87.

43. Richer, *Histoire*, 4.24 (2:182–83).

neric letter of consolation to a congregation that had lost its bishop.[44] Gerbert's twentieth-century English translator altered the ordering of the letters in the collection to strengthen the sense that Gerbert and Adalbero were carefully monitoring the vital signs of the German bishops by immediately following this with a letter to the archbishop of Trier congratulating him on his restoration to health.[45]

When Adalbero of Reims died, the vacancy of his see undoubtedly appeared to offer Gerbert the perfect opportunity to achieve his episcopal ambitions. Gerbert's letter collection gives ample evidence that he had hopes of this sort. Not only did he hint at his hopes in his own letters, but he succeeded in persuading others to write letters on his behalf.[46] The monks of Fleury must have been surprised when Hugh selected Arnulf, a nephew of Charles of Lorraine, instead. In the months between January and April, Abbo and his monks, along with the rest of the northern French ecclesiastical community, must have hastily weighed the advantages and disadvantages of Arnulf's appointment. Arnulf was rumored to be the illegitimate son of Lothar and hence the half brother of Louis V, Hugh Capet's predecessor.[47] Although relatively young, Arnulf had already served as Lothar's chancellor.[48] Arnulf's intellectual background and spiritual character were far less impressive than Gerbert's. He was under the canonical age for consecration, with no particular intellectual attainments or reputation for holiness. His best qualification for the position

44. Lattin, letters 125–26 and 125nn1–2; Weigle, letters 117–18.
45. Lattin, letter 127; Weigle, letter 126.
46. Lattin, letters 158 and 162; Weigle, letters 150 and 154.
47. Gerbert, "Acta Consilii Remensis," c. 25 (MGH SS 3:670): "Arnulfus, regis Lotharii ut dicunt filius."
48. Richer described Arnulf as having "utpote adolescentis mores" (*Histoire*, 4.27 [2:186–87]). Robert T. Coolidge, "Adalbero, Bishop of Laon," *Studies in Medieval and Renaissance History* 2 (1965): 38n60, thinks that Arnulf may have been in his early thirties at this time. The editor of Richer, *Histoire*, cites Lot (*Derniers Carolingiens*, 246n4), who puts his age at twenty-four or twenty-five. Note, however, that Richer's reference is to Arnulf's habits (*mores*) and not his chronological age; even if Arnulf were in his thirties, he may still have had the maturity of an *adolescens*.

was political; he was apparently willing to promise loyalty to the Capetian kings over the claims of his relative Charles of Lorraine, thus securing the city of Reims and simultaneously weakening the familial claims of Hugh Capet's challenger. Abbo, and certainly those monks of Fleury who had studied with Gerbert, would have been disappointed in Hugh's choice. Personally, Abbo may have been relieved that the king had passed over Gerbert, who had had no hesitation in meddling in Fleury's affairs as Adalbero's assistant. Perhaps, as well, Arnulf's youth and inexperience would have appeared advantageous to members of a reformed monastic community longing to be free of episcopal interference. On the other hand, since the archbishop of Reims, though politically influential, did not have direct jurisdiction over Fleury or the Orléanais, the Fleurisians could have regarded the appointment with detached interest, regardless of their feelings for either Arnulf or Gerbert.

Abbo probably made the journey to Reims himself for Arnulf's consecration. Even with the cares associated with his abbacy, Abbo had several motives for visiting Reims. The archbishop of Reims was arguably the most important prelate of northern Francia, someone whom the abbot of the premier monastery of the kingdom could not afford to ignore. The city itself was well known to Abbo, who had studied there before going to England.[49] Abbo almost certainly knew several of the minor clergy and teachers of Reims from his days as a student, even if he were not personally acquainted with the archbishop-elect. Constantine's correspondence with Gerbert of Reims indicates that Fleury probably continued to have educational ties with Reims.[50] In light of Gerbert's interest in Fleury, Abbo may have found it politic to reassure Gerbert's successful rival of Fleurisian support. Even if he could not applaud Hugh's choice of archbishop, Abbo could not diplomatically have neglected to show his support to the kings,

---

49. Aimoinus, *VsA*, c. 3.
50. See Weigle, letters 86, 142, 143, and 191.

especially when he had the opportunity to renew his ties with the scholars of Reims and the influential churchmen of the realm. By March the roads would have been passable, though possibly muddy. Even then, numerous problems could beset a traveler on the road. Abbo's contemporary Richer, for example, described a journey from Reims to Chartres in which a horse died, a bridge was in such disrepair as to be nearly impassable, and heavy rainfall made the journey miserable.[51] Under good conditions, the journey itself would have taken just over a week (Reims lay just over 250 kilometers, or about 150 miles, north of Fleury), and Abbo could have traveled with other churchmen going north to witness the event, absenting himself from Fleury for perhaps a month all told.[52]

Along the road to Reims, Abbo would have had plenty of time to meditate on why Hugh Capet had chosen Arnulf, who had recently been a partisan of Charles of Lorraine, Hugh's chief rival for the throne, for such a powerful position. The archbishopric of Reims was important to any claimant to the West Frankish throne because of the historical role of the archbishop in the consecration of kings.[53] Hugh's accession in 987 depended in some measure on his alliance with Archbishop Adalbero of Reims, a remarkable politician and administrator whose machinations very nearly brought him to grief with the last Carolingian kings, Lo-

---

51. Richer, *Histoire*, 4.50 (2:224–31).

52. Pierre Riché calculated that in Carolingian times most travelers covered between 30 and 40 kilometers a day, though he cited an exceptional instance in which someone had covered 120 kilometers in a night (*Daily Life*, 22–23). Riché's estimates (especially the last one!) appear to represent optimal conditions: fresh horses, good weather, good roads, little or no baggage. Road conditions probably did not improve between the height of Carolingian power and the collapse of the Carolingian dynasty in France two centuries later. Fernand Braudel noted that means of transportation changed very slowly even in the early modern period (*Civilization and Capitalism, 15th–18th Century*, vol. 1, *The Structures of Everyday Life*, trans. Siân Reynolds [New York: Harper and Row, 1982], 422).

53. Olivier Guillot, "La papauté, l'église de Reims et les Carolingiens," in *Xeme siècle: Recherches nouvelles*, ed. Pierre Riché, Carol Heitz, and François Heber-Suffrin, Contribution au Colloque Hugues Capet, 987–1987, cahier VI, Centre de recherches sur l'antiquité tardive et le Haut Moyen Age (Paris: Centre national de la recherche scientifique, 1987), 17–20.

thar (954–986) and Louis V (986–987). Louis V had been close to condemning Adalbero for conspiring with the Ottonians against royal interests in Lorraine, when (fortunately for Adalbero) Louis died suddenly in the spring of 987. The death of the king left the question of Adalbero's culpability in suspension. Since Louis left no sons, the hasty election of Hugh Capet, a supporter of Adalbero, secured the alliance between the two.[54] Hugh Capet gained a supporter from Charles of Lorraine's previous allies, while Adalbero was assured that all inquiries into his previous actions would be dropped. Since Adalbero's position in Francia was powerful but precarious, the first Capetian king knew that he would be able to rely completely upon the prelate's support.

Meanwhile, Hugh faced opposition to his rule from Charles of Lorraine, who claimed the throne as the brother of Lothar and uncle of Louis V. Despite his ties of blood to the former kings, Charles's claim to the throne was hindered by his alliances with the Ottonians, the rivals of the west Frankish lords, and his marriage to a woman of low rank.[55] Hugh, in contrast, had taken advantage of Louis's unexpected death and had astutely used his position as a powerful landholder and heir to former kings (the Robertians) to secure his election and coronation as king.[56] Nevertheless, Charles quickly proved himself a serious threat to

---

54. Hallam, *Capetian France*, 21–23; Fawtier, *Capetian Kings*, 48. Fawtier coupled his insistence on Adalbero's role in the king's election with an assertion that Hugh played a small role in his own promotion and that the nobility who elected him had no idea that he would found a royal dynasty. Lewis, *Royal Succession*, 16–18, presents a very different view of these events, in which Hugh's political influence and the likelihood that he would be able to pass on the crown to a son were important aspects of the nobility's decision to support his bid for the throne. Although Lot initially accorded Adalbero of Reims a large role in Hugh's election (*Derniers Carolingiens*, 204–10), he later reconsidered his position in light of the problematic nature of Richer's account (*Hugues Capet*, 1–2n3).

55. Richer, *Histoire*, 4.11 (2:160–61), attributed this charge to Adalbero of Reims.

56. Adalbero urged Hugh's election on the grounds of his nobility and his ability both to promote the public good and to support his retainers in private matters (Richer, *Histoire*, 4.11 [162–63]): "Promovete igitur vobis ducem, actu, nobilitate, copiis clarissimum, quem non solum rei publicae, sed et privatarum rerum tutorum invenientis."

Hugh by capturing the city of Laon and temporarily imprisoning its bishop, Adalbero (the nephew of Archbishop Adalbero of Reims) in the spring of 988.[57]

When Archbishop Adalbero of Reims died in January 989, Hugh Capet hoped to use the filling of this powerful see to strengthen his position in northern Francia. Although Gerbert would have been a strong candidate to succeed Adalbero, Hugh took the advice of the late archbishop's nephew, Bishop Adalbero of Laon, and passed over Gerbert in favor of Arnulf, a close relative of Hugh's chief rival, the Carolingian Charles of Lorraine.[58] Although this appointment was politically risky, Hugh may have had good reason to believe that Charles could not depend upon his relatives to be his strongest supporters. Several prelates with blood ties to Charles proved to be strong supporters of Hugh in the long run.[59] Arnulf, as it turned out, was not among them. By 988, just a year before his elevation to the see of Reims, he had proven himself a partisan of his uncle, Charles, by helping him capture Laon and expel Bishop Adalbero of Laon from the see. To add to the political obstacles to his election, Arnulf was relatively young and inexperienced, hardly a likely candidate for such an exalted post in such an unstable time.[60] As a cautious politician, Abbo may well have recognized that Hugh's attempt to buy Arnulf's loyalty with the archbishopric was imprudent, to say the least.

Hugh and Adalbero of Laon clearly foresaw the potential problems that might arise from Arnulf's election, but their motives in the elevation of Arnulf to the see of Reims are obscure.

---

57. Coolidge, "Adalbero," 33–34.
58. Ibid., 38–40, describes Arnulf as Charles's nephew, while Lewis, *Royal Succession*, 18, described him as his half brother.
59. Hugh's supporters at the Council of Saint-Basle, for example, included Bishop Bruno of Langres, a nephew of Lothar and cousin of Charles (Gerbert, "Acta Consilii Remensis," c. 5 [MGH SS 3:660–61]). Several other bishops at the council were Carolingian appointees: Guy of Soissons, Adalbero of Laon, Gotesman of Amiens, Walter of Autun, Milo of Mâcon, Seguin of Sens, Arnulf of Orléans, and Herbert of Auxerre (Gerbert, "Acta Consilii Remensis," c. 1 [MGH SS 3:659–60]). See Lot, *Hugues Capet*, 40–41.
60. Coolidge, "Adalbero," 38, noted that Arnulf had been Lothar's chancellor.

Regional Politics 99

According to Robert Coolidge, the most likely explanation for this unlikely choice was that Arnulf tried to "persuade Hugh and Adalbero that he [Arnulf], who had delivered Laon into Charles' hands, would betray him and deliver it back again."[61] Whether Hugh depended on Arnulf for the return of Laon or not, the prospect of neutralizing a close relative and potential supporter of Charles was apparently attractive enough to risk Arnulf's appointment as archbishop.[62] Hugh was too canny a politician to be easily convinced of Arnulf's loyalty, however, and before allowing the consecration, he exacted an oath from Arnulf to support the Capetian kings in their defense of the throne:[63]

I, Arnulf, with the intervening grace of God, archbishop of Reims, promise to the kings of the Franks, Hugh and Robert, that I will preserve most pure faith, [and] provide counsel and aid, according to my knowledge and ability, in all affairs, [and] not knowingly aid their enemies either by counsel nor assistance in their infidelity. I promise these things, standing in the presence of divine majesty, and of the blessed spirits, and of the entire church, [I, who] will receive the rewards of eternal blessing for those things well upheld. If indeed—which I do not wish and which should not be—I were to deviate from these things, may all of my blessing be changed into a curse, and may my days be few, and may another accept my episcopate. May my friends desert me, and may they be perpetually enemies. Therefore, I will subscribe to this chirograph, written by me in witness of my blessing or curse, and I ask that my brothers and sons subscribe [to it]. I, Arnulf, archbishop, have subscribed.[64]

---

61. Ibid., 38–39.
62. Schneidmüller, *Karolingische Tradition*, 180.
63. Coolidge, "Adalbero," 39.
64. Gerbert, "Acta Consilii Remensis," c. 8 (MGH SS 3:661–62): "Ego Arnulfus gratia Dei praeveniente Remorum archiepiscopus, promitto regibus Francorum, Hugoni et Rotberto, me fidem purissimam servaturum, consilium et auxilium, secundum meum scire et posse in omnibus negotiis praebiturum, inimicos eorum nec consilio nec auxilio ad eorum infidelitatem scienter adiuturum. Haec in conspectu divinae maiestatis, et beatorum spirituum, et totius aecclesiae assistens promitto, pro bene servatis laturus praemia aeternae benedictionis. Si vero, quod nolo et quod absit, ab his deviavero, omnis benedictio mea convertatur in maledictionem, et fiant dies mei pauci, et episcopatum meum accipiat alter. Recedant a me amici mei, sintque perpetuo inimici. Huic ergo cyrographo a me edito in testimonium benedictionis vel maledictionis meae subscribo, fratresque et filios meos ut subscribant rogo. Ego Arnulfus archiepiscopus subscripsi."

Although Arnulf, as a new prelate, would have sworn an oath of loyalty in any case, this oath is notable for its specific provisions against aiding the enemies of the kings and for the severe penalties attending any violation.[65] For the moment, Arnulf's loyalty had to be assumed. If Abbo were unaware of any of the details of Arnulf's selection, his colleagues at Reims undoubtedly were eager to explain the background to their out-of-town visitor.

When Abbo arrived in Reims, he found that the validity and the expediency of such an oath were already being hotly debated. Several bishops had insisted that Arnulf not only swear the oath but that he receive the Eucharist and pledge his eternal damnation if the oath should be broken. That this was an extreme view is attested by Richer's comment: "It was believed by several of those [bishops] with clearer minds that this was impious and against the right of faith."[66] The dissenting bishops particularly objected to the Eucharist being used as a means of coercion and possibly of damnation. Although pledges of loyalty were common, almost essential, in holding together medieval society, Arnulf's oath to Hugh Capet, written up as a chirograph, or formal document, clearly fell outside normal practice.[67]

Abbo must have found Arnulf's oath striking, particularly in light of later events. He later wrote a treatise on oaths in the form of a letter addressed to an unnamed bishop.[68] Although the recip-

---

65. In addition to the religious motivation to keep oaths, societal pressures were also strong; see Koziol, *Begging Pardon*, 156. Fawtier, *Capetian Kings*, 73, cited Arnulf's oath as having set a precedent for future archbishops of Reims but says nothing of the circumstances or the disastrous results of Arnulf's consecration.

66. Richer, *Histoire*, 4.30–31 (2:190–93): "Nonnullis tamen quorum mens purgatior erat, nefarium et contra fidei jus id creditum est."

67. The exact meaning of "chirograph" in this case is unclear. The classical meaning is simply an autograph copy, but by the Middle Ages, it generally referred to a charter. Niermeyer's lexicon offers as well the meaning of "record of a solemn promise in the form of an indenture" and cites the summary of Arnulf's case by Richer of Reims as an example of such a usage (see Lewis and Short, *Latin Dictionary*, under *chirographum*, 327; Niermeyer, *Lexicon minus*, under *chirographum*, 176, especially definition 4).

68. Abbo, letter 10. The bishop addressed is not named. In the printed editions of the letter, it is addressed to *N... episcopo*. The only surviving manuscript (London, BL Add 10972, f. 11r), however, begins "Domino singulariter unanimi episcopo."

ient and the exact date of the letter are in doubt, Abbo probably wrote with this oath in mind.[69] Abbo began by providing a justification for a philosophical approach to questions of this sort; in his view, philosophy anticipates problems that the ignorant cannot even imagine. He went on to distinguish between oaths concerning things about which the oath taker can be sure, that is, things that have already happened, and things about which the oath taker cannot be sure, including future actions. In the first case, it is possible to swear with certainty, as a witness in a judicial proceeding, but in the second, a person could be trapped by changing circumstances. Clearly Arnulf's oath fell into this second category; regardless of whether Arnulf intended to keep the oath, he could not know what future events might lead him to break it. Next, Abbo addressed the question of the circumstances behind the oath. Certain people could not on their own authority keep oaths. Abbo gave the example of a woman who was still under her father's rule. Arnulf, though not legally of age to become bishop, was old enough to be held accountable for his actions. Furthermore, breaking an oath taken under coercion was far less

69. Speculation about the date and the intended recipient of the letter raises several possibilities. Abbo may have addressed this letter to Arnulf himself. If so, the letter must have been written after the consecration, since the addressee is a bishop. Abbo may have been responding to a request for advice on whether Arnulf was bound by the oath, though there is no record of Abbo's having taken an interest in Arnulf before Arnulf's deposition. Another possibility is that Abbo was writing to one of the bishops who supported Arnulf's deposition, perhaps to persuade him not to proceed or (if written after the deposition) to encourage leniency in punishing Arnulf. Abbo could also have been writing about another oath. Shortly before the deposition of Arnulf of Reims, Bishop Adalbero of Laon, for example, broke an oath to support Charles of Lorraine. Although this is possible, there is no evidence indicating that Abbo took an active interest in events at Laon. Abbo also wrote a letter to Bernard, abbot of Beaulieu and Solignac, on an oath Bernard had made to go on pilgrimage to Jerusalem but now was compelled to break. Since Abbo did not include specific references, he may have intended the letter as a general introduction to a subject that had raised many difficult questions in tenth-century Francia. Cousin, *Abbon de Fleury-sur-Loire,* identified three possible occasions on which Abbo could have composed this letter: as a lesson while he was a teacher at Fleury, on Adalbero of Laon's breaking of an oath to Charles of Lorraine, or upon Arnulf's inquiring as to the validity of his renunciation of his office. Cousin declined, however, to choose between them or to speculate on the identity of the recipient (218nn1–2).

serious than breaking an oath freely given, though Abbo held out the possibility of mercy in some circumstances (Peter's denial of Christ, for example). Arnulf appears to have been under no coercion except that of his own ambition, but if he were sincere in his initial oath, he might still merit some indulgence for succumbing to an unexpected temptation. Whether written for the occasion or not, Abbo's letter can highlight some of the problems faced in evaluating Arnulf's oath and his subsequent breaking of it.

If Hugh had hoped to win Arnulf's loyalty through an oath, he was quickly disappointed. Arnulf was consecrated in March 989 and by November of that year had betrayed Hugh and turned over the city of Reims to the forces of Charles of Lorraine. Initially, Arnulf appeared to be as much of a victim as any of the inhabitants of the city, but by March 990 Hugh and the bishops of the province realized that he had almost certainly participated willingly in the capture of Reims. They lost little time in summoning him to answer their questions.[70] When Arnulf failed to appear, Hugh sent an envoy to the pope to explain Arnulf's crimes. According to Robert Coolidge, these crimes were twofold: Arnulf's failure to fulfill his secular duties to Hugh and his spiritual duties to the Church.[71] Despite the seeming increase in tensions between the parties, they managed to reach an agreement of sorts in early 991. Hugh pardoned Arnulf and allowed him to resume his office as archbishop of Reims, Charles of Lorraine reinstated Adalbero as bishop of Laon, and Charles agreed to hold Laon from Hugh Capet. Charles never had an opportunity to fulfill his promise to Hugh, however, because Adalbero, through trickery, orchestrated the capture of Charles, his family, and Arnulf on Palm Sunday 991.[72]

With the imprisonment of Charles, Hugh had brought under control the most serious threat to his kingship and, at the same time, lost any reason for supporting Arnulf as archbishop of Re-

---

70. Richer, *Histoire,* 4.33 (194–95); Coolidge, "Adalbero," 40–41; Lewis, *Royal Succession,* 18.
71. Coolidge, "Adalbero," 51.
72. Ibid., 43–51.

ims. Arnulf's spiritual qualifications for the post had never been outstanding, and he had proven himself an unstable ally, at best. Hugh could not simply keep Arnulf in prison, however, as he did Charles. Arnulf was the consecrated archbishop of Reims, Hugh's own choice for the position. As long as Arnulf remained in Hugh's custody, he could not perform his spiritual functions as archbishop of Reims, and as long as he remained in office, Hugh could not appoint a sympathetic replacement. Furthermore, many in the Church, though not necessarily sympathetic to Arnulf, felt that Hugh could not unilaterally deprive an archbishop of his see.[73] Nevertheless, Hugh and the bishops of northern Francia decided that Arnulf's treachery could not go unpunished. On 17 June 991, thirteen bishops convened a council at the church of Saint-Basle of Verzy, outside Reims, to try Arnulf for his crimes.

Two accounts of this council have come down to us. The first and longer is Gerbert's account of the proceedings. As he was an eyewitness, this is the closest view of what happened in the council that we have. Gerbert, however, was an active participant, someone who benefited greatly from the outcome of the council, as he took over the see of Reims after Arnulf's deposition. Gerbert's account of the council is, not surprisingly, largely unsympathetic to Arnulf and his supporters. His account was substantially abridged and reworked by the monkish historian Richer of Reims for inclusion in his histories. Although Richer almost certainly did not attend the council, he had access to both Gerbert's account and to later discussion of the situation among the ecclesiastics of Reims and Chartres. His point of view is harder to judge, but overall he seems more sympathetic to Arnulf as a man torn by loyalties to Hugh Capet and to his uncle, Charles of Lorraine. Unlike Gerbert, Richer suggests that the bishops had some doubts from the beginning both about whether they had the authority to judge and punish Arnulf and whether Arnulf was truly guilty of the charges.[74]

---

73. Richer, *Histoire*, 4.51 (2:230–35).
74. Glenn, *Politics and History*, gives a detailed comparison of the two accounts in appendix C, "Richer's Account of the Synod of Saint-Basle," 276–84.

Though Abbo did not appear in any descriptions of the affair up to this point, Gerbert's account of the council makes clear that Abbo headed a well-defined faction and considered himself a major participant in the debate.[75] Abbo probably began to follow the succession to the see of Reims with close interest shortly after the capture of Reims in November 989. Abbo and other abbots and scholars, according to Richer, were so disturbed by the imprisonment of the archbishop of Reims that they composed texts in Arnulf's defense.[76] This is probably the context in which Abbo composed his letter on oaths.[77]

Hugh realized that he could not afford to ignore the complaints of these churchmen and therefore issued a royal decree ordering that "all bishops of Gaul, who are able and especially those of the same province [as Arnulf of Reims], are to come together as a body."[78] The council convened near Reims at the church of Saint-Basle in Verzy on 17 June 991.[79] According to Gerbert, thirteen bishops, in addition to Arnulf, attended the council. Six of these were bishops from the archdiocese of Reims; there were

---

75. Gerbert, "Acta Consilii Remensis," MGH SS 3:658–86. Gerbert wrote his description of the council in part to clear himself of rumors that he had orchestrated Arnulf's deposition so that he could take over the see of Reims. This may explain why he never mentions his own role in the council; clearly, he wished to leave the impression that the bishops had reached their conclusions without any interference from him. Koziol made the Council of Saint-Basle the centerpiece of his work on rituals and politics in the early Middle Ages. For his summary of the events of the council, see Koziol, *Begging Pardon*, 1–4.

76. Richer, *Histoire*, 4.51 (2:230–31). Abbo later collected texts in support of his claims for monastic immunities and to convince the kings of their duties as Christian monarchs.

77. Abbo, letter 10. Marco Mostert suggests that the letter was written to someone who regretted having taken an oath and wanted to know if the oath was binding (*Political Theology*, 64). In that case, one could even imagine Abbo advising Arnulf in advance of his betrayal of the Capetians, but if so the question of Abbo's motive becomes murkier. Another possible context for this is the dilemma of Bernard of Beaulieu, who had promised to go on pilgrimage to Jerusalem but later found political obstacles would prevent his fulfilling that vow without risking complete disorder at his monastery. Abbo wrote at least two letters of advice to Bernard, which are discussed in chapter 7.

78. Richer, *Histoire*, 4.51 (2:230–33): "edicto regio decretum est ut episcopi Galliae omnes qui valent et maxime qui comprovinciales sunt in unum conveniant."

79. Verzy is just southeast of Reims on the road to Châlons-sur-Marne.

Regional Politics 105

also two archbishops from neighboring archdioceses, Dagobert of Bourges and Seguin of Sens, along with two of Seguin's suffragans, Arnulf of Orléans and Herbert of Auxerre. The three remaining were bishops from the archdiocese of Lyon, to the south.[80] The bishop who came the farthest was Milo of Mâcon, who had traveled over five hundred kilometers (or about three hundred miles) from his see. Despite Milo's heroic effort, the bishops gathered at this council were hardly a representative sample of "all the bishops of Gaul," as Hugh had specified in his decree.[81] The composition of the council, in fact, illustrated the extent of Hugh Capet's influence. Nearly half of the bishops, as might be expected, came from the archdiocese of Reims, which was an area key to Capetian interests. The bishops of Orléans and Auxerre came from the ancestral center of Capetian power and represented some of Hugh's earliest and strongest supporters. Their archbishop, Seguin of Sens, had been reluctant to support Hugh initially, but by 991 had apparently been won over, albeit grudgingly. The remaining prelates, with the exception of the bishop of Autun, held bishoprics in which the Capetian kings reserved the right to appoint the bishops.[82]

Abbo decided to appear in Arnulf's defense at the council. He probably met along the road to Reims two other defenders

---

80. Gerbert, "Acta Consilii Remensis," c. 1 (MGH SS 3:659). The bishops were Guy of Soissons, Adalbero of Laon, Hervé of Beauvais, Gotesman of Amiens, Ratbold of Noyon, Odo of Senlis, Dagobert of Bourges, Walter of Autun, Bruno of Langres, Milo of Mâcon, Seguin of Sens, Arnulf of Orléans, and Herbert of Auxerre.

81. Ibid. noted that Hugh had settled for a much smaller number "because all the bishops of the Gauls had not been able to come there": "omnes Galliarum episcopi eo convenire non poterant."

82. Hallam, *Capetian France,* map 3.1 (79), shows the royal principality of the Capetians as including Orléans and Senlis as part of the royal domain, and the bishoprics of Laon, Reims, Beauvais, and Noyon as being episcopal lordships by the mid-eleventh century. Hallam, *Capetian France,* map 3.3 (81), shows the ecclesiastical domain of Henry I (1031–1060), including the right of the king to select bishops for the sees of Senlis, Orléans, Sens, Auxerre, Bourges, Mâcon, Langres, Laon, Noyon, Beauvais, and Reims. By the eleventh century, the Capetian king exercised power over every bishopric represented in the council except Autun, Soissons, and Amiens. Lot, *Hugues Capet,* also noted the pro-Capetian bias of this council (32), though he remarked as well that of the fourteen prelates attending the council, we have little information about eight (40).

of Arnulf, Jean of Auxerre and Romulf of Sens. Little is known about Abbo's two companions. Jean was the head of the school of Auxerre and had studied with Gerbert at Reims.[83] Ferdinand Lot speculated that Romulf was the abbot of Saint-Remi of Sens and might have been the same person as Renard, abbot of Saint-Pierre-le-Vif and nephew of Archbishop Seguin of Sens.[84] Gerbert corresponded with an Abbot Romulf, who may be the same person.[85] These three were the only ones arguing against Arnulf's deposition in Gerbert's account of the council.[86] Their reasons for defending the accused archbishop are unclear, though their support for Arnulf was clearly tied more to the interests of reformed monasticism and papal prerogatives than to the merits of the individual case. Bishops Arnulf of Orléans, Herbert of Auxerre, and Archbishop Seguin of Sens were probably all too familiar with the independence of the abbots from their diocese.

The bishops began the council in closed session. Abbo and his colleagues probably waited outside the church of Saint-Basle until the private business was completed.[87] Perhaps the abbots discussed their strategy for defending Arnulf. Jean of Auxerre may also have taken the opportunity to renew his acquaintance with his old teacher Gerbert, though he may have felt awkward arguing against his former master. When the council came into session, Abbo discovered that the bishops had selected his archbishop, Seguin of Sens, to preside over the council.[88] This selection

83. Pfister, *Robert le Pieux*, 189.
84. Lot, *Hugues Capet*, 39n4. Although the identification of Romulf of Sens with the abbot of Saint-Remi or the abbot of Saint-Pierre-le-Vif rests on a tenuous similarity of names, Gerbert referred to all three men as *abbates*, and they clearly were well educated and respected churchmen.
85. Lattin, letters 124, 175, and 179; Weigle, 116, 167, and 170. In the second and third letters, the recipient is definitely identified as an abbot of Sens, though the specific house is not mentioned.
86. Gerbert, "Acta Consilii Remensis," c. 19 (MGH SS 3:666).
87. Gerbert stated that the abbots of several cities were invited to enter after the "solitariam episcoporum diputationem" ("Acta Consilii Remensis," c. 2 [MGH SS 3:660]). Richer also stated that after a "solitariam sui disputationem" the abbot and other clergy entered the council (*Histoire*, 4.51 [2:234–35]).
88. Gerbert, "Acta Consilii Remensis," c. 1 (MGH SS 3:660): "dignitas praelaturae ac potestas quasi iudiciaria stetit penes archiepiscopum Seguinum."

was in many ways politically astute. Seguin, although his see lay near the heart of Hugh Capet's area of influence, had been slower than many prelates to accept Hugh's claim to the throne, though he had by this time acknowledged Hugh's accession.[89] The archbishop of Sens was also, since at least the ninth century, the recognized leader of the bishops of Gaul. Because of Seguin's aloofness from Capetian interests and the traditional primacy of the archbishop of Sens, his presidency over the council gave the appearance (at least) of impartiality and legitimacy.[90] In their closed session, the bishops had elected Bishop Arnulf of Orléans to serve as prosecutor.[91] In the bishop of Orléans, Abbo would have recognized a formidable rival and a powerful man with whom his monastery had already come into conflict. One scholar has suggested that Archbishop Seguin of Sens brought together the abbot of Fleury and the bishop of Orléans at this council in order to bring their mutual grievances to a head and perhaps clear the air.[92] The meeting at Verzy was supposedly a broad provincial council, convened to decide the fate of the archbishop of Reims, but the president (Seguin), the leader of the prosecution (Arnulf), and the main defenders of Arnulf of Reims (Abbo, Jean of Auxerre, and Romulf of Sens) were all from the archdiocese of Sens and the center of Capetian power.

The initial question before the council was the nature of the crime with which Arnulf of Reims was charged and the appropriate punishment. Arnulf of Orléans began by reminding the council that divine and human law should be followed in making decisions, and that council participants should judge justly in deciding whether Arnulf of Reims committed the serious crimes with which he was charged. Specifically, he noted that Arnulf had broken his faith as a bishop. Arnulf of Orléans initially explained the crime as one against the inhabitants of Reims but then went on to

89. Lattin, letter 114; Weigle, 107.
90. Lot, *Hugues Capet,* 41–42.
91. Gerbert, "Acta Consilii Remensis," c. 1 (MGH SS 3:660): "ordinis custos ac omnium gerendorum interpres."
92. Riché, *Abbon de Fleury,* 139.

note that this disgraced the reputation of bishops as a whole and called into question their loyalty to their kings.[93] Although the council eventually turned to a discussion of the religious nature of the crimes alleged against Arnulf of Reims, it is significant that its first consideration was Arnulf's crimes against his king.

The debate on this point revealed the aristocratic family background of the bishops. This appears most clearly in the argument of Bruno of Langres. Bruno was the nephew of King Lothar and the cousin of Arnulf of Reims.[94] By his own testimony, he had pledged himself as guarantor of Arnulf's fidelity and was now shamed by Arnulf's breaking of his faith.[95] Bruno's response, like the introductory comments of Arnulf of Orléans, emphasized the secular rather than the ecclesiastical crimes of the archbishop of Reims. The wording of Arnulf's oath also reinforces the impression that this is primarily a case of treason rather than ecclesiastical malfeasance. Arnulf promised to observe pure faith and to give counsel and aid to the kings, as well as to deny aid to the kings' enemies—specifically, Charles of Lorraine. The charges against Arnulf are very similar to the ideas of Fulbert of Chartres, propounded thirty years later, on the duties of fidelity. Fulbert stressed the duty not to injure one's lord—neither in his body, his possessions, nor his rights, or in Fulbert's words, to remember to do only what is "safe and sound, secure, honest, useful, easy, possible."[96] The bishops' decision to act hinged upon their desire to prove their support for the new king, to avoid appearing as accomplices in Arnulf's betrayal, and to claim the prerogative of trying Arnulf themselves rather than allowing Hugh to act unilaterally, as he almost certainly would in the absence of their own

---

93. Gerbert, "Acta Consilii Remensis," c. 2 (MGH SS 3:660): "Si, inquiunt, iustis episcopi utuntur legibus fidissimique suis regibus sunt."

94. Lot, *Hugues Capet*, 40.

95. Gerbert, "Acta Consilii Remensis," c. 5 (MGH SS 3:660–61).

96. Fulbert of Chartres, letter to William of Aquitaine (1020), in *The Letters of Fulbert of Chartres*, ed. and trans. Frederick Behrends (Oxford: Oxford Medieval Texts, 1976), no. 51, 90–93; also quoted and discussed in F. L. Ganshof, *Feudalism*, trans. Philip Grierson, foreword by F. M. Stenton (London: Longmans, Green, 1952), 76.

Regional Politics 109

action.⁹⁷ Clearly, in giving up the city of Reims to Hugh's enemy, Charles of Lorraine, Arnulf had violated his oath of faithfulness to the kings.

Once the bishops had decided that the case was a serious one, and within their jurisdiction, they quickly brought witnesses to prove the facts of the case. In addition to Arnulf's oath to the kings, the bishops examined the priest who had opened the gates of Reims to Charles of Lorraine, allegedly on the orders of Arnulf.⁹⁸ Almost as damning was Arnulf's own *anathema* against the plunderers of the church of Reims. Walter of Autun noted that Arnulf did not condemn the most serious crimes (including violation of the church and his own imprisonment as archbishop), only the destruction or theft of certain movable goods, and promised forgiveness if restitution were made for these. Furthermore, the evidence suggested that Arnulf had continued to administer Communion to the plunderers even though they had not made even this small restitution, and even though the Council of Senlis had condemned them (and he knew of it).⁹⁹ By this point, Lot argued, Seguin had allowed the discussion to turn from breaking of the oath to questions of ecclesiastical misbehavior,¹⁰⁰ and the bishops quickly found passages from previous Church councils to support their condemnation of Arnulf's behavior.¹⁰¹

Once the evidence for Arnulf's guilt had been presented, both Arnulf of Orléans and Seguin called for Arnulf's defenders to present their arguments. Gerbert's description of the defense of Arnulf makes clear the weakness of Arnulf's support. Though Seguin and Arnulf of Orléans specifically called for defenders from the clergy of Reims and from the abbots, only Abbo and his two companions stepped forward to defend Arnulf.¹⁰² Gerbert's description of their presentation is striking: "Therefore, when there was silence, sud-

97. Koziol, *Begging Pardon*, 1.
98. Gerbert, "Acta Consilii Remensis," c. 11 (MGH SS 3:662).
99. Ibid., cc. 13–15 (MGH SS 3:663–65).
100. Lot, *Hugues Capet*, 50.
101. Gerbert, "Acta Consilii Remensis," c. 16 (MGH SS 3:665).
102. Ibid., cc. 17–18 (MGH SS 3:666).

denly numerous volumes of books appeared from all sides. Many were brought into the middle, many were consulted by those sitting together, and they proved to be a great sight."[103] Gerbert's emphasis on the books of the abbots underlines the fact that no one disputed the facts of the case; the abbots were arguing technicalities of the law. The bishops also must have had books since not only did they quote Church councils at length, they even lent a book to the abbots.[104] Nonetheless, Gerbert did not comment on either the quantity of books cited by the bishops or their assiduousness in consulting them. Instead, he emphasized the documents written by the participants in the crisis and the damning evidence of the priest, Adalgar, who had opened the gates of Reims at Arnulf's behest. Gerbert particularly emphasized the evidence provided by Adalgar by noting that the bishops had time to read through a document while waiting for him and then interrupted their discussion as soon as he was available for questioning.[105] Gerbert also minimized the impact of the abbots' words by not indicating who made which arguments. Whereas the bishops appeared as individuals, Abbo and his supporters appeared as a faction, arguing from ignorance and only on pain of excommunication.[106] Although he painstakingly reproduced the texts quoted by the abbots, Gerbert sent the subtle message that the arguments of the texts could not undermine the fact of Arnulf's guilt; they served only to call into question the procedures used to condemn him.[107]

According to Gerbert's summary of the evidence, the abbots had four major objections to Arnulf's condemnation. First, they argued that Arnulf should not have been deprived of his see un-

---

103. Ibid., c. 19 (MGH SS 3:666): "Facto itaque silentio, diversarum partium multiplicia librorum volumina subito apparuerunt. Multa denique in medium prolata, multa inter considentes collata, ingens spectaculum praebuerunt."
104. Ibid., c. 22 (MGH SS 3:668).
105. Ibid., cc. 6, 10, 11 (MGH SS 3:661–62).
106. Gerbert stated that Seguin urged the defenders of Arnulf forward with a threat of excommunication to any who withheld evidence (ibid., c. 18 [MGH SS 3:666]).
107. Ibid., cc. 20–23 (MGH SS 3:666–69), is almost entirely quotations from the proceedings of other councils.

til his case had been examined. Second, Arnulf should have received a legal notification of the charges against him. Third, the bishops should have presented the case to the pope. Finally, the abbots argued that "the accused, the accusers, the witnesses, and the judges should be set apart in a general synod."[108] Gerbert's presentation of this material suggests that the abbots structured their arguments around these four points, but I would argue that Gerbert imposed this structure upon the abbots' arguments in order to strengthen the refutation of these arguments. Gerbert elsewhere suggested that there was another group of defenders who argued that Arnulf had already been pardoned for his crimes by the king at Senlis and should not be punished for them.[109] He did not mention this faction in his summary of the council, so it is unclear whether this argument was actually put forward in the council itself, though the participants may have heard it informally well before the council had convened.

Gerbert rendered ambiguously the final charge of the abbots, that the accusers and the judges should not be the same people.[110] The word Gerbert used in his summary of their argument, *discernendos* (from *discernere*), could mean either that the "accusers, witnesses, and judges" should "separate, part, divide" themselves or alternatively that these three groups should "judge ... settle."[111] The first sense clearly echoes the councils cited by the abbots, but the phrasing of the sentence and Gerbert's rendering of the bishops' response suggest that the abbots were again emphasiz-

---

108. Ibid., c. 23 (MGH SS 3:669): "tum accusatum, accusatores, testes, ac iudices, in magna synodo discernendos."
109. Lattin, letter 201. Weigle, letter 217, cites but does not give the text of the letter (arguing that it is not a letter but a treatise).
110. Gerbert, "Acta Consilii Remensis," c. 21 (MGH SS 3:667): "Accusatores vero et iudices non idem sint, per se accusatores, per se iudices, per se testes, per se accusati, unusquisque in suo ordinabiliter ordine" (from the Pseudo-Isidorian decretals, supposedly from a letter from Damasius to Stephen). Lot, *Hugues Capet*, discusses these decretals briefly in a footnote (52n6).
111. Gerbert, "Acta Conicilii Remensis," c. 23 (MGH SS 3:669). See Lewis and Short, *Latin Dictionary*, under *discerno*, and Niermeyer, *Lexicon minus*, under *discernere*, respectively.

ing the need for a large and impartial council. The bishops responded to the last point by claiming that Arnulf's accuser was worthy.[112] The possibility that this ambiguity was intentional is reinforced by the summary of this point given by Richer in his *History of France:* "and finally, the entire crime should be discussed in a general synod with the authority of the pope."[113] By giving an ambiguous summary of the abbots' argument, Gerbert has created a straw man that the bishops (and Gerbert's audience) could quickly dismiss.

According to Gerbert, the bishops replied fully to each of the four points raised by the abbots, though not in the order in which the arguments were presented. They began with the last point, asserting that Arnulf's accusers were indeed suitable, and that their council was, indeed, a legitimate venue for Arnulf's trial. In response to the abbots' second point, the bishops noted that Arnulf had been informed of the synod nearly a year ahead of time—far longer than the six months prescribed in Church councils. As for the abbots' first argument, that Arnulf must be restored to his see before the trial could continue, the bishops justified their actions on two counts. Their pursuit and capture of Arnulf were completely legal under canon law in the case of treason. Furthermore, Arnulf could not be restored to his see without the intervention of the pope because he had vacated it for more than a year.[114]

The most serious charge of the abbots, after their claim that the synod was unfairly biased against the accused, was that the pope had full jurisdiction over the deposition of bishops. Abbo must have listened with great interest when the bishops made their case that the kings had appealed to the pope but had not received a satisfactory response. In support of their case, the bishops produced a copy of the letter of King Hugh Capet to Pope

---

112. Gerbert, "Acta Consilii Remensis," c. 23 (MGH SS 3:670).
113. Richer, *Histoire,* 4.67 (2:256–57): "et postremo pontificis Romani auctoritate in generali sinodo totum facinus discutiendum." Even a usually careful reader like Ferdinand Lot was misled by Richer's summary of the arguments: "accusé, accusateurs, témoins et juges devaient être examinés dans un grand concile" (*Hugues Capet,* 53).
114. Gerbert, "Acta Consilii Remensis," c. 23 (MGH SS 3:670).

John XV (985–996) and another written by the bishops to the pope. This may have been the first Abbo and his fellow abbots had heard of either of these letters.

In his letter, Hugh stressed that the circumstances of Arnulf's deposition were highly unusual. Hugh noted that if not resolved there would be a loss of kingly power, since Hugh had been like a parent to Arnulf and had received an oath of loyalty from him. Hugh briefly summed up Arnulf's betrayal of Reims and finished by asking the pope what actions should be taken.[115] The letter of the bishops began by apologizing for not consulting the pope earlier. They claimed that they had been occupied with numerous tyrants, clearly a reference to Charles of Lorraine and his followers, but perhaps also a more general reference to the unsettled political situation in Francia. The bishops went on to complain of Arnulf's betrayal of Adalbero of Laon, his complicity in the capture of Reims, and his abandonment of his own flock. They concluded by appealing to the pope, as the successor of Peter, to take action against Arnulf who, they claimed, had acted through a tyrannical faction to bring tyranny to Reims.[116]

Abbo and the other abbots clearly had not heard of either the letters or the pope's response to them. They asked when the letters had been sent and what response the legation to the pope had received. They cannot have liked the response to either question. The legation had been sent eleven months ago, certainly enough time for the pope to make some sort of response. The answer the legation received was even less satisfactory. Although John XV initially seemed prepared to receive their complaints, legates of Count Herbert of Vermandois bribed him not to hear their pleas. Herbert's legates, according to the bishops, offered a beautiful white horse as well as several smaller gifts. The result was that the legates from the bishops and the kings waited outside the doors to the papal palace for three days before leaving without being granted an audience. The representatives of Bishop Bruno re-

---

115. Ibid., c. 25 (MGH SS 3:670).
116. Ibid., c. 26 (MGH SS 3:671).

counted a similar experience with the pope, whose ministers had asked for a bribe of ten *solidi* and then suggested that a thousand *talenta* would be more appropriate if they wished to avoid delays.[117] If the abbots had hoped to make a case for the supremacy of the papacy over the episcopate, they could hardly have chosen a less cooperative pope than John XV.

Bishop Arnulf of Orléans weakened the abbots' case still further by describing canonical precedent in cases in which the pope either cannot or will not respond to requests for guidance. Gerbert took the liberty of combining into a single speech all of Arnulf's arguments.[118] Although Gerbert claimed that he made this change in order to make the proceedings easier to understand and more useful for study, he undoubtedly had other motives. By consolidating Arnulf's remarks, Gerbert did, of course, give an impression of rhetorical unity, but he also made Arnulf's remarks appear to be directed more against corrupt popes than against the very institution of the papacy. He furthermore gave the impression of relative unity among the bishops on this point. According to Gerbert, Arnulf began by affirming his support of the papacy, though he also noted that the early Church councils would ultimately take precedence over papal action (or inaction). He made a particularly strong argument for not vesting responsibility for the entire Church in one man. Arnulf praised several good popes but then noted that recent popes had not been worthy of much praise. He singled out for condemnation John XII, Benedict V, Boniface VII, and John XIV. Arnulf concluded by noting that, although matters of this sort should be put before the pope if possible, councils of bishops always have the option of taking affairs into their own hands if the pope is unwilling or unable to decide promptly and justly.[119] The bishop of Orléans's remarks re-

117. Ibid., c. 27 (MGH SS 3:671).
118. Ibid., c. 28 (MGH SS 3:671). Richer, *Histoire*, 4.68 (2:256–57), omitted Arnulf's condemnation of the papacy, possibly because it was not in his interest at that time to denigrate the papacy. Since Arnulf's long speech is, in fact, a pastiche created by Gerbert, Richer's account may be a truer reflection of the impact of Arnulf's arguments.
119. Gerbert, "Acta Consilii Remensis," cc. 28–29 (MGH SS 3:671–77).

flect a concern in the assembly that Arnulf of Reims would appeal the council's decision to the papacy.[120] Though Arnulf perfunctorily acknowledged papal prerogatives, Abbo and his companions must have recognized that acceptance of his arguments would give bishops almost unlimited discretion in disciplining their fellow bishops (at least as long as the papacy remained corrupt).

At this point, according to Gerbert, the abbots apologized for having taken up the time of the council and for not having previously investigated the case carefully.[121] The abbots also asserted that they had testified not from love of controversy but because the bishops had called upon anyone who could defend Arnulf to step forward under threat of anathema. Gerbert's insertion of the abbots' apology immediately after Arnulf's speech once again marginalizes the arguments of the abbots. Careful reading of the text suggests that the areas in which the abbots were ill informed were the attempts already made to persuade the pope to pass judgment and to persuade Arnulf to answer the charges made against him.[122] However, by placing their apology after the speech of Arnulf of Orléans, Gerbert makes it appear as though the abbots were apologizing for their ignorance of the papal and conciliar history that Arnulf cited. Furthermore, Gerbert subtly suggested that the threat of anathema, by which the bishops had asserted their desire for a fair trial, actually cast doubt on the relative worth of any testimony made on Arnulf's behalf, since none of the witnesses would otherwise have thought it worthwhile to mount even a feeble defense. By the time of their apology, Abbo and the other abbots may also have realized that the bishops would not accept their defense of Arnulf. It may have seemed the better part of valor to rest their case humbly rather than to continue the fight.

Only after the abbots had finished their testimony was Arnulf of Reims himself called upon to testify. Arnulf of Orléans reminded the assembled clergy of the young archbishop's crimes against

120. Koziol, *Begging Pardon*, 1.
121. Gerbert, "Acta Consilii Remensis," c. 30 (MGH SS 3:677).
122. Ibid., cc. 23–27 (MGH SS 3:669–71).

the monarchy, once again stressing the secular crime rather than the ecclesiastical. Arnulf's defense of himself was weak at best. He began by denying all wrongdoing and, when confronted with the testimony of the priest Adalgar, claimed that the priest had lied under pressure from the council. When the priest countered that he had come freely to testify the truth, Arnulf tried to turn the discussion by claiming that he was isolated from his bishops and abbots, in a hostile council. When the presence of all of his bishops and abbots was pointed out to him, Arnulf admitted that he had not seen them and seemed confused. Bishop Guy of Soissons then attacked Arnulf fiercely for not having responded to repeated summonses to explain his actions before the kings and the bishops, despite guarantees of safe conduct. After this onslaught, Arnulf's only defense was to blush.[123]

The bishops next called in Arnulf's household to testify against him. The testimony of the first, Raynerius, was so damaging that the abbots asked permission, which the bishops granted, for Arnulf to consult separately with some trusted advisers before responding to the charges. Arnulf's choice of advisers, given the course of the proceedings, is a little surprising. He chose to consult with four of the prosecuting bishops, Arnulf of Orléans, Seguin of Sens, Bruno of Langres, and Gotesmann of Amiens.[124] Perhaps, in the end, Arnulf felt more at ease with his social equals and fellow bishops, including his cousin Bruno, however hostile, than with the idealistic reformed abbots. More to the point, he may have wanted to consult with those who had the authority to moderate his punishment.

While Arnulf and the four bishops were conferring in the crypt of Saint-Basle, the rest of the clergy kept themselves occupied by reading over various canonical works that had been brought to the council. Abbo and his companions must have real-

---

123. Ibid., c. 30 (MGH SS 3:677–78).
124. Ibid., c. 30 (MGH SS 3:678–79). Richer, *Histoire*, 4.69 (2:258–59), summarized the interrogation of Arnulf only briefly and completely omitted any mention of Arnulf's repentance in the crypt of the cathedral.

ized that the decision of the council was unlikely to be favorable. Arnulf and his advisers were absent long enough for the remaining bishops and abbots to read and discuss several lengthy passages from the Council of Toledo of 656.[125] Abbo may also have taken the opportunity to examine in more detail the pseudo-Isidorian decretals that Bishop Ratbold of Noyon had brought from Lotharingia, perhaps even arranging to have relevant passages copied out for future reference.[126]

When the bishops finally emerged from the crypt, it was not to return to the council but to call others to join them down below. Arnulf had voluntarily confessed to his crimes and had requested that he be removed from the priesthood. The bishops invited thirty of the most religious of the abbots and the clergy to hear Arnulf's confession for themselves.[127] Abbo and his companions may well have been among those abbots who witnessed Arnulf's confession in the crypt. As the leading defenders of Arnulf, their presence would have been essential for giving legitimacy to the proceedings, and curiosity and a desire to verify Arnulf's confession would have compelled them to accept the invitation. Since Arnulf had freely confessed to judges of his own choosing, Gerbert argued that the only decision left was what punishment and what rites were appropriate in Arnulf's case. The bishops consulted several works for precedents, and the council adjourned for the day.[128]

Lodgings for the night must have been scarce. In addition to the thirteen bishops and their entourages, there were at least thirty abbots and clergy.[129] Many of the latter probably came from

---

125. Gerbert, "Acta Consilii Remensis," cc. 32–39 (MGH SS 3:679–81). The passages cited from the proceedings of this council come from the false decretals of Pseudo-Isidore (Lot, *Hugues Capet*, 70n2).
126. Gerbert, "Acta Consilii Remensis," c. 22 (MGH SS 3:668).
127. Ibid., c. 40 (MGH SS 3:681).
128. Ibid., cc. 40–48 (MGH SS 3:682–83).
129. Heinrich Fichtenau, *Living in the Tenth Century: Mentalities and Social Orders*, trans. Patrick J. Geary (Chicago: University of Chicago Press, 1991), 56–57, discusses the importance of retinues for royalty, nobility, and bishops; according to Fichtenau, certain abbots also claimed the right to travel with a large retinue.

the region of Reims, but most of these would not have had time to return to their homes for the night. Saint-Basle was far enough outside of Reims (nearly twenty kilometers) that even those resident in Reims could not return to the city for the night, nor could the entourages of those who came from farther afield hope to rent lodgings within the city or request hospitality from the bishop or monks of the city. The monastery itself probably served as the main lodging for those attending the council. According to the Rule of St. Benedict, a monastery should be prepared to receive guests, both great and small because, as Christ said, "I was a stranger and you welcomed me" (Mt 25:35), and Benedict then went on to explain how guests could be properly fed and lodged without disturbing the monastic routine.[130] The monastery of Fleury provided separate accommodations for wealthy and poor visitors, though smaller monasteries might not have had the same resources.[131] The abbots and bishops probably had the best lodgings in the guest rooms of the monastery of Saint-Basle. The monks and servants in their entourages likely found less comfortable lodgings in the church or possibly in barns or in tents, taking advantage of the warm June nights. As one of the leading abbots of the council, Abbo probably had some of the better lodgings. He and his companions undoubtedly discussed the events of the day. They may even have begun considering how to mitigate the effects of the unfortunate precedent of episcopal authority set by the council.

Gerbert's account of the council stressed the efforts of the bishops to consider the legitimacy of the proceedings and to grant Arnulf of Reims as fair a trial as possible. His emphasis on these considerations was largely dictated by events several years later, when a new pope, Gregory V (996–999), had taken a much more active role in challenging the proceedings and demanding Arnulf's restoration to the see of Reims. Geoffrey Koziol's analysis of the council, however, indicates that the bishops were primar-

130. Benedict, *RB 1980*, c. 53.
131. Thierry, "Le coutoumier de Fleury," cc. 13–14 (194–99).

ily concerned with preserving the prestige of the episcopacy and the monarchy by resolving the issue of Arnulf's treason through a public ritual. Only thus could they hope to maintain public order and stability.[132] In Koziol's analysis, the Council of Saint-Basle "was at the center of a conscious program, developed by the Capetians and their bishops, that used pageantry to communicate their vision of a society restored to peace by a new spirit of cooperation among its leaders."[133]

When the council reconvened the next day, the bishops began considering the practical question of how Arnulf should be punished. Abbo, along with the rest of Arnulf's defenders, seems to have given up active participation in the council by this point, though he undoubtedly listened to all that passed with great interest. As had been established the day before, Arnulf had committed serious crimes that brought shame upon the entire episcopate and also threatened monarchical power in the kingdom. When it came to sentencing Arnulf, however, the bishops were inclined to mercy. Some argued that Arnulf deserved mercy because of his youth, others because of his family. Gerbert, however, took a cynical view of these protestations, suggesting that the bishops were afraid that any punishment imposed upon Arnulf might one day be imposed upon them.[134] Abbo, a religious man of nonnoble birth, may also have felt some surprise at the arguments. The same bishops who had argued that a corrupt pope need not be consulted now argued that a corrupt bishop should be spared on the grounds of birth and age.

While the bishops were debating Arnulf's punishment, someone sent word to Hugh Capet and Robert that the council had finished judging Arnulf's case.[135] The bishops were still deliberating

132. Koziol, *Begging Pardon*, 2–3.
133. Ibid., 7.
134. Gerbert, "Acta Consilii Remensis," c. 40 (MGH SS 3:683): "Unusquisque enim casum eius ex se ipso metiebatur, seque ab infamia liberari putabat, si is, qui publice impetebatur, a criminibus liber foret [vel periclitari, si causam perderet.]" (The section in brackets is missing from one of the manuscripts.)
135. Richer, *Histoire*, 4.70 (2:258–61).

over Arnulf's punishment when the kings arrived at the church.¹³⁶ Koziol believed that the early arrival of the kings upset the orderly proceedings of the council, which had hoped to preserve the semblance of independence. The French "episcopate . . . was too proud of its autonomy to grant a free hand to a leader whose entire generation had been tainted by the civil wars. . . . This was an episcopal affair, they thought, and interference by the kings would only make matters worse."¹³⁷ Hugh and Robert thanked the bishops for carefully considering a case of great importance to the kings. They requested a summary of the events of the council and then suggested that the time had come to sentence Arnulf.¹³⁸ Arnulf of Orléans briefly summarized Arnulf's withdrawal with the bishops and his confession and offered to have the archbishop of Reims publicly repeat his confession to the kings.¹³⁹

Arnulf, along with the people of Verzy, entered the church, the bishops asked for silence, and another humiliating interrogation began. Arnulf of Orléans urged Arnulf of Reims to speak, but the unhappy archbishop muttered in such a low voice that he could barely be understood. The bishop of Orléans pressed him:

—Are you still of the opinion in which we recently left you?
—I am.
—Do you understand that you abdicate from the honor of priesthood, which you have up to now abused?
—As you say.¹⁴⁰

At this point, one of Hugh Capet's retainers became impatient. Count Bouchard of Vendôme asked angrily,

136. Gerbert, "Acta Consilii Remensis," c. 50 (MGH SS 3:683–84).
137. Koziol, *Begging Pardon,* 127.
138. Richer, *Histoire,* 4.70 (2:258–61). Gerbert, "Acta Consilii Remensis," c. 50 (MGH SS 3:683–84), described the entry of the kings and their request for a summary of the council but did not indicate why they arrived when they did or that they had ordered the sentence to be passed against Arnulf.
139. Gerbert, "Acta Consilii Remensis," c. 51 (MGH SS 3:684).
140. Ibid., c. 52 (MGH SS 3.684): "ait pater Arnulfus: Esne adhuc in sententia, in qua te sero reliquimus?—Sum, inquit—Visne te abdicare a sacerdotii honore, quo hactenus abusus es? Et ille: Sicut dicitis." In this and the following translation, I have omitted words indicating a change of speaker.

Regional Politics 121

—What is this "As you say"? Let him speak clearly, let him confess clearly, so that he will not soon assert that the bishops had fabricated whatever crimes they wished [and] deny that he has confessed.
—I say clearly and I confess that I have erred and that I have fallen away from royal fidelity. But I ask that you trust that lord Arnulf [of Orléans] speaks for me.[141]

Bouchard persisted in demanding a full public confession. The bishop of Orléans, however, understood Arnulf's desire to avoid further humiliation and argued that full confession was due only to a priest, which Bouchard certainly was not.[142] Arnulf of Orléans probably feared that Bouchard's demands for full public confession from Arnulf would threaten the compromise that they had worked out in the privacy of the crypt with Arnulf.[143] If Arnulf withdrew his confession, the process of reconciliation would fall apart. Additionally, Arnulf of Orléans may have wished to minimize the kings' interference lest the council appear a tool of the secular government rather than an independent meeting of the Church. Instead, the bishop again asked Arnulf if he had confessed, and had the archbishop prostrate himself before the kings and beg for mercy.[144] According to Richer, whose account was more sympathetic to Arnulf than Gerbert's, the entire assembly was by this time in tears.[145]

A debate quickly ensued over how Arnulf should be punished. Archbishop Dagobert of Bourges urged lenience. He asked not only that Arnulf's life be spared but that he not be threatened with chains unless he fled. By this point, indefinite detention was inevitable; Dagobert sought merely to preserve Arnulf's life and what little remained of his dignity. This, however, was not enough for the other bishops. They feared that a young man such as Ar-

---

141. Ibid.: "Tum comes Brochardus: Quid est, inquit istud: 'Sicut dicitis?' Palam eloquatur, palam confiteatur, ne postmodum episcopos criminia quae voluerint finxisse dictitet, se confessum esse abneget Et ille: Palam, inquit, dico et profiteor, me errasse, et a fidelitate regia deviasse. Sed peto, ut domno Arnulfo pro me loquenti credatis."
142. Ibid., c. 52 (MGH SS 3:684–85).
143. Koziol, *Begging Pardon*, 3–4.
144. Gerbert, "Acta Consilii Remensis," c. 53 (MGH SS 3:685).
145. Richer, *Histoire*, 4.70 (2:260–61).

nulf could easily be persuaded to flee and would as a result soon find himself condemned to death. The kings agreed that Arnulf would not be executed unless he committed some fresh crime. Arnulf returned to the kings and the bishops whatever secular and ecclesiastical honors he had received from each, and read and signed a confession and resignation of his office.[146] Arnulf left the assembly a prisoner of the kings, though not in chains or under heavy guard.[147]

All that remained for the council was the punishment of the chief witness against Arnulf, the priest Adalgar. By his own confession, Adalgar had opened the gates of Reims to the enemy and entered the church violently. The bishops were not inclined to deal mercifully with him. They held him directly responsible for Arnulf's treason, first through giving the archbishop bad advice and then for actually opening the gates himself, albeit on Arnulf's orders. They offered him the choice between perpetual anathema and being stripped of his priestly office. He chose the latter on the condition that he suffer no violence.[148] With the degradation of Adalgar, the council adjourned.

Shortly afterward Gerbert became archbishop of Reims, possibly within a week of the adjournment of the council, but certainly by the end of August.[149] If Gerbert's consecration immediately followed the council, Abbo may have remained to see the ceremony, but it seems unlikely that Abbo would have remained in Reims until August to witness a consecration that he clearly believed to be illegal.

Though the outcome may have disappointed him, Abbo was probably not completely dissatisfied with the council. The abbots had stated their case for papal prerogatives firmly. The only real objection made to their claims was that the pope in this instance

---

146. Gerbert, "Acta Consilii Remensis," cc. 53–54 (MGH SS 3:685).
147. Richer, *Histoire*, 4.70 (2:260–61).
148. Gerbert, "Acta Consilii Remensis," c. 55 (MGH SS 3:685–86).
149. Lattin, letter 191 (and note on dating); Weigle, letter 179 (dated "Ende Juni–August 991").

was not cooperative. Furthermore, the bishops were clearly uncomfortable with the decision by the end of the council. Their hesitation when the question arose of deposing Arnulf and their desire to treat him leniently reflected their own discomfort with the process and held out the possibility that this council would not set a precedent for future relations between the bishops and the papacy. Finally, the outcome of the council was clearly motivated by secular concerns rather than purely ecclesiastical ones. Arnulf was condemned primarily for having broken his oath to Hugh and hence casting doubt on the loyalty of the French episcopate, and only secondarily for having forsaken his spiritual duties as archbishop. The possibility remained that the pope or another council could invalidate the decisions of this council.

Abbo's political position at the close of the council was ambiguous. The men whom he defended, Archbishop Arnulf of Reims and Pope John XV, hardly deserved his support. Arnulf, according to surviving accounts, was distinguished neither by spiritual nor administrative merits. In fact, the most generous construction that can be put on his actions was that he was young, inexperienced, and easily swayed by conflicting loyalties. John XV is in some ways even harder to defend. He became pope while very young and seems to have been completely unfit for the office by education and temperament. Arnulf of Orléans was not the only one to attack the pope's moral character. Abbo's biographer, Aimoinus, also described John as unworthy to hold the office of pope due to his shameful desire for bribes.[150] On the other side, Abbo found himself ranged against some of the most powerful and well-respected figures in West Frankish secular and ecclesiastical politics. Hugh Capet's family had long been patrons of Fleury and one of the most influential families in the Orléanais. Hugh himself, as king, had supported Abbo in his election as abbot and confirmed the election. Gerbert's credentials were impeccable, whether as a scholar, a teacher, or an adviser to the archbishop of

150. Aimoinus, *VsA*, c. 11.

Reims. In addition, the most important bishops of the realm, including Arnulf of Orléans and Seguin of Sens, spoke in opposition to Arnulf of Reims.

On the other hand, the abbots had not openly opposed either the kings or the bishops on issues of secular power and prerogatives. They had defended neither Arnulf nor his actions, but only his right to be judged by the pope. Gerbert's account indicates that both the bishops and the kings were willing to regard the arguments of the abbots as motivated by an idealistic desire to give even a miserable miscreant a fair defense. In the short run, the kings had gained political stability and had neutralized at least one important supporter of Charles of Lorraine. In the long run, the abbots' arguments laid the groundwork for further assertions of papal supremacy and hence, of monastic freedom from secular and episcopal power. If the reformed abbots were to claim independence from local secular pressures (and the episcopacy came overwhelmingly from the local aristocracy at this time), councils of bishops, from which abbots were largely excluded, could never be allowed precedence over papal prerogatives. Eventually, both sides won. Hugh Capet and Robert gained time to consolidate their power through Arnulf's imprisonment, and Abbo and the abbots ultimately gained their goal of strengthening papal authority.

5

ROYAL POLITICS

ALTHOUGH ABBO did not prevail at the Council of Saint-Basle in 991, over the next six years he became a major figure in the politics of reformed monasticism and experienced firsthand the violence inherent in the politics of his age. After the Council of Saint-Basle, the party of monastic reform was clearly in a weak position in West Francia.[1] The kings, though probably sympathetic to the ideals of reform, had far more practical concerns. Now that the claims of Charles of Lorraine were no longer a threat, they could concentrate on consolidating their power throughout West Francia.[2] They needed the support of the bishops, and could not risk losing that support by encouraging monastic reformers in their assertions of the independence of monasteries. A marital crisis had distracted the Capetians from the problems confronting the monastic community. King Robert had repudiated his first wife, Rozala Suzanna, in about 992. Appeasement of the bishops was particularly important if the kings were to persuade the

---

1. Lemarignier, *Gouvernement royal,* 52, suggests that the inverse may have been true as well: that the monasteries had neglected the monarchy because they were preoccupied with their own concerns ("probablement parce que la réforme monastique distrait ceux-ci vers d'autres tâches").

2. Lot, *Hugues Capet,* 30, noted that Charles had died in prison by 993, though the exact date and manner of his death are unknown.

Church to recognize the repudiation and sanction a subsequent marriage. When added to the Capetians' already strong strategy of forming alliances with the bishops, this additional impetus to conciliate the bishops left Abbo and his supporters in a delicate position as the monastic reform movement found its concerns increasingly subordinated to episcopal prerogatives.

Fleury was most vulnerable from the demands of its own bishop, Arnulf of Orléans. Bishop Arnulf was not only one of Hugh Capet's strongest supporters, he was also one of the strongest opponents of the demands of reformed monasteries.[3] Hugh Capet needed a strong episcopate and would not wish to weaken the power base of any of his episcopal supporters, particularly not one as strategically placed as the bishop of Orléans. Since Abbo was the abbot of one of the most prestigious monasteries in the Loire valley and Arnulf's near neighbor, he had to walk a thin line between protecting the interests of his monastery and appeasing the episcopal party. Abbo clearly could not count on the support of the papacy, given Pope John XV's embarrassing lack of action on the deposition of Arnulf of Reims. Instead, Abbo concentrated on protecting Fleury's existing privileges and on making the case for monastic prerogatives to the kings and bishops without specific reference to the pope.

Maintaining good relations with Arnulf of Orléans had never been easy, given the natural conflict between an independent monastery and a controlling bishop, but by November of 991 or 992, Abbo discovered that infuriating his bishop could have physical as well as political consequences.[4] According to Aimoinus's account,

---

3. Hallam, *Capetian France,* 100, based on Arnulf of Orleans's support of the deposition of Archbishop Arnulf of Reims and his relationship with Fleury, both of which are discussed in more detail below. For a more detailed discussion, see Barbara Rosenwein, Thomas Head, and Sharon Farmer, "Monks and Their Enemies: A Comparative Approach," *Speculum* 66.4 (1991): 780–84.

4. Aimoinus does not date any of the events in Abbo's life except his death, but this incident probably happened before the Council of Saint-Denis in the spring of 993. Aimoinus, *V&A,* places the violent attack on Abbo before his discussion of the

Royal Politics 127

it happened that the followers [*satellites*] of the said bishop [Arnulf of Orléans], attacking by night, inflicted serious wounds on this same man of God [Abbo], while he was traveling to the festival of St. Martin of Tours [11 November], and certain men of his retinue were wounded fatally. The said bishop did not react to this matter at all unworthily, as was proper (when in his remaining deeds he showed that he always prevailed in honorable behavior); indeed, because of a rumor among the common folk, he brought some of those who carried out this crime before him [Abbo], as if for punishment so that they would be subjected to [beating with] staffs. But the servant of God, believing that this was not done from good motives, and also remembering the Lord saying in the scriptures: "I shall vindicate myself and I shall repay," was unwilling to accept what was offered, and, because he declined to exact revenge through himself, he earned the right to be vindicated by the Lord. For we learned by common report that some of them were stricken with sudden death, found dead in their beds, others were driven mad.[5]

Aimoinus did not give a motive for this attack, but he did suggest that Abbo's problems did not lie entirely with the bishop. Aimoinus hinted that jealous monks (whom he declined to name) may also have been behind many of Abbo's problems.[6] Although

---

Council of Saint-Denis. In his defense of his actions at the council, Abbo referred to Arnulf's earlier violence, which must have preceded the council, but probably not by much. Cousin, *Abbon de Fleury-sur-Loire,* places the Council of Saint-Denis in October 993 (near the feast of St. Denis on 9 October) and the attack on Abbo in November of the same year (134–35 and 213). Most other scholars place the council in the spring of 993 on the basis of an allusion to Easter in a letter of Gerbert on the subject (for example, Lattin, letter 194 [228n3]; Weigle, letter 190 [227]).

5. Aimoinus, *VsA,* c. 8: "actum est, ut satillites memorati pontificis, eumdem virum dei Turonis ad festivitatem SANCTI MARTINI properantem, noctanter agressi, gravibus afficerent contumeliis, quibusdam obsequii illius hominibus ad necem usque vulneratus. Quam rem prefatus antistes, cum in reliquis actibus suis, honestis semper se demonstraret pollere moribus nequaquam ut pareret indigne tulit. Verum propter vulgi famam aliquos eorum qui hoc perpetraverant scelus, quasi pro satisfactione ut virgis cederentur, ante eum adduxit. Sed dei servus perpendens, hec non recta fieri intentione, simulque memor domini per scripturam dicentis, mihi vindictam, ergo retribuam, que offerebantur accipere noluit. Et quia vindicatam sumere per semet distulit, ut a domino vindicaretur emeruit. Et enim quosdam ex ipsis morte subita interceptos, in lectulis suis repertos mortuos, alios in rabiem esse versos, fama vulgante didicimus."

6. Ibid.: "a quibusdam quoque aliis presulibus necnon nostri ordinis viris videlicet monachis quos nunc nominibus propriis designare supervacuum fore credimus." There are numerous possibilities, both within Fleury and without, for the identification of these monks. The faction of monks at Fleury that opposed Abbo's election

it is possible that the bishop's men had attacked Abbo's party without knowing whom they had targeted for their brigandage, it seems much more likely, given the tensions between Fleury and the see of Orléans, that Abbo's retinue was singled out by Arnulf's followers for political reasons, possibly with the connivance of monks from Fleury or another monastery. Another possibility is that followers of Arnulf's nephew, Arnulf of Yèvre, rather than the bishop's own household, saw an opportunity to resolve a long-standing dispute over some revenues from a vineyard belonging to Fleury.

Abbo's reluctance to see his attackers punished is at first glance puzzling in light of the violent nature of the attack and the relatively mild punishment that Arnulf offered (beating rather than outright execution). When seen in the larger context of ritual punishment and pardon, however, this was a strategic move on Abbo's part.[7] By offering punishment Arnulf had ritually taken the role of prosecutor; by refusing the punishment, Abbo was both undermining Arnulf's role and taking for himself the power of pardoning. The subsequent punishment of the perpetrators by God (something that Aimoinus knew of only by rumor) underlined the guilt of Arnulf's followers while removing from him the merit of having enforced the punishment. Aimoinus hinted that the abbot saw Arnulf's offer to punish his attackers as a diplomatic move rather than a serious attempt to punish the true offenders. As the victim of the attack and the head of a monastic community, Abbo would not, by his own standards, have been the appropriate person to judge and punish Arnulf's followers. In several places in his writings, he clearly stated that one and the same person should not be both accuser and judge.[8] While it is tempting to see Abbo as attempting a reconciliation with the bishop,

---

and Abbo's possible conflict with Constantine of Fleury (and through him with Gerbert) have already been discussed (see chapters 2–3). Abbo also had serious problems with a monk of Fleury named Frederick, who is discussed in chapter 6.

7. Koziol, *Begging Pardon*, 13–16.

8. Abbo, *Apologeticus,* London, BL Add 10972, f. 21v (= *PL* 139:469), but more directly in *Collectio canonum,* c. 44.

the subsequent actions of both Abbo and Arnulf suggest the opposite. Abbo probably felt that beating was an inappropriate punishment; excommunication would be more fitting for those attacking an abbot and his retinue, or possibly execution as more than one of Abbo's entourage were mortally wounded. The punishment of beating was more appropriate for a servile person, and suggested both that the attackers acted on their own initiative and that the harm suffered was relatively minor. Abbo's writings reveal that Arnulf's superior, Archbishop Seguin of Sens, and Bishop Odo of Chartres both excommunicated Abbo's attackers, but that Arnulf ignored their excommunication.[9] Arnulf's unwillingness to enforce a sentence of excommunication and Abbo's subsequent complaint suggest that Abbo refrained from demanding a more appropriate punishment for reasons of politics rather than mercy.

In the spring of 993, while Abbo was still disputing the status of the villa at Yèvre with Arnulf's nephew, violence erupted again, this time over the question of monastic and episcopal rights at the Council of Saint-Denis. The council probably took place shortly before Easter, which fell on 16 April in 993,[10] at the monastery of Saint-Denis, about ten kilometers north of the Ile de la Cité, the center of medieval Paris. We owe our knowledge of the dramatic events of the council to Aimoinus's description in the *Vita sancti Abbonis*. Aimoinus gives no hint of who called the council or why, but his account makes clear that in his view the bishops were not discussing legitimate issues: "When they ought to have conversed on the purity of faith, [and] the correction of their depraved behavior and that of their subjects, as the popu-

---

9. Abbo, *Apologeticus,* f. 21v (= *PL* 139:469). Also quoted in Aimoinus *VsA,* c. 8. Seguin of Sens was a lukewarm supporter of the Capetians at best; see chapter 4. It seems likely that Bishop Odo of Chartres was a relative or at least a supporter of Count Odo of Blois and Chartres (who was a serious threat to the Capetians), though his family background is not known. I am grateful to Amy Livingstone for this information.

10. On the date of this council, see Lot, *Hugues Capet,* 184n1 (in 992 or 993); Mostert, *Political Theology,* 48n27 (February 994); Riché, *Abbon de Fleury,* 141 (993, before Easter).

lar proverb says, they turned all their talk to Church tithes which they [were] attempting to take away from the laity and the monks serving God."[11] Abbo (and Aimoinus) clearly felt that the subject of tithes, whether collected by the laity or monasteries, were not the concern of the bishops, but the history of monastic tithes indicates that the issues were much more complicated. Tithes were originally intended to provide for the parish clergy, but over time, due to many historical factors, bishops, monks, and even laymen came to have the right to collect tithes from parishes for their own use. Historically, bishops had overseen the collection and use of tithes, with the responsibility of distributing a certain portion to the parish priests to maintain the fabric of the church and as charity to the poor of the parish.[12] The bishops undoubtedly felt that they were within their rights in discussing tithes, which had been diverted from their original function in order to provide for the monasteries and the laity. The monks, however, probably felt that it was the bishops who were making unreasonable demands in order to exert control over the monasteries, for which tithes were a long-standing source of revenue.

No direct record survives of the arguments made in the council, probably because of its disorganized adjournment. Abbo apparently addressed the council on the subject of monastic tithes, but the debate was never completed.[13] Rumors quickly spread that

---

11. Aimoinus, *VsA*, c. 9: "Qui cum de fidei puritate, de corrigendis tam suis, quam subditorum pravis moribus, sermocinari debuissent, iuxta vulgare proverbium. Cunctum suum sermonem, ad decimas verterunt ecclesiarum. Quas laicis ac deo servientibus monachis auferre moliti."

12. Giles Constable, *Monastic Tithes: From their Origins to the Twelfth Century* (Cambridge: Cambridge University Press, 1964), 1–56 (for early theories on tithes), 57–83 (for the development of monastic tithes). Constable explains very clearly early systems of dividing tithes into quarters or thirds according to their intended use, and how these systems were misunderstood in the tenth century. See Bachrach, "*Facultates Monachorum*," 41–42. Cousin, *Abbon de Fleury-sur-Loire*, 131–32, noted the uses to which monasteries put tithes, such as sheltering travelers and the poor, thus clarifying the monkish rationale for continuing the practice of collecting monastic tithes.

13. Cousin, *Abbon de Fleury-sur-Loire*, 132–33, suggested that Abbo's arguments can be found in a letter written to Abbot G. (whom Cousin identified as Gauzbert of Tours). The letter is undated, and even the recipient cannot be known with any cer-

the bishops were planning to prevent the collection of tithes by monks and secular authorities. The potential loss of income must have been great, and the crowd that gathered responded with proportionate violence. A group of laymen and monks attacked the assembled bishops, catching one group of prelates just as they were sitting down to a large meal. The bishops quickly scattered in several directions, some fleeing as far as the walls of Paris, ten kilometers (or just over six miles) away. The archbishop of Sens, Seguin, had a particularly disturbing experience: "Among them, Seguin, archbishop of Sens, who held the position of first bishop of Gaul in that synod, was also the first in flight. And in flight he barely escaped, after he had been hit between the shoulder blades with a hatchet and covered with mud by the crowd."[14] Seguin did not die from his wounds (he lived until 999), although he must have been considerably shaken by the experience. In his account of the riot, Abbo expressed particular distress at the fate of his ally, the white-haired Archbishop Seguin, but was curiously silent on the actual participants in the riot.[15]

Almost immediately after the riot, each side accused the other of being responsible for the disturbance. The correspondence of Archbishop Gerbert of Reims and Bishop Arnulf of Orléans suggests that the kings had sided with the monks against the bishops. Gerbert and several other bishops apparently excommunicated the monks of Saint-Denis and refused to say Mass for them.[16] The kings, for their part, criticized Arnulf of Orléans for his role in this incident. Arnulf suspected that Gerbert was responsible for the kings' accusations against him and apparently accused his onetime ally of betrayal. Gerbert quickly wrote back, however, re-

---

tainty. For these reasons, I discuss this letter in more detail in the next chapter in the context of Abbo's interactions with other abbots.

14. Aimoinus, *VsA*, c. 9: "Inter quos SEVUINUS Senonum archiepisopus, primatum gallie in ea sinodo sibi usurpans, primatum quoque fuge arriperuit. Et inter fugiendum, securi inter scapulas ictus, lutoque a popularibus oblitus egre evasit."

15. Abbo, *Apologeticus*, London, BL Add 10972, ff. 20v–21r (= PL 139:468).

16. Gerbert refers to the displeasure this had caused the kings (Lattin, letter 194; Weigle, letter 190).

assuring him of his loyalty and support.[17] Shortly after the riot at Saint-Denis, Arnulf (presumably with Gerbert's connivance) accused Abbo of having incited the riot through his declarations at the council.[18] Abbo probably responded first in person, while at the royal court. He followed up his advantage by addressing a written *Apologeticus* to the kings, in which he defended himself from charges of having incited the riot and reminded Hugh of Arnulf's own attacks on Abbo.[19] Arnulf responded, in turn, with his own diatribe, the curiously titled *De cartilagine* (On Cartilage).[20] Hugh Capet soon found himself faced with an open quarrel between Arnulf of Orléans and Abbo of Fleury.

Abbo had chosen his quarrel well in this instance. Given Hugh Capet's need of episcopal support, he and Robert might have been expected to support the actions of the bishops in most matters. Nevertheless, since Aimoinus indicated that lay tithes as well as monastic tithes were in question, the Capetians may have had a personal interest either in preserving their own rights to tithes or (more probably) in preserving the rights of their lay supporters in the region around Saint-Denis and Paris. On the oth-

17. Gerbert clearly addressed his letter to Arnulf, but midway through he states his loyalty to "A," whom most editors have identified as Arnulf himself (Lattin, letter 194; Weigle, letter 190). Cousin, *Abbon de Fleury-sur-Loire*, 135, however, identified "A" with Abbo. To accomplish this, he also had to change the usual reading of the line from "antistem tuum . . . A" (Your Bishop A) to "artificem tuum . . . A" (Your artist A).

18. Evidence for this is derived from Abbo's *Apologeticus* (London, BL Add 10972, f. 20v [= *PL* 139:468]), Aimoinus's testimony in the *VsA*, c. 9, and from Arnulf's own counterattack, the strangely titled *De cartilagine*, ed. Ph. Lauer, in "Le manuscrit des *Annales de Flodoard*, Reg. Lat. 633 du Vatican," *Mélanges, d'archéologie et d'histoire de l'École française de Rome* 18 (1898): 492–95.

19. Aimoinus quoted this in *VsA*, cc. 8 and 9. There is a complete edition in *PL* 139, cols. 461–72. The manuscript version is BL Add MS 10972. Aimoinus indicated that Abbo wrote this as a response both to accusations arising from the Council of Saint-Denis and to the earlier attack on Abbo and his entourage by Arnulf of Orléans's supporters. In a letter introducing his *Apologeticus* (Abbo, letter 8, addressed to King Robert), Abbo indicated that he had eaten with Robert on at least one occasion in the past.

20. This treatise survives in fragmentary form in the MS Vat Reg. Lat. 633.1, under the title "Incipit epistola Arnulfi episcopi Aurelianensis de cartillagine; quid sit cartillago," and is edited and discussed briefly in Lauer, "Le manuscrit," 492–95. This document is discussed fully below.

er hand, Hugh's supporters among the episcopacy would have exerted pressure to keep tithes in the hands of bishops and parish churches.[21] Furthermore, since the monastery of Saint-Denis was near Paris, which was, along with Orléans, one of the main centers of Capetian power and influence, the kings had important personal and political ties with both the monks and the laity of Saint-Denis.

Abbo's *Apologeticus* is, at first glance, an incredible potpourri of accusations against his enemies, defense of his own actions, political philosophy, theology, and reminiscence, sprinkled with quotations from the Bible, Church councils, and the Church Fathers. After an introduction in which he reminded King Robert of a previous meeting, in which they had sat down to a friendly meal together, he began with a general complaint on the current problems of the world, without reference to any specific event. He continued his *Apologeticus* with a brief study of the structure of society and then bemoaned the ills that he had suffered in the preceding year or two, as well as social problems that he had observed in his adolescence. Abbo closed rather abruptly with a list of ecclesiastical concerns that ought to be discussed at Church councils. On the face of it, the *Apologeticus* is abstract and theoretical, since Abbo mentions very few specific events, but at the same time it is a response to the concerns of the moment, without any clear overall theoretical argument.[22]

Abbo's rhetorical strategy in the *Apologeticus,* however, is much more sophisticated than it first appears to be. His omission of specific names and details, though surprising in a work that (Aimoinus tells us)[23] was intended to clear his own name and to condemn the actions of his adversaries, was the basis of a strategy of reconciliation. In his opening remarks Abbo did not once mention the

---

21. Hubert of Angers, for example, included tithes among his numerous sources of revenue. See Fanning, *A Bishop and His World,* 80.
22. Cousin, *Abbon de Fleury-sur-Loire,* 136, for example, noted Abbo's long canonical digressions before summarizing the substance of Abbo's defense (136–38), Abbo's division of Christian society (139–40), and simony (140–41).
23. Aimoinus, *VsA,* cc. 8–9.

Council of Saint-Denis or monastic tithes, probably not his strongest point in any case. Instead, he began by discussing the spiritual turmoil caused by the misfortunes of the world and the errors in judgment that many people make as a result. In particular, he pointed out that under stressful conditions, people often speak without thinking, saying things that would have been better kept to themselves and neglecting to say what is proper.[24] Since Abbo did not specify what was said or who said it, the kings, as recipients of the *Apologeticus,* were free to decide for themselves which speeches were or were not appropriate. Taken in one way, Abbo in his *Apologeticus* was making a general apology for his actions without renouncing any specific statement. On the other hand, he was also making a conciliatory gesture toward his opponents. If the kings or Arnulf of Orléans or any other bishops at the council had condemned Abbo or made other inflammatory statements, then Abbo was sending the message that he was willing to overlook their rash words in light of the troubled times. He was thus giving both sides the opportunity to moderate their positions and renounce any personal attacks they may have made without sacrificing their prestige. Abbo unquestionably saw himself as a peacemaker. Later in the *Apologeticus,* he specifically complained that he had been unfairly singled out for criticism, when he, above all others, had sought peace through legates and personal supplication.[25] Within the early medieval context, ritual supplication served both as an acknowledgment of authority and as a means of establishing authority. Abbo's claim to have engaged in personal supplication was a clear statement that he, of all people, recognized and respected the kings' prerogatives and would be active in defending them.[26]

In order to reinforce his image as a peacemaker, Abbo painted a picture of social and political turmoil from which he could

24. Abbo, *Apologeticus,* f. 15v (= *PL* 139:461).
25. Ibid., f. 21r (= *PL* 139:469). Abbo admitted, however, that he was willing to obey only reasonable commands that did not infringe upon the rights of Fleury.
26. For more on supplication and its political context, see Koziol, *Begging Pardon,* especially 13–16.

escape only briefly into the tranquility of philosophy.[27] In sharp contrast to the peaceful study of philosophy, Abbo evoked images of those who jealously attacked him. In his guise as a philosopher, Abbo used the imagery of the Roman Republic to defend his own position as the upholder of the Senate of monks and the preserver of the Republic.[28] The implication is that those who rioted, with whom Abbo linked those who falsely accused him, had resorted to exactly the same sort of extralegal actions as had the assassins of Julius Caesar. Abbo is clearly making an allusion to the Church councils, probably with reference to Saint-Denis, in which Abbo upheld what he saw as the legitimate rights of monks. Abbo did not mention particular people who had attacked him or particular issues that had been raised in the attacks. By putting his reference in vague terms, Abbo presented himself as the champion of abstract ideals while avoiding any allusion to specific events that may have shown him in a bad light.

Abbo also made clear that attacks on him were not only verbal but physical. He had been violently attacked, he claimed, by those who did not respect royal majesty, but was refused the opportunity to defend himself in a fair trial, where he knew that he would prevail. These references to royal prerogatives and a fair trial also suggested that Abbo was a strong supporter of the rights of the kings and the Capetian strategy of increasing royal authority. Abbo emphasized the pettiness and injustice of those who criticized him by using the diminutive (*possessiuncula* and *furniculi* rather than *possessiones* and *furnimenta*) to indicate the relative poverty of the possessions and furnishings that his opponents had sought to appropriate.[29] Even though in this instance the kings

---

27. Abbo, *Apologeticus*, f. 15v (= *PL* 139:461). See also Mostert, *Political Theology*, 125.

28. Abbo, *Apologeticus*, f. 16r (= *PL* 139:461): "nec aliud contra me immurmurant, nisi quod monachorum senatum salvum esse volui, nostrae reipublicae augmentum quaesivi." Marco Mostert noted that "Abbo clearly preferred to use the classical word rather than the post-classical whenever possible" (*Political Theology*, 81). For the self-conscious use of Roman republican and imperial imagery in the tenth and eleventh centuries, see Bachrach, *Fulk Nerra*, especially xiii–xiv, 256–69.

29. Abbo, *Apologeticus*, f. 16r (= *PL* 139:461).

could not have doubted that Abbo's attackers were the followers of Arnulf of Orléans, Abbo did not mention the bishop by name. The vague, theoretical tone of the *Apologeticus* once again allowed Abbo to present his case without embarrassing himself politically. Arnulf of Orléans was one of Hugh Capet's strongest supporters, and Abbo surely realized that he had slight hope of gaining the king's favor by attacking Arnulf directly. Aimoinus's account suggested that Arnulf had no personal knowledge of the attack on Abbo, and Abbo may have been taking advantage of the ambiguity of the situation to condemn the attack and its motives without specifically condemning Arnulf.[30]

Abbo opened the next major section of the *Apologeticus* with a discussion of his own faith and the problem of heresies.[31] He cited the Council of Chalcedon under the emperor Marcian in 451 as the model of a Church council. He noted that the council dealt entirely with matters of faith and apostolic teaching, that six hundred or possibly twelve hundred bishops had attended the council, and that the secular powers, the emperor and his wife, had supported the decisions of the council with a legal document.[32] This council was in direct contrast to the two most important councils of Abbo's career, the Council of Saint-Basle and the Council of Saint-Denis. Both of these councils had consid-

---

30. Aimoinus, *VsA*, c. 8. Aimoinus stated that Arnulf had always behaved honorably and had even offered to punish the culprits but that Abbo had refused the offer. Aimoinus is probably presenting Arnulf more favorably than Abbo would have done at the time.

31. Mostert, *Political Theology*, 92, noted Abbo's frequent preoccupation with heresies, which were undoubtedly a reflection of the spiritual and institutional turmoil of the tenth-century Church but also an ominous foreshadowing of the heresies that erupted in Orléans shortly after Abbo's death. For more on the heresies of Orléans in the eleventh century, see Robert-Henri Bautier, "L'hérésie d'Orléans et le mouvement intellectuel au début du XIe siècle: Documents et hypothèses," in *Actes du 95e Congrès national des sociétés savantes*, Comité des travaux historiques et scientifiques, Reims, 1970, section de philologie et d'histoire jusqu'à 1610, vol. 1, *Enseignement et vie intellectuelle (IXe–XVIe siècles)* (Paris: Bibliothèque nationale, 1975), 63–88.

32. Abbo, *Apologeticus*, f. 16v (= *PL* 139: 462). Mostert, *Political Theology*, 130, noted that Abbo always included the names of the popes who ratified the proceedings of the councils, thus emphasizing the necessity of papal authority for conciliar legitimacy.

Royal Politics

ered secular affairs, both had involved a relatively small number of bishops (a mere dozen at Saint-Basle in contrast to the twelve hundred whom Abbo imagined at Chalcedon), and in the Council of Saint-Denis the kings seemed to have held aloof from the proceedings. Abbo thus made the case that he was not an opponent of episcopal councils per se, while still expressing his contempt for the small, hastily convened gatherings that his opponents tried to pass off as legitimate councils. Only much larger and diverse meetings were legitimate venues for deciding important ecclesiastical questions. Abbo must have known that this call for a broader, more geographically diverse group of bishops went against the trends in the monarchy, as the early Capetians oversaw the continuation of the late Carolingian trend of geographical contraction of royal power.[33] Whether Abbo suggested this in order to take Church councils out of the hands of a single secular ruler or to encourage the Capetian kings to expand their geographical sway remains in doubt.

From this discussion of councils, Abbo moved easily to his next topic, the divisions of Christian society. Abbo's tripartite division of Christian society in the *Apologeticus* is perhaps the most thoroughly studied part of Abbo's writings. Georges Duby, Jacques LeGoff, and Marco Mostert have all discussed the divisions and their place in the history of philosophy and political thought in great detail.[34] Although his work is fascinating in the context of political philosophy, Abbo's divisions of society served a practical purpose as well. Abbo divided men into three groups—laymen, clerics (including bishops), and monks.[35] As Mostert has

---

33. Lemarignier, *Gouvernement royal*, 38–41.
34. Duby, *Three Orders*, 87–92; LeGoff, *Time, Work, and Culture*, 53–57; Mostert, *Political Theology*, especially 87–107; Jean Batany, "Abbon de Fleury et le théories des structures sociales vers l'an mille," *Etudes ligériennes d'histoire et d'archéologie médiévales*, Mémoires et exposés présentés à la Semaine d'études médiévales de Saint-Benoît-sur-Loire, 3–10 July 1969, ed. René Louis, Publication de la Société de fouilles archéologiques et des monuments historiques de l'Yonne (Paris: Clavreuil, 1975), 9–18.
35. Abbo, *Apologeticus*, f. 17r (= *PL* 139:463). Abbo first noted that men and women were divided into virgins, the continent, and the married, then said, "There are like-

noted, Abbo's social hierarchy was a moral rather than a functional one, with monks clearly superior to other classes of society by virtue of their greater commitment to chastity.[36] In the context of quarrels between Abbo, as a representative of the monastic party at the councils of Saint-Denis and Saint-Basle, and the episcopal party headed by Arnulf of Orléans, the *Apologeticus* is clearly making a case for the moral superiority of the monks' position.

Given the Capetian reliance on episcopal support under Hugh Capet and Robert, Abbo's argument initially seems ill advised or, at best, likely to be ignored. In fact, however, Abbo was proposing a realignment of power in northern Francia, one that Robert, if not Hugh, eventually accepted. The first few years of Abbo's abbacy, up until at least 993, were filled with wars, contentious councils, and petty violence, of which the attack on Abbo by Arnulf's supporters was just one example. In contrast to the grim reality surrounding him, Abbo presented an ideal world in which the laity served the Church. Christian farmers labored for the nourishment of the Church, and Christian warriors fought not each other but the enemies of the Church. Abbo also proposed a supportive role for the bishops and other clerics. He compared them to Martha, who represented the active life and whose labors made possible the contemplative life chosen by Mary and by the monks.[37] Later in the *Apologeticus,* Abbo offered the argument that the power of the bishops should be balanced by that of the kings.[38] Through this argument Abbo suggested that the kings were too heavily dominated by the bishops and offered them an excuse to exert their power more firmly. Within this framework Abbo indicated that the kings could enjoy both monastic and episcopal support. Indeed, in the words of Marco Mostert, "The purpose which a strong monarchy had to serve, in Abbo's view, was the

---

wise three grades or orders of men" (Virorum tantum similiter tres sunt gradus vel ordines). Women were specifically excluded from this scheme.

36. Mostert, *Political Theology,* 89.

37. Abbo, *Apologeticus,* f. 18r (= *PL* 139:464). See Mostert, *Political Theology,* 180, for the importance of hierarchy in Abbo's writings.

38. Abbo, *Apologeticus,* f. 20r (= *PL* 139:467).

Royal Politics 139

protection and furthering of the church, of the monks, and, especially, of St. Benedict."[39] Although his construct clearly favored the monks, it also offered the possibility of a strengthened royal position, with monastic support giving the kings a source of power and legitimacy to balance their dependence on the bishops.

From his vision of a peaceful and unified Christendom, Abbo returned to the issues facing him in the wake of the Council of Saint-Denis. Foremost of these was the question of possession of Church property. Though Abbo did not specifically mention monastic tithes, he undoubtedly intended the kings to remember both the arguments of the Council of Saint-Denis and his recent quarrel with Arnulf of Yèvre over Fleury's claims to customary dues at Yèvre, as well as simony, the sale of Church offices. The main argument that Abbo made was that the possessions of the Church belong not to individual humans, but to God. Therefore, he reasoned, the bishops and their allies, through their attempts to alienate the property of the monks (the poor of Christ), were eroding the very foundation of the Church and abandoning the most important business of the Church, the salvation of souls.[40]

The unnamed villain in the piece is clearly Bishop Arnulf of Orléans.[41] Without mentioning specific people or events, Abbo complained of a series of attacks, verbal and physical, each one of which corresponded to one actually perpetrated by Arnulf or his followers. The abbot condemned those who had attacked him murderously, those who had refused to acknowledge the excommunication of Abbo's attackers by other bishops, those who had falsely accused Abbo of having started a riot merely by express-

39. Mostert, *Political Theology*, 155.
40. Abbo, *Apologeticus*, f. 18v (= *PL* 139:465).
41. Abbo never mentioned Arnulf by name in this document, but other sources (the correspondence of Gerbert, the *VsA* of Aimoinus, and Arnulf's own response, *De cartilagine*) make clear that Arnulf was the supposed perpetrator of all of the crimes against monasticism enumerated in the document. The intentional ambiguity of Abbo's rhetoric is partially lost in translation; Latin requires no subject pronouns (except for emphasis), so Abbo's statements about the actions of Arnulf do not include even a definite indication of gender. This is the equivalent (though much more graceful rhetorically) of putting the entire work in the passive voice in English.

ing his support of monastic prerogatives and, finally, those who had declared Abbo excommunicated because he had consorted with those who had themselves been excommunicated following the riot. This last charge, Abbo maintained, revealed the true hypocrisy of his enemy, since Arnulf had quite willingly consorted with those who had attacked Abbo on the road to Tours even after they had been excommunicated by both Archbishop Seguin of Sens and Bishop Odo of Chartres.[42] Despite the specificity of the charges, Abbo maintained his policy of not mentioning Arnulf by name. His diatribe had less the air of a demand for personal retribution than of a plea for general reformation of behavior.[43]

After condemning Arnulf's actions, Abbo defended his own. Abbo had been accused of consorting with the excommunicated (and thence had incurred excommunication for himself), but Abbo noted that the bishops had so abused their power of excommunication that at this rate the entire kingdom would be under excommunication in a short time.[44] He noted that although he had been accused of inciting a riot (presumably at Saint-Denis) with inflammatory rhetoric, he had not noticed that other participants at the council had opened their books or consulted texts in an effort to make a reasoned argument. Abbo and his fellow monks apparently were more inclined to consult texts at councils than were bishops. Gerbert also noted that a number of books suddenly appeared when the abbots arose to testify at the Coun-

42. Abbo, *Apologeticus*, London, BL Add 10972, ff. 20v–21r (= *PL* 139:468–69). Given his previous reticence in naming names, it is interesting that Abbo identified both Seguin and Odo by name in this passage.

43. The only other exception to Abbo's policy of not naming names is the curious reference to Letald of Micy. According to Abbo, Arnulf (still unnamed) had gone beyond his episcopal prerogatives in questioning Letald unjustly (though he did not mention about what). See also Head, *Hagiography*, 217–18. According to Mostert, *Political Theology*, 36, the dispute between Letald and Arnulf arose over Arnulf's demand that Letald take an oath of loyalty to Arnulf as his bishop, which Letald eventually did. Mostert does not give a source for this interesting piece of information. Lot, *Hugues Capet*, 37–38n4, indicated that Arnulf of Orléans had clashed with the monastery of Micy as well as Fleury, and had treated Letald harshly. In corrections to the text, however, he noted: "It is by mistake that it was said that he [Letald] had been persecuted by the bishop of Orléans" (444).

44. Abbo, *Apologeticus*, ff. 21v–22r (= *PL* 139:470).

Royal Politics

cil of Saint-Basle.[45] This suggests a fundamental disagreement about the nature of judicial proceedings and evidence. Abbo and his bookish allies were more concerned with finding legal rules and precedents, while his opponents were more interested in uncovering any exceptional circumstances that might require special treatment. Abbo further noted that he, more than many others, had reason to regret the riot; his ally Seguin of Sens was the most severely injured of any. Abbo pointed out that he had made no arguments encouraging the riot and was certainly not a magician capable of casting spells on people's minds. Abbo concluded his defense by noting his own role as a peacemaker and Arnulf's harsh treatment of another monk, Letald of Micy.[46] Clearly Abbo believed that the best defense is a strong offense, but ultimately he hoped for a society in which bishops and abbots could work together without the need for defensive or offensive measures.[47]

Abbo ended his *Apologeticus* with a plea for councils about the truly pressing needs of the Christian Church. He urged the kings to play a leading role in the councils, as good Christian monarchs. He then appended a short and somewhat eccentric list of suitable topics for councils, which he urged his newfound allies the kings to present to the bishops: the nature of the Holy Ghost, heresies about the imminent end of the world, and the proper date for the beginning of Advent.[48] These topics differed markedly from the subjects of recent councils. Whereas the councils of Saint-Basle and Saint-Denis addressed political and administrative questions, such as the deposition of an archbishop and the distribution of tithes, Abbo's ideal councils addressed theological questions of concern to Christians of all times and places. Two of his topics had to do with calendrical calculations, one of Abbo's intellectu-

---

45. Gerbert, "Acta Consilii Remensis," c. 19 (MGH SS 3:666).

46. Abbo, *Apologeticus*, f. 21r (= *PL* 139:469).

47. See Mostert, *Political Theology*, 125, for Abbo's preference for cooperation rather than strife.

48. This list is so eccentric and brief that Marco Mostert has argued that Abbo's original intent was to append a much longer and more fully explained list of topics: "The list of recommendations promised at the end of the *Liber Apologeticus* seems irretrievably lost" (ibid., 51).

al interests, while the third harked back to the time of the Council of Chalcedon, which aimed to refute the Monophysite heresy by establishing orthodox teaching on the nature of the Trinity.[49] All of these concerns have to do with unifying the Church across political boundaries. Abbo's concern with the nature of the Trinity arose from his observation that English and French churches recited a slightly different formula concerning the Holy Ghost. This may have been a problem that struck him while at Ramsey in England or one that arose subsequently, as more English monks arrived at Fleury. The Church could not, he believed, be at odds with itself on something so fundamental to Christian teaching. His second concern also recalled to him a scene from his earlier life, when as a student he had heard a preacher claiming that the year 1000 marked the end of time and rumors of a larger group claiming that the conjunction of certain ecclesiastical festivals would mark the end of the world. These heresies may have led to his study of computus and continuing interest in the calendar. Abbo eventually corrected the anno Domini dating of Bede by twenty-one years, arguing that the year 1000 had actually come and gone in 979, and carried forward the reckoning of days in his own calendrical tables up to 1576. In these two actions Abbo fell into an Augustinian pattern for refuting those who imagined that the end of the world was approaching rapidly. Rather than claiming that the end could not be known (though that argument often accompanied this), the Augustinian would point out that the date was actually much more distant than originally believed or (as in Abbo's case) that it had already passed without incident.[50] Finally, Abbo worried that not all Christian congregations were celebrating Advent at the same time. Again, as monks traveled for their educations and monasteries sought to establish uniform practice, this diversity of Christian practice would create factions and divisions within the greater Christian community.

49. Abbo, *Apologeticus*, ff. 22r–22v (= *PL* 139:470–72).
50. Aimoinus, *VsA*, c. 13; Arno Borst, *The Ordering of Time: From the Ancient Computus to the Modern Computer*, trans. Andrew Winnard (Chicago: University of Chicago Press, 1993), 52–54; Landes, "Fear of an Apocalyptic Year 1000," 250–54.

Royal Politics 143

One could argue about the relative importance of his concerns. These were clearly three issues of importance to Abbo, though probably not an exhaustive list of his concerns. The theological question of the nature of the Trinity was clearly central, as it went to the heart of the Christian understanding of God as well as reflecting the most troubling heresies of the past. The apocalyptic heresies (since Abbo mentions more than one) came second in his estimation. These potentially divided Christians not just between communities but within a single geographical radius. When he spoke of one apocalyptic movement that spread over almost all the world, he was not claiming that a large proportion of his community believed the heresy (evidence is lacking on the numbers of believers) but that the heresy was found in many parts of Europe. Finally, Abbo urged the regularization of the yearly calendar so that all parts of the world would celebrate Advent at the same time. Once again, he called for a unification of the Christian community. Ultimately, Abbo offered these suggestions to the Capetian kings to provide an alternative to the worldly topics that the bishops chose to address. The removal of tithes from a monastery's possession was a question more concerned with wealth and the growth of worldly power than with spiritual issues. Each of Abbo's alternatives dealt with timeless religious issues (even though two of the three involved calendars) rather than fleeting temporal concerns. With this brief suggestion for the improvement of the world, Abbo ended his *Apologeticus*.

Abbo's argument in his defense was apparently successful and was probably what provoked a biting letter from Arnulf of Orléans. In his letter, with the curious title *On Cartilage,* Arnulf vehemently attacked those who seemed to be practicing virtues when they were, in fact, practicing sins. Because of its unusual title, this letter was long ignored by political historians and cited by historians of science (who had clearly never read past the title) as evidence for the teaching of medicine in tenth-century France.[51] In fact, the letter begins with a quotation from Job, "His sinews like

---

51. Lauer, "Le manuscrit," 493, does not mention specific historians.

bars of iron."[52] This phrase began a repetitious, but rhetorically powerful, comparison of apparently virtuous behavior and truly virtuous behavior. Among other things, Arnulf condemned those who disguised their unwillingness to punish as mercy and those who claimed to exercise humility in speech but who actually failed to speak out through timidity or laziness. Like Abbo's *Apologeticus,* this letter does not mention any particular person, but its editor, Lauer, has asserted that it refers to the conflict with the monks of Fleury.[53] Certainly Arnulf's phrasing strongly echoes the opening of Abbo's *Apologeticus,* where Abbo noted that under certain circumstances someone might "relate not those things which one ought to say, but ... those things which one ought not to say."[54] Arnulf's reference to the "unwillingness to punish" of some suggests his dissatisfaction with Abbo's ritual pardoning of the perpetrators, as does his reference to inaction disguised as "humility," an indication as well of impatience with the monastic claims to humility before authority.

Similarities between Arnulf's letter and Abbo's *Apologeticus* do not end with phrasing. Like the *Apologeticus,* Arnulf's letter does not mention any names or specific circumstances. If this letter does indeed refer to Abbo's *Apologeticus* and the disturbances at the Council of Saint-Denis, Arnulf may have had several motives for his vagueness. Like Abbo, Arnulf probably wished to avoid openly accusing his rival. Instead, he suggested that things that had been perceived as virtues were actually signs of weakness, if not actually vices. In this way, he left open the question of who had committed serious offenses and who had merely been de-

52. This is Jb 40.18 in the New Revised Standard Version or Jb 40.13 in the Vulgate. The Oxford Annotated Bible translates the full verse as "His bones are tubes of bronze, his limbs like bars of iron," but I am grateful to Paul B. Harvey for pointing out that the term *cartilago* is ambiguous in the Vulgate, as is its Greek counterpart in the Septuagint. The original Hebrew term probably referred to the spinal column, which (like cartilage) was flexible. Arnulf's purpose in citing this passage was to contrast the seeming firmness of *cartilago* with the actual firmness of bone.

53. Lauer, "Le manuscrit," 493. Lauer gives no basis for this suggestion, but most subsequent scholars have agreed with him; for a recent and important example, see Head, *Hagiography,* 246.

54. Abbo, *Apologeticus,* f. 15v (= PL 139:461).

Royal Politics 145

ceived.⁵⁵ Arnulf probably hoped that King Hugh would hold Abbo responsible for the riot at Saint-Denis. If, however, Abbo were ultimately successful in persuading Hugh to strengthen his ties to the monks, Arnulf would not want to have attacked him directly, and could claim that Abbo had merely been overly naive in supporting the position of the monks and laity at Saint-Denis. Both Abbo and Arnulf clearly had motives for avoiding further direct confrontations, and both also had strong motives for presenting their defenses to Kings Hugh and Robert and to the ecclesiastical community of northern Francia.

The immediate effect of Abbo's appeal was to gain him small concessions on minor matters and to begin the process of integrating monastic and royal interests. Shortly afterward, Abbo appeared as a witness to a royal charter in which the kings recognized a donation from Walter, count of Amiens, Vexin, and Valois, to Saint-Crépin of Poitiers.⁵⁶ This puts Abbo at the heart of the royal court, a position usually reserved only for bishops during the reign of Hugh Capet.⁵⁷ Abbo also laid the groundwork for reconciliation with the kings on the issue of Arnulf of Reims, though this was not achieved until after Hugh's death in 996.⁵⁸

Abbo's new philosophy bore fruit almost immediately, as may

---

55. The lack of specificity in both Arnulf's and Abbo's writings at this time is curious. A possible explanation is that references were omitted by later editors or copyists who wished to downplay tensions between Fleury and the see of Orléans. Both works survive in eleventh-century manuscripts; if they were edited, it must have been very shortly after their composition. Abbo's *Apologeticus* did, however, contain references to Letald of Micy (f. 21r [= *PL* 139:469]), and is quoted extensively by Aimoinus as a defense against Arnulf (*VsA*, c. 9). The more likely explanation is that both Abbo and Arnulf had strong motives for not mentioning each other by name, at least at this time.

56. Paris, BN Coll. Moreau 16, ff. 19r–20r. The date of the charter is uncertain, but William Mendel Newman dated it between 7 January 992 and 24 October 996 (death of Hugh Capet), based on the presence of Bishop Fulk of Amiens and Bishop Guy of Soissons as witnesses (*Catalogue des actes de Robert II, roi de France* [Paris: Recueil Sirey, 1937], no. 8, pp. 8–9).

57. Lemarignier, *Gouvernement royal*, 46; note that Lemarignier identified Count Walter of Amiens as one of Hugh Capet's most important retainers (50).

58. Mostert, *Political Theology*, 55, noted that Robert did not develop the same interdependent relationship with bishops (particularly Arnulf of Orléans) as had his father, so that after Hugh Capet's death, "the influence of the bishop waned, enabling Abbo's influence to wax." See also Cousin, *Abbon de Fleury-sur-Loire*, 120.

be seen in a charter drafted in the summer of 993. This document records the settlement of a long-standing dispute between Fleury and Arnulf of Yèvre, a nephew of Bishop Arnulf of Orléans. Fleury claimed that it had for many years held an estate at Yèvre, just east of Pithiviers and about fifty kilometers (or thirty miles) from Fleury. Sometime before 993 and probably before the siege of Melun in 991, the younger Arnulf had claimed the right of *advocatia* and *vicaria* for some lands of Fleury in Yèvre, and had wrongfully (in the eyes of the monks) attempted to exact payments from the estate and to carry off goods from Yèvre.[59] Such claims of lay "protection" of monastic lands through advocatia or vicaria were more often than not excuses to plunder them. When Abbo complained of this behavior to the kings, Hugh sent Robert to investigate the charge and to bring the lands back into Fleury's control under royal protection.[60]

By 993 the situation at Yèvre had become more complicated. In 991 Count Odo of Chartres had laid siege to Melun, and the kings needed whatever support they could muster in the region.[61] As Hugh stated in the charter:

---

59. The exact meanings of *advocatia* and *vicaria* in this context are unclear. The definitions in Niermeyer, *Lexicon minus*, under *advocatia* and *vicaria* suggest that these terms referred to rights of revenue collection associated with secular or ecclesiastical estates, rights of legal jurisdiction, and protection of ecclesiastical estates. The context indicates that Arnulf of Yèvre was certainly claiming the right to collect revenues from Yèvre, though whether as a secular lord or as a monastic advocate is unclear. Abbo's writings on the predatory habits of lay advocates of monasteries, however, suggest that he may have been acting in the latter capacity (see especially his *Apologeticus*, ff. 19v–20v [= *PL* 139:465–68]).

60. Prou and Vidier, *Recueil des chartes de Saint-Benoît-sur-Loire*, no. 70 (993, after 1 June). This is one of the few charters of Fleury that still existed in the original when Prou and Vidier published their edition early in the twentieth century. The dating clause of this charter states that the charter was "enacted publicly in the *civitas* of Paris, in the year of the incarnation of the Lord 993, in the sixth indiction, in the seventh regnal year of the most glorious King Hugh and his renowned son Robert." On the basis of this, Prou and Vidier place the date of the charter in 993, "after 1 June," the anniversary of Hugh's consecration. The dating can be further limited by the reference to the indiction. Since the indictional year changed in September, the charter must have been enacted during the summer of 993.

61. See Lot, *Hugues Capet*, 159n1, for the date of the siege of Melun.

Royal Politics   147

Meanwhile, since Count Odo [of Blois and Chartres] had begun a dispute against me, we furthermore called Arnulf, bishop of Orléans to our aid—along with our other relatives and retainers in our retinue whom we called together; for this reason he [Bishop Arnulf] asked that we return the customary payments to the said Arnulf, his nephew, just as he had previously held [them], though violently; since I did not wish to offend him because of his service, when I had called the said abbot [Abbo], I asked that he pay thirty *modii* of wine, as a wine tax from this holding to that Arnulf, as long as the bishop, his uncle, lived, for our salvation.[62]

This charter makes clear that Abbo and Hugh both found themselves in a difficult position. For Hugh to capitulate on his support for Fleury against Arnulf of Yèvre would be a clear admission of his own weakness. On the other hand, the form of the charter suggests great royal power. The charter is dated by their regnal year and the incarnation, contains no witnesses other than Hugh and Robert, contains the monograms of both kings, and is sealed with a large wax seal (now missing from the manuscript, though its traces are still visible).[63]

Hugh must nevertheless have chafed under the pressure from the bishop, which would have compromised his relationship with Fleury. The monastery had traditionally had close ties with the

---

62. Prou and Vidier, *Recueil des chartes de Saint-Benoît-sur-Loire*, no. 70 (993, after 1 June): "Interea orta contentione Odonis, comitis, adversus me, inter ceteros necessarios et fideles nostros quos in apparatu nostro commonuimus, etiam Arnulfum, episcopum Aurelianensem, in adjutorium nostrum promonuimus; qua de causa petiit ut predicto Arnulfo, nepoti suo, redderemus consuetudines, sicut prius ipse licet violenter tenuerat, quem offendere pro suo servitio nolens, evocans predictum abbatem rogavi ut XXX modios vini in vindemii solveret de ipsa potestate ipsi Arnulfo quamdiu viveret episcopus, avunculus ejus, pro salvamento nostro."

The term *salvamentum* is problematic. Niermeyer, *Lexicon minor*, under *salvamentum* (definition 7), defines this as *"redevance coutumière* exigée pour prix de la garde exercée par un seigneur—a *tribute* exacted in respect of protection afforded by a baron" and gives as an example of this usage Hugh's charter to Fleury in 993. The overall meaning is clear: if Hugh arranges for Fleury to make this payment, then Arnulf of Yèvre will support Hugh. The exact meaning of salvamentum in this passage is less clear. It could refer to the protection that Hugh will accord Fleury in return for Fleury's paying Arnulf, or it could refer to the protection that Hugh hopes to receive from Arnulf. Niermeyer's French definition suggests the former; the English suggests the latter.

63. See notes to charter in Prou and Vidier, *Recueil des chartes de Saint-Benoît-sur-Loire*, no. 70 (993, after 1 June). See also Dunbabin, *France in the Making*, 129.

Capetians and could also serve as a center for pro-Capetian propaganda. The deciding factor was the importance of Melun to Hugh in the face of an attack by Odo of Blois. The loss of this territory would have divided the Capetian base of Ile-de-France to the north from their holdings in the Orléanais to the south, while uniting Odo's territories to the southwest and the northeast.[64] Abbo, for his part, had strong reasons for not relinquishing any rights that Fleury might claim on the lands of Yèvre. As writings from Fleury make clear, an abbot's reputation rested largely on his ability to preserve and increase the wealth of the monastery. Although Abbo's main claim to fame was his subsequent martyrdom, his biographer took care to note as well the gifts that he attracted to the monastery and various building projects carried out during his abbacy. Likewise, in the biography of Abbo's successor, Gauzlin of Fleury, the first book (consisting of fifty-six chapters) is almost entirely devoted to his additions to the wealth and privileges of Fleury.[65] Abbo would hardly need to spell out these considerations to a savvy politician such as Hugh. On the other hand, after opposing Hugh Capet at the Council of Saint-Basle, Abbo knew that he could hardly afford to antagonize both his king and his bishop by outright refusal to accept the terms offered. Abbo may also have feared the growing power of Odo of Blois. If Capetian territory were fragmented and Fleury cut off from Capetian protection, Abbo did not have any reason to hope that the counts of Blois would be more generous or sympathetic patrons than the kings of West Francia. Since Arnulf of Yèvre was willing to use force to take possession of the property, Abbo's opposition to the proposal would in any case have served only to embarrass Hugh, without guaranteeing any of Fleury's prerogatives.

The compromise reached in the charter reflects the ambiguity of the situation. Fleury was to pay thirty *modii* of wine to Arnulf of Yèvre, but only so long as his uncle, Bishop Arnulf, was

---

64. Melun lay forty-eight kilometers (about thirty-two miles) southwest of Paris on the Seine River. See Bachrach, *Fulk Nerra*, 37; Lot, *Hugues Capet*, 159.

65. Aimoinus, *VsA*, cc. 6, 11–12, 15; André, *Vie de Gauzlin*.

alive. The reference to the lifetime of Arnulf of Orléans indicates that his influence was the important factor in this decision, not the leverage of his nephew. Furthermore, the charter includes an implicit recognition of the weakness of the younger Arnulf's claims by noting that he held these rights "violently," that is, by force rather than by legal claims. The amount of wine may have been a purely symbolic payment (as Thomas Head has argued), but without more specific information of the size and yield of the land, we cannot assert this with absolute certainty. Assuming that relative measures of volume remained constant throughout late antiquity and the early Middle Ages (a questionable assumption), each *modius* contained sixteen *sextarii* or thirty-two *heminae*. Since one *hemina* was the measure of wine allotted daily to monks by St. Benedict, 30 *modii* (or 960 *hemina*) would be enough to keep two or three monks in drink for a year.[66] While giving up this much wine would not impoverish Fleury, it would require a noticeable adjustment in bookkeeping and would set a very bad precedent for future dealings with Hugh Capet's supporters. Fleury also ran the risk of the younger Arnulf trying to extend his collection of the wine after the death of his uncle—a claim that it would not be unreasonable to expect in a society governed by custom and precedent. The monks of Fleury were willing to run this risk, according to the charter, for Hugh's sake (*pro salvamento nostro*). Clearly, Hugh agreed to the charter only to placate the bishop of Orléans, and Abbo agreed only to retain Hugh's support. By holding out the promise that Fleury would have to pay the younger Arnulf for only a limited period of time, Abbo avoided permanently alienating the rights of Fleury to Yèvre, while Hugh put off confronting Arnulf of Yèvre until much later, when Arnulf's powerful uncle would be dead and Hugh's own position (he must have hoped) would be much stronger.[67] In the meantime, Hugh

---

66. For relative measures, see Lewis and Short, *Latin Dictionary*, under *hemina, modius*, and *sextarius*. For the amount of wine consumed daily by monks see Benedict, *RB 1980*, cc. 39 and 49 (the latter for lesser rations during Lent); Fichtenau, *Living in the Tenth Century*, 282.

67. For a slightly different reading of this charter, see Rosenwein, Head, and

was able to retake Melun,[68] and Abbo continued his efforts to increase the influence of the monastic party in Francia.

In the course of the three years following the Council of Saint-Basle, Abbo had succeeded in strengthening his monastery's position in Francia. The attack on his traveling party by followers of Bishop Arnulf of Orléans, although upsetting, provided him with an opportunity to assert his authority to pardon the perpetrators while maintaining the sympathy of other prelates. Both Archbishop Seguin of Sens, Arnulf's superior, and Bishop Odo of Chartres had excommunicated his attackers. In the question of monastic tithes, Abbo again turned physical violence, the riot at Saint-Denis, to his advantage, even though this time the perpetrators were his allies. His *Apologeticus* went beyond his immediate defense to propose a reevaluation of both royal and episcopal behavior. An incidental benefit of the affair was the cooling of relations between Arnulf of Orléans and Gerbert of Reims, whom Arnulf suspected of having brought accusations against him. Finally, though Abbo made great concessions relative to Fleury's lands at Yèvre, he also gained a certain amount of political capital with the kings.

Farmer, "Monks and Their Enemies," 781. For more on this charter as a compromise, see Mostert, *Political Theology*, 38–39.

68. See Lot, *Hugues Capet*, 158–62.

6

PAPAL POLITICS

THE COUNCIL of Saint-Basle and its aftermath made clear to Abbo that Fleury needed a stronger and more reliable patron than the kings if he were to achieve his goal of monastic independence. Abbo's weariness with the quarrels of the world came through clearly in his *Apologeticus*. Despite his public and private attempts to establish a more cooperative relationship with the monarchy, his efforts bore fruit only slowly. If anything, the period following the composition of his *Apologeticus* involved him in nearly as many controversies as the years preceding it. The deposition of Arnulf of Reims remained a source of tension between Abbo and the papacy on the one hand and the kings and Gerbert on the other. Likewise, although Fleury had temporarily settled its differences with the bishop of Orléans, Abbo had no guarantee that Fleury's rights would be respected in the future. Fleury needed a patron with great authority, something that the Carolingian kings had let wane and the Capetian kings could not regain easily. Increasingly, Abbo looked to the papacy for support.

The development that hit closest to home in the months following the riot of Saint-Denis was the death of Abbot Maiolus of Cluny in 994. The death of Maiolus marked the end of an era in the monastic reform movement. Even those who lived entirely in the cloister would have been moved by the death of the great abbot. Maiolus had become abbot of Cluny thirty years earlier, in 964, and had managed Cluny for the ailing Abbot Aymard for a decade before that.[1] Maiolus had inspired a great affection among his contemporaries, causing one recent historian to describe him as "one of the most attractive figures of the age and the warmest of all the abbots of Cluny, striking everywhere an authentic note of holiness."[2] The monk Syrus quickly produced a *Vita*, telling of his saintly life and miracles, which formed the basis for two more editions by the monk Aldebald as well as an abridged version of the *Vita*.[3] In the tenth century, the recognition of a saint was still an informal process, not the bureaucratic canonization procedure that began to grow up in the eleventh century. Instead, popular veneration combined with official assent allowed for the proliferation of cults and shrines.[4] Within a few years of his death, a papal charter referred to him as "saint"; he was the first abbot of Cluny to be called a saint, though Abbot Odo, who had reformed Fleury a generation earlier, eventually received that honor as well.[5] Maiolus, through his life and through the accounts of that life by Syrus and others, set the standard for a holy abbot in the tenth-century tradition of monastic reform. The traits that marked him as holy were bookishness, personal poverty coupled with spiritual wealth, the embrace of solitude and the peace of the monastery as a means to union with God through prayer, and a spiritual fatherhood, as he governed his monks with strictness tempered with paternal love.[6] Aimoinus would emphasize many of these traits, especially the love of study and spiritual fatherhood, when little more than a decade later he sat down to write Abbo's *Vita*.

In addition to his reputation for holiness, Maiolus was an en-

---

1. Rosenwein, *Rhinoceros Bound*, 51.
2. Noreen Hunt, *Cluny under Saint Hugh* (London: Edward Arnold, 1967), 23. For a discussion of hagiographical literature on Maiolus, see Head, *Hagiography*, 279.
3. Jean Leclercq, "Saint Majolus and Cluny," in *Aspects of Monasticism*, ed. Jean Leclercq, trans. Mary Dodd, Cistercian Studies Series 7 (Kalamazoo, Mich.: Cistercian Publications, 1978), 207–8.
4. Ward, *Miracles and the Medieval Mind*, 184–87.
5. Hunt, *Cluny under Saint Hugh*, 23.
6. Leclercq, "Saint Majolus," 209–24. Dominique Iogna-Prat, *Agni Immaculati:*

Papal Politics 153

ergetic administrator. Under his leadership Cluny participated in the reform of numerous monasteries, including Marmoutier and Saint-Julien of Tours, Paray-le-Monial in Burgundy, Lérins on the Mediterranean coast, and three monasteries in Italy.[7] Probably as a result of the riot at Saint-Denis in 994, in which Abbo had played such an important role, Hugh Capet requested Maiolus to come north to reform the monastery. This was Maiolus's last attempt at monastic reform; he died on the road north in 994.[8] Abbo almost certainly would have attended the funeral of so distinguished a monk and abbot, and it may have been there that he first met Maiolus's successor, Odilo of Cluny, who, during his fifty-five-year abbacy, was to make at least as important a mark on the monastic community as Maiolus had in his day.[9] Immediately following the death of Maiolus, however, Cluny's influence in the north must have waned. The abbots of both Marmoutier and Saint-Julien of Tours were among Abbo's correspondents in later years, and after 998 he seems to have filled the role of leader of the monastic houses of the Loire valley as the millennium drew to a close.[10]

Undoubtedly, the death of the powerful and energetic abbot of Cluny left both houses in Tours without important outside advice and support. The passing of Maiolus made Abbo's intervention in their affairs almost a foregone conclusion.

Even while Abbo mourned the great abbot, he must have found himself and Fleury benefiting from the need for a new leader in monastic politics. Shortly after the riot at Saint-Denis, the French bishops came together at a synod in Chelles, twenty-five kilometers (about sixteen miles) east of Paris.[11] King Robert him-

---

Recherches sur les sources hagiographiques relatives à Saint Maieul de Cluny (954–994) (Paris: Editions du Cref, 1988), 319–39, put monastic virtue at the center of this hagiographical tradition, though with greater emphasis on abandonment of self and virginity.

7. Rosenwein, *Rhinoceros Bound*, 51–55, and maps on xiv–xv; Philibert Schmitz, *Histoire de l'Ordre de Saint Benoît*, vol 1, *Origines, difussion et constitution jusqu'au XIIe siècle*, 2nd ed. (Maredsous and Namur: Editions Maredsous, 1948), 144.

8. Rosenwein, *Rhinoceros Bound*, 55.

9. Two letters from Abbo to Odilo survive (letters 7 and 12).

10. Riché, *Abbon de Fleury*, 235.

11. Lot, *Hugues Capet*, 88n2, suggests that the council took place either in 993 or

self presided over the council, and Gerbert directed the discussion. The other participants at the council included Archbishops Seguin of Sens, Dagobert of Bourges, and Archembald of Tours with their suffragans.[12] While Dagobert and Seguin had been present at the Council of Saint-Basle, the archbishop of Tours had not been represented there, a reflection, perhaps, of the evolution of Capetian relations with the northern French episcopate. Abbo probably attended this council, but even if he were not able to do so, he certainly would have learned of its decisions quickly, since the bishops concentrated on topics that were of great interest to him. In the years since the Council of Saint-Basle in 991, the supporters of Arnulf of Reims had tried numerous times to revoke the decision of that council and to reinstate him as archbishop of Reims. Councils had been attempted at Aachen, Rome, and Grenoble without result.[13] In the aftermath of the Council of Saint-Denis, the French bishops undoubtedly felt a strong need to reassert their authority. The bishops needed to work together in cases of excommunication. Abbo could not have been alone in complaining of bishops who did not honor excommunications made by other bishops but sought to add to the excommunicated those who failed to recognize their own actions.[14]

994: after Robert's divorce from Rozala Suzanna (992), according to Richer, and probably after the Council of Aachen and the summons from Rome (992–993) but before the wars between Odo of Blois and Fulk of Anjou, which ended in early 996. Our only source of information about the council is Richer, *Histoire,* 4.89 (2:290–91). In his edition of Richer, Latouche noted that the council is difficult to date, since Richer uses phrases such as *hujus temporis diebus* to facilitate transitions between topics rather than chronological relationships. Possible dates for this council range from 992 to 995 (Richer, *Histoire,* 4:89 [2:290–91n1]).

12. Richer, *Histoire,* 4.89 (2:290–91). Lot, *Hugues Capet,* 150, suggested that Gerbert himself had argued for holding this council.

13. Lot, *Hugues Capet,* 82–87, noted the ineffectiveness of the Council of Aachen and of the pope's summons of the kings and the French bishops to Rome (probably with the encouragement and support of the German court). Gerbert had written a letter to Pope John XV on behalf of Hugh Capet, asking for a meeting in Grenoble to discuss the deposition of Arnulf of Reims (undated, but both Lattin and Weigle in their editions of Gerbert's letters suggest late 992 or early 993). See Lattin, letter 193; Weigle, letter 188.

14. Abbo, *Apologeticus,* ff. 20v–21r (= *PL* 139:468–69).

The necessary unity came at last at the Council of Chelles. The bishops agreed here that only a united council of bishops could condemn a churchman who had abused his office, and that once a council of bishops had excommunicated someone, only a council could readmit that person to Communion.[15] This decision was significant in its affirmation of the rights of bishops (and no others) to oversee the actions of other bishops, while at the same time addressing complaints of episcopal abuse of the power of excommunication through unilateral action. In addition to restoring episcopal dignity after the riot at Saint-Denis (994), the council also considered the continuing attacks on the decision of the Council of Saint-Basle (991) to depose Arnulf. The Council of Chelles strongly reaffirmed the legitimacy of Arnulf's deposition and declared that the decision to depose him as archbishop of Reims and elect Gerbert in his stead was irrevocable, and any decision of the pope that contradicted the decrees of the Church Fathers was invalid.[16] The decisions of the Council of Chelles strongly reaffirmed the Capetian position on papal and episcopal power.

Ferdinand Lot exaggerated only slightly when he called this council "a declaration of war on the Papacy."[17] By asserting the primacy of Church canons, which were based primarily on the decisions of councils of bishops, the prelates gathered at the Council of Chelles had in effect subjected every decision of the papacy to the scrutiny of the episcopate. This reaffirmation of episcopal and conciliar primacy was a serious blow to the interests of reformed monasticism as well. As Abbo well knew, a strong bishop, such as Arnulf of Orléans, could dominate the internal affairs of a monastic establishment and threaten the possessions of the

---

15. Richer, *Histoire*, 4.89 (2:290–91).

16. Ibid.; the context suggests that the assembly's main concern was decrees made in Church councils.

17. Lot, *Hugues Capet*, 150, though he also noted that problems in Italy prevented the papacy from responding to this affront for at least two years (88). Contrast this with Cousin, *Abbon de Fleury-sur-Loire*, 118–19, which describes the council's support of Gerbert as contributing to "a latent hostility" between the king and the papacy.

monks in pursuit of his own policies or in the interests of his relatives. Abbo had firmly placed his hopes for monastic reform in Francia on the observation of papal prerogatives and the recognition of the rights of monks to appeal to the pope, rather than relying on local lords and bishops for protection. Although Abbo had already recognized the importance of a strong monarch in his *Apologeticus,* he continued to argue that papal authority was paramount in securing monastic independence from local politics. As the papacy's strongest advocate in Francia, Abbo cannot have approved of the judgments reached at Chelles, but already ecclesiastical politics were beginning to turn in his favor.

Despite the vote of confidence at Chelles, by the spring of 995 Gerbert could no longer ignore the challenges to his position as archbishop of Reims. When Pope John XV and the papal legate Leo called a council at Mouzon on 2 June 995 to discuss Gerbert's position, Gerbert decided to attend to make his case.[18] The location for the council was carefully chosen. Mouzon lay on the Meuse River in the Ottonian Empire but was also part of the archdiocese of Reims. Mouzon was thus a legitimate venue for hearing a case involving the archbishop of Reims but was safely outside of Capetian territory, and thus safe from direct Capetian pressure, as Saint-Basle of Verzy and Chelles were not.[19] Although Mouzon lay a mere ninety-six kilometers (about sixty-four miles) northeast of Reims and near the border between Capetian and Ottonian lands, Gerbert was the only French prelate in attendance at Mouzon. The other bishops at the council were

---

18. Richer's account of the events leading up to the council appears to have been based entirely on his reading backward from the written account of the council, not always accurately. Latouche argued that Richer erroneously developed a narrative in which the French bishops had refused to attend a synod in German territory and had absented themselves from both the Council of Aachen in 992 and that of Mouzon in 995 because of commands from Hugh Capet (Richer *Histoire,* 4.95 [2:302–3n3]). Lot, *Hugues Capet,* 90, although discounting the fantastic plots that Richer wove into his narrative, argued that it was highly likely that Hugh Capet did forbid the French bishops to attend the council.

19. Cousin, *Abbon de Fleury-sur-Loire,* 119.

from Trier, Verdun, Liège, and Münster.[20] Despite Mouzon's convenient location, with the exception of Gerbert and the bishop of Münster, the other bishops were all from Lorraine, the center of power of Charles of Lorraine, whom Arnulf had aided in the taking of Reims.[21] Also present, in addition to the papal legate Leo, were several secular rulers, including Count Geoffrey of Verdun (the only one named) and "the not ignoble abbots of several cities" (not named).[22] Given that no bishops from the Capetian kingdom attended the council, it is unlikely that any French abbots or nobles were present, though not impossible.[23] Gerbert was alone at Mouzon in his efforts to defend his actions as well as the policies of Kings Hugh and Robert.

The surviving account of the Council of Mouzon consists almost entirely of Gerbert's defense of himself. Gerbert began his argument by claiming that his accession as archbishop of Reims had been undertaken despite warnings of possible danger from his colleagues, and that he had done so only out of concern for the people of Reims. In fact, he argued, Archbishop Adalbero of Reims had, before his death, intended Gerbert as his successor, and his selection had been ignored only because of simony, which had led to Arnulf's selection instead. Gerbert had not, of course, known of his designation as heir during the late archbishop's lifetime—that would have been a violation of canon law, which forbade bishops to name their own successors. Nevertheless, Gerbert had served Arnulf faithfully until he had discovered his misbehavior, at which point Gerbert had severed relations with him. Upon the deposition of Arnulf at the Council of Saint-Basle, Gerbert had only reluctantly agreed to take his place

20. Johannes Dominicus Mansi, ed., *Sacrorum Conciliorum nova et amplissima collectio* (Venice, 1774; facsimile Paris, 1902), "Concilium Mosomense," 19:193.
21. Lot, *Hugues Capet*, 90.
22. Mansi, "Concilium Mosomense," in *Sacrorum Conciliorum*, 19:193: "diversarum urbium abbates non ignobiles."
23. Although Abbo probably did not attend the council, he presumably was able to receive detailed accounts of it from German abbots and monks, at least some of whom were in attendance.

as archbishop.²⁴ Once he had established the sequence of events, Gerbert then turned to the legitimacy of Arnulf's deposition and his own elevation. He argued that he had neither participated in Arnulf's betrayal of Reims nor brought evidence against Arnulf (with whom he had had no contact after leaving his service). Furthermore, Arnulf had been given every consideration in preparing his defense, including recourse to the pope, though the pope did not respond to repeated requests for guidance in the handling of the case.²⁵

When Gerbert had finished his defense, the bishops, together with Count Geoffrey of Verdun, withdrew to consider the case. Their decision was inconclusive, probably as a reflection of the difficulty of enforcing a decision against Gerbert without the support of the French bishops. The bishops asked Gerbert to see that a certain John, one of Abbot Leo's monks, be received fittingly by Hugh Capet and Robert. They also declared that a synod should be held at Reims on 1 July to consider the affair further.²⁶ Finally, Leo requested that Gerbert not partake of Communion until then. At this harsh stipulation, Gerbert protested that he had cooperated with the council and had not been condemned for any misconduct. Leo then agreed that Gerbert need refrain only from celebrating Mass until after the synod.²⁷ Although the bishops had not reached a firm decision, Leo's final request to Gerbert suggested that he, as a representative of the pope, had not wavered in

---

24. Mansi, "Concilium Mosomense," in *Sacrorum Conciliorum*, 19.193–94.

25. Ibid., 19.195–96. Lot, *Hugues Capet*, 94, found Gerbert's discourse filled with pretentious rhetorical flourishes that cast doubts on his sincerity without promoting his cause. Lot later (151), with uncharacteristic hyperbole and anachronism, accused Gerbert of abandoning his principles for the sake of worldly promotion, to the point of advocating Protestantism.

26. Lot, *Hugues Capet*, 90, noted that the council cannot, in itself, have had much independent authority, since neither the French kings nor the French bishops had attended, and later (94) added that the synod was too small to render a decision. Although size may have been a factor, the composition of the council was at least as important. Of those present, only Gerbert was from the archdiocese of Reims, or even from Capetian territory. The actions of the council were unlikely to be effective unless it could gain the support of the West Frankish bishops or the West Frankish kings.

27. Mansi, "Concilium Mosomense," in *Sacrorum Conciliorum*, 19:196.

his conviction that Gerbert should relinquish the see of Reims in favor of Arnulf, who had been deposed without papal sanction.

Between the Council of Mouzon in early June and the Council of Reims on 1 July 995, Gerbert wrote several works defending his position. Within a week of the Council of Mouzon he had redacted the proceedings of the Council of Saint-Basle, probably in order to present his case more clearly before the papal legate, the kings, and the French bishops. Although it is highly unlikely that Gerbert composed the entire proceedings of the council in the week following the Council of Mouzon, he did circulate these proceedings publicly for the first time shortly before 9 June.[28] Gerbert may also at this time have written letters to two bishops of Lorraine, Wilderod of Strasbourg and Notker of Liège, in which he discussed the Council of Saint-Basle more briefly.[29] As at the Council of Mouzon, he emphasized the seriousness of Arnulf's actions, the many opportunities that had been given to both Arnulf and Pope John XV to respond to the charges against Arnulf, the fairness of the proceedings, and Arnulf's condemnation of himself at the end of the council. Gerbert also maintained his position that he had not personally been responsible for the prosecution of Arnulf and therefore could not be accused of having conspired to convict the archbishop so that he could take his place.

Gerbert's publication of the proceedings of the Council of Saint-Basle brought an immediate and harsh response from Leo and a later and somewhat milder response from Abbo. Leo's reaction to reading the proceedings was anger and astonishment at their condemnation of the pope's actions and their support of the (in his eyes) illegitimate Council of Saint-Basle. He clearly ex-

---

28. Lot, *Hugues Capet*, 96. Abbot Leo claims to have seen the proceedings for the first time on 9 June, so Gerbert must have written and sent them to Leo at least a day or two earlier.

29. Lot, ibid. suggested that this account of the council as well as two letters (Lattin, letters 201–2; Weigle, letters 193 and 217) containing a briefer summary of its proceedings were both written in June 995. Both Lattin and Weigle date the letters much later, to late 995 or early 996, when Gerbert had already left Reims and was still attempting to orchestrate his return. (Weigle does not give the text of letter 217 since he regards it as more of a treatise or apologia than a true letter.)

pressed his distress to the French kings, Hugh Capet and Robert: "on the day of Pentecost [9 June] a *libellus* was brought to us in which was included your synod, made against Arnulf, ultimately against the Roman church, completely full of outrages and blasphemies. When we had seen it, stunned with astonishment and amazement, we immediately thought that we would return to the apostolic lord [Pope John XV], and bring this *libellus* of apostasy to him."[30] His anger was somewhat appeased after he had received a conciliatory letter from the two kings, and he decided to attend the Council at Reims after all.[31] Leo went on to condemn the participants in the Council of Saint-Basle as "Antichrists" and to compare them to the scribes and the Pharisees. Furthermore, he condemned those who (unlike the early followers of Christ) studied Plato, Vergil, and Terence. He singled out whoever wrote the account of the council as one "who dared to write such things against the Roman church which the Arian heretics never presumed [to say]." Leo also argued vigorously that opposition to the pope, as the heir to Peter, to whom God had entrusted the keys of the kingdom of Heaven, was in essence opposition to God himself.[32] His complaint was directed against all of those who partici-

---

30. Leo, abbot and papal legate, "Leonis abbatis et legati ad Hugonem et Rotbertum reges epistola," in *Annales, chronica et historiae aevi Saxonici*, ed. Georgius Heinricus Pertz, MGH SS, vol. 3 (Hanover, 1839), 686: "die sancto pentecosten ablatus est nobis libellus, in quo vestra synodus contra Arnulfum facta continebatur, immo adversus Romanam ecclesiam, tota iniuriis et blasphemiis plena. Quo viso, admiratione et stupore attoniti, cogitavimus statim ad domnum apostolicum reverti, et ipsum ei apostaticum libellum portare." See also Cousin, *Abbon de Fleury-sur-Loire*, 119–20.

31. Leo, "Leonis legati epistola," MGH SS 3:686.

32. "Ibid., 3:687–88: "tanta contra Romanam ecclesiam ausi sunt scribere, quod nec Arriani heretici aliquando presumpserunt." On the Antichrist, Leo quoted I Jn 2.18, "Many antichrists have been made, and therefore we know that it is the last hour," to justify his application of the term to the entire council of bishops. He then defined Antichrist broadly as anyone who was contrary to Christ (*contrarius Christo*). Leo appears not to have known that it was Gerbert who had authored the "Acta Consilii Remensis." Lot, *Hugues Capet*, 96–97, suggested (correctly, I think) that Gerbert did not attach the preliminary letter identifying himself to the proceedings of the council, but that Leo, though feigning ignorance of the author, probably suspected that the work was Gerbert's. For an overview of papal prerogatives in this period, see Geoffrey Barraclough, *The Medieval Papacy* (Norwich, England: Harcourt Brace and World, 1968), especially 51–70; Walter Ullmann, *A Short History of the Papacy in the Middle Ages*

pated in the Council of Saint-Basle, but Gerbert, as the only major participant with a reputation for great learning, was certainly Leo's main target, though, as a teacher versed in classical literature himself, Abbo may have secretly felt that Leo had cast his net a bit wide (or perhaps had underrated his ally's own accomplishments). Leo continued with a biting attack on the kings themselves. The kings, he said, alone of all Christians, had failed to honor and respect the papacy as was fitting. The letter concluded with a brief argument against the legitimacy of Arnulf's deposition. Although Gerbert and his supporters had claimed that Arnulf had freely confessed, Leo noted that since Arnulf had been threatened with death unless he did so, his confession was hardly a valid indication of his guilt. In fact, Leo noted, Arnulf had maintained his innocence until threatened by the bishops, and the only witness against him was a priest—whose testimony must surely be worth less than that of an archbishop.[33] The extreme language of Leo's letter indicates that, whatever Gerbert might have hoped, his account of the Council of Saint-Basle worsened his position rather than bettered it.

Abbo's response to Gerbert's arguments may be inferred from his *Collectio canonum*. Although the date of this collection is not known, many of the issues Abbo raised in this work seem to speak directly to Gerbert's case. Marco Mostert has argued that Abbo began keeping a dossier of quotations from the Church councils and patristic works around the time of the Council of Saint-Basle in 991. Certainly Abbo cited the same sources repeatedly in different contexts.[34] Abbo's *Collectio canonum* was directed to Kings

---

(London: Methuen, 1972), especially 99–108; Bernhard Schimmelpfennig, *The Papacy*, trans. James Sievert (New York: Columbia University Press, 1992), especially 109–14.

33. Leo, "Leonis legati epistola," MGH SS 3:690.

34. Mostert, *Political Theology*, 70–71. Mostert noted that certain patristic writings were referred to repeatedly in Abbo's *Apologeticus*, in his *Collectio canonum*, and in his letters. As time went on, Mostert argued, Abbo added excerpts from the letters of Gregory the Great, Roman law, and early Church councils.

The dating of the *Collectio canonum* is determined by Abbo's prefatory letter to Kings Hugh and Robert. Abbo referred to his earlier *Apologeticus*, probably written in 994. Since Hugh Capet died in October 996, the *Collectio canonum* was written be-

Hugh Capet and Robert as a guide to Christian rulership within the medieval genre of a mirror for princes.[35] His approach in this instance is in marked contrast with his earlier inflammatory oratory at Saint-Basle and Saint-Denis. Clearly, he had learned that stable and peaceful results are more likely to come from prior persuasion than from impassioned speechifying. Abbo ranged widely in the *Collectio canonum,* but the unifying theme in the work was his concern with the proper ordering of Christian society, from the relationship between secular and ecclesiastical powers to proper understanding of laws to the nature and source of the authority associated with the offices of kings, bishops, and abbots.[36] Within this framework, many of Gerbert's arguments were implicitly refuted.

Abbo's *Collectio canonum* contained responses to Gerbert's main claims. Gerbert's writings emphasized the legitimacy of episcopal councils, the need to act independently of the pope under certain circumstances, and the desire of the late Archbishop Adalbero of Reims that Gerbert succeed him. Abbo argued strongly for papal primacy and specifically noted that Church councils were not valid unless ratified by the pope.[37] On the proper election of bishops, he noted that bishops should be selected by the people and clergy of the city, without regard for material concerns or friendship (which could include political alliances).[38]

---

tween 994 and 996. As the work seems to be at least partially a response to the arguments made by Gerbert at the Council of Mouzon and in his account of the Council of Saint-Basle, the work was probably begun shortly after Abbo heard these arguments, possibly after the Council of Reims in July 995. See Mostert, *Political Theology,* 53.

35. Abbo, *Collectio canonum.* Cousin, *Abbon de Fleury-sur-Loire,* 141–56, summarized the main issues addressed in Abbo's *Collectio canonum.* He saw (156) the *Collectio canonum,* the *Apologeticus,* and Abbo's letter 14 to Abbot G. as forming a handbook for the clergy.

36. Mostert, *Political Theology,* 53, said of the *Collectio canonum,* "There seems to be no order to speak of in its presentation," and later (54) noted that "Abbo's preoccupation with the struggle for exemption of his monastery is apparent on every page."

37. Abbo, *Collectio canonum,* c. 8.

38. Ibid., c. 4. For the definition of friendship in the Middle Ages, see Brian Patrick McGuire, *Friendship and Community: The Monastic Experience, 350–1250* (Kalamazoo, Mich.: Cistercian Publications, 1988), xvii–l; for Cicero's conception of friendship as partly political, see xxxiii.

Abbo did not need to say that if the Capetians had followed these precepts earlier, Arnulf of Reims would not have been appointed to begin with. Furthermore, Abbo explicitly noted that bishops should not choose their own successors. If someone were to be designated by a bishop as his successor, he was not guaranteed the position on the death of the bishop. Instead, he would have to undergo the process of election and confirmation according to the canons.[39] Although Gerbert never explicitly argued that his selection by Adalbero gave him a claim to the archiepiscopal see of Reims, that argument was implicit in his speech at Mouzon. Abbo's work must have served as a reminder both to the kings and to Gerbert that Adalbero's wishes were irrelevant in this instance. On the other hand, Abbo's argument that bishops should be selected without regard for anything other than their moral and canonical qualifications may have been a subtle hint to the kings that if they had chosen the archbishop of Reims according to spiritual rather than political qualifications, they could have avoided much trouble.[40] Finally, near the end of the *Collectio canonum*, Abbo raised an argument that he had made at the Council of Saint-Basle and in his *Apologeticus:* in a fair hearing, the accusers, the witnesses, and the judges should not be the same people.[41] By the time Abbo actually wrote out the *Collectio canonum* and presented it to the kings, many of these issues had been decided, but Abbo was clearly inspired in part by the affair of the archbishop of Reims and the need to draw lessons from the experience.

After the exchanges between Gerbert, Leo, and Hugh Capet in June, none of the participants can have been surprised at the course of the Council of Saint-Remi of Reims, which convened

39. Abbo, *Collectio canonum*, c. 42.
40. See chapter 4 for Arnulf's lack of qualifications for the position of archbishop. Abbo never addressed the question of Arnulf's qualification for office; he merely maintained that once elected and consecrated Arnulf could not be deposed without a trial before a full council of bishops under the direction of the pope.
41. *Collectio canonum*, c. 44. The heading on this chapter begins "How accused priests should be examined." This chapter probably also refers to the degradation of the priest Adalgar, who testified against Arnulf at the Council of Saint-Basle (see chapter 4). Cousin, *Abbon de Fleury-sur-Loire*, 119–20.

on 1 July 995. No full account of the proceedings of the council survives, though Gerbert's arguments have been preserved separately.[42] Gerbert, possibly as a result of Leo's vigorous denunciation of the proceedings of the Council of Saint-Basle, moderated his arguments considerably, at least as far as his criticism of the papacy was concerned.[43] Many of his previous claims remained, however. He continued to maintain that Arnulf's confession of guilt was valid. Furthermore, although he acknowledged the papacy's interest in the matter, he argued that the dominance of papal business by the corrupt Crescentius family precluded immediate action by the pope. Given the corruption in Rome, according to Gerbert, the bishops were justified in adjudicating the matter on their own. As it turned out, there was ample precedent for the actions of the bishops in the councils of the Church. Gerbert cited several African councils but also the case of Ebo of Reims, who had been deposed under similar circumstances. The popes who had presided over the councils had set a clear precedent for papal behavior in matters of this sort. Although neither the pope nor his legates could be present at the Council of Saint-Basle, Gerbert contended that the council had not been undertaken without consideration of the papal position. Gerbert ended with a plea to Leo for mercy in deciding the matter, particularly in light of the difficulty of consulting the pope as long as the Crescentius family controlled Rome. The tone of the council suggests that Gerbert may still have harbored hopes of convincing Leo.

42. Gerbert of Aurillac, "Acta Consilii Causeiensis," in *Annales, chronica et historiae aevi Saxonici,* ed. Georgius Heinricus Pertz, MGH SS, vol. 3 (Hanover, 1839), 691–93. On the peculiar name of the council, see Lot, *Hugues Capet,* 99–100n5; Latouche, in his edition of Richer, *Histoire,* 2:328–29n2. Richer's history, which has filled in many gaps in our knowledge of the tenth century, ends with the Council of Mouzon (*Histoire,* 4.107 [2:328–29]). Richer made notes for subsequent chapters that he never completed (4.108 [2:328–33], especially Latouche's textual notes). The highly anti-Capetian "Historia Francorum Senonensis," in *Chronica et annales aevi Salici,* ed. Georgius Heinricus Pertz, MGH SS, vol. 9 (Hanover, 1851), 368, suggests that Gerbert's deposition was agreed upon at this council, though the proceedings of the council and subsequent events prove this account misleading at best.

43. Lot, *Hugues Capet,* 100.

Papal Politics 165

The response of Arnulf's defenders has not been preserved but can be reconstructed plausibly. If Abbo spoke at the council, he probably addressed it in much the same terms as at Saint-Basle four years earlier.[44] He would undoubtedly have continued to emphasize the primacy of Rome and the importance of clearly separating accusers from witnesses and judges. He was much better prepared, however, to present his ideas effectively. He could have referred to his own *Collectio canonum* rather than having to borrow books from the other participants as he had at Saint-Basle. He also could be confident that the kings and bishops were already familiar with his main points from his published works dedicated to the kings. His arguments, as such, were probably not a major subject of debate, but they were a reminder to the participants of his earlier arguments, both at the Council of Saint-Basle and subsequently. For his part, Leo undoubtedly reiterated the points made in his letter to Hugh and Robert.[45] In Leo's eyes, Arnulf's confession was invalid because it was obtained under threat of death. Although Leo had explained the slow response of the papacy as due to problems with the Crescentii, he would not have accepted the problems in Rome as a valid reason for ignoring the papacy completely, especially when a year later Leo, as a papal legate, had tried to call a council in Aachen, which the French bishops had refused to attend. Leo's eloquence on this occasion impressed Abbo so greatly that he commented on it repeatedly in a letter that he wrote to Leo nearly a year later.[46] The results of the council could have been anticipated. Leo demanded that Arnulf be freed from prison and Gerbert stripped of the office of archbishop, but no action was taken by either the kings or the bishops to carry out his demands.[47]

---

44. See chapter 4.
45. See above, this chapter. Leo, "Leonis legati epistola," MGH SS 3:686–90.
46. Abbo, letter 15. One could argue that Abbo (who was requesting Leo's aid in securing a papal privilege for Fleury) was flattering Leo as a matter of policy rather than out of sincere admiration. On the other hand, Abbo evidently agreed with Leo's position at the council and repeated his praises several times in a relatively short letter.
47. The only direct source we have for the council is Gerbert's arguments ("Acta

While at the council, Abbo had time for at least one private conversation with the papal legate. He could have counted on a sympathetic ear, since he was one of only three supporters of the papal position mentioned in Gerbert's account of the Council of Saint-Basle, which had so enraged Leo. The abbot of Fleury was always "mindful of the needs of the place which he ruled," and undoubtedly saw a golden opportunity to gain the favor of an influential man.[48] Abbo took advantage of his meeting with Leo to discuss the possibility of Pope John XV confirming the privileges of Fleury.[49] Periodic papal and royal confirmation of a monastery's privileges was, by the tenth century, a standard means of reaffirming the monastery's place in society and ensuring institutional support for a monastery's rights. Monasteries might also take the opportunity to ask the papacy to expand on their privileges or at least to spell out their rights a little more clearly. Fleury's privileges had already been confirmed by Popes John VIII in 878 and Leo VII in 938,[50] and by Frankish kings from the time of Pepin I to that of Hugh Capet.[51] Given Abbo's long-standing support for

---

Consilii Causeiensis," MGH SS 3:691–93). Richer's history ended just before his proposed treatment of the council; Richer, *Histoire*, 4.108 (2:328–33), contains only very abridged notes of topics he intended to cover, beginning with the council at Reims (which Richer placed in his notes at Senlis). Lot, *Hugues Capet*, 102n2, pointed out that the results of the council are not known, but that Gerbert continued to function as archbishop and Arnulf remained in prison for several years after the council.

48. Aimoinus, *VsA*, c. 12: "memor utilitatis loci quem regebat."

49. Abbo, letter 15.

50. Prou and Vidier, *Recueil des chartes de Saint-Benoît-sur-Loire*, nos. 29 (5 September 878) and 44 (9 January 938). Prou and Vidier include other papal confirmations of the privileges of Fleury, but the privileges of John VIII and Leo VII are the only ones of undisputed authenticity. See Prou and Vidier's notes on the authenticity of charters granted by Gregory IV (no. 18 [April 829]), Leo VII (no. 45 [14 August 938–July 939]), and Benedict VII (nos. 55 [5 June 967] and 56 [5 June 967]). See also Marco Mostert, "Die Urkundenfälschungen Abbos von Fleury," in *Fälschungen im Mittelalter: Interntionaler Kongress der Monumenta Germaniae Historica*, Munich, 16–19 September 1986, vol. 4, *Diplomatische Fälschungen (II)* (Hanover: Hahnsche Buchhandlung, 1988), 287–309, on the authenticity of these papal charters.

51. Prou and Vidier, *Recueil des chartes de Saint-Benoît-sur-Loire*, nos. 4 (November 751–24 September 768), 8 (9 October 768–28 January 814), 14 (27 July 818), 34 (30 October 900), 55 (5 June 967), 56 (5 June 967), 60 (974, before 12 November), 64 (979), and 69 (987).

papal prerogatives and conviction that monastic reform depended on his monastery's independence from local ecclesiastical and secular pressures, his desire for papal recognition of Fleury's privileges makes perfect sense.[52]

In pursuit of his goals and presumably with Leo's encouragement, Abbo traveled to Rome shortly after the Council of Saint-Remi at Reims.[53] Abbo probably followed one of the routes usually used for trade and pilgrimage to the south. He could have made use of water travel or have traveled on foot or horseback along the surviving Roman roads.[54] His journey would have been facilitated by the network of reformed monasteries that had grown up since the foundation of Cluny early in the tenth century. Abbo may have stopped at Cluny for several days. If he had, he would have been reminded of the problems that the late Abbot Maiolus had encountered when crossing the Alps more than twenty years earlier. Maiolus had faced the usual problems of climbing to the heights of the Alpine passes, but his biggest obstacle was human. In a narrow pass, he had been waylaid and held for ransom by Saracens.[55]

---

52. It is noteworthy that although Fleury received five royal confirmations of its privileges from three kings in the twenty years prior to Abbo's accession as abbot, no royal charter confirming its privileges exists for his abbacy. Either one was never granted or else Abbo or one of his successors allowed it to be lost.

53. For the date of Abbo's first journey to Rome, see Lot, *Hugues Capet*, 266–71. Lot placed the journey after the Council of Saint-Remi, the earliest date at which Abbo could have met Leo in person, and before Leo's return to Rome, probably after the Council of Ingelheim in February 996 (since Abbo could not enlist Leo's aid in dealing with Pope John XV). Because travel across the Alps would have been difficult in the winter, I have hypothesized that Abbo left for Rome in the late summer or early fall of 995. Riché, *Abbon de Fleury*, believed that there had been three journeys to Rome (203), the first undertaken while Pope John XV was well and healthy, the second about the time of John XV's death, and the third shortly after the accession of Gregory V. Most other historians have interpreted the evidence as indicating only one journey before the accession of Gregory V.

54. N. J. G. Pounds, *An Historical Geography of Europe* (Cambridge: Cambridge University Press, 1990), 139, 181, though Pounds argues that the Roman roads by this period would not have been well maintained or suited to medieval forms of transport, but Jean Hubert, "Les routes du Moyen Age," in *Les routes de France depuis les origines jusqu'à nos jours*, Colloques: Cahiers de civilisation (Paris: Association pour la diffusion de la pensée française), 28–29, argued for the continued heavy use of Roman roads in France.

55. Syrus, *Vita sancti Maioli*, 3:1, PL 137:763–65.

Although imperial intervention had eliminated the dangers from Saracens, Abbo's journey nevertheless covered rough roads, frequently in poor repair, with the crossing of the Alps, which could take several days even in good weather, added to the normal problems of medieval travel.[56] The distance from Orléans to Rome was nearly 1,400 kilometers (about 850 miles). If Abbo had traveled at the relatively fast pace of 30 kilometers (about 20 miles) a day, the journey would have taken at least a month and a half each way, assuming that he did not spend more than one night at each stop along the route.[57] Adalbert of Prague, traveling the somewhat shorter distance from Rome to Mainz (about 1,250 kilometers or 775 miles) in the preceding year, had needed two months for his journey.[58] A journey south of the Alps was no minor undertaking, but Abbo felt secure of his petition, given Leo's assurances and his own efforts on behalf of the pope.

According to Aimoinus, Abbo's main goal in seeking out the pope was to have the privileges of Fleury confirmed.[59] Abbo had already heard much about John XV. At the Councils of Saint-Basle and of Saint-Remi, the French bishops had complained frequently of Pope John XV's corruption and his unwillingness to act promptly and decisively. John's legate Leo, however, had painted a very different picture of the situation in Rome. He portrayed John as a responsible man whose dilatory behavior was due to the constant attempts of the Crescentius family in Rome to dominate the papacy. Abbo's own experiences with pressures from the local nobility of the Orléanais would have made this explanation of the pope's behavior perfectly comprehensible to him. Abbo soon learned that the picture painted by the French bishops was the more accurate one. Pope John would not give Abbo a hear-

---

56. Pounds, *Historical Geography*, 140. Pounds notes that in the Middle Ages people often crossed the Alps in winter, despite the hazards of the journey.

57. See chapter 4, my description of Abbo's journey to Reims in 991, for a discussion of the problems of travel in the Middle Ages.

58. "Vita, auctore monacho coevo ex Codice MS Prageus: collato cum variis editionibus," *AASS* 3.187–88, under 23 April.

59. Aimoinus, *VsA*, c. 11.

Papal Politics 169

ing on his privileges. In Abbo's words: "I came, on bended knee, to the magnificent chambers of the prince of the apostles; but I found—alas, o woe—the Roman Church widowed of a worthy shepherd."[60] Aimoinus described the situation much more precisely. John XV refused to consider any request without a suitable bribe.[61] If nothing else, Abbo had learned never again to approach Rome empty-handed.[62] After his support of the papacy against the French bishops, Abbo probably felt that John's treatment of him was ungrateful at the very least. He did not waiver in his support of the papacy, but his opinion of this particular pope certainly plummeted. He had hoped for help from Leo in winning the pope's approval, but Leo had not yet returned to Rome.[63] Abbo later described himself as wandering aimlessly around Rome, "like a chick crying because it had lost its mother."[64] In consolation for his loss, Abbo then visited the holy places of Rome and, unwilling to return to his monastery empty-handed, he bought several particularly handsome silk vestments for use at Fleury before taking the long road back home.[65]

Abbo returned to Francia in the spring of 996. After Abbo left Rome, the situation there changed rapidly, but Abbo could have kept abreast of the news through pilgrims coming north from Italy, such as Adalbert of Prague, who visited Fleury in 996 while on a tour of the shrines of the region.[66] The first important piece of information was that Pope John XV had passed away in April 996,

---

60. Abbo, letter 15: "magnifica principis apostolorum membra supplex adii; sed Romanam Ecclesiam digno viduatam pastore, heu proh dolor! offendi."
61. Aimoinus, *VsA*, c. 11.
62. Riché, *Abbon de Fleury*, 198.
63. Lot, *Hugues Capet*, 103, 271, suggested that Leo had attended the synod of Ingelheim in February 996, and so did not arrive back in Rome until at least the spring of 996.
64. Abbo, letter 15: "sicut . . . fetus gallinae, conquerens . . . abstractum esse . . . matris suae praesidium."
65. Aimoinus, *VsA*, c. 11.
66. Adalbert of Prague had resided in Leo's monastery of Saints Bonifacius and Alexius in Rome before his final mission to eastern Europe. In 996 he had traveled north to the Ottonian court and had then visited the shrines of western Francia, including those of St. Denis (Paris), St. Martin (Tours), St. Maurus (at the monastery

shortly after Abbo had left Rome.[67] It was in the spring of 996 as well that the German ruler, Otto III, traveled to Italy, where he reasserted imperial control over the Italian peninsula (which had lapsed during his minority), had himself crowned emperor, and had his young relative Bruno consecrated as Pope Gregory V.[68] Gregory V was a very different man from his predecessor. The German emperor had appointed the serious young man pope in part to break the hold of the Crescentius family on the papacy. Although Gregory was not always successful in his battles with the Crescentii, his actions indicated that he was far more favorably inclined toward Abbo's position than John had been.

Probably in the summer of that year, Abbo wrote to the papal legate Leo. He began his letter by praising Leo's eloquence at the Council of Saint-Remi. This was a good strategy, since in addition to flattering Leo, Abbo was reminding him that they were allies in their efforts to revoke the Council of Saint-Basle, and also that they had conversed privately while Leo was in Francia. At this point Abbo turned to the main subjects of his letter. He first mentioned that he was sending proof of Fleury's possession of the relics of St. Benedict, the founder of Western monasticism, whose remains gave Fleury great prestige in the monastic world.[69] He then went on to complain briefly of his experiences with John XV. From any other French cleric, Leo might have regard-

---

bearing his name), and St. Benedict (at Fleury). It seems likely that Leo and Adalbert traveled together for much of this journey. See "Vita auctore monacho coevo ex codice MS Prageus," 187–88, and "Alia vita, auctore altero monacho coaevo, Ex codice MS Pragensi cum editione Suriana collato," 195, both in *AASS*, vol. 3 under 23 April. See also Lin Donnat, "Recherches sur l'influence de Fleury au Xe siècle," in *Etudes ligériennes d'histoire et d'archéologie médiévales,* Mémoires et exposés présentés á la Semaine d'études médiévales de Saint-Benoît-sur-Loire, 3–10 July 1969, ed. René Louis, publication de la Société de fouilles archéologiques et des monuments historiques de l'Yonne (Paris: Clavreuil, 1975), 169, which noted that Fleury was a common stop for German pilgrims to Saint-Martin of Tours.

67. For a refutation of the theory that John XV had died during or before Abbo's visit to Rome, see Lot, *Hugues Capet,* 269.

68. Gerd Althoff, *Otto III,* trans. Phyllis G. Jestice (College Park: Pennsylvania State University Press, 2003), 59.

69. This was probably the *MsB* by Adrevald of Fleury. Adrevald's work forms only

Papal Politics 171

ed this as insolence, but given Abbo's record as a supporter of the papacy (of which Abbo had carefully reminded him), he was unlikely to take offense. Abbo dwelt at greater length on the last theme of his letter, the consecration of a new pope, who, Abbo had heard, possibly from Adalbert of Prague or some other pilgrim passing through Fleury in 996, was a man truly worthy of the office.[70]

Abbo's letter to Leo was part of his strategy for gaining important privileges for Fleury. Abbo was attempting to convince Leo, and through him the new pope, of Fleury's unique position among French monasteries. Not only was its abbot, Abbo himself, the foremost defender of papal prerogatives in Francia, but Fleury possessed the relics of the most important figure in Western monasticism, St. Benedict himself. The privileges that Abbo worked to secure for Fleury included nearly complete autonomy from episcopal control. So extensive were the privileges that Fleury was eventually to secure that many modern scholars have doubted their authenticity.[71] Eventually, Abbo had to travel to Italy to convince Gregory V in person of the merits of approving Fleury's privileges.

In the summer of 996, however, Abbo remained in Francia, where he undoubtedly continued his policy of rapprochement with the royal court. This may have been the period in which he presented his *Collectio canonum* to the kings.[72] Although the *Collectio canonum*, as noted above, was heavily influenced by the controversy over the archbishopric of Reims, Abbo used it as a vehicle to address broader issues of the government of a kingdom and the relationship between secular and ecclesiastical institutions. As Abbo made clear in his introductory letter, Hugh Capet and Rob-

---

the first book of the miracles, which were added to by Aimoinus and others under Abbo's successors at Fleury.

70. Abbo, letter 16.
71. Mostert, "Urkundenfälschungen," 4:288.
72. The dating of the *Collectio canonum*, as noted above, is uncertain. It was composed after Abbo's *Apologeticus* (which Abbo mentioned in his prefatory letter) and before the death of Hugh Capet, that is, roughly between 993 and October 996.

ert had endured many challenges from within the kingdom in the first years of their reign. Now, Abbo argued, since the kings had successfully met those challenges and had become supporters of the monastic order, it was only fitting that he dedicate his collection of church canons to them, so that they could build upon their successes as Christian kings. As did Abbo's other works, the *Collectio canonum* stressed the importance of monastic independence, consistent and fair application of the rule of law, and respect for societal hierarchies, particularly the need for people to obey and support their king, abbot, and pope, as the situation demanded.[73]

The probability that Abbo's view of Christian social relations would bear fruit increased with the death of Hugh Capet in October 996. Hugh's power had depended heavily on episcopal support, particularly the support of Arnulf of Orléans, an opponent of monastic independence. King Robert, however, was in a very different situation. Unlike his father, Robert had succeeded to the kingdom as the legitimate heir of the previous king and had even been elected and crowned within his father's lifetime. Furthermore, by this time Charles of Lorraine, the only serious Carolingian claimant to the throne, had died in prison.[74] Robert, then, did not have to face the same challenges to his authority that his father had. On the other hand, by the time of Hugh's death, the prestige of the French monarchy had been seriously damaged by the dispute with the papacy over the archbishop of Reims as well as Robert's repudiation of his first wife, Rozala Suzanna. Robert had married this much older woman for political reasons when he was just an adolescent and had repudiated her without consummating the marriage. Now Robert needed to improve his image with the educated elite of the kingdom; the reformed monasteries, with their schools and scriptoria, could help him achieve that

---

73. Abbo, *Collectio canonum*. For a discussion of Abbo's recommendations, see Mostert, *Political Theology*, especially cc. 11–12.

74. Lot, *Hugues Capet*, 30n1, noted that no reliable record of Charles's death survives, but that he was almost certainly dead by 993, when an unsuccessful plot centered around the claims of his son, Louis.

Papal Politics 173

end. In addition, Abbo had identified Robert as sympathetic to his point of view several years before Hugh's death.[75]

Robert soon had other reasons for cultivating his friendship with Abbo. Probably before Hugh's death, Robert had begun an affair with Bertha, the widow of Count Odo of Blois, who had died in the spring of 996.[76] Eventually the two decided to marry, but the match was problematic for both ecclesiastical and political reasons. Robert and Bertha were second cousins, well within the Church's prohibited degrees of kinship, which insisted that marriages between relatives closer than sixth cousins was incestuous. In addition, Robert had stood as godfather to one of Bertha's children by Odo. He was thus related to Bertha spiritually as well as by blood.[77] Georges Duby has argued that the medieval nobility did not embrace the same view of incest as did the Church.[78] Constance Bouchard, has pointed out, to the contrary, that the nobility of this period went out of their way to avoid incestuous marriages (though they often contracted marriages between fifth cousins rather than insisting on a relationship as distant as sixth cousins).[79] The match also complicated the political situation.

---

75. Abbo, letter 8. It is important, however, not to overstate Robert's support of Abbo's positions. Abbo's successor at Fleury, Gauzlin, was a strong ally, perhaps even a blood relative of King Robert, and our knowledge of Abbo's career is heavily influenced by Aimoinus's life of Abbo, written during Gauzlin's abbacy. The monks of Fleury, in looking back on Abbo's career, had strong motives for portraying Abbo as an earlier and a stronger supporter of the Capetians than was, in fact, the case.

76. Lot, *Hugues Capet,* 178n2. For a romanticized account of this affair, see Pfister, *Robert le Pieux,* 47–51. It is not clear whether the liaison between Robert and Bertha had begun during Hugh's lifetime or not. Lot, *Hugues Capet,* 108, suggested that Robert openly rebelled against his father over his marriage to Bertha. Lot based his hypothesis on a passage in Rodolfus Glaber's history, in which Robert was reminded (on the occasion of his own son's rebelliousness) of his youthful indiscretions. The passage quoted by Lot gives no hint as to the nature or date of Robert's "rebellion" against Hugh. Cousin, *Abbon de Fleury-sur-Loire,* 121, picked up this interpretation without citing any sources.

77. Pfister, *Robert le Pieux,* 49; Cousin, *Abbon de Fleury-sur-Loire,* 121.

78. Georges Duby, *The Knight, the Lady, and the Priest: The Making of Modern Marriage in Medieval France,* trans. Barbara Bray (New York: Pantheon, 1983). His treatment of Robert's marriages (75–85) is unfortunately somewhat superficial.

79. Constance Bouchard, "Consanguinity and Noble Marriages in the Tenth and Eleventh Centuries," *Speculum* 56.2 (1981): 268–87.

Hugh Capet had been an ally of Fulk Nerra, the count of Anjou, and an enemy of the counts of Blois.[80] Both Abbo and Gerbert strongly discouraged this match, probably on theological rather than strictly political grounds.[81] Since Robert could not persuade Gerbert to consecrate the marriage, he had to rely instead on Archbishop Archembald of Tours.[82] When, at the Council of Pavia in early 997, Pope Gregory V condemned the match and excommunicated Robert and Archembald, it was clear that Robert would have to try to justify his marriage to the papacy.[83]

One of the earliest results of Robert's new alliance with the house of Blois was the dispute between the canons of Saint-Martin of Tours and Archbishop Archembald of Tours. The city of Tours and its religious houses had for over a year been a point of contention between Count Fulk of Anjou and the house of Blois-Chartres. Fulk Nerra had temporarily lost the support of the canons of Saint-Martin after he violently entered their cloister in the course of taking Châteauneuf of Tours. The canons protested by restricting access to St. Martin and his relics and by ritually humiliating the saint. By 998, however, Fulk had made his peace with the canons.[84] The canons had in the meantime begun to resent King Robert's appointment of Walter, a man firmly within the Blésois sphere, to the important position of treasurer of Saint-Martin of Tours, especially since the king had rejected the canons' own choice of Peter, who happened to be a supporter of Fulk, as *presul* of Tours.[85] As a result of the shifting political alli-

80. Bachrach, *Fulk Nerra*, 64. Lot, *Hugues Capet*, 183, suggested that Hugh had opposed this match and that relations between him and Robert were strained during the last few months of Hugh's life over this issue.

81. For Gerbert, see Richer, *Histoire*, 4.108 (2:328–33); this is Richer's last chapter, with only fragmentary notations of themes that he probably intended to expand on. For Abbo, see Helgaud, *Vie de Robert le Pieux*, c. 17 (pp. 94–95).

82. Pfister, *Robert le Pieux*, 51; Cousin, *Abbon de Fleury-sur-Loire*, 121.

83. For the excommunication of Robert and Archembald, see Gregory V, "Litterae de Synodo Papiensi," in *Annales, chronica et historiae aevi Saxonici*, ed. Georgius Heinricus Pertz, MGH SS, vol. 3 (Hanover, 1839), 694. See also Cousin, *Abbon de Fleury-sur-Loire*, 122.

84. Bachrach, *Fulk Nerra*, 62–64.

85. Ibid., 64, 84.

Papal Politics

ances, the canons found themselves in direct opposition to Archbishop Archembald of Tours, who had consecrated Robert's marriage to Bertha of Blois and had continued to support Capetian policies in the region.[86]

Abbo's interest in the affairs of Tours lay both in his friendship with Hervé, a canon of Tours (and later treasurer of Saint-Martin of Tours) and in his desire to create a balance of power between Capetian and Angevin interests. Hervé and other canons of Saint-Martin had evidently written to Abbo, asking for his support against their archbishop and his presence at the royal court to which the canons had been called to resolve the dispute.[87] Unfortunately, as Abbo complained in his reply to them, they had not included adequate information, so he was not able to prepare a defense from the writings of the Church Fathers, which he had at hand. Without more detailed knowledge of the dispute, he argued, how could he formulate an adequate defense of the canons' position?[88] He went on, however, to explain that he had heard rumors of the dispute between the canons and the archbishop. Rumor had it that the archbishop had infringed on the rights of Saint-Martin, although Abbo expressed his disbelief that someone of Archembald's stature would go against the decrees of the

---

86. Ibid., 64, 91, briefly mentioned Archembald as a Capetian supporter. Gerbert, in his letters, also referred to a quarrel between the canons and the archbishop of Tours (Lattin, letters 213 and 215; Weigle, letters 207 and 209). Weigle dates these letters to the spring of 994, in opposition to most of the secondary sources in his critical apparatus, which place the incident between 995 (at the earliest) and 997. Weigle did not explain his reason for this dating, but it may lie in a reference in one of Gerbert's letters (Weigle, letter 209) to a council at the church of Saint-Paul, which is probably the one at the monastery of Saint-Denis. He is evidently confusing a later council with the riotous Council of Saint-Denis in 994 (see above, this chapter). Since Bachrach, *Fulk Nerra*, 64, placed Fulk's expulsion from Tours by King Robert in 997 and since Robert's marriage to Bertha did not occur until late 996 or early 997, it seems most likely that these events happened in the early summer of 997.

87. Abbo, letter 5. Gerbert wrote to the canons of Saint-Martin at about this time to request their presence at the royal court at Chelles to settle the dispute (Lattin, letter 215; Weigle, letter 209). See also Cousin, *Abbon de Fleury-sur-Loire*, 160–61.

88. Abbo, letter 5. This passage supports the hypothesis of Mostert, *Political Theology*, 70–71, that Abbo had prepared a dossier of excerpts from patristic and other sources upon which he based his written and oral arguments in the disputes with which he was confronted in the course of his career as abbot of Fleury.

pope and the rights of St. Martin. After discussing the importance of precedent and of the superiority of the Roman pontiff, Abbo closed with an injunction that the canons consider the merits of both the pope and the archbishop of Tours.[89] With this ambiguous ending to his letter, Abbo hinted at his support for the canons without actually promising them anything.

The dilemma faced by Abbo at Tours stemmed from more than a mere dearth of information from the canons who had appealed to him. In the wake of his rapprochement with the Capetians, Abbo would not have wanted to attack directly King Robert's policies at Tours or elsewhere. On the other hand, since Abbo had clearly disapproved of Robert's marriage to Bertha of Blois, he may not have wished to encourage the establishment of Blésois supporters at Tours, particularly over the objections of the canons of Tours. Another complicating factor was the allegiance of the abbot's main correspondent at Tours, Hervé—who was also the brother of Robert of Buzançais, a longtime supporter of the Angevins.[90] Abbo could not support his friend and fellow religious, Hervé, without opposing his king, Robert. Likewise, to side with either Robert or Count Fulk Nerra would have served only to exacerbate the strife, which it was in Fleury's interests to avoid. By this time, as well, Abbo had learned that direct public confrontation was not always as effective as quiet, behind-the-scenes persuasion. The abbot of Fleury found himself caught between Capetian, Angevin, and monastic interests.

Meanwhile, the situation of the archbishop of Reims had not been resolved. Gerbert had probably left Reims for Rome in 996, possibly in the entourage of Otto III, who traveled to Italy in the spring of 996 and remained there for the summer.[91] Possibly as

---

89. Abbo, letter 5.   90. Bachrach, *Fulk Nerra*, 84.

91. The dating of the events from the synod of Saint-Remi until Abbo's second journey to Rome, in November 997, is uncertain. The most plausible scenario is that developed by Lot, *Hugues Capet*, 102–24 (general narrative), 266–79 (dating of journeys of Abbo to Rome), 286–97 (date of Gerbert's final departure from Francia), and 298–303 (date of Hugh Capet's death); for Otto's and Gerbert's movements in 996, see 104–6.

Papal Politics

early as fall 996 Gerbert had returned to Reims, disappointed in his hopes of convincing the new pope, Gregory V, of the legitimacy of his election.[92] On the contrary, Gregory seems to have taken steps to invalidate Gerbert's claims conclusively. In early 997 Gregory called a council at Pavia, which the French bishops declined to attend, to settle the situation at Reims. The result was an overwhelming decision against Gerbert's election and in favor of the reinstatement of Arnulf of Reims.[93]

With the decisions of the Council of Pavia against both his remarriage and his choice of archbishop, King Robert must have realized that he would have to concede something to the papacy. He was willing to yield on the issue of Reims. Arnulf of Reims was no longer the threat that he had been six years earlier. Charles of Lorraine, to whom Arnulf had betrayed Reims, was dead, and the Capetians were slowly gaining strength. Gerbert, too, was a less attractive choice for archbishop than he had been in 991. His defense of his position in Reims had led him to antagonize the papal legate Leo, while his refusal to consecrate Robert's marriage to Bertha cannot have won him the favor of the king. Robert seems to have briefly considered appointing a third man, Gibuin, the nephew of the bishop of Châlons-sur-Marne, as archbishop of Reims.[94] Fear of an action of this sort had led Gerbert to flee Francia by the summer of 997: neither Arnulf nor Gibuin was likely to be sympathetic to the deposed usurper's plight.[95] Ultimately, Robert was willing to consider the reinstatement of Arnulf, undoubtedly in the hope that the pope would in return recognize Robert and Bertha's marriage. Rather than entrust negotiations to Leo, Robert turned to Abbo, who departed for Rome late in the summer of 997.[96]

Abbo's decision to revisit Rome rested on the probability that such a visit would be in the interests of Fleury. Abbo had, by this

---

92. Lot, *Hugues Capet*, 106.
93. Gregory V, "Litterae de Synodo Papiensi," 3:694.
94. Lot, *Hugues Capet*, 116.
95. Lattin, letter 221; Weigle, letter 181.
96. Aimoinus, *VsA*, c. 11; Helgaud, *Vie de Robert le Pieux*, c. 17 (94–95); Abbo, letter 1.

time, several reasons to expect a better reception than he had received on his last visit. The decisions of the Synod of Pavia indicated that Gregory shared Abbo's strong disapproval of the deposition of Arnulf and the marriage of Robert and Bertha. Abbo probably had the opportunity to consult the legate Leo further, either by letter or in person, when Leo returned to Francia to announce formally the decisions of the Council of Pavia.[97] From Leo Abbo probably learned something of Gregory's character and whether he would be sympathetic to granting far-reaching privileges to Fleury. Although Crescentius still controlled Rome, Gregory had publicly declared his intention to defy him at the Council of Pavia.[98] Given Gregory's problems in Rome and Abbo's strong support of the papal position on both the archbishop of Reims and the marriage of the French king, Abbo, probably with Leo's encouragement, had good reason to hope that the pope would be willing to reward his supporter with extensive privileges for his monastery. Finally, by 997 Abbo had had time to prepare a forged charter that would validate Fleury's claims to extraordinary privileges, including the right to exemption from excommunication, a particularly important concern in the wake of Gregory V's excommunication of the French prelates over Robert's marriage.[99]

Abbo could not have undertaken his second journey to Rome lightly. He already knew, from his experience two years earlier, that the journey was a difficult one. Furthermore, by the time of his second journey, Abbo was probably in his forties or fifties and had gained enough weight to make travel difficult, ostensibly as the result of his sojourn in England a decade earlier.[100] He must also have

97. Lot, *Hugues Capet*, 115. Lot based his assumption that Leo had made yet another journey north, probably in order to speak with Robert personally, on an ambiguous phrase in one of Gerbert's letters. The assumption, however, seems valid in light of papal interests, Leo's continuing involvement in the affair, and Robert's decision to concede on this matter soon afterward.

98. Gregory V, "Litterae de Synodo Papiensi," 3:694. Otto III had driven Crescentius from Rome in 996, but soon after Otto's return to Germany, Crescentius had driven Gregory out of Rome (Lot, *Hugues Capet*, 282–83).

99. Mostert, "Urkundenfälschungen," 287–318.

100. Aimoinus, *V&A*, c. 11. Although Aimoinus mentioned Abbo's weight in con-

known from Leo that the pope's position in Rome was not secure. In fact, upon reaching Rome, Abbo found the papacy under the control of an antipope, John Philagathus (John XVI), who had been set up by the Crescentius family.[101] Abbo was forced to search for Gregory V in the countryside. He finally found the young Pope Gregory in Spoleto, about 120 kilometers (about 80 miles) north of Rome.[102] Despite the difficulties of the journey, once Abbo had finally located the pope, his reception was warm. According to Aimoinus, Gregory greeted Abbo effusively, embracing him and promising to agree to anything Abbo suggested. Abbo owed this friendly reception to reports Gregory had heard of Abbo's learning and good character.[103] Although Gregory was far superior to Abbo in the Church hierarchy, his relative youth coupled with a lack of experience and confidence would have assured his dependence on the learning and political experience of the much older abbot.

Although Aimoinus's account suggested that Abbo's reputation had spread throughout Europe, Gregory's eagerness to meet Abbo was largely due to Abbo's shrewd political maneuvering. The most probable source of reports of Abbo's character was the papal legate Leo, who had met Abbo at least once in Francia and had exchanged letters with him. Gregory was probably already aware of Abbo's role in the Councils of Saint-Basle and Saint-Remi. In addition, at Abbo's prompting, Leo made a strong case to Gregory that Abbo was not merely a supporter of the papacy but was also key to the achievement of the pope's goals in Francia. Leo also would have told Gregory of Fleury's claims to possess the relics of St. Benedict and to be the leading monastery in the ecclesiastical province of Gaul.[104] As a result of Abbo's relationship with Leo, Gregory was

---

nection with Abbo's journey to Rome, the process of weight gain had clearly started many years earlier, while Abbo was in England, as he attributed the gain to the change in diet. See chapter 3.

101. Giuseppe Sergi, "The Kingodm of Italy," in *The New Cambridge Medieval History*, vol. 3 (c. 900–c. 1024), ed. Timothy Reuter (Cambridge: Cambridge University Press, 1999), 362.

102. Aimoinus, *VsA*, c. 11.   103. Ibid.

104. For Fleury's possession of the relics of St. Benedict, see Abbo's letter 16 to

already familiar, even before Abbo's arrival in Spoleto, with the basis for the privileges that Abbo would request for Fleury.

Abbo was not, however, willing to rely solely on Gregory's goodwill toward him and his monastery. In order to be sure that Gregory would approve the privileges that Fleury sought and that the prelates of Francia would be unable to challenge those privileges in the future, Abbo had to establish a precedent for these actions. Abbo brought with him to Italy a charter purportedly from Pope Gregory IV (827–844), which Abbo had had forged at Fleury before his journey.[105] Abbo's forgery was, for its time, sophisticated. He took the formulae for the charter from a charter that Pope John VIII had granted to Fleury in 878 and one that Leo VII had granted in 938.[106] For the specific provisions of the charter, Abbo relied on a variety of sources, including royal charters, the writings of Pope Gregory the Great, which he had already mined for his dossier, and proceedings of Church councils. The resulting document provided not only a basis for Fleury's claims but also a model for the wording of Gregory V's genuine charter of November 997.[107]

The need for the elaborate documentation that Abbo provid-

Leo, written shortly after the Council of Saint-Remi, and his letter 4 to Gregory. For Fleury's claims to be the leading monastery in Gaul, see Prou and Vidier, *Recueil des chartes de Saint-Benoît-sur-Loire,* no. 71 (November 997). The term *Gallia* is used in accounts of Church councils and charters in the late tenth century to refer to those ecclesiastical provinces that fell within the bounds of Roman Gaul.

105. Prou and Vidier, *Recueil des chartes de Saint-Benoît-sur-Loire,* no. 18 (April 829), list this as an "acte suspecte," on the basis of its date, its unusual claims, and its similarity to later documents. For a discussion of previous analyses of this charter, see Mostert, "Urkundenfälschungen," especially 287–89; for the attribution of this forgery to Abbo's abbacy, see 299. Unless otherwise indicated, I am relying on Mostert for parallels between the charters of Fleury, either genuine or forged.

106. Mostert, "Urkundenfälschungen," 299; these are Prou and Vidier, *Recueil des chartes de Saint-Benoît-sur-Loire,* nos. 29 (5 September 878) and 44 (9 January 938).

107. Mostert, "Urkundenfälschungen," 301–3. Mostert included a comparison in parallel columns of charters purportedly granted by Pope Gregory IV and Benedict VII, as well as the genuine charter of Pope Gregory V, as an appendix to his article (309–18). These are Prou and Vidier, *Recueil des chartes de Saint-Benoît-sur-Loire,* nos. 29 (5 September 878), 55 (5 June 967), and 71 (November 997). The supposed charter of Benedict VII was a later forgery based on the other two charters (Mostert, "Urkundenfälschungen," 304–5).

Papal Politics

ed becomes clear upon examination of the specific provisions of the charter Gregory V approved for Fleury.[108] The charter contains a conventional opening, taken word-for-word from a charter of Pope John VIII to Fleury (dated 878), which was also the source for the opening to Abbo's forgery.[109] Gregory V went on to recognize Fleury's possessions and its right to freedom from outside interference. He further recognized Fleury's special status among monasteries. Fleury's abbot was the foremost of the abbots of Gaul. The monks of Fleury had the right to elect their abbot freely. If an abbot were accused of criminal conduct, he had a right to trial by a provincial council. Any monk of Fleury who had received clerical orders would not be allowed to exercise his powers over the monks of Fleury. Finally, as a center of monastic reform, Fleury also had the right to receive monks fleeing from monasteries that had been disrupted or that practiced a more lax rule.

At first glance Gregory's confirmation of Fleury's possessions appears unexceptional. After all, King Lothar had granted almost identical recognition to the possessions of Fleury, as had several other French kings before him.[110] Such a recognition by a pope, however, was unusual. Only two genuine papal privileges to Fleury survive from before 997.[111] The first of these, from John VIII, in 878, recognized and reaffirmed the actions of the Frankish emperors Charlemagne and Louis the Pious in favor of Fleury and the freedom of the monks of Fleury to elect their own abbot. The second, from Leo VII in 938, came at the request of the Abbot Odo of Fleury and of Hugh, duke of the Franks (the father of

---

108. Prou and Vidier, *Recueil des chartes de Saint-Benoît-sur-Loire*, no. 71 (November 997).

109. See ibid., no. 29 (5 September 878).

110. See ibid., nos. 4 (November 751–24 September 768) and 5 (November 751–24 September 768) for Pepin, 7 (9 October 768–28 January 814) and 8 (9 October 768–28 January 814 for Charlemagne, 14 (27 July 818) and 15 (27 July 818) for Louis the Pious, 34 (30 October 900) for Charles the Simple, 55 (5 June 967) and 56 (5 June 967) for Lothar, 64 (979) for Louis V, and 69 (987) for Hugh Capet. The texts of nos. 4, 5, 7, and 8 do not survive, but the general content of the charters has been inferred by Prou and Vidier from the text of nos. 14 and 15.

111. Ibid., nos. 29 (5 September 878) from John VIII and 44 (9 January 938) from Leo VII.

Hugh Capet). The duke of the Franks had just overseen the reform of Fleury according to the Rule of St. Benedict and the example of Cluny, and had installed Odo, already abbot of Cluny, as abbot of Fleury as well. The main provisions of this second charter were the freedom of the monastery from local authority other than that of the king, the right to free election of the abbot, and inalienability of the lands of the monastery. Both of these charters, though they contain provisions similar to those granted by Gregory V in 997, confirm not the specific possessions of the monastery but rather the monastery's right freely to administer its possessions (which are partially enumerated in the second papal privilege and not at all in the first). The charter that Abbo persuaded Gregory V to issue goes farther than either of the others in designating the pope as the protector of the monastery's lands as well as its position in society.[112] Both men must have been pleased with this clause, which both strengthened the position of the papacy and increased the independence of Fleury.

Gregory V's charter for Fleury was also unusual in the special status that it granted Fleury among the monasteries of Gaul. The claim that the abbot of Fleury was the foremost (*primus*) abbot of Gaul arose from Fleury's possession of the relics of St. Benedict. An enterprising monk of Fleury had rescued them from their neglected grave in Italy more than three centuries earlier and brought them to Fleury. Since the refounding of St. Benedict's monastery at Monte Cassino, the Italian monks had hotly contested this claim.[113] The monks of Fleury had long been proud of possessing Benedict's bones. They mentioned them in several charters, including the charter from Pope Leo VII in 938, and a monk of Fleury had written a book recording the translation and

---

112. H. E. J. Cowdrey, *The Cluniacs and the Gregorian Reform* (Oxford: Clarendon, 1970), 32, noted that although the charter did not convey "exemption in the twelfth-century sense, [it] effectively met Abbo's desire to break the coercive power of the bishop of Orléans over his monastery," but went on to argue that the privileges granted to Fleury by Gregory V set a precedent for monastic exemption as it eventually developed in the twelfth century.

113. For the earlier history of the relics of St. Benedict at Fleury, see Ward, *Miracles and the Medieval Mind*, 46–56, and Geary, *Furta Sacra*, 145–49.

Papal Politics 183

miracles of St. Benedict, which validated their claim to possessing the genuine relics and the goodwill of the saint.[114] Abbo himself had emphasized Fleury's possession of Benedict's relics in his correspondence with the papal legate Leo.[115] Abbo stressed the importance of Benedict's relics to Gregory as well and promised the pope an account of their translation to Fleury.[116] Fleury's special relationship with St. Benedict had in the past also been used to justify another clause in Gregory's charter to Fleury—the right of monks to leave more permissive monasteries for the purer and stricter rule of Fleury.[117] Fleury's special status among monasteries was made clear in yet another clause of the charter, which exempted the monastery from any excommunication that might be placed on the rest of Francia due to the actions of the kings and bishops.[118] Since the archbishop of Tours and the king of West Francia had suffered papal excommunication over King Robert's second marriage without much effect, Abbo may well have anticipated needing to invoke this provision in the near future. By accepting Fleury's claims to preeminence among French monasteries, Gregory was greatly strengthening the hand of his foremost supporter in Francia, Abbo of Fleury.[119]

The charter also contains provisions for the proper appointment and (if necessary) deposition of abbots at Fleury. An abbot was to be elected by the congregation of the monastery, without

---

114. *MsB*. The first book of miracles, by André of Fleury, was composed many years before Abbo's abbacy. Abbo's biographer, Aimoinus, composed two more books of miracles under Abbo's successor, Gauzlin. Other monks of Fleury composed subsequent books over the next century.

115. Abbo, letter 16.   116. Abbo, letter 4.

117. This argument is implied by Prou and Vidier, *Recueil des chartes de Saint-Benoît-sur-Loire*, no. 44 (9 January 938), though it is not spelled out in Gregory V's charter of November 997 (no. 71). In Gregory's charter several clauses separate the reference to St. Benedict and the provision for monks leaving other monasteries for Fleury.

118. This provision undoubtedly was inspired by Gregory's excommunication of the bishops who had upheld the deposition of Arnulf of Reims and the election of Gerbert in his place, as well as the excommunication that threatened Robert the Pious over his marriage to Bertha of Blois.

119. Lot, *Hugues Capet*, 274–75, argued that Abbo was almost the sole supporter of the papacy in Francia and that Gregory, as a young man in his twenties, was highly susceptible to the arguments of the older man.

bribery or regard for worldly status. Once elected, an abbot could not be deposed except by a provincial council of bishops. Abbo's own contested election as abbot of Fleury undoubtedly prompted at least some of his research and writing on the subject. Not surprisingly, both of these provisions appear in Abbo's *Apologeticus* and his *Collectio canonum,* supported by quotations from Church councils and the Church Fathers, particularly the writings of Pope Gregory I (590–604), known as "the Great."[120] Since Abbo had written both of these works at least in part to support his claims at the Council of Saint-Basle in favor of the papal position on Arnulf of Reims, Gregory V's inclusion of these clauses in the charter not only stabilized Abbo's position as abbot of Fleury but also gave added legitimacy to his arguments at the Council of Saint-Basle.

Pope Gregory V clearly had good reasons for favoring even the most extraordinary claims made in the charter that he granted to Fleury in 997. Ferdinand Lot has portrayed Gregory as a young man who was easily persuaded by the older and more politically astute Abbo, who was also indispensable in Gregory's attempts to revive respect for papal authority in Francia.[121] Gregory's very name promised a friendly reception. Pope Gregory I had come out of a monastic environment and had promoted the cult of St. Benedict in his own writings. By choosing the papal name of Gregory, the current pope was signaling that he would be sympathetic to the arguments of the abbot of a reformed Benedictine monastery. In the course of Abbo's stay with the pope in Spoleto, the two men undoubtedly discussed both the theoretical and practical implications of the charter. The young pope must certainly have relied heavily on the learning of the older and more experienced abbot in his decision to ratify the charter. Abbo's ability to produce precedents, in the form of his forged charter, must have swayed the pope as well. As noted above, the provisions of

120. For the sources used in the forgery, on which this charter is based, see Mostert, "Urkundenfälschungen," 309–18. For a fuller discussion of the sources of Abbo's ideas, see Mostert, *Political Theology,* 65–76.

121. Lot, *Hugues Capet,* 274–75; Cousin, *Abbon de Fleury-sur-Loire,* 129, follows Lot's analysis.

that charter strengthened both the theoretical position of the papacy and gave material strength to the pope's strongest supporter, Abbo of Fleury. Abbo's record as a supporter of papal prerogatives in the Capetian kingdom, his impressive documentation, and his correspondence with the papal legate Leo must surely have impressed the more experienced members of the papal bureaucracy as well.[122] Although granting the charter to Fleury may have been politically expedient, it was also in the long-term interests of both the papacy and the monastic reform movement.

Despite the care that Abbo took to legitimize the claims of Fleury, these claims were still controversial enough a decade later for his biographer, Aimoinus, to feel the need to justify the radical provisions of this charter.[123] Aimoinus began by noting that Gregory had already heard of Abbo's learning and virtue. Gregory then promised, according to Aimoinus, "For I wish you alone to know that I receive well your legation, and that I will do whatever you have recommended," because "I also knew that you were not going to ask anything contrary to human and divine law."[124] In this short passage Aimoinus made two important points: first, that Gregory was willing to grant whatever Abbo asked, even the extraordinary privileges of the charter, and second, that Abbo was not asking anything that could not be justified by tradition and Church law. Only then did Aimoinus proceed to enumerate the specific provisions of the privileges that Abbo had obtained for Fleury from the pope.[125] Aimoinus noted specifically Fleury's freedom from episcopal interference and its exemption from interdict if the rest

---

122. Although the pope undoubtedly had strong reasons for supporting monastic reform in France, Teta E. Moehs, *Gregorius V, 996–999: A Biographical Study*, Päpste und Papsttum (Stuttgart: A. Hiersemann, 1972), 3, surely overstated the case: "the action leading to the reform is to be found particularly among the French monks who revolted during the political upheavals caused by the collapse of the Carolingian power and the rise of the Capetian dynasty."

123. Aimoinus, *VsA*, c. 11. See Mostert, "Urkundenfälschungen," 307.

124. Aimoinus, *VsA*, c. 11: "Porro unum te volo nosse, legationem tuam me benigne suscipere, et queque suaseris, me facturum fore.... Novi namque nil te contra ius fasque postulaturum."

125. Ibid., c. 12.

of Gaul were to be condemned. He then quoted, as support, the letters of Gregory the Great, which Abbo had cited in his earlier works as a basis for Fleury's claims.[126] The extraordinary nature of the privileges granted to Fleury can be measured by the pains that Aimoinus took to defend them nearly ten years later. He may quite rightly have regarded this as Abbo's most valuable legacy to Fleury.

Although securing Fleury's privileges was Abbo's main goal in traveling to Rome, he had other business to transact as well. The situation at Reims was still not regularized. By 997 King Robert seems to have relented on the question of Arnulf of Reims, in the hope (probably encouraged by the papal legate Leo) of having his marriage to Bertha of Blois recognized or at least of improving relations with the papacy.[127] Gregory formally entrusted to Abbo the archiepiscopal pallium, an important symbol of office, to take back to Arnulf, but he did not relent on the question of Robert's marriage.[128] Abbo, though possibly relaying the king's petition, probably advised Gregory against approving the marriage on canonical grounds.[129] Abbo also presented the pope with a request from the Angevin count, Fulk Nerra. Fulk had fallen afoul of the Church frequently through his policies of violently capturing ecclesiastical institutions and appropriating Church property to reward his lay followers.[130] When he heard that Abbo was to trav-

126. Ibid. For Abbo's use of Gregory's letters, see Mostert, *Political Theology*, 71–75.

127. Abbo's interest in Robert's marriage is indicated by Abbo's letter 1, to Gregory V (shortly after Abbo's return to Francia), and a passage in Helgaud, *Vie de Robert le Pieux*, c. 17 (94–95), which indicates that Abbo opposed the union with Bertha. For negotiations between Robert and the papal legate Leo, see Lot, *Hugues Capet*, 115, which relies on a letter of Gerbert (Lattin, letter 221; Weigle, letter 181).

128. Aimoinus, *VsA*, c. 11. Aimoinus did not indicate why Arnulf had been deprived of his see or who was responsible; he merely indicated that Arnulf had been expelled without proper procedure having been followed. Aimoinus said nothing at all about Robert's marriage.

129. See Helgaud, *Vie de Robert le Pieux*, c. 17 (94–95), which attributes Robert's final abandonment of Bertha to Abbo's influence. The exact date of Robert's renunciation of Bertha is open to debate, and may have occurred after Abbo's death in 1004. Even so, the *Vie de Robert le Pieux*, which was written at Fleury, probably reflects a valid tradition of Abbo's opposition to the marriage. Cousin, *Abbon de Fleury-sur-Loire*, 122–23, mistakenly presents Abbo as a supporter of Robert's marriage, who traveled to Rome specifically to resolve the questions of the marriage and the archbishop of Reims.

130. Bachrach, *"Facultates Monachorum,"* 41–42; Bachrach, *Fulk Nerra*, 76.

Papal Politics 187

el to Rome, he availed himself of the opportunity to ask Abbo to carry a *mandatum* to the pope. Since Robert's marriage to Bertha of Blois, the balance of power had shifted in Francia, and the Angevin count may have found it politic to cultivate the favor of the Church.[131] As a result, Fulk wished to gain papal sanction for his policy of restoring old monasteries rather than building new ones. Abbo presented his case but also suggested to Gregory that Fulk's promises were hollow. At Ferrières, an Angevin monastery in the diocese of Sens, Abbo reminded Gregory, Fulk himself was responsible for impoverishing the monks by giving their possessions to his vassals. To use a modern topos, Fulk was behaving like the man who, "having killed his mother and father, throws himself on the mercy of the court because he is an orphan."[132] Gregory took the matter into consideration but did not decide immediately.[133] Given the rapidly shifting political alliances following Robert's marriage to Bertha of Blois and his concomitant forsaking of his Angevin alliance, Abbo may have felt that favoring neither side too strongly was the best policy to follow.

Abbo stayed with Gregory in Spoleto for just over a week.

---

131. Bachrach, *Fulk Nerra*, 62, noted that almost immediately after cementing his alliance with the Blésois, King Robert moved against the lands of the Capetians' sometime ally Fulk. Bachrach (70–71) provides a good example of the conflict of political and religious interests among the French nobility in the case of Bouchard of Vendôme—though in Bouchard's case it was his alliance with King Robert that compromised his religious scruples.

132. Leo Rosten, *The Joys of Yiddish* (New York: McGraw-Hill, 1968), 92, cited such a case as the "classic definition of *chutzpa*." Rosenwein, *Neighbor of St. Peter,* especially 12, has amply documented the pattern of families' giving, taking, and then returning land to monasteries as a way of renewing the relationship between Cluny and the families of the Mâconais in succeeding generations. Fulk's alienation of monastic property seems to have been more permanent than the sort of alienation described by Rosenwein. See Bachrach, *"Facultates Monachorum,"* 41–42.

133. Abbo, letter 1, written shortly after Abbo's return to Francia in 998. Since Abbo felt it necessary to remind Gregory of Fulk's request and Abbo's own arguments, Gregory appears not to have made a pronouncement immediately. Since Gregory died in the following year, he may never have decided whether Fulk's offer to restore the monasteries that he had previously despoiled was genuine or worthy of papal support. Although papal condemnation (and possibly excommunication) of Fulk would have been in Capetian interests, Bachrach, *Fulk Nerra*, 73, probably overstates the involvement of King Robert in pressure to have Fulk's request denied, since Abbo and Robert had only just begun to seek common ground in their policies.

Unlike his predecessor, who had so disappointed Abbo, Gregory courted Abbo eagerly. The two often dined together and must have had several long discussions of the situation in Francia and Abbo's various petitions to the pope. Gregory may also have discussed philosophical and theological matters with Abbo. Certainly, the young pope had a great need of whatever arguments he could find to bolster the position of the papacy, and who could better provide these than the papacy's foremost supporter in Francia? When Abbo finally left after not quite eight days, he carried with him Fleury's charter and a pallium for the archbishop of Reims as well as many gifts from the pope, including a chasuble and incensory for use during Mass.[134]

When Abbo returned to Fleury early in 998, after having been gone for more than four months, his position in Francia was significantly stronger. He carried an important privilege for Fleury that vindicated almost all of the theoretical claims he had made in the past seven years. He also carried tangible tokens of the pope's goodwill in the form of costly presents for Fleury's altar. If any had doubted his influence with the successor of St. Peter, Abbo had prevailed upon the pope to accept his arguments on King Robert's second marriage and the restoration of Arnulf of Reims. By giving Abbo the job of formally presenting Arnulf of Reims with the archiepiscopal pallium, Pope Gregory had conferred upon Abbo the prestige of being an official papal representative. Abbo now had both the responsibility and the means to exercise his power as the leading abbot of Gaul for the good of the monastic reform movement and for the stability of the French realm.

    134. Aimoinus, *VsA*, cc. 11–12. Cousin, *Abbon de Fleury-sur-Loire*, 125, stated that Abbo left Rome having achieved what he desired, but glossed over the fact that Gregory did not relent on the marriage of Robert and Bertha (127), approval for which Abbo had, in Cousin's view, sought from the pope. Aimoinus's statements make more sense if one assumes that Abbo agreed merely to present King Robert's arguments, even though his goal was to persuade the pope to reject the king's plea.

7

MONASTIC POLITICS

WHEN ABBO returned from Rome in early 998, he was for the first time well equipped to exercise independent leadership within northern Francia. Royal and episcopal attitudes toward Abbo and the administration of Fleury seem to have softened. Certainly, in the remaining six years of his life, Abbo and the monks of Fleury did not see the open and violent hostility that had characterized the first half of his abbacy. The formal recognition of the Fleurisian abbot's status as the premier abbot of Gaul coupled with Abbo's friendly relationship with Pope Gregory V gave Abbo a basis for exerting his influence more aggressively in the monastic community outside of Fleury. Furthermore, the monastery's more secure position in the Capetian realm allowed the flowering of scholarship that made Fleury one of the most important centers of learning in Francia in the eleventh century. In the final years of Abbo's abbacy, he came closer than ever to attaining his vision of an ideal society, with the divisions of the Christian Church (monks, secular clergy, and laymen) all working together for a peaceful Christian kingdom. Upon his return to Fleury from Spoleto, Abbo quickly began following up on his accomplishments in Italy. In his capacity as the leading abbot of Gaul and the confidant of the pope, Abbo was able to play a much more influential role in ecclesiastical politics. He duly delivered the pope's responses to the petitions of King Robert and Count Fulk Nerra and had the honor of presenting the archiepiscopal pallium to Arnulf of Reims. Furthermore, Abbo used his improved position to intervene in disputes between several bishops and the religious houses in their dioceses. Finally, Abbo realized that the pope could be an effective leader of Christendom only if he were freed from the exigencies of local Roman politics. For this reason, Abbo wrote to the German emperor Otto III, urging him to take a more active role in ensuring peace and stability in Rome and hence in the papacy.

Abbo approached his first task with a certain degree of trepidation. He later wrote of having delivered the pope's unfavorable judgments despite the anger of the king. Helgaud of Fleury, writing after the death of Abbo (but in Robert's lifetime), indicated that Abbo broached the subject of Robert's marriage without fear of death, almost as if one might normally expect to provoke violence when delivering such news to such an important personage.[1] King Robert had made a significant concession to the pope when he had agreed, shortly before Abbo's departure to Rome, to restore Arnulf to the archiepiscopal see of Reims. Not only had he reinstated a man openly hostile to the Capetians to a position of power and authority within his kingdom but, more important by this time, Robert was also admitting that the proceedings of the Council of Saint-Basle were flawed. By 998, the death of the Carolingian pretender Charles of Lorraine had considerably weakened Carolingian claims to the throne. There was almost no chance that Arnulf of Reims would have another opportunity to betray Reims to the Capetians' enemies. Robert's theoretical concessions were much greater. By allowing Arnulf to be restored to his see, the king had also tacitly conceded that jurisdiction over the treason of a bishop lay in the pope's domain rather than that

---

1. Abbo, letter 1, to Pope Gregory V; Helgaud, *Vie de Robert le Pieux,* c. 17 (94–95). Lot, *Hugues Capet* 125–26, however, noted that Robert not only refrained from attacking Abbo but quickly acceded to his demands that Arnulf be freed from prison and restored to his see.

of the king or the bishops—an admission that was certain to antagonize many of the bishops who had supported the Kings Hugh and Robert at the Council of Saint-Basle. While the kings may have occasionally felt hemmed in by the demands of the bishops, they also depended on them. In the short run royal power would suffer from the loss of episcopal power. The Capetians were not yet in a position to calculate the effects of this concession in the long run.

In light of his capitulation on the question of the archbishop of Reims, Robert must have hoped to receive concessions from the papacy regarding his marriage to Bertha of Blois. Pope Gregory V, presiding over the Council of Pavia of 997, had condemned the marriage on the grounds of consanguinity and ordered Robert to repudiate Bertha.[2] The decision of this council, however, seems to have had little effect on Robert and his supporters. In the late tenth century the French nobility, according to the French historian Georges Duby, did not entirely embrace the ecclesiastical notion of marriage. In Duby's model, the nobility had a fundamental commitment to producing legitimate male heirs and were willing to circumvent ecclesiastical rules concerning divorce, remarriage, and consanguinity.[3] Robert evidently expected that the pope would approve his marriage in light of his concessions to the papacy. Now that he had moved toward the papal camp, Robert may have reasoned, the pope would wish to strengthen the position of the French monarchy. A marital alliance between Robert and Bertha of Blois would be highly advantageous. In addition to her Blésois connections, Bertha could also add legitimacy

   2. Gregory V, "Litterae de Synodo Papiensi," 3:694.
   3. Duby, *Knight,* 35–53; for Robert's case in particular, see 75–85. Note that Duby's book, written for a popular audience, contains little documentation and no systematic consideration of the reconstruction of the events of the late tenth and early eleventh centuries—a period in which even major events are ambiguously recorded in the sources. For a good example of the difficulties of working in this period, see the chronological studies of Lot, *Hugues Capet,* 249–303. Bouchard, "Consanguinity," 268–87, however, suggests that the nobility was only slightly less narrow in its understanding of incestuous unions than the papacy. Robert may have hoped that royal marriages would have received special consideration.

to the Capetians' rule through her descent from the Carolingian King Louis IV.[4] Abbo had the unpleasant task of telling Robert that Pope Gregory V had refused to recognize the marriage, and that Robert must repudiate Bertha or face excommunication.[5] So great was the importance of this alliance (and Robert's preference for Bertha) that Robert chose to risk excommunication rather than give up the marriage. Thus, at a council held in Rome in the spring or summer of 998, Gregory was forced to make good his threat and excommunicate Robert and the bishops who had recognized the marriage.[6] If the pope had ever felt the need to extend his excommunication to the entire kingdom, Abbo had the comfort of knowing his papal exemption had made Fleury safe.

Despite his continuing disagreement with the pope over his marriage, Robert fulfilled his promised restoration of Arnulf to the see of Reims. The king had contemplated the release of Arnulf for some time,[7] probably because Arnulf's threat to Capetian power had diminished to the point that his continued imprisonment had become more of a political liability than a benefit. In anticipation of Arnulf's release, Gerbert had left Reims and Francia, fearing that his life would be in danger. Gerbert may have exaggerated for dramatic effect, but certainly he was not mistaken in his belief that if Arnulf were restored, Gerbert as his supplant-

---

4. Lot, *Hugues Capet,* 170n3.
5. Abbo, letter 1. Gregory had threatened excommunication at the Council of Pavia, "Litterae de Synodo Papiensi," MGH SS 3:694.
6. Mansi, "Concilium Romanum," in *Sacrorum Conciliorum,* 19:225. Robert did not repudiate Bertha for at least three years, possibly longer. See Lot, *Hugues Capet,* 127; Pfister, *Robert le Pieux,* 55; Bachrach, *Fulk Nerra,* 73, 84; Hallam, *Capetian France,* 71; Duby, *Knight,* 77. Duby, *Knight,* 83, makes the curious and unsupported statement that Robert, contrary to popular belief, was never actually excommunicated. Although the Council of Pavia in 997 and the Council of Rome, probably in 998, threatened excommunication, rather than actually imposed it, since Robert did not comply with the clearly stated conditions of the councils, there is no reason to assume that Gregory did not carry out his sentence. Whether the clergy of Francia actually enforced Robert's excommunication is another question entirely.
7. Gerbert wrote a letter to King Robert's mother, Adelaide, in hopes of dissuading her (and hence her son) from doing just this, probably in the spring or summer of 997 (Lattin, letter 221; Weigle, letter 181).

Monastic Politics 193

er would be unwelcome in Reims.[8] With Charles of Lorraine dead, Gerbert in self-imposed exile, and the papacy taking an active interest in the see of Reims, Robert had no reason to postpone Arnulf's restoration and several good reasons for acceding to the pope's demands. Abbo had the honor of presenting Arnulf with the archiepiscopal pallium, which the abbot had received from the pope himself.[9]

The papal pronouncements that Abbo relayed probably did not please Count Fulk Nerra, Robert's enemy, any better than they did Robert. Fulk had asked Abbo to present Gregory with a *mandatum* in which Fulk, who needed to atone for his previous attacks on the Church, had offered to restore religious houses that had fallen into decay, rather than found new houses. Gregory had not given Abbo a satisfactory response to Fulk's request, so Fulk had sent another message to Gregory requesting absolution if he restored religious life at old establishments.[10] When, shortly after his return to Fleury, Abbo wrote Gregory, he reminded the pope that Fulk had a history of despoiling religious houses and that restoring what he himself had brought to ruin was not a particularly meritorious act.[11] Bernard S. Bachrach has argued that Abbo in this instance was acting on behalf of King Robert, who hoped that Fulk's excommunication would enable the monarchy to establish someone more sympathetic to its position in the Angevin lands.[12] Although Robert may well have hoped for this outcome, Abbo's dealings with the king suggest that he had other motives for urging the pope to condemn Fulk. If, as Aimoinus suggested, Gregory allowed himself to be guided by Abbo's advice in his French policy, then Abbo appears to have also encouraged the excommunication of Robert for his marriage to Bertha and to have insisted

---

8. Gerbert, letter to Adelaide (Lattin, letter 221; Weigle, letter 181).
9. Abbo, letter 1.
10. Ibid. For the circumstances surrounding the request, see Bachrach, *Fulk Nerra*, 73.
11. Abbo, letter 1.
12. Bachrach, *Fulk Nerra*, 73.

that Robert take the embarrassing step of restoring Arnulf to Reims.[13] Rather than giving Robert a position of moral superiority over Fulk, Abbo actually managed to maintain a balance between them. Both stood to be excommunicated for their actions. Abbo's real motive for encouraging the pope to condemn Fulk probably lay both in his hopes of maintaining a balance of power between the two sides and in his idealistic commitment to monastic stability, papal prerogatives, and moral Christian rulership within a peaceful realm—though neither the king nor the count might have appreciated Abbo's evenhandedness.

Abbo's continuing commitment to his ideal Christian society appears clearly upon a careful reading of his first letter to Pope Gregory V. Abbo's deference to the papacy and his commitment to being a reliable emissary are clear from the opening of the letter: "To Lord Gregory, always venerable in Christ, bishop of the Roman and apostolic see, and thence doctor of the universal Church, his own Abbo, rector of Fleury, greetings in Christ."[14] Abbo clearly regarded Gregory as someone worthy of personal respect as a good Christian as well as the respect due to his position as pope. Abbo's reference to Gregory as a "doctor of the universal Church" recalled the former doctors of the Church, including Augustine and Jerome, but also Pope Gregory I, one of the most respected popes of the Middle Ages, in whose honor Gregory V took his papal name. The reference to the universal Church was a reminder to Gregory that Abbo was a supporter of a unified Church, serving all Christians, in contrast, perhaps, to the fragmented Church that Abbo foresaw if episcopal conciliarism held sway in Francia. The greeting is also interesting for what it does not say. In almost all of his other letters, Abbo refers to himself by some variant of the formula "lover of the lovers of Christ," which is reminiscent of the standard papal formula in which the pope

---

13. Aimoinus, *VsA*, cc. 11–12.
14. Abbo, letter 1: "Domino semper in Christo venerabili Gregorio sanctae Romanae et apostolicae sedis praesuli, ac ideo universalis Ecclesiae doctori, suus illius Abbo, Floriacensium rector, salutem in Christo."

Monastic Politics 195

referred to himself as "the servant of the servants of God."[15] In his letters to Gregory, however, Abbo omitted this formula, referring to himself merely as the "rector of Fleury."[16] By abstaining from this formula when writing to the pope and his representative Leo, Abbo was tacitly acknowledging the pope's position as the leading servant of God on earth, a courtesy and admission of humility that the abbot did not employ when addressing his other correspondents.

The substance of Abbo's letter to Gregory, as well as the form, indicated Abbo's respect for both Pope Gregory V and the institution of the papacy. Abbo reported that he had faithfully rendered Gregory's message to Robert, omitting nothing, without altering a word, lest he misinterpret the pope's actual wishes. Gregory may have smiled at this passage since the evidence suggests that the pope's policy for the French Church was molded largely by the advice of Leo and Abbo. Nevertheless, he would also have recognized that Abbo was careful to preserve the authority of the papacy, both in his letter to Gregory and in his presentation to the king. Abbo also pointed out that King Robert had complied with Gregory's wishes by freeing Arnulf of Reims from prison and allowing Abbo to present to him the archiepiscopal pallium that

---

15. See, for example, Gregory V, letter 12, to Abbo (*PL* 137, col. 920; this is letter 2 in BL Add Ms 10972, a collection of Abbo's letters): "Servus servorum dei." See also papal charters to Fleury in Prou and Vidier, *Recueil des chartes de Saint-Benoît-sur-Loire,* nos. 18 (Gregory IV in April 829; forgery by Abbo; see chapter 5), 29 (John VIII on 5 September 878), 44 (Leo VII on 9 January 938), and 71 (Gregory V in 997). On the importance of rhetorical titles of this sort, see Leonard E. Boyle, "Diplomatics," in *Medieval Studies: An Introduction,* ed. James M. Powell, 2nd ed. (Syracuse, N.Y.: Syracuse University Press, 1992), 95, where he noted that "the papal tendency from the ninth century onwards of describing the pope as 'servus servorum Dei' probably represents a growing sense of primacy based on a rather unabashed exegesis of Mark 10:44, 'Qui voluerit . . . primus esse . . . erit omnium servus.'"

Of Abbo's fourteen surviving letters, nine contain a variant of this formula: "amatorum Christi amator Abbo" (letters 5, 10, 11, 12, and 14); "Abbo . . . famulorum Dei famulus" (letter 6); "famulorum Christi famulus Abbo" (letters 7 and 9); "servus servorum Dei Abbo" (letter to Bernard of Beaulieu, quoted in Aimoinus, *VsA,* c. 10). The only letters that Abbo did not begin with a variant of this formula are his letters to Gregory V (letters 1, 3, and 4), and his letter to the papal legate Leo (letter 15).

16. Abbo, letters 1, 3, and 4: "Floriacensium rector Abbo."

Gregory himself had entrusted to Abbo's care. Finally, Abbo appealed to Gregory's wisdom and authority by requesting that he instruct Arnulf on the proper conduct for an archbishop (something that Arnulf's previous record indicated he sorely needed) and how most quickly to restore peace and prosperity to the archdiocese of Reims after the years of dispute—for which both Gerbert and Arnulf bore some responsibility. Now that Arnulf had been restored to his see, Abbo was free to admit Gerbert's worth and Arnulf's culpability; he confided that "because I considered and still consider each of them a friend, if I found anything in either of them worthy of censure, even if it were displeasing to them, I would not be silent."[17] Abbo carefully omitted any mention of Robert's marriage, though his earlier claim that he omitted nothing when speaking to the king left Gregory to draw his own conclusions as to the reasons for Robert's continued relations with Bertha. Abbo's narrative made very clear that, though he could congratulate himself on Robert's compliance regarding Arnulf of Reims, he would not accept blame for Robert's perseverance in defying the papacy on the subject of his marriage.

After describing the results of his mission to the king, Abbo's letter rather abruptly turned to problems facing religious houses in Francia. He reminded Gregory of Fulk's desire to avoid ecclesiastical censure by restoring neglected religious houses. He also brought up a new subject. Geoffrey, count of Gâtinais, who was the son of the count of Amiens, Valois, and Vexin and the second cousin of Fulk Nerra of Anjou,[18] had attacked the lands of Fleury. Abbo requested that Gregory persuade Geoffrey's uncle, Walter of Gâtinais, to exercise his influence with the younger man. Abbo advised Gregory to threaten Geoffrey with excommuni-

---

17. Abbo, letter 1: "quia utrumque et amicum et colo et colui, si qua in eis reprehensione digna comperi, quamvis eis displiceret, non tacui." This is the only surviving evidence that Abbo knew either man more than slightly. It also gives some insight into Abbo's ideas on the duties of friendship.

18. Bachrach, *Fulk Nerra*, "Genealogy 2," 262; for the family of the counts of Amiens in the tenth century, see Philip Grierson, "L'origine des comtes d'Amiens, Valois, et Vexin," *Le Moyen Age* ser. 3, 10.1 (1939): 95–122

cation should Walter's influence fail. While this may have been a routine matter of despoiling monastic lands for political or military gain from Walter's perspective,[19] for Abbo this was symptomatic of the problems facing monasteries in a politically unstable kingdom. Both cases illustrated the need for monastic establishments, especially those with far-flung holdings, to have a reliable and powerful ally outside of the give-and-take of French politics. The most important noble families in western Francia in the late tenth century were the counts of Blois, the counts of Anjou, and the counts of Vexin, Amiens, and Valois.[20] Robert's recent marriage to Bertha of Blois had moved the Capetian kings into the camp of the house of Blois and out of the camp of the Angevins. Given the political realignment, Abbo could not expect material help from the Capetian kings. In the cases of Fulk and Walter, Abbo made clear that harassment of religious houses was unacceptable and should be punished by the leader of the Christian world, no one other than the pope himself. Abbo's inclusion of these matters in his letter to Gregory indicated that, in his opinion, the recent violence and upheaval in Francia could be cured only by the proper exercise of papal, royal, and comital power—and, above all, with respect for the lands of the Church, especially monastic lands.

Once Abbo had carried out Gregory's commissions in Francia, he turned his attention to strengthening the pope's position in Rome. The abbot's two brief visits to Italy and his attempts to promote papal authority in Francia had given him ample opportunity to observe how the independence of the papacy was compromised by the machinations of the powerful Roman nobility. His appeals to the bishops that they respect papal supremacy failed largely because of the inactivity of the papacy—which, in turn, was due to problems with the Roman nobility. On his first journey to Rome in 995, Abbo's attempt to meet with Pope John XV gave

19. Bachrach, *Fulk Nerra*, 65, disposes of this incursion in a single sentence as part of a longer description of the military maneuvers of Fulk and his allies in 997.
20. Lemarignier, *Gouvernement royal*, 50.

him fresh proof of the potential for venality in a papacy completely subservient to the exigencies of local politics. Although Gregory V differed from John in character and temperament, he, too, was largely at the mercy of the local nobility. In order to continue to function with a degree of independence, Gregory had been forced to flee Rome, with the result that Abbo had had to seek him out in Spoleto. Abbo realized that Gregory owed his consecration as pope in 996 entirely to the influence of Gregory's kinsman, the German emperor Otto III. Gregory's subsequent retreat from Rome corresponded almost exactly with Otto's departure from Italy for the north.[21]

In order to bolster Gregory's position in Rome, Abbo saw that he would have to appeal to Otto's sense of responsibility as emperor for the security of papal authority. Probably in the summer of 998, Abbo composed a poem in which he called upon Otto to take up his responsibilities in Italy as a Christian emperor. The form of the poem itself expressed Abbo's overriding theme. According to Aimoinus, Abbo had purposely written his poem following the example of Porfyrius, a poet of the age of Constantine the Great.[22] Porfyrius was noted for his composition of technopaegnia to Constantine, poems "in which the author hid a message which the inscriber revealed by picking out the letters forming the significant pattern in inks of different colors."[23] Abbo's decision to imitate

---

21. Althoff, *Otto III*, 62.
22. Aimoinus, *VsA*, c. 13, described the poem as forming the greater part of a letter to Otto. The letter in which the poem was embedded has not survived. Aimoinus did not discuss the content or the context of the poem. The poem itself is not included in the MSS or the *PL* text of the *VsA*, but is included in *PL* 139:519–20 and in Gian Andri Bezzola, *Das Ottonische Kaisertum in der französischen Geschichtsschreibung des 10. und beginnenden 11. Jahrhunderts* (Graz, Austria: Hermann Böhlaus, 1956), 199. Bezzola's edition is based on the manuscript Vat. Reg. Lat. 1864, ff. 73r–73v. More recently, the poem has been included in Scott Gwara, "Three Acrostic Poems by Abbo of Fleury," *Journal of Medieval Latin* 2 (1992): 227. Gwara includes several textual emendations based on comparison of the manuscript evidence and a detailed discussion of the manuscript tradition, Abbo's poetic models, and the form of the poem (203–14).
23. Timothy D. Barnes, *Constantine and Eusebius* (Cambridge, Mass.: Harvard University Press, 1981), 47. The full name of the poet is Publilius Optatianus Porfyrius. For his career, see A. H. M. Jones, J. R. Martindale, and J. Morris, *Prosopography of the Lat-*

Monastic Politics 199

Porfyrius sprang from more than a desire to display his poetic virtuosity. Porfyrius had written his first poem to Emperor Constantine the Great (d. 337) shortly after the emperor had established his supremacy over his rivals in 313, due, according to imperial propaganda, to his adoption of the symbols of Christianity.[24] The use of Porfyrius's poetic form in Abbo's letter to Otto very strongly suggested a comparison with Constantine, the first Christian emperor and one who had interested himself greatly in strengthening and unifying the Church. Since Porfyrius had written his poems in order to secure his own return from exile, they were particularly apt coming from the supporter of an exiled pope. Furthermore, imitators of Porfyrius had been common during the Carolingian renaissance, again mainly in works designed to praise the imperial majesty of the emperor.[25] Abbo's use of dactylic hexameters recalled the works of Vergil and other poets of the Augustan age, the high point of the Roman Empire. Abbo was thus simultaneously comparing Otto to the emperors Augustus, Constantine, and Charlemagne. Since Otto had been a student of Gerbert and continued to maintain a well-educated entourage, the young emperor must have quickly recognized the allusion.

The most striking aspect of the poem was the highlighted lettering. Aimoinus's description indicates the high degree of technical expertise necessary for the poem's composition:

"Otto, o ye powerful Caesar, heed our tragic poem" [*Otto valens caesar nostra tu cede coturno*]. Indeed, this line ended in the same letter with which it began. And thus it happened that it fell in the shape of a cross, hav-

---

er Roman Empire, vol. 1 (A.D. 260–395) (Cambridge: Cambridge University Press, 1971), 649; Barnes, "Publilius Optatianus Porfyrius," *American Journal of Philology* 96.2 (1975): 173–86. The standard modern edition and commentary of the poems is Publilius Optatianus Porfyrius, *Publilii Optatiani Porfyrii Carmina*, ed. Iohannes Polara, 2 vols., Corpus scriptorum Latinorum paravianum (Turin, Italy: Io. Bapt. Paraviae et sociorum, 1973).

24. Barnes, *Constantine* 46–47.

25. Carolingian poets employing this verse form include Alcuin, Boniface, Josephus Scottus, and Theodulf of Orléans. See, for example, Ernst Dümmler, ed., *Poetae Latini aevi Carolini*, vol. 1, MGH Antiquitates, Poetae Latini medii aevi (Hanover, 1881), 17, 153, 155, 157, 159, 225, 227, 482.

ing [the initial letters of the first line repeated] up and down [at] the beginnings and the ends of all the lines and also through the middle of the work, and likewise across, while it [i.e., the repeated line] also brought an end to the poem. And in this manner it happened that it [the repeated line] might be read in six different directions, and it outlined four squares in the epistle. In these squares four names, placed up and down, might be read. In two [of these squares], indeed, [were written] Otto and Caesar, and in the others Abbo and abbot.[26]

The two features that undoubtedly struck Otto and his court immediately were the shape of the cross outlined by the highlighted letters and the four words written in highlighted letters in the four squares outlined by the cross. The shape of the cross naturally reminded Otto of his role as a Christian monarch, while the names written within the squares would have suggested the duties of Otto as emperor (*caesar*) and Abbo as abbot.[27] The poem itself was a call to Otto to assume his responsibilities as a Christian emperor. Abbo invoked Otto's ancestry several times as well as the traditional imperial titles Augustus and Caesar. Abbo's cover letter for this epistolary poem has, unfortunately, been lost. In it, the French abbot probably explained the appropriateness of this form as well as his reason for writing it.

The political context of the poem is, however, unambiguous. By February of 997, Pope Gregory V was still in exile, due to the machinations of the Crescentii, while an antipope, John Philagathus, an adviser to Otto III, had declared himself in Italy. Meanwhile, Otto III was planning an expedition to the Slavic lands to

---

26. Aimoinus, *VsA*, c. 13: "Otto valens c[a]esar, nostro tu cede coturno. Is nempe versus, in eadem desinebat littera, qua etiam incipiebatur. Sicque fiebat, ut ipse principia versuum omnium finemque tenens, per medium quoque epistolae erectus, itemque in transversum, in modum crucis incederet, ipse nichilominus clausula camnis fieret. Atque hoc modo contingebat, ut et ipse sexies diversis modis legeretur, et quatuor quadrangulos in aepistola [*sic*] faceret. In quibus quadrangulis quatuor nomina erectim posita legebantur. In duobus quidem, Otto et C[a]esar, in aliis vero Abbo et abba[s]."

Abbo addressed a poem similar in form to Dunstan, which one editor called "[a] curious specimen of misdirected ingenuity" (Stubbs, *Memorials of St. Dunstan*, 410).

27. The functional and moral social hierarchy of Abbo's *Apologeticus* and his *Collectio canonum* is suggested by these titles, although no evidence exists that Abbo's works ever circulated in Otto's empire.

the east, which could delay his restoration of order in Italy indefinitely.[28] Gregory, however, desperately needed the support of the emperor at this juncture, and Abbo probably wrote his poem with these circumstances specifically in mind. Certainly, the central theme of the poem is the emperor's responsibility to the Church and its rector, the pope. Unfortunately, the effect of Abbo's letter and poem are unknown. Teta E. Moehs has argued that the poem had little effect: Otto did not postpone his eastern expedition and attended to affairs in Italy only upon completion of the campaign.[29] In general, Geoffrey Barraclough argued that though Otto III was "not unconscious of the glories of ancient Rome, such ideas did not directly influence Italian policy or imperial policy," though he acknowledged the prominence of references to the *renovatio imperii Romanorum* in imperial propaganda.[30] Scott Gwara made a similar argument when he described the poem as "less a plea for help than an affirmation of Roman, Carolingian and Ottonian Hegemony."[31] On the other hand, though Otto did not immediately remedy Gregory's position, he ultimately did seriously rethink his policies in Italy. In 998 he launched a second expedition to Italy and initiated a policy of strengthening German influence in the Italian Church and restricting alienation of Church lands in Italy by appointing officials loyal to imperial policy to important ecclesiastical positions there.[32]

Abbo's continuing correspondence with Gregory V reflects the pope's improved situation in Rome after 998 as well as the abbot's increased prestige as a confidant of the pope. Only one brief

---

28. Moehs, *Gregorius V*, 55. Bezzola, *Das Ottonische Kaisertum*, 160, places the composition of the poem in the autumn of 996, while Abbo was visiting Gregory V. Although his visit undoubtedly inspired the poem and he may even have composed a rough draft at the time, it seems unlikely that Abbo could have completed a piece of such technical complexity while away from home and engaged in complicated negotiations over the charter that he eventually obtained for Fleury.

29. Moehs, *Gregorius V*, 55–56.

30. Geoffrey Barraclough, *The Origins of Modern Germany* (New York: W. W. Norton, 1984), 61.

31. Gwara, "Three Acrostic Poems," 213–14.

32. Barraclough, *Origins*, 60–62.

letter from Gregory to Abbo survives, but in it the pope clearly expressed his affection and esteem for his French correspondent. Gregory opened by bemoaning the short period of time that Abbo's messenger was able to spend in Italy and closed by calling Abbo his "special friend," for whose kindness (*beneficium*—already mentioned once in the letter) he would never be ungrateful. The brevity of the letter suggests that the pope had sent more detailed instructions, perhaps through his messenger. Abbo had apparently asked the pope for permission to send an unidentified monk to the papal court, a request that Gregory readily granted. Furthermore, Gregory hoped to hear from this monk of events in the north, including the behavior of the French king and reports on the health of both Abbo and the archbishop of Canterbury.[33] Finally, as a personal favor, Gregory asked that Abbo send some of his finest missal books "so that I might remember my special friend during the celebration of mass."[34] The tone of the letter suggests continued cooperation between Abbo and the papacy. Gregory's gratitude may stem from Abbo's support in the affair of Arnulf of Reims or from Abbo's letter urging Otto's support for the papacy. In either event, he surely succeeded in flattering the abbot of Fleury with his open expressions of gratitude and his assumption that Fleury's scriptorium produced missals of such quality as to make them welcome additions to the papal collection.

Gregory's letter, coupled with Abbo's successful mission to the papal court, ensured that many petitions to the papacy passed through Abbo's hands. The abbot of Fleury's two remaining letters to Gregory reflect his increased prestige. Abbo began one letter by remarking on the large number of petitions he had received from people who believed that Abbo had influence with the

---

33. I have not been able to identify more precisely the monk, identified in the letter only as "brother Ri." Given that Gregory expected him to be a reliable informant on both Abbo and the archbishop of Canterbury, this monk must have traveled considerably, and may have been an English monk who had sought Fleury as a center of learning.

34. Gregory V, letter 12, *PL* 137:920: "ut . . . inter missarum solemnia . . . specialis amici memor sim."

pope.³⁵ Both letters recalled the meeting of the two churchmen in Spoleto, their only face-to-face encounter, and one that evidently impressed both men deeply.³⁶ In the first letter, Abbo asked Gregory to receive favorably a woman of his acquaintance, possibly a relative, named Ildegard.³⁷ Abbo described this woman to Gregory as "a sinner ... and noble, but not, however noble because a sinner, but, in fact, a sinner because noble." She had, however, atoned for her sins by building two monasteries, one for men and one for women, dedicated to Sts. Peter and Andrew.³⁸ Now Ildegard wished to visit Rome and had called upon the abbot of Fleury, as her friend and the confidant of the pope, to write a letter of introduction for her. Abbo's next surviving letter to Gregory contained a similar request on behalf of someone named Humbold, about whom Abbo gave no information beyond his name. Once Humbold's petition had been disposed of, Abbo immediately began discussing a verse account of Benedict's translation to Fleury (which he appended to the letter) and some vessels for Mass that he was sending Gregory.³⁹ Abbo's successful mission to Rome and his continuing correspondence with Gregory had made him an important contact for the faithful of northern France wishing to present their petitions to the head of the Church.

With his reputation as a Church leader firmly established, Abbo turned his attention to the problems of monastic communities. The religious communities of the city of Tours had close ties with Fleury. Tours lay just over one hundred kilometers (about sixty miles) downstream from Fleury along the Loire River, on which the monks of Fleury had held transport rights since at least the time of Charlemagne's father, Pepin I (reigned 741–

---

35. Abbo, letter 3.
36. Abbo, letters 3 and 4.
37. Abbo, letter 3. According to this letter, Ildegard had asked a favor of Abbo "jure propinquitatis." This could mean "by right of friendship" or "by right of kinship." I have not been able to identify her more precisely.
38. Oddly enough, I can find no reference to houses with this dedication founded at this time.
39. Abbo, letter 4.

768, as king from 751).[40] It had been while he was traveling to celebrate the feast of St. Martin at Saint-Martin of Tours that Abbo had been attacked by the followers of Bishop Arnulf of Orléans. Abbo also regarded the young Hervé of Saint-Martin (later treasurer of Saint-Martin) as a friend, to whom he had earlier offered advice when the canons had a dispute with their bishop. The religious situation at Tours in the last decade of the tenth century was highly politicized. The Capetian kings, as lay abbots, had strong interests in Saint-Martin, but the positions of dean and treasurer of the monastery were usually held by supporters of either the counts of Blois or the counts of Anjou. Likewise, the ancestors of the Capetians had been lay abbots of Marmoutier but had turned over their authority to the counts of Blois, who had, in turn, called in the monks of Cluny to reform the monastery.[41] The monastery of Saint-Julien of Tours retained close ties with the archbishop of Tours (who had officiated at Robert's marriage to Bertha of Blois), despite the house's reform by monks from Cluny earlier in the tenth century.[42] The city itself had passed by force of arms from the count of Blois to the count of Anjou in 996, but since the Touraine was of strategic importance to King Robert (who was now allied with the comital house of Blois), the royal forces waged a successful offensive to retake Tours in the summer of 997.[43] Now, probably in 998, the abbot of Fleury had heard of a serious dispute between the monks of Marmoutier, just outside of Tours, and their abbot, Bernier. Abbo took an immediate interest in the situation and wrote two letters, the first to Abbot Gauzbert of Saint-Julien of Tours and the other to Bernier himself.[44]

Abbo began his letter to Gauzbert, as he had begun his *Apol-*

40. Prou and Vidier, *Recueil des chartes de Saint-Benoît-sur-Loire,* nos. 5 (November 751–24 September 768), 8 (9 October 768–28 January 814), and 15 (27 July 818); nos. 5 and 8 are lost, but have been hypothesized on the basis of no. 15, which gives the monks of Fleury exemption from royal tolls for four boats on the Loire River.
41. Farmer, *Communities of Saint Martin,* 34–35.
42. Ibid., 30.
43. Bachrach, *Fulk Nerra,* 59, 62–65.
44. Abbo, letters 8 and 9, are the main sources for this dispute. These are summarized in Cousin, *Abbon de Fleury-sur-Loire,* 162–67.

Monastic Politics 205

ogeticus, with a contrast between the quiet study that he desired and the necessity that the evils of the time had forced upon him.[45] The evil of the present age, in his opinion, was the abuse of monasteries by those who sought refuge from worldly responsibilities without a proper commitment to the religious life. He described such monks as "wolves in sheep's clothing" who corrupted those who had entered the monastery out of true devotion. "Lovers of the holy religion," such as Abbo and Gauzbert, had a responsibility to intervene in the affairs of other monasteries when disruptive forces took hold. At the time of writing, Abbo may not yet have been fully briefed on the source of the conflict. Nowhere in this letter did he indicate that he had heard the charges brought against the abbot of Marmoutier. In fact, he asked Gauzbert to describe the circumstances more fully—particularly whether Bernier had signed a letter of resignation and whether he had been prejudged and violently expelled from the monastery.[46]

What little Abbo had heard was disturbing enough. One rumor that reached his ears was that the monks of Cluny had been expelled from the monastery and that a certain Frederick, a former monk of Fleury, may have instigated their expulsion, along with that of the abbot.[47] Even though Abbo was merely speculating on Frederick's involvement, he was adamant in warning Gauzbert against the former Fleurisian's evil tendencies: "And perhaps one of our former [monks], Frederick, jealous of good brothers, a most terrible schemer, established factions of this sort among you to such an extent that just as from Arius Arians, from Gnato Gnatonites, so also his disciples, from Frederick, Fredericians."[48] He

---

45. Abbo, *Apologeticus,* f. 15v (= *PL* 139:461).
46. Abbo, letter 8.
47. Thirteen monks from Cluny had been sent to reform Marmoutier by Maiolus (*GC* [1856] 14:199–200; Rosenwein, *Rhinoceros Bound,* 54).
48. Abbo, letter 8: "At fortassis ille quondam noster Fredericus bonorum aemulus fratrum, insidiator pessimus, hujusmodi apud vos scholas instituit; quatenus sicut ab Ario Ariani; a Gnatone Gnatonici; ita sui discipuli a Frederico Frederici." The only known controversy within Fleury during Abbo's tenure as abbot was the opposition to his election (following the opposition to the election of Abbo's predecessor Oylbold). Though it is tempting to identify Frederick as one of the instigators of this con-

did not describe Frederick's activities at Fleury, but the extreme tone of the letter indicates that in Abbo's eyes Frederick was not a lone deviant but a dangerous corrupter of naive monks. The expulsion of Bernier was made worse by the procedure that had been followed. Abbo had heard that Bernier had been tortured and had undergone an ordeal by hot iron.[49]

Procedural issues were clearly paramount in Abbo's mind as he wrote to Gauzbert. As in the trial of Arnulf of Reims, Abbo insisted on correct judicial procedure in the trial of an abbot, warning of the incompetence of monks to oversee that trial. It would be, Abbo wrote derisively, as if "the sheep had judged the shepherd." As he had argued in other cases, in order for a trial to be fair, the same people cannot simultaneously be accusers, witnesses, and judges.[50] To justify his own intervention in the affairs of a distant monastery, Abbo cited a letter of Pope Gregory the Great (as well as the charter that Fleury had recently received from Pope Gregory V), in which the pope insisted that abbots could not be expelled unilaterally but must have a fair hearing before a council.[51]

Bernier's actions also came under scrutiny. Abbo clearly was not sure to what extent Bernier had acquiesced in his own expulsion. Clearly, if Bernier had submitted a written repudiation (*libellus repudii*) of his office, the situation became more complicated legally, especially if, as Abbo suspected, the repudiation had been exacted under torture. Abbo was also concerned by the rumor that Bernier had undergone a trial by hot iron. This particular form of ordeal was practiced at least occasionally in the tenth century. Various participants at the Council of Saint-Basle in 991 had, in fact, offered to verify their testimony by carrying heated iron in their bare hands.[52] The use of this ordeal was usually re-

---

troversy, the existing evidence is not full enough either to support or to refute such a reading.

49. Ibid.

50. For other contexts in which Abbo made this argument, see his *Collectio canonum*, c. 44.

51. Abbo, letter 8.

52. Gerbert, "Acta Consilii Remensis," cc. 11, 30 (MGH SS 3:662, 678); Rob-

served for cases that could not be decided by other means—often when sexual purity or heresy were at issue.[53] Abbo clearly objected to the use of ordeal in this case, though he did not explain why. He may have felt that the ordeal had pagan origins and unduly tempted God. He may merely have objected to the use of the ordeal in this situation—either because Bernier was a churchman or because other legal procedures had not been attempted first or because official misconduct rather than heresy was the issue. In view of the questionable legality of the proceedings, Abbo then requested a full summary of the events at Marmoutier from Gauzbert, who had a responsibility as the abbot of a neighboring monastery to investigate the charges against Bernier.

Shortly after Abbo's letter had reached Gauzbert, Bernier evidently communicated directly with Abbo. If he had heard anything about Abbo's letter to Gauzbert, he may have hoped to enlist the abbot of Fleury in support of his cause. By doing so, he would have gained the backing of the leading monastery in the realm by virtue of Fleury's papal charter of the previous year. If so, the tone of Abbo's response must have quickly disabused him of that notion. Abbo had addressed Gauzbert as "the most beloved brother and fellow abbot, G." in contrast to Abbo, "the humble rector of Fleury."[54] Abbo's response to Bernier, however, emphasized the power of the Fleurisian abbot, who imitated the papal style of address, "Abbo, servant of the servants of Christ," while he accorded a minimum of respect to his addressee, who was simply "Bernier." After this chilly introduction, Abbo began chastising Bernier for his actions and his excuses. As someone who had been brought up in the Church, Bernier ought to behave better,

---

ert Bartlett, *Trial by Fire and Water: The Medieval Judicial Ordeal* (Oxford: Clarendon, 1986), 14–15.

53. Bartlett, *Trial*, 20, 26–27. Jeffrey A. Bowman, *Shifting Landmarks: Property, Proof, and Dispute in Catalonia around the Year 1000* (Ithaca, N.Y.: Cornell University Press, 2004), 129, found only nine appeals to judicial ordeal in charters from the Province of Narbonne betwen 950 and 1100. In most of those, the ordeal did not take place, as the case was settled before the date set for it. In the few where the ordeal did take place, the results were ambiguous.

54. Abbo, letter 8.

and he certainly should have known better than to try to escape the consequences of his actions by hiding behind the protection of the monastery and his religious profession. Quite the contrary, Bernier ought to realize that he would be held to a higher standard of conduct because of his position in the religious life.

Bernier's crimes appear to have included the corruption of the monks of his monastery. His defense, if Abbo understood rightly, was that no monks had actually been corrupted by his actions, not that his behavior was above reproach. Abbo's response to Bernier's defense of himself was scathing:

But what does it matter whether you committed part of the deed or the [whole] deed, when all praise this little verse, all wisely esteem this saying: "Well begun is half done" [Horace, ep. I.2,40]? . . . A crime which was committed in a brothel with the wife of someone else, the husband calls one thing, the accused something else; for the one complains of adultery, the other claims not adultery, but that what he did in the brothel was allowed. . . . You say that you contaminated many of the flock entrusted [to you] with your sickness, you prove that you lost [many of the flock] by the leprosy of that most foul disease, saying nothing other than that you began but did not complete: with the sword you pierced a companion, a son even, and him who chose you as the protector of his life; you offered poison to him; you cast fire into the sacred rooms; if he, pierced with a sword, survived, if the poison which he drank did not kill [him], if the fire did not take hold, you said that you did not sin.[55]

Although Abbo's fiery reprimand of Bernier may be taken as evidence that the abbot of Marmoutier had been accused of attempted homicide and arson as well as frequenting brothels, the truth was probably less sensational, though equally serious from

---

55. Abbo, letter 9: "Sed quid prodest utrum partem facti, an factum habeas, cum illum versiculum 'Dimidium facti qui coepit, habet,' omnes laudent, omnes sapienter dictum existiment. . . . scelus quod in prostibulo perpetratum est cum uxore alicujus aliter vir, aliter reus nominat; alter enim de adulterio queritur, alter non adulterium, sed quod fecit in prostibulo, licuisse fatetur. . . . Plurimos commissi gregis tuo morbo contaminasse diceris, lepra foedissimae contagionis perdidisse convinceris, nihil aliud dicens nisi quia fecisti, sed non perfecisti: ferro socium immo filium, et eum qui te suae titae tutorem elegerat, transfixisti; venenum ei porrexisti; ignem sacris aedibus injecisti: si ferro transfixus evasit, si venenum potatum non extinxit, si ignis non convaluit, te pecasse negas."

a spiritual point of view. When Abbo wrote of Bernier taking the life of someone entrusted to his care, he was referring not to a literal murder but to the spiritual death of the young man. Although Abbo's own experience indicated that violence among monks was possible, even likely, in the later tenth century, the evidence indicates that Bernier was probably not charged with crimes of violence.

Abbo does not appear to have heard the charges against Bernier and the fact that Bernier attempted to clear himself of the crime through ordeal until some time after his expulsion from Marmoutier. In the first case, if the rumor of the expulsion of an abbot had traveled up the Loire River to Fleury, it seems highly unlikely that the even more sensational news of attempted murder and arson on the part of the abbot would not have reached Fleury. Furthermore, trial by ordeal was rare except in cases where no witnesses existed,[56] and attempted murder and arson are both crimes in which witnesses are likely to be abundant. As far as the charge that Bernier had visited a brothel, Abbo clearly intended this as an example of a case in which both parties might dispute the legal crime committed, not as a direct reference to the case at hand. Abbo did not specify the exact nature of Bernier's crimes, though they clearly threatened the spiritual life at Marmoutier. They may have been of a sexual nature or possibly involved heretical beliefs, both of which were often decided by ordeal.[57] Abbo closed by advising Bernier to come to his senses and confess, rather than disgracing all monks and abbots with his infamous conduct, and submit his resignation to the monks and the bishop.

Abbo did not address the political ramifications of the disturbance at Marmoutier in either of his letters. Sharon Farmer speculated that the count of Blois or possibly King Robert had been instrumental in the expulsion of Bernier and noted that Gauz-

---

56. Bartlett, *Trial*, 26–27.
57. The hypothesis that Bernier had espoused heretical doctrines is the most attractive, in light of Abbo's ongoing concern with heresy in the French Church, and subsequent heretical outbreaks in Orléans. See Bautier, "L'hérésie d'Orléans," 63–88.

bert, who eventually succeeded Bernier as abbot, was related to the counts of Blois.[58] The counts of Blois had, however, initially supported Bernier as abbot of Marmoutier. The counts had supported the Cluniac reform of Marmoutier earlier in the century, and Bernier appears to have been originally a monk of Cluny. Furthermore, the counts and the archbishop of Tours had arranged exchanges of land and had made gifts to Marmoutier during Bernier's abbacy.[59] Bernier's crimes, whatever they may have been, undoubtedly provided the impetus for the monks, and possibly the counts, to seek his removal from office. If there were a political motive for Bernier's removal from office, neither Abbo nor the monks mentioned it—nor, significantly, does Bernier appear to have put forth such motives in his defense of himself.

This incident clearly illustrates the use to which Abbo put his newfound power and influence in the French Church. While his initial reaction to Bernier's expulsion was to condemn the undermining of abbatial authority, upon receiving fuller information he encouraged Bernier to admit his crimes and step down peacefully. Throughout he emphasized the importance of following proper procedures, whether for the reinstatement of a wrongly expelled abbot or for the removal of a guilty one. Not coincidentally, both actions would have maintained the current political orientation of Marmoutier as a house loyal to the counts of Blois. Abbo's interests lay not in overthrowing the current political order but in maintaining a peaceful balance between competing political interests in order to ensure the political stability necessary to facilitate the uninterrupted practice of monastic life.

Abbo continued to maintain and strengthen his position as

58. Farmer, *Communities of Saint Martin*, 68. Farmer has not delineated the political situation in the tenth century as clearly as for later centuries. She does not differentiate between the comital houses of Anjou and Blois or consider the relatively young age of Odo II of Blois or discuss fully their changing relationship with the Capetians, referring to both as "the principal rival of the Capetians" (65). Her account of the episode of Bernier's expulsion is so general as not to mention his name or the charges against him (she merely reported that the Cluniac monks had been expelled), much less cite Abbo's letters to Bernier and Gauzbert (68).

59. *GC* 14 (1856), col. 200.

leader of the monastic world right up until his death in 1004. No longer was he a lone voice, more often disregarded than not, calling for cooperation between monks and secular rulers or for papal supremacy. He now led the monastic world from the position of a respected statesman whose advice was actively sought. Ironically, he outlived his protégé and ecclesiastical superior, the young Pope Gregory V, by several years. Gregory's sudden death in 999 threatened to undo Abbo's careful work at securing the status of the papacy. Fortunately, by this time Otto III, perhaps partly due to Abbo's advocacy, had committed himself to providing strong support for the papacy. In order to secure the papacy during the emperor's absence, Otto had implemented a policy of staffing the important ecclesiastical offices in Italy with men who could support imperial policy and papal independence in Italy against the exigencies of local Italian politics. A brilliant example of this policy was his elevation of Abbo's old adversary, Gerbert of Reims, to the archbishopric of Ravenna. By placing Gerbert on the archiepiscopal throne, Otto had rewarded his old tutor and secured a reliable ally and shrewd politician in a key diocese. From the papal perspective, Otto had also solved a major political problem by removing any concern that Gerbert might try to reverse the papacy's reinstatement of Arnulf in the see of Reims.

Now, with the death of Gregory V, Otto promoted Gerbert to the pontificate, as Pope Sylvester II.[60] Abbo must have regarded this appointment with mixed feelings. On the one hand, no one could fault Gerbert on the basis of either his learning or his personal integrity (despite the controversy over Reims), but on the other hand, Gerbert's arguments in the wake of the Council of Saint-Basle, less than a decade earlier, had been unequivocally hostile to the notion of papal supremacy. Abbo need not have feared. One of Gerbert's first acts upon becoming pope was to grant a formal pardon to Archbishop Arnulf of Reims and to recognize Arnulf's right to perform all of the offices of archbishop.[61] Gerbert

60. Barraclough, *Origins*, 60–61.
61. Sylvester II, in Lattin, no. 244 (326–28). Gerbert is almost unique among

could not very well admit that his own accession as archbishop of Reims during Arnulf's imprisonment had been illegal. On the other hand, his interests as pope made it expedient for him to support claims of full papal jurisdiction in the affair. Thus, without admitting that the arguments of the bishops at the Council of Saint-Basle had been faulty, his pardon of Arnulf paved the way for reconciliation between King Robert, the archbishop of Reims, and the papacy, thus bringing closure to the unfortunate affair. Abbo must have breathed a sigh of relief. When Gerbert, who had been in ill health for many years, died in 1003, Abbo may have had nearly as much cause to regret his death as that of Gregory V, a mere four years earlier.

Certainly in 1003 Abbo found many more immediate concerns to occupy his attention. Although usually laconic, the "Annales Floriacenses" vividly describe a series of strange portents and disasters for the year 1003: "In the year of the Incarnation of the Lord 1003, the season of winter was longer than usual, and there was a serious inundation of rain, and in many areas the rivers rose much beyond their usual banks. Indeed, in contrast with others, the Loire so greatly exceeded its banks that it shook everything in the area with the fear of death, by penetrating the ramparts, by uprooting houses together with men, by destroying solid bridges and enclosures, by submerging oxen with plowmen, sheepfolds with sheep and shepherds, so that one would have thought it was the Flood."[62] The chronicler went on to describe the appearance of a phantasmal city and a monstrous birth before concluding by noting the death of Gerbert in 1003 and

---

popes in being better known by his original name than by his name as pope. Many modern writers continue to refer to him as Gerbert, even when referring to his actions as Pope Sylvester II, in order to avoid confusion; Gerbert's career as Sylvester II was brief and, in comparison with his earlier career, uneventful.

62. Vidier, *L'historigraphie,* appendix 3, 220: "anno ab incarnatione domini .M. IIIo. et qualitas hiemis longior solito pluuiarumque inundatio extitit gravior, atque diuersis in regionibus flumina suos ultra modum preterierunt terminos. Pre ceteris uero liger in tantum faceret, ualla penetrando, casas una cum hominibus eruendo, pontes firmos sepesque eradicando, boues cum bubulcis, ouilia cum ouibus et pueris demergendo, ita ut diluuium esse crederetur."

Monastic Politics 213

of Abbo in the following year. The chronicler certainly had motives for exaggerating the portents of 1003 in order to underscore the tragedy of losing both Gerbert and Abbo within less than two years. Whether the writer saw this as the beginning of the end times or merely the beginning of a downward cycle is impossible to say. Certainly other marginal and interlinear entries in the "Annales" indicate a long-standing obsession with disasters, such as the fire at Fleury in 979, and portents, such as blood on the moon in 956.[63] Regardless of the annalist's interpretation, the flooding of the Loire must have been devastating to Fleury, which lay on the fertile land of the floodplain and which depended on the river for transportation and fishing.[64] The flood would not only have damaged the buildings and fields of Fleury, it would have cut off access to needed supplies from outside the monastery because of the disruption of river transport. A natural disaster of this sort would have occupied all of the abbot's time, as he supervised the salvaging of Fleury's goods from the floodwaters, arranged for alternate transport routes, and rationed any goods that were in short supply.

Despite the devastation of 1003, Abbo found himself in the following year mediating disputes at Saint-Père of Chartres and Saint-Mesmin of Micy. The monks of Saint-Père of Chartres had refused to accept the abbot appointed by Count Thibault, the bishop-designate of Chartres and the older of the two surviving sons of Count Odo of Blois-Chartres.[65] In a now-lost letter, Abbo wrote to Fulbert (c. 970–1028), then a canon of Chartres, for more details. Fulbert sent a full account of the affair.[66] While the abbot of Saint-Père lay on his deathbed, a monk named Magenard had persuaded Thibault, as bishop-designate of Chartres, to appoint

63. Ibid., appendix 3, 219.
64. Prou and Vidier, *Recueil des chartes de Saint-Benoît-sur-Loire,* no. 15 (27 July 818), is a charter of Louis the Pious granting rights to transport along the Loire.
65. Lot, *Hugues Capet,* 179, 180n1.
66. Fulbert, *Letters,* letter 1. This is the only surviving correspondence between these two great ecclesiastical figures of that region. Their careers apparently overlapped by only a few years.

him as the next abbot. The monks protested that the proceedings went against the monastic rule since not only was their abbot still living but they had certainly not elected Magenard.[67] As a result, they refused to accept the new abbot. When Thibault attempted to impose Magenard on the congregation by force, the monks fled Saint-Père and took refuge in the cathedral of Chartres.

How Abbo became interested in the plight of Saint-Père is unknown. He may initially have heard about their flight from a traveler: Chartres lay just over one hundred kilometers (about sixty-five miles) from Fleury. Perhaps the monks of Chartres or Magenard himself had requested Abbo's mediation. Certainly, Abbo's extensive work on Church canons, his status as the leading abbot in the Capetian kingdom, his prominent role in the Councils of Saint-Basle and Saint-Denis, and his involvement in disputes at the monasteries of Tours all made him an attractive choice to mediate the dispute. The situation at Chartres appealed to Abbo's interest in the proper election of Church officials and the relations between monks, bishops, and secular officials. The dispute was further complicated by the character of Magenard, who appears to have been a hitherto exemplary monk. Fulbert described him as someone "previously very dear to me," who had been led astray by two less honorable and less well-educated monks.[68] Throughout his career, Abbo never seems to have abandoned his role as teacher and mentor to young monks, as can be seen from his letters to the monks of Cluny and Bernard of Beaulieu.[69] The case of Magenard, as a young monk temporarily led astray by evil counsel, would very likely have appealed to these paternal feelings.

Abbo's response to this affair is a mystery. Abbo died less than a year later, and no subsequent document linking him with the

---

67. For the election of abbots, see Benedict, *RB 1980*, c. 64 (280–85); Abbo, *Collectio canonum*, c. 14. Neither Abbo nor Benedict addressed the question of whether an abbot can be appointed or elected before the death of his predecessor, though Abbo made the case that a bishop could not select his own successor, even on his deathbed (*Collectio canonum*, c. 40 [c. 42 in *PL* 139]).

68. Fulbert, *Letters*, letter 1: "ante michi non mediocriter carus."

69. Abbo, letters 7 and 16 (quoted in the *VsA*).

decision survives. Count Thibault died even before Abbo did, and the affair was settled by compromise: Magenard resided in the episcopal palace until his behavior had shown him worthy of the office of abbot, as it subsequently did.[70] Abbo would probably have approved of this resolution. It recognized the importance of following proper procedures in electing an abbot as well as the legal interest and responsibilities of the bishop. On the other hand, justice was tempered with mercy toward Magenard, whose main fault seems to have been a certain degree of youthful gullibility. Furthermore, the decision acceded to the interests of the house of Blois, which controlled the bishopric, thus preserving the delicate balance of power between Capetians, Angevins, and Blésois. Robert had by this time given up Bertha of Blois to marry the count of Anjou's relative Constance. A diminishing of Blésois authority in the religious institutions of Chartres could have further weakened the house of Blois, thus upsetting the balance that Abbo had been attempting to nurture between the three families.

The other major dispute that Abbo mediated in early 1004 was between the monks of Micy, an abbey near Orléans, and their abbot. The monks had incited the bishop of Orléans against Robert, the abbot of Micy, and attempted to engage the sympathy of the monks of Fleury in their cause. Abbo quickly put to rest any hopes that they might have of his sympathy in a letter addressed to the monks of Micy, especially Constantine, their dean, about their rebellion.[71] He began by chastising them for publicly airing their private disputes with their abbot. Abbo noted that the Fleurisian monks were little inclined to sympathy, as might be seen by their rejection of Frederick, who had some time earlier tried to incite a similar uprising at Fleury.[72] He reminded the monks of their

---

70. *GC* 8:1219–20, suggests that Abbo urged the compromise that resolved the conflict but does not cite the source for this.

71. Abbo, letter 11. The letter from the monks of Micy to those of Fleury is, unfortunately, lost.

72. This was apparently the same Frederick mentioned in Abbo's letters about Bernier of Marmoutier. Unfortunately, we have no further information about Frederick's activities at Fleury.

vows of obedience, and particularly of their duty to try to correct problems privately before making them public. Above all, he stressed the importance of following proper channels for charging and deposing an abbot. Monks were no more competent to judge their abbots than sheep were to judge their shepherd. Even if the charges against Robert were true, Abbo argued, the monks could not on their own authority have him removed from office. On a theoretical level, Abbo's arguments were of a piece with his earlier writings on the importance of respecting the authority of the abbot and of following proper procedure in the accusation, trial, and deposition of churchmen.

The situation at Micy, however, also had strong political overtones. Robert was abbot not only of Micy but also of Saint-Florent of Saumur, by the appointment of the count of Blois, and was a strong supporter of the Blésois and the Capetians against Angevin interests.[73] King Robert's selection of the abbot of Saint-Florent as abbot of Micy in about 997 was an astute political move in terms of uniting Capetian and Blésois interests, but one unpopular with the brothers of Micy. Constantine, Gerbert's correspondent and a former monk of Fleury, had temporarily governed Micy immediately prior to Abbot Robert's appointment and was apparently popular with the monks. To add to the new abbot's unpopularity, evidence exists that he had diverted some of the wealth of Micy to Saint-Florent. When King Robert renounced his marriage to Bertha of Blois, probably early in 1003, in favor of Constance of Arles, who was the cousin of Fulk Nerra, count of Anjou, the political dynamics changed drastically, and the monks of Micy were able to mount an attack on Abbot Robert's authority.[74]

Abbo addressed both the canonical and political dimensions of the affair. Although he wrote with remarkable restraint and

---

73. Bernard S. Bachrach, "Robert de Blois, Abbot of Saint-Florent de Saumur and Saint-Mesmin de Micy (985–1011): A Study in Small Power Politics," *Revue bénédictine* 88 (1978): 126, 132–33.
74. Ibid., 132–34.

even a hint of affection to the monks of Micy, it was clear that their arguments would not sway him. On the question of canonical deposition of an abbot, there was no room for compromise. As in the case of Magenard of Saint-Père, Bernier of Marmoutier, and Arnulf of Reims, duly appointed Church officials, regardless of their qualifications and personal morality, had the right to a fair hearing before a competent judge before they could be deposed. Political expediency was never a just cause for deposition. Behind these concerns lay equally important political considerations. Abbo had devoted his career as abbot to establishing the political stability necessary for monasteries to flourish. Without the balance of power between the Angevins and the Blésois, Abbo feared that the violence and instability of the first years of his abbacy would return. To allow Robert's removal from Micy would weaken the Blésois while strengthening the Angevins, just when the Blésois, because of Bertha's divorce from King Robert, were most vulnerable. Though Abbo undoubtedly favored the end of the king's incestuous marriage to Bertha, he was not prepared to jeopardize peace in the Loire valley now that King Robert was allied by marriage with the count of Anjou. Given the propensity of the leading families of the realm to change alliances and invade each other's territories, monastic stability demanded an abbot independent of all parties or at least (since true independence was unlikely) minimally acceptable to all. Abbo's appeal was successful; Abbot Robert returned to govern Micy until his death in 1011.[75]

Abbo's external political activities should not be permitted to overshadow his accomplishments within Fleury. He continued to pursue his own studies at Fleury, often as a release from his political concerns but also in pursuit of his ideal society in which monks studied and prayed in peace for the benefit of all Christians. Many of the monks at Fleury during his abbacy had studied

---

75. *GC* (facsimile: Paris, 1531), 8:1531; Head, *Hagiography*, 223–27. Bachrach, "Robert de Blois," 123.

under him when he had been a teacher in the monastic school. He probably continued to instruct them, though in a limited fashion, after becoming abbot, and he certainly encouraged the efforts of Fleury's new teachers. For his own part, he continued to make his own works, especially his poetry, public at irregular intervals. Finally, he did not neglect the physical fabric of Fleury, the resting place of St. Benedict and the home of many monks.

Abbo continued to correspond with his former pupils long after they had left Fleury. Hervé, a canon and later treasurer of Saint-Martin of Tours, for example, received a letter from Abbo in response to a request for assistance in combating the claims of the archbishop of Tours against the house of canons.[76] Abbo's most extensively documented correspondence, however, is with Bernard of Beaulieu, a former pupil who had left Fleury to become abbot first of Solignac and then of Beaulieu-sur-Dordogne as well, probably in about 980.[77] Twice after leaving Fleury, Bernard faced serious moral dilemmas in which he sought the advice of his former teacher and fellow abbot. In 989 the count of Toulouse, William Tailleferre, offered to sell him the bishopric of Cahors. Though tempted by this offer, Bernard first wrote to Abbo, who reminded him that the goods of the Church could not be bought and sold like temporal property, with the result that Bernard refused the offer.[78]

Several years later, in about 995, Bernard once again turned to his old teacher for advice. He had wished to go on a pilgrimage to Jerusalem, but he found that affairs in his monastery could not be neglected for an extended period of time and so decided to go no farther than the Gargano Massif in Italy, the site of Monte Sant'Angelo, where the archangel Michael was reported to have appeared to some shepherds. Bernard visited his old school at

---

76. Abbo, letter 5.
77. Cousin, *Abbon de Fleury-sur-Loire*, 100n28, placed Bernard's departure from Fleury during the lifetime of Abbot Richard, who died in 978 or 979. *GC* 2 (1873), col. 569, placed his accession as abbot of Solignac in about 983. The main source for Bernard's correspondence with Abbo and his stay at Fleury is Aimoinus, *VsA*, c. 10.
78. This letter survives in fragmentary form in Aimoinus, *VsA*, c. 10.

Fleury before setting out on his journey and took several monks from Fleury with him. They had not been gone many days, however, when one of them returned, out of breath and barely able to talk because of his haste. One of Bernard's companions had died on the road, and Bernard himself was ill and feverish. The problems on the road had brought Bernard to a personal crisis. He sought Abbo's advice on whether he should give up his abbacy entirely so that he could continue on his pilgrimage unhindered, or whether he should return immediately to his abbey, where wars and factions were likely to erupt in his absence.[79] After expressing sympathy for Bernard's situation and concern for his health, Abbo began a serious consideration of the biblical and legal precedents for keeping one's vow and for abdicating one's position as a spiritual leader. As a good teacher, however, Abbo was compelled to point out that the situation could not be resolved easily. He cited an example from Martianus Capella that indicated that often the choice was not between good and evil but between conflicting goods.[80] In the end, Abbo refused to make the difficult decision for him but assured Bernard that whatever decision he made would be a good one, so long as he consulted his ability and the needs of his soul and the souls of his monks.[81]

Two important biographical works were written at Fleury under Abbo's successor, both authored by monks who had lived at Fleury during his abbacy. Helgaud of Fleury wrote the *Epitoma vitae Rotberti Pii* in honor of King Robert, and André of Fleury wrote the *Vita Gauzlini*, in which he commemorated the accomplishments of Gauzlin, who had become abbot of Fleury on the death of Abbo in 1004.[82] These two works, along with Aimoinus's *Vita sancti Abbonis*, bear witness to the extreme fruitfulness of biographical writing at Fleury in the late tenth and early eleventh centuries. Helgaud's work, in particular, with its emphasis on the

79. Ibid.
80. Quoted in ibid. Abbo did not cite Martianus Capella by name, but the source is identified by Mostert, *Political Theology*, 70.
81. Aimoinus, *VsA*, c. 10.
82. Helgaud, *Vie de Robert le Pieux;* André, *Vie de Gauzlin.*

sanctity of the king, carries on Abbo's ideas about the close relationship between ecclesiastical and secular concerns in the ideal Christian state. Not surprisingly, both of these works, especially the *Vita Gauzlini*, by and about contemporaries of Abbo, contain important information about life at Fleury during his abbacy and that of his successor.

André of Fleury began his life of Gauzlin with a list of scholars who worked at Fleury "in that time."[83] André implied that the luminaries of Fleury had flourished during Gauzlin's abbacy, but several of them did their most important work during Abbo's lifetime. Constantine, for example, had actually left Fleury to become abbot of Micy shortly after Abbo's accession as abbot.[84] Likewise, although Aimoinus wrote both the *Vita sancti Abbonis* and his contribution to the *Miracula s. Benedicti* at Gauzlin's request, he lived only a few years into Gauzlin's abbacy and had spent most of his monastic career under Abbo.[85] André's inclusion of monks who had passed their careers almost entirely under Abbo's rule—or in the case of Constantine under the rule of Abbo's predecessors and never under Gauzlin—suggests that his catalog of Fleurisian scholars is most reliable as a measure of the continuing intellectual tradition of Fleury from before Abbo's time to well after his death. When viewed in this light, it is an important index of how scholarly traditions fared under Abbo and gives a particularly clear picture of the sort of intellectuals with which he surrounded himself as a teacher and as an abbot.

Of the monks mentioned by André, Constantine is probably the most well known. He already had a reputation as a serious scholar when Abbo became abbot of Fleury, and he carried

83. André, *Vie de Gauzlin*, bk. 1, c. 1: "ea tempestate."
84. Ibid., bk. 1, c. 2h. Elsewhere, Bautier and Labory dated Constantine's departure to Micy to probably 988 but certainly before 995 (introduction to Helgaud, *Vie de Robert le Pieux*, 23n4). See also Warren, "Constantine."
85. André, *Vie de Gauzlin*, bk. 1, c. 2a. See Aimoinus, *VsA* and *MsB*. Aimoinus became a monk at Fleury under abbot Amalbert (978–985) and died in about 1005. For more on Aimoinus, see A. Courty, "Un compatriote méconnu: Aimoinus, moine fleurisien, hagiographe et historien des Xe et XIe siècles," *Revue historique et archéologique de Libournais* 23 (1955): 87–96.

Monastic Politics 221

on a lively correspondence with Gerbert of Aurillac, his former teacher.[86] While a monk of Fleury, Constantine had also studied music. Perhaps due to conflict with the monastery, he left Fleury shortly after Abbo's election to become the abbot of Saint-Mesmin of Micy, near Orléans. Constantine later left Micy to become abbot of Nouaillé, again probably for political reasons.[87] Some have argued that Constantine left Fleury because of Abbo's election—either because he had hoped for the abbacy himself or had disapproved of the choice of Abbo.[88] The evidence for personal rivalry or enmity between the two men is circumstantial, resting, as it does, largely on Constantine's departure almost immediately upon Abbo's election. It may be significant, however, that a musical setting that Constantine had written at Fleury was not actually performed until Gauzlin's abbacy.[89]

André, in his *Vita Gauzlini*, mentioned many other monks who may have been at Fleury under Abbo's abbacy. Gauzlin himself had almost certainly been a monk at Fleury before he succeeded Abbo in 1004. According to Adhemar of Chabannes, Gauzlin was an illegitimate half brother of King Robert who had been raised at Fleury.[90] André, however, noted only that Gauzlin came from one of the most illustrious families of Gaul and said nothing at all about his upbringing or earlier career.[91] Whether raised

86. Lattin contains several letters not included in Weigle.
87. Head, *Hagiography*, 217. See also Bachrach, "Robert de Blois."
88. Warren, "Constantine," 287, saw Abbo as a patristic thinker who had little patience with Constantine's more classically and scientifically oriented studies. Head, *Hagiography*, 217, suggested that Constantine left Fleury because his own aspirations to be abbot had been thwarted.
89. André, *Vie de Gauzlin*, bk. 1, c. 2h. Warren, "Constantine," 288, saw this as evidence of repression of Constantine's work under Abbo.
90. Adémar, *Chronique*, bk. 3, c. 39 (p. 161).
91. André, *Vie de Gauzlin*, bk. 1, c. 1 (32–33). Bautier and Labory, introduction to Helgaud, *Vie de Robert le Pieux*, 25, noted with skepticism that Adhemar is the sole source for Gauzlin's relationship with Robert (which Helgaud never mentioned), but did not question Adhemar's evidence of Gauzlin's upbringing (for which Adhemar is again the sole source). This is not an appropriate forum for discussing Gauzlin's relationship with the Capetian dynasty. Nevertheless, it is interesting to note that Robert, Hugh Capet's legitimate son and heir, had been educated not at Fleury but at episcopal schools (Pfister, *Robert le Pieux*, 13).

at Fleury or not, Gauzlin must surely have been a monk there by late 1004 and, given his later support of scholarly pursuits at Fleury, had probably enriched intellectual life there in some fashion during Abbo's abbacy. André also mentioned Aimoinus, Abbo's biographer, as one of the leading scholars of Fleury, famous not only for the *Vita sancti Abbonis* but also for a work on the history of the Franks, two additional books of miracles of St. Benedict, and a now-lost history of the abbots of Fleury.[92] Since Aimoinus probably did not live for more than four or five years into Gauzlin's abbacy, most of these works must have been begun during Abbo's abbacy.[93] Two other monks were Gerald and Vitalis, who were probably the recipients of two letters of Abbo's on astronomy.[94] Other monks mentioned in the *Vita Gauzlini* included Arnulf, Oddo, Isembardus, and Hisembertus.[95] Although all of these monks were not necessarily at Fleury in Abbo's day, they represent the continuing scholarly traditions under Gauzlin that would not have been possible without the foundations laid by Abbo.

Abbo's own accomplishments are often lost in the long catalog of literary and scholarly attainments at Fleury, but they were considerable even after he became abbot. Despite the cares of abbacy, he continued his work on astronomy and the calendar as well as composing poetry and answering the rather mundane questions posed by curious monks at Fleury and elsewhere. Aimoinus noted that from the beginning of his abbacy, Abbo had insisted on study among his monks as a safeguard against vices, and for his own part continued his studies even after becoming abbot.[96] Abbo's facility

---

92. André, *Vie de Gauzlin*, bk. 1, c. 2a–b (32–35).
93. Le Stum, "L'*Historia Francorum*," 89, placed Aimoinus's death "après 1008." A somewhat earlier scholar suggested a date of about 1010; see Courty, "Un compatriote méconnu," 95. Both of these suggestions appear to be based on the evidence of Aimoinus's writings, whose internal references indicate a date *post quem*, while his cessation of activity suggests that he died within a few years of his last work.
94. André, *Vie de Gauzlin*, bk. 1, c. 2d–e (34–37); see Bautier and Labory's excellent comments on these two monks in their editorial notes to this work (35n6, 35–36n7). Abbo's letters are preserved in Paris BN n.a. lat. 469, ff. 136r–140r.
95. André, *Vie de Gauzlin*, bk. 1, cc. 2b, 2c, 2f, 2g.
96. Aimoinus, *VsA*, c. 7.

at composing polemical texts had served a very practical purpose in responding to the challenges raised by the trial of Arnulf of Reims, the riot at Saint-Denis, threats to the papacy, and dissension within the monasteries of Tours. His surviving works, however, suggest that his interests were much broader than mere promotion of his political agenda. The complexity and subtlety of his poetic and scientific works reveal a man who truly sought an escape from the cares of the world in his studies.

One of the most telling instances of Abbo's continuing commitment to intellectual inquiry is his letter to Odilo of Cluny (994–1049).[97] The letter is not dated but clearly was written after a visit to Cluny. Abbo may have spent time at Cluny on his way to or from Rome, or possibly he paid a visit following the funeral of Odilo's predecessor, Maiolus of Cluny, at Souvigny (near Moulins) in 994. Whatever the occasion of the visit, Abbo had clearly engaged in a serious scholarly discussion with some of the younger monks. Several monks of Cluny had asked Abbo to explain the use of the canon tables that grace so many medieval pandects and gospel books. Time had not permitted Abbo to give them a full or satisfactory answer during his visit. Nevertheless, Abbo kept their questions in mind and soon after his return to Fleury wrote a letter to their abbot, Odilo, to clarify his meaning. After rehearsing his frequent and sincere lament that he was not often enough able to escape from his cares to the refuge of spiritual philosophy, Abbo carefully explained for the benefit of his young acquaintances how one could use the canon tables to find parallel passages in the three synoptic Gospels, Matthew, Mark, and Luke, giving a series of detailed examples. This letter clearly expressed Abbo's love not only of learning but of teaching and his willingness to take time from his busy life to clarify a simple but important technical point for eager students.

In a very different vein was his letter to someone identified only as "G," possibly Gauzbert of Saint-Julien of Tours.[98] Abbo's

97. Abbo, letter 7.
98. Abbo, letter 14. For the identification of "G," see Cousin, *Abbon de Fleury-sur-*

correspondent was certainly a churchman, probably a monk or abbot, someone whom Abbo could address as "most dear brother." Abbo began this letter by commiserating with his correspondent on the problems that beset him, for he had acquired "as enemies those who ought to have been his friends."[99] Specifically, he complained that people who claimed to be Christians had carried off the goods of the Church. If "G" was indeed Gauzbert, many incidents in Tours, whose religious houses suffered greatly from the Angevin-Blésois rivalry, could have inspired Abbo to write. Whoever "G" might have been, he was clearly in a difficult political situation, and Abbo's letter to him is a small treatise on the Church and the clergy. After sympathizing with "G" on his difficulties, Abbo provided him with a detailed discussion of the alienation of Church property, specifically monastic rights, before concluding with an equally detailed discussion of the importance of celibacy and moral behavior in the clergy. This lengthy letter touched on nearly all of the major concerns of Abbo's career, beginning with the nature of Church possessions. He specifically discussed the belief that kings or bishops could possess the property of the Church, when in fact, he argued, only Christ could possess the goods of the Church. Likewise, he reiterated his arguments, made in the context of the Council of Saint-Denis, on the proper dispersal of tithes. Within this context Abbo consistently reiterated

---

Loire, 156n87; Jean-François Lemarignier, "L'exemption monastique et les origines de la réforme grégorienne," in *A Cluny: Congrès scientifique, fêtes et cérémonies liturgique en honneur des saints abbés Odon et Odilon*, 9–11 July 1949 (Dijon: Bernigaud et Privat, 1950), 288–334, 309–10; and Mostert, *Political Theology*, 63. Cousin prefers Gauzbert of Saint-Julien; Lemarignier suggests Gauzlin, who succeeded Abbo as abbot of Fleury; and Mostert opts for Gauzbert. Lemarignier's argument in favor of Gauzlin relies on Abbo's use of the phrases "liber huius *nostri* monasterii" and "*nostrae* utilitates" (emphasis added) as evidence that Abbo was writing to a monk of Fleury. It seems more likely that by *nostri* and *nostrae* he was referring to himself and the other monks of Fleury, not necessarily to himself and his correspondent. For a detailed treatment of this letter, see Lemarignier, "L'exemption monastique," 309–10, which puts Abbo's works in the context of monastic exemption and as a prelude to the Gregorian reforms of the later eleventh century, and Mostert, *Political Theology*, 63–64, which disputes Lemarignier's contention that letter 14 was itself Abbo's dossier, which he used to justify the extraordinary privileges he had sought from the pope on his second journey to Rome.

99. Abbo, letter 14: "inimicos sustines quos amicos habere debueras."

Monastic Politics 225

the major contentions that he had made in defense of monastic property in his *Apologeticus* and his *Collectio canonum* as well as in his testimony at Church councils and other letters. As in his other works, he relied heavily on the letters of Gregory the Great to support his claims for monastic privileges and monastic exemptions.[100] Above all, Church property and tithes could not be arbitrarily alienated by officials either of the laity or of clergy.

At this point, Abbo turned from the property of the Church to the clergy. As he had in his *Apologeticus*, he emphasized the central role of chastity in the moral hierarchy of Christian society. He continued to quote extensively from the works of Gregory the Great. Abbo clearly saw the issues of monastic liberties and chastity as closely related. In his *Apologeticus*, he had supported his claims for monastic exemption by formulating a view of the world in which monks, because of their celibacy and renunciation of the world, occupied the highest position in the moral hierarchy of Christian society.[101] In this letter, Abbo once again made a connection between monastic exemption and chastity. He went further, however, and advocated chastity for all churchmen, not just the regular clergy, from bishops down to parish priests. Clerical celibacy had been a major feature of theological writing throughout the early Middle Ages, though without much effect on actual clerical practice.[102] The canonists of the tenth century, however, seem to have paid scant attention to questions of sex or marriage.[103] Nevertheless, the rise of reformed monasticism at the

100. For Abbo's use of Gregory the Great, see Lemarignier, "L'exemption monastique," 304–13.
101. See Duby, *Three Orders*; Le Goff, *Time, Work, and Culture*, 53–57; Mostert, *Political Theology*.
102. James A. Brundage, *Law, Sex, and Christian Society in Medieval Europe* (Chicago: University of Chicago Press, 1987), 150. For an analysis of the role of attitudes toward women in the early medieval discussion of clerical celibacy, see Suzanne Fonay Wemple, *Women in Frankish Society: Marriage and the Cloister, 500–900* (Philadelphia: University of Pennsylvania Press, 1985), 129–36.
103. Brundage, *Law*, 172, singles out Regino of Prüm, writing in about 906, as the only tenth-century canonist to treat questions of sex. He mentions Abbo's *Collectio canonum* as an example of a work that said little or nothing on the topic, but he is apparently unaware of Abbo's treatment of celibacy in his letter to "G."

beginning of the century appears to have played a major role in the insistence on celibacy among the secular as well as the regular clergy.[104] Abbo's purpose in this second major section of his letter was clearly to provide his correspondent with a moral basis for arguing for monastic rights.

Still further examples of Abbo's intellectual vigor, despite political and administrative distractions, are his works of acrostic poetry. The most notable of these was his poem to the German emperor Otto III described above. Although this poem had a decidedly political purpose—to persuade Otto to provide the material and military support necessary to ensure the independence of the papacy—the work is also a measure of Abbo's familiarity with various poetic forms and their historical context. His poems imitated the style of the poet Porfyrius, who had written poems in honor of Constantine and whose works had inspired several poets of the Carolingian renaissance, including Theodulf of Orléans. Abbo's model, Publilius Optatianus Porfyrius, had been a senator in the fourth century whom, for reasons unknown, the emperor Constantine had exiled. To regain the emperor's favor, he had composed a series of thirty-one remarkable poems. By controlling the number of letters in a line, choosing his words carefully, and highlighting certain letters in color, he made his poems into a visual display in which the highlighted letters could be read separately to spell out words and phrases relating to the theme of the poem while at the same time creating a picture from the colored letters. The most elaborate of these is probably Carmen 19, in which the highlighted letters outline a ship, complete with oars and a mast in the shape of a Chi-Rho symbol, and are themselves a short poem on sailing, with the Latin letters of the square poem doubling as Greek letters in the ship-shaped poem.[105] Several of his poems incorporate the Chi-Rho, which was an important aspect of Christian-imperial propaganda in Constantine's day and later.[106]

---

104. Ibid., 174.
105. Porfyrius, *Carmina,* no. 19, pp. 72–75.
106. Ibid., nos. 8, 14, and 24, pp. 32–36, 57–60, and 93–96.

Monastic Politics 227

Porfyrius found few imitators in succeeding centuries, though interest in his poems never completely died out. The surviving manuscripts of his poems range in date from the ninth to the seventeenth centuries, while each century since the sixteenth has produced at least a partial edition of his work.[107] Several scholars of the early Middle Ages, including Ennodius, Fortunatus, and Theodulf of Orléans, admired his poems enough to imitate them.[108] Modern literary critics have not, however, been so respectful of Porfyrius's accomplishments. In discussing Porfyrius, F. J. E. Raby commented that the "corruption of triviality had eaten deeply into poetry," categorizing the poems as "ridiculous verses" and "the triumph of the poet's futility."[109] William Stubbs, commenting on one of Abbo's earlier efforts at Porfyrian poetry, was only slightly kinder, describing a poem to Archbishop Dunstan of Canterbury as "[a] curious specimen of misdirected ingenuity."[110] W. Levitan has more recently provided a considerably less contemptuous reading of Porfyrius's poetry, though even he admitted, "Frankly, the poems make entirely unremarkable, even banal, reading.... But it is not *reading*, as the word is commonly understood, that the poems invite; rather *wonder*, to say the least, at the appalling genius responsible for them."[111]

What most modern commentators fail to appreciate, however, is not only the enormous facility with language required to execute the poems but the role of the poetic form as a vehicle for propaganda. By choosing to write poetry in this style Abbo was connecting himself with the world of past poets. Constantine had become the embodiment of the ideal Christian ruler. To imitate the poems of Porfyrius was to tie oneself to the first Christian

---

107. Polara, introduction to Porfyrius, *Carmina*, xxxv–xxxvi.
108. F. J. E. Raby, *A History of Secular Latin Poetry in the Middle Ages*, 2nd ed. (Oxford: Clarendon, 1957), 1:45–46; Peter Godman, *Poetry of the Carolingian Renaissance* (London: Duckworth, 1985), 19–20.
109. Raby, *Poetry*, 1:45.
110. Stubbs, *Memorials of St. Dunstan*, 410n1.
111. W. Levitan, "Dancing at the End of the Rope: Optatian Porfyry and the Field of Roman Verse," *Transactions of the American Philological Association* 115 (1985): 246.

emperor and to remind one's readers of the strong ties that had united Church and State in Constantine's day. By the tenth century, Abbo's imitation of Porfyrius recalled not only Constantine's world but also the world of the Carolingian renaissance, and particularly of Theodulf of Orléans, whose association with Fleury and its environs was very much a part of the living sense of history in the Loire valley. A Latin inscription over the south entrance to the church of Germigny-dès-Prés commemorated Theodulf's role in building it and is still a conspicuous feature of the present church, which is a fairly faithful nineteenth-century reconstruction of the Carolingian building.[112] Evidence suggests as well that the well-endowed library of Fleury probably owned at least one copy of the poems of Porfyrius.[113] The linguistic virtuosity necessary to compose such poems is itself a testimony to the flourishing of Latin learning in the monasteries: the poems not only contained elegant figures, they also obeyed rules of meter. Finally, production of the poems can be read as a sort of conspicuous consumption—apart from the investment of time in composing them, they required a substantial investment in labor on the part of highly skilled scribes. As Levitan said of the work of Porfyrius: "As impressive as the poems are as finished products, they are irresistibly more impressive as activities. How much time, how much intellectual labor, how many discarded versions, how much paper [sic], how much ink has been so conspicuously consumed for this gigantic enterprise? and finally, to what purpose and under what strange compulsion?"[114] By any of these measures, the poems of both Abbo and Porfyrius were worthy gifts for an emperor.

Abbo's poem to Otto III was not his first attempt at Porfyrian poetry. His earliest surviving acrostics consist of a series of

112. For a description of the church and its reconstruction, see Jules Banchereau, *L'église de Saint-Benoît-sur-Loire et Germigny-des-Prés* (Paris: Henri Laurens, 1947), 83, 88. Theodulf had also been Fleury's abbot (Head, *Hagiography*, 30n).
113. Berne, Burgerbibliothek 207, a ninth-century manuscript containing some works of Porfyrius, was almost certainly written at Fleury. See Polara, introduction to Porfyrius, *Carmina*, xxxv; Mostert, *Library of Fleury*, BF110 63.
114. Levitan, "Optatian Porfyry," 266.

Monastic Politics 229

three poems to Dunstan, the archbishop of Canterbury, probably written during or shortly after Abbo's stay in England. These poems follow the format of some of Porfyrius's less complicated endeavors. The first, like his poem to Otto, contains the form of a cross within a square, in which the sides of the square and the bars of the cross spell out a greeting to Dunstan. Of all of his acrostic poems this most exactly parallels the form and meter of Porfyrius's Carmen 2, including a grid of thirty-five characters across and thirty-five down, as well as the exact placement of the highlighted message within that grid.[115] The second of these is simpler still, with the first, middle, and last letters of each line spelling out the same phrase.[116] Abbo's poem to Otto follows the pattern of the first of his poems to Dunstan, but with added words reading down within each square. All three poems are testament to Abbo's continuing love of Latin literature and his devotion to writing, despite the enormous demands on his time from his official duties as premier abbot of Gaul.

If Abbo's Porfyrian poems illuminate the high level of literary achievement at Fleury, his work on computus, astronomy, and syllogisms reflects the monastery's high level of scientific achievement. He probably completed much of his work on astronomy and computus before becoming abbot, and modern commentators have dated his most important works to that early period in his life.[117] Aimoinus, however, made clear that Abbo continued

---

115. Gwara, "Three Acrostic Poems," 209.
116. Stubbs, *Memorials of St. Dunstan,* 410–11. The first poem, as well as Abbo's poem to Otto III, follows essentially the pattern of poems nos. 2 and 11 (pp. 8–11 and 46–49 in Polara's edition). It should, perhaps, be noted that although Abbo's poetry is written in proper hexameters, it does not, at first glance, re-create Porfyrius's poetic scheme; the lines vary in length and the highlighted letter in each line is not always in the exact middle of the line. Gwara's edition of his poem to Otto III, however, has restored the suspensions and abbreviations necessary for the poem to appear as a square in the manuscript ("Three Acrostic Poems," 227).
117. Cousin, *Abbon de Fleury-sur-Loire,* 215–17 (appendices on chronology), placed all of Abbo's scientific work, except for a revision of paschal tables and his two letters to Gerald and Vitalis, before 987; for his discussion of specific works, see 80–90. Cousin is undoubtedly basing his argument on *VsA,* c. 3, in which Aimoinus followed a description of Abbo's early education with a list of his major works.

his studies and writing even while abbot, often as an escape from the worldly cares of his office: "He hardly ever let pass any time when he did not read, write, or dictate."[118] Aimoinus went on to note that Abbo turned from astronomy and computus to scriptural and patristic studies shortly after becoming abbot, but later mentioned his revised table of dates as the most noteworthy of Abbo's nonscriptural writings as abbot.[119] Toward the end of his life, in 1003 and 1004, Abbo wrote two letters to monks of Fleury, Gerald and Vitalis, concerning the Dionysian era, a continuation of his long-standing interest in questions of time and dates, probably inspired by the need to refute apocalyptic movements of his day.[120] Although it has been said that "[a]ll who have studied the astronomical treatises of Abbo agree that they are highly derivative,"[121] Abbo's scientific works do, in fact, bear his individual stamp. He consistently provided his students with concrete examples of how to apply his general theories as well as graphic presentations of the material.[122] The abbot's continued work in these areas could not have been possible without both his own willingness to pursue his studies in his spare time and the resources of the library of Fleury.

Abbo's scholarly and artistic works, whether in the form of letters, poems, or treatises, though very different in purpose, provide insight into the abbot's continuing commitment to intellectual endeavors, both as an escape from the political challenges of his day and as a tool in fighting the forces that threatened his goals of monastic exemption and papal primacy. These works furthermore demonstrate the extensive resources of the library of Fleury, on which Abbo drew for inspiration, models, and authori-

118. Aimoinus, *V&A*, c. 7: "nullum pene intermitebat tempus, quin legeret, scriberet, dictaretve."
119. Ibid., c. 13.
120. Abbo, "Oeuvres inédits," 154–58.
121. Abbo, "Two Astronomical Tractates," 115.
122. See Wallis, "Abbo of Fleury," on Abbo's computistical manuscripts. Lutz, *Schoolmasters of the Tenth Century*, noted that tenth-century teachers, including Abbo and his student Byrhtferth, frequently composed their own textbooks (5–10) and made extensive use of diagrams (153).

tative quotations. Abbo's literary and scientific endeavors established him (and hence his monastery) as a leader in the intellectual community of northwestern Europe. Quite apart from any personal satisfaction or specific political advantage to be gained from such work, Abbo and Fleury needed this intellectual output to maintain prestige, authority, and influence among the intellectual and political elites of his day.

Upon his return from his second journey to Rome, Abbo had become one of the most important churchmen in the Capetian realm and did not hesitate to employ his newfound power. He consistently used his status and influence to strengthen monasticism throughout the region. He did this not only by careful attention to internal problems of monastic governance but by paying close heed to the delicate political balance between the major ruling families of western Francia: the Capetians, the Blésois, and the Angevins. Within the limited peace that he achieved by these means, Fleury flourished as a center of learning. The prosperity of Fleury must have been particularly dear to him, as he continued to seize whatever spare moments he could for pursuit of his own studies. For a few brief years, he came close to fulfilling the role that he had worked so hard to achieve, as the leader of the monastic community in a peaceful Christian kingdom.

8

THE MAKING OF A MARTYR

DURING THE LAST MONTHS of his life Abbo turned from outside concerns to the problems of monastic discipline at one of Fleury's dependent houses, the priory of La Réole in Gascony. Such challenges to the authority of the abbot of a reforming monastery were common in the tenth century, but the case of La Réole seems to have been particularly severe. Abbo's predecessors had repeatedly attempted to resolve problems at the Gascon priory, but the monks of La Réole remained recalcitrant. Although Abbo appears to have allowed matters to rest at La Réole in the early years of his abbacy, he was compelled to visit the priory personally twice in the last year of his life. In the end, he gave his life trying to bring La Réole into proper monastic practice.

The priory of La Réole lay on the Garonne River in the borderlands between Gascony and the land of the Franks. The linguistic, legal, and cultural distinctions between these two regions could hardly have been greater. Linguistic evidence even today draws a clear boundary between the characteristically Gascon pronunciations of the southwest and the French dialects to the north and east. These are not minor differences between regional dialects, however. These differences are so extreme as to indi-

The Making of a Martyr 233

cate instead a separate language.¹ The Gascons also had distinctive legal institutions. Paul Ourliac's work on medieval French legal customs indicates that, although the entire south of France has been portrayed as the domain of Roman law, the southwest of France possessed a distinctive tradition of customary law, different both from that of the north and from the legal traditions of the southeast.² Elsewhere he proposed that differences in legal traditions in the southwest roughly corresponded with linguistic boundaries.³ This region was isolated politically as well. The nobility of the region had a reputation for being independent and unwilling to submit to central authority in either secular or religious matters.⁴ La Réole was not only isolated by virtue of its Gascon character, it was out of the way even by Gascon standards. In an innovative study of centrality in southwestern France, Charles Higounet has applied Christaller's central-place theory to the villages and markets of Gascony. This theory allows geographers to describe and explain the disparity in size and division of services among different towns and cities in the same region. Each central place serves an outlying hinterland, with the larger centers including the smaller centers within their hinterland. Higounet's application of this theory suggests that even within Gascony, La Réole

---

1. Henri Guiter, "Limites linguistiques dans la région bordelaise," *Actes du 104e Congrès national des sociétés savantes,* Bordeaux, 1979, section de philologie et d'histoire, vol. 2, *Etudes sur la Gascogne* (Paris: Bibliothèque nationale, 1981), 63–66, maps 1, 2, 4 (61, 62, 65).

2. Paul Ourliac, "Les coutumes du Sud-Ouest de la France," in *Etudes d'histoire du droit médiéval* (Paris: A. et J. Picard, 1979), 3–15 [originally published in Spanish in the *Anuario de historia del derecho espanol* 23 (1953): 407–22].

3. Paul Ourliac, "Coutumes et dialectes gascons (note sur la géographie coutumière du Sud-Ouest au Moyen Age)," in *Etudes d'histoire du droit médiéval* (Paris: A. et J. Picard, 1979), 17–29 [originally published in *Droits de l'antiquité et sociologie religeuse, Mélanges . . . Henry Lévy-Bruhl* (1959), 459–70]. Ourliac specifically highlighted rules regarding descent, division of inheritance, and inheritance of women (22) and isoglosses for medial *ll* and *r*, final *ll* and *t*, disappearance of *f* and *r* in initial position, and absence of *v* (23).

4. Christian Lauranson-Rosaz, "Réseaux aristocratiques et pouvoir monastique dan le Midi aquitain du IXe au XIe siècle," in *Actes du premier colloque du CERCOR [Centre européen de recherches sur les congregations et ordres religieux],* Travaux et recherches 1 (Saint-Etienne, France: Publications Université Jean Monnet, 1991), 354–55.

was on the edge of a vacuum between the hinterlands of central places.[5] These factors must have made the administration of Fleury's distant priory even more of a challenge than was normally the case with the reform of far-off dependencies.

According to a tenth-century charter, La Réole was an early foundation, originally called Squirs, which had suffered serious damage during the Norman invasions.[6] In 977 Bishop Gumbald of Gascony, with his brother Guillaume Sanche, duke of Gascony, had given La Réole to Fleury in order to restore and reform monastic life there.[7] The language of this charter makes clear that La Réole is located in territory distinct from the northern Frankish kingdom of the Loire valley. In lamenting the destruction of monasteries by the Normans, the charter noted their devastation in both Gaul and in Aquitaine, as if the two regions were quite separate.[8]

---

5. Charles Higounet, "'Centralité', petites villes et bastides dans l'Aquitaine médiévale," in *Les petites villes du Moyen-Age à nos jours,* Colloque international CESURB, Bordeaux, 25–26 October 1985 (Paris: Centre national de la recherche scientifique, 1987), 44–45 and figure 3 (48).

6. Charles Higounet, "A propos de la fondation du prieuré de La Réole,"in *Actes du Colloque millénaire de la fondation du prieuré de La Réole,* La Réole, 11–12 November 1978 (Bordeaux: Société des bibliophiles de Guyenne, 1980), 7–11, summarizes the debate over the foundation of La Réole. According to Higounet, textual traditions linking La Réole with Charlemagne or St. Momolus are almost certainly without factual basis.

7. Prou and Vidier, *Recueil de chartes de l'abbaye de Saint-Benoît-sur-Loire,* no. 62 (977). Prou and Vidier discuss in detail objections to the authenticity of this charter but conclude that though the surviving text contains several interpolations, the basic import of the act is authentic. (Though the charter's claims that Fleury had had jurisdiction over La Réole before the destruction wrought by the Normans are usually regarded as extravagant.)

8. Aimoinus, *VsA,* c. 16, called Guillaume the duke of Gascony (*dux Vasconie*). The terminology in the medieval sources is ambiguous. *Wasconia* or *Vasconia* appear to apply both to the inhabitants of Gascony and to the Basques. Aimoinus and the author of the anonymous *Vita Ludovici Pii* both indicate that the Garonne River is the boundary between the Franks and the Wascones, but the author of the *Vita Ludovici* also refers to the inhabitants of the Pyrenees as Wascones. Linguistically and ethnically, however, though both groups were clearly distinct from the Franks to the north, they are also distinct from each other. For the anthropological and linguistic identity of the Basques, see Roger Collins, *The Basques,* Peoples of Europe, 2nd ed. (Cambridge, Mass.: Blackwell, 1990), 3–12; for the title *Dux Vasconum,* see 127–28.

The Making of a Martyr   235

In the decade between its refoundation and Abbo's abbacy, the southwestern priory had given the abbots of Fleury more than its share of trouble. Aimoinus reported that the priory had been given to Fleury in the time of Abbot Richard and had caused much trouble for Richard as well as for his successors, Amalbert and Oylbold. Abbo had regarded La Réole as so unmanageable that he refused to visit it at the beginning of his abbacy. He responded jokingly to those who urged him to do so "that he would go there when he had begun to have enough of life."[9]

When the counts of Gascony, Bernard Guillaume and Sanche Guillaume, asked him to investigate matters at La Réole, Abbo cannot have been either surprised or pleased at the need for further intervention. According to Aimoinus, Abbo did not turn his attention to La Réole on his own initiative but at the request of Counts Bernard and Sanche, the sons of Guillaume Sanche, who had granted La Réole to Fleury twenty-seven years earlier. In either 1003 or early 1004, the abbot of Fleury traveled to Gascony to consult with the counts, who appear not to have granted him sufficient authority to effect reforms.[10] The journey of 550 kilometers (or about 330 miles) would have taken nearly a month each way, and was an arduous one through inhospitable territory. When Abbo returned to the north, he left behind a small number of monks from Fleury to supervise the priory. He seems to have chosen badly. According to Aimoinus, the monks were unwilling to stay and frightened of the Gascons. The Gascons, in turn,

---

9. Aimoinus, *VsA*, c. 16: "respondebat cum ioco se illuc iturum quando eum societas coepisset vitae." Aimoinus's *VsA* is the only source for most of the details of Abbo's journeys to La Réole. Although Aimoinus wrote with the aim of glorifying Abbo and his monastery, he was also an eyewitness to most of the events described, and therefore provides an unusually clear and immediate picture of the last weeks of Abbo's life.

10. The significance of the dates is particularly important in dating the beginning of Abbo's abbacy, for which we have only Aimoinus's statement that Abbo visited La Réole after being abbot for sixteen years (Aimoinus, *VsA*, c. 16) and an entry in tyronian notes in the "Annales Floriacenses" which places the beginning of his abbacy in 987, seventeen years before his final journey to La Réole in the autumn of 1004. For an analysis of these seemingly contradictory data, see chapter 3.

took advantage of the monks' fears to harass them. As a result, the Fleurisian monks almost immediately returned home with reports of the unmanageability of the Gascons. Abbo decided that the fault lay mainly in the monks' incompetence or perhaps laziness (*inertiae*) and sent other monks in their stead.[11] In Aimoinus's account Abbo appears blameless, but subsequent events indicate that Abbo underestimated the hostility of the residents of La Réole as well as the ability of his own monks to negotiate a delicate position between competing regional and monastic ideologies.

The second group of monks did not fare much better among the Gascons. They almost immediately sent word back to Abbo that they would have to leave the priory if the abbot did not send them aid quickly. They did, however, offer hope of improvement in the situation. The counts were now willing to grant Fleury greater autonomy in the administration of La Réole. They put Viscount Amalguin at Abbo's disposal as an advocate and promised to remove, by force if necessary, anyone whom the abbot wished to have expelled from La Réole.[12] Such expulsions had been a prominent feature of reform programs at both Continental and English monasteries in the tenth century. Although in retrospect purifications by force were seen as salutary when successful, at the time monks were strong in their denunciations of attacks on monastic freedom. Abbo himself had frequently criticized episcopal and lay intervention in monasteries and reserved special hostility for unscrupulous lay advocates. If he saw any iro-

---

11. Aimoinus, *VsA*, c. 16, did not indicate whether the troublemakers were the Gascon monks of La Réole, the people of the village, or both; nor did he indicate what *injuriae* the Gascons had perpetrated on the Fleurisians.

12. Ibid. The use of technical legal terms (*mandant* and *liberiorum ... potestatem*) suggests that the counts had offered to cede these rights formally in a charter. The passage in question is therefore worth quoting in the original: "Unum hoc sibi ex sententia comitum notum fore mandant, liberiorem sibi quam primis affuturam loci potestatem si semel eos adeat et tam comitibus quamque AMALGUINO vicecomiti quem ipse eis advocatum dederat, quid ipse velit verbo tenus dedaret. Quos manere decreverit mansuros, quos exire iudicaverit memoratos polliceri principes vi se expulsuros."

ny in his acceptance of a viscount to help regulate monastic affairs, no record of it survives. Not coincidentally, the champion offered to Abbo, Viscount Amalguin, had close ties with Fleury. His wife, Rosemberga, was a relative of Aimoinus of Fleury.[13] The seriousness of the situation may be gauged by the counts' sudden decision to expand the abbot's authority at La Réole and by the proposed expulsion of recalcitrant monks by force.

In mid-October, two days after receiving this message, Abbo and a small entourage set out for La Réole. This second journey seems to have been conducted in far more haste than had been the first. Two days is scant time to prepare a suitable retinue, especially as the number and composition were important for protection on the road and in establishing authority.[14] Because of his haste Abbo may have taken a far smaller group than was usual. Aimoinus mentioned only three monks in Abbo's entourage by name, though he indicated that messengers had been sent ahead to alert the counts of Abbo's plans.[15] Aimoinus did not indicate the size of the entourage, but a total of at least sixteen monks and servants, with their horses, returned north from Gascony after Abbo's death.[16] These may, however, have included some who had previously been sent to La Réole, not necessarily members of Abbo's entourage in the fall of 1004. The abbot's desire for speed may have been dictated by the season as well as by the urgency of the situation. With winter approaching, the roads between Fleury and La Réole would not be easily traversed for much longer. If Abbo had hoped to solve the problems at La Réole and return to Fleury before Christmas and the heavy snows and rains of winter, he would have had little choice except to travel quickly and lightly. Even greater haste would have been needed to return in time for the feast of the Translation of St. Benedict on 4 December.

---

13. Ibid., c. 21.
14. Fichtenau, *Living in the Tenth Century*, 56–57.
15. Aimoinus, *VsA*, c. 17.
16. Ibid., c. 21: "verum etiam eorum servientibus atque equis, qui omnes xvi erant numero." This total includes only the injured monks and their servants.

The journey from Fleury to northern Aquitaine was a familiar one to the monks. Aimoinus did not think it necessary to describe the route taken by Abbo between Fleury and Poitiers, even though he recorded almost every stop along the road from Poitiers to La Réole in detail.[17] Abbo almost certainly traveled down the Loire valley, either by boat or along an old Roman road that ran along one bank, possibly along the same route that he had taken to Saint-Martin of Tours in the early 990s, when the followers of Bishop Arnulf of Orléans had made a murderous attack on him. This trip seems to have been relatively uneventful. Abbo and his retinue could have stayed along the way at any of the numerous monasteries of the Loire valley, possibly spending a night at Tours itself, the city whose religious houses had so interested the Fleurisian abbot in the past decade. The journey from Fleury to Poitiers, nearly 250 kilometers (about 150 miles), probably took about a week if the monks' pace in the earlier part of the journey was as rapid as in the later stages. The extremely fast rate of travel suggests that Abbo and his companions were able to exchange horses at regular intervals along the route.

Given the haste with which the Fleurisians proceeded south, one would have expected them to take the most direct route available. Patrice Cousin, however, has argued that Abbo's route through Poitiers was rather indirect. A route following Roman roads through Bourges, Argenton-sur-Creuse, Limoges, and Périgueux would, he felt, have been more efficient.[18] Although this would certainly be the quickest route in terms of total distance, the route chosen would have allowed Abbo to follow the Loire River, perhaps even traveling by boat, as far as Tours before heading south to Poitiers. Furthermore, the twelfth-century pilgrimage route from Fleury to Santiago de Campostella traveled through

---

17. Ibid., c. 17. The itinerary of Abbo's final journey occupied *VsA*, cc. 17–20. Aimoinus's interest in recording the final journey is undoubtedly due in part to his own participation. His work must also be understood, however, in light of Abbo's subsequent death at La Réole and the martyrological and hagiographical traditions, which emphasized the final suffering and death of martyrs. Furthermore, Aimoinus's work is clearly intended as a vindication of Fleury's claims for Abbo's sanctity.

18. Cousin, *Abbon de Fleury-sur-Loire*, 177.

The Making of a Martyr 239

Tours and Poitiers before turning south to Bordeaux.[19] In fact, Abbo's route through Poitiers was probably the safest and most direct, at least for the beginning of the journey, lying as it did in territory familiar to him and his monks, with lodgings and possibly changes of horses available at friendly monasteries along the way.

Cousin was not wrong, however, in noting the importance of Abbo's brief layover at Poitiers. According to Aimoinus, Abbo wished to consult Count William of Aquitaine (995–1030) about problems that Fleury's priory at Saint-Benoît-du-Sault had encountered with its lay advocate.[20] Abbo's real concern while at Poitiers may have been to discuss the political situation in the south with William. Cousin exaggerated William's powerful position in France—"next to whom his cousin, Robert II of France, cut a small figure"[21]—but William nevertheless would have been able to provide the abbot with vital information on the political situation to the south, and Abbo may have hoped to persuade the important man to use his influence in the region to ensure the successful completion of the Fleurisians' mission.

In addition to his discussions with the count on Saint-Benoît-du-Sault and the situation in Gascony, Abbo helped a relative and fellow abbot while in Poitiers. Gislebert, the abbot of Saint-Cyprien of Poitiers, had been falsely accused of several serious crimes, apparently by one of his own monks and a prostitute. According to Aimoinus, Gislebert had asked Abbo to consider the case. Abbo was not impressed with the probity of the witnesses and wrote an indignant letter on Gislebert's behalf to Odilo, the abbot of Cluny, the monastery on which Saint-Cyprien was dependent.[22] Unfortunately, Abbo's letter did not specify the charges, but clearly his concern rested on the character of the witnesses

---

19. Hubert, "Les routes du Moyen Age," 25–56, especially plate 1 (facing p. 25), and maps on 27 and 43.
20. Aimoinus, *VsA*, c. 17.
21. Cousin, *Abbon de Fleury-sur-Loire*, 177: "Robert II de France, son cousin, faisait petite figure auprès de lui." For the contrary view, see Bernard S. Bachrach, "Toward a Reappraisal of William the Great, Duke of Aquitaine (995–1030)," *Journal of Medieval History* 5 (1979): 11–21.
22. Aimoinus, *VsA*, c. 17.

and the impropriety of a monk accusing his own abbot: "Indeed where is it written that monks and priests of the Lord be condemned by the accusation of a prostitute? What monk compelled his abbot, by the authority of the Fathers, to secular judgment?"[23] As in other cases of this sort, Abbo concluded with an allusion to Pope Gregory the Great's injunction that accusers, witnesses, and judges should not be the same people.

By the time Abbo had concluded his business in Poitiers with Count William and Abbot Gislebert, five days had passed. After celebrating the feast of All Saints (1 November), which fell on a Wednesday in 1004, Abbo and his entourage departed at a brisk pace. They passed through Charroux on Friday of that week and stayed the night in the small monastery of Nanteuil, dedicated to St. Benedict. The following day they reached Angoulême. From Angoulême, the party traveled south through Aubeterre, crossed the Isle River, and spent a night at the small town of Francs, where Aimoinus's mother entertained them. She was delighted to meet the man who was at once the abbot of Fleury and her son's mentor. The next day Abbo's party crossed the Dordogne River into Gascony. They arrived in La Réole on 9 November, a Thursday, two days before the feast of St. Martin of Tours. They had traveled just over three hundred kilometers (about two hundred miles) in eight days, at a rate of nearly forty kilometers (about twenty-five miles) a day.[24]

Aimoinus clearly intended, in his description of Abbo's final journey to La Réole, to impress upon his readers a sense that Fleury's priory in Gascony was distant from Fleury geographically, culturally, and linguistically. The region around Aubeterre, for exam-

23. Abbo, letter 12: "Quo certe lectum est monachos et sacerdotes Domini damnatos esse accusatione meretricis? quis monachus auctoritate Patrum abbatem suum ad saeculare judicium compulit?"
24. Aimoinus, V&A, cc. 17–19. These calculations are based on the distances between the cities mentioned along modern roads, and on the assumption that Aimoinus recorded the dates of their departure from Poitiers and their arrival at La Réole accurately. For the latter, since he is recalling important holidays in the ecclesiastical calendar, it seems unlikely that he would be mistaken as to where and how these feast days were celebrated.

The Making of a Martyr 241

ple, was clearly unknown territory to the monks, as they found themselves on the road without a place to stay. Fortunately, the lord of the *castrum* of Aubeterre, Girald, appeared at an opportune moment and entertained them graciously.[25] The monks had not, however, entered into truly foreign and hostile territory, in Aimoinus's account, until they had crossed the Dordogne River the day after meeting Aimoinus's mother. In Aimoinus's account, they soon encountered their first indication that the place itself was hostile to the travelers from the north. While entering a boat to cross the Droth River, not long before they reached La Réole, Abbo nearly fell in and drowned but was miraculously saved from even getting his feet wet.[26]

The very site of La Réole emphasized its foreignness and perilousness. Aimoinus described at length the priory's strong defensive position. "The monastery of La Réole, dedicated to God in honor of the prince of the apostles, is located on a mountain; this mountain is itself surrounded by other mountains on three sides, the east, the north, and the west. Furthermore, it is defended on the south by the Garonne River and by a dangerous chasm of the valley. . . . The place of La Réole, because of its position, as described, is not easily exposed to being taken by the enemy, except that a small plain lies to the north of it."[27] Abbo, surveying La Réole's strong strategic location and meditating on the limited power of the French monarch in Gascony, noted laughingly that "now I am more powerful than our lord the king of the Franks, within these boundaries where no one possessing such a house fears his rule."[28] The image Aimoinus conveyed was one of a remote, lawless land, where the peaceful monks could not rely on any other protection than the strength of their walls.

25. Ibid., c. 18. 26. Ibid., c. 19.
27. Ibid., c. 20: "Monasterium Regule in honore principis apostolorum deo dicatum, in monte est positum, qui videlicet mons a tribus lateribus orientali, aquilonali, et occidentali, aliis cingitur montibus. Porro a meridie Garonna vallatur flumine, periculosaque vallis voragine. . . . Locus sane Regule, ob supradictam positionem, non facile hostium patuisset accessui nisi ab aquilone parva ei adiaceret planities."
28. Ibid.: "Homo dei conspicatus admiransque leto nobis adridens vultu infit.

Aimoinus's account underscores not only the remoteness of La Réole but the barbarity of its inhabitants, both monks and laymen, in contrast to the more civilized "Franks" from Fleury. In his initial description of the monastery, he underlined the presence of earlier generations of Franks at the site: "On the east, between this and another mountain there is a very narrow valley through which a spring flows which the natives call the Moselle. It is likewise watered, on the east, by the rapid stream of another spring whose name is the Meuse. These names are thought to have been given by the Franks who were left there by Charlemagne for the protection of the province."[29] Aimoinus went on to mention other sites of interest from the campaign of Charlemagne. Not far from La Réole lay Chasseneuille, a Carolingian royal *villa* (later a palace), where Charlemagne's wife (the mother of Louis the Pious) had stayed during Charlemagne's campaigns in Spain, and which belonged to the dukes of Aquitaine by 1028.[30] His specific reference to the campaigns of Charlemagne recalls the height of Frankish dominance in the area but also the attack on Charlemagne's baggage train in the Pyrenees by the Wascones—just as Abbo was later to be slain by treacherous Wascones on the banks of the Garonne. In Aimoinus's account of Abbo's final days, the villagers and monks of La Réole become indistinguishable from each other but differentiated from the civilized monks of Fleury by their barbaric names and customs.

Aimoinus's disdain for the language and customs of the Gas-

Potentior inquiens nunc sum domino nostro rege Francorum intra hoc fines ubi nullus eius veretur dominium, talem possidens domum." This passage has been quoted in just about every major survey of early Capetian power in the past fifty years: Lemarignier, *Gouvernement royal*, 41; Dunbabin, *France in the Making*, 177 (who calls this a "much-quoted comment"); Hallam, *Capetian France*, 94, to give just a few examples.

29. Aimoinus, *VsA*, c. 20: "Ab oriente inter ipsum et alterum montem, vallis existit per angusta per quam fons meat quem incole Mosellam nuncupant. Simili modo ab occidente alterius fontis rapido alluitur cursu, cui Mosa nomen est. Haec nomina a Francis illis inposita estimantur, qui a magno KAROLO ad tuitionem provintie ibi relicti sunt."

30. Jane Martindale, "The Kingdom of Aquitaine and the 'Dissolution of the Carolingian Fisc,'" *Francia* 11 (1983–1984), 155, 164.

cons are all the more interesting because of his own background. He was a monk of Fleury but was a native of the small town of Francs, located just under fifty kilometers (about thirty miles) from La Réole. Although Aimoinus's home was near the Dordogne River (the beginning of Wasconia), Aimoinus was very careful to note that it was only after leaving his mother's home that Abbo crossed into Wasconia.[31] The name of the town, Francs (*Ad Francos* in Latin), suggests that this was a Frankish settlement, perhaps the site of one of the garrisons left by Charlemagne after his expedition to Spain. Clearly, Aimoinus saw himself as a civilized Frank among barbarous Gascons even if at La Réole he were only a few kilometers from his hometown.

Aimoinus's perception of himself as significantly different in background from the people of La Réole is borne out by recent research into the language of the region. The boundary between characteristically Gascon pronunciations and the Occitan dialect of French runs close to the Dordogne, not far, in fact, from Aimoinus's hometown of Francs, and represents an extreme difference in language, not just a boundary between two French dialects.[32] Aimoinus's sense that the people of La Réole spoke an alien and barbarous tongue is not merely the judgment of a monk who had succeeded in the north and was disavowing his southern upbringing. Linguistically, the French of the Loire valley was probably considerably closer to Aimoinus's native tongue than Aimoinus's dialect was to that of people who lived only a few kilometers south of his hometown. His knowledge of the toponymic traces of Charlemagne's armies and the sites associated with Carolingian activities suggests that there was a strong living tradition among the southwestern Franks of differentiating themselves from their Gascon neighbors.

Abbo undoubtedly wished for some rest after arriving at La Réole. He was a heavy man who found traveling difficult and un-

31. Aimoinus, *V&A*, cc. 18–19.
32. Henri Guiter, "Limites linguistiques," maps 1 and 2 (61 and 62), and 63–66, esp. map 4 (65).

comfortable.[33] By 1004 he must have been in his late fifties or sixties, and his journey from Fleury to La Réole on horseback was one that would have taxed the strength of a younger and more athletic man. He was not to enjoy much rest at the end of this journey. The monks of Fleury quickly found themselves embroiled in a series of seemingly minor conflicts with the natives. Though their first day at La Réole passed quietly, on the evening of the second the monks of Fleury found themselves at odds with those of La Réole over the feeding of their horses. When Abbo heard of this the next day, he upbraided his party sternly: "Why do you, unarmed and among a people hostile to you, stir up trouble?"[34] He insisted that they exercise patience until the lay advocate, who was charged with enforcing their authority, arrived. His reference to arms suggests as well that he feared physical attacks, though whether from the monks or others at La Réole is not clear.

The next few days passed quietly. The feast of St. Martin of Tours (11 November) fell on Saturday that year, and Abbo celebrated a Mass in the saint's honor without incident. The next day, Sunday, after celebrating Mass yet again, he took a walk up the mountain to view the defenses of the monastery. On Monday, the advocate had not yet arrived, and Abbo found himself faced with a problem of monastic discipline. One of the monks of La Réole, named Anezan, had violated the Benedictine Rule by eating outside of the monastery without the permission of the abbot.[35] Although this may appear a minor infraction, it struck at the core of monastic life. The Rule of St. Benedict presents the ideal of a family of monks in which the monks share their fare under the guidance of the abbot—a strict but caring father, a benevolent paterfamilias. To violate the rule about eating outside the monastery was to undermine the communal life of the monastic

---

33. Aimoinus, *VsA*, c. 11.
34. Ibid., c. 19: "Cur inermes, et inter infensam sibi gentem bella cierent?" It is probably not a coincidence that one of the people killed in the riot in which Abbo died was the servant in charge of the horses (*custos equorum*).
35. Ibid., c. 20; Benedict, *RB 1980*, c. 51 (254–55).

family, introduce outside familial ties and loyalties, and weaken the authority of the abbot. Gregory the Great, in his dialog on St. Benedict, explicitly mentioned an incident in which Benedict miraculously discovered that a pair of monks had transgressed the rule about eating outside of the monastery. In Gregory's story, the monks were penitent and Benedict pardoned them.[36] The case of the Gascon Anezan, however, appears to have been more of an instance of open defiance. The monks in Gregory's story were unavoidably delayed while on a legitimate journey and tempted by a well-meant offer of hospitality. Anezan seems purposefully to have left the monastery to dine with relatives in the neighborhood. As an abbot, Abbo felt that he could not ignore the threat to his authority (despite his earlier advice of patience) and reprimanded the erring monk, who appeared to take his reprimand calmly and humbly. After this encounter, Abbo apparently felt the need of some quiet intellectual diversion, so he retired to a room in the monastery to study his computus.[37]

As Abbo pored over his tables and figures, however, the situation quickly deteriorated. Anezan may have appeared to take his punishment with equanimity, but in fact the delinquent monk had subsequently spoken with great recalcitrance to those who had been present. Aimoinus characterized Anezan as "barbarous in descent and name" even treating his name as a foreign term by not troubling to make it conform to Latin case endings.[38] Anezan's barbarous name was further emphasized by Aimoinus's reference to him later in the same chapter as a monk in name only. Anezan was true to his barbarous name but false to his monkish profession, supported by an equally barbarous and unruly populace. While Anezan was expostulating with the monks of Fleury, the women of the town raised a Gascon cry that denoted the death of a man or the beginning of an uprising. Aimoinus later discovered that the riot outside the monastery had arisen when

36. Gregory, *Dialogues*, c. 12 (20–21).
37. Aimoinus, *VsA*, c. 20.
38. Ibid.: "gente barbarus et vocabulo."

the Frankish monks and the Gascons had gotten into a squabble, the cause of which is unknown. After some initial exchanges, for which both sides bore the blame, one of the Fleurisians foolishly struck one of the Gascons with his staff. Both sides began throwing stones at each other. Anezan, according to Aimoinus, feared that he would be held responsible for the riot but did nothing to stop it. "Then that traitor, a monk in name only, spoke to those who stood around him, saying, 'Now it is being said that this outrage arose at my urging.' One of those who were present said to him, 'If you fear this, come with us to quiet these disturbances.'"[39] Aimoinus implied that the monks and people of La Réole had conspired between themselves to attack the Fleurisians. "Then the faction of evil-doers, who had inflicted injuries on those whom that holy father had sent to that place, now conspired that, once a disturbance had been created, for whatever reason, such an outrage of bloodshed might afflict his [Abbo's] companions, that neither he nor any other would dare to come against them. But it is not known for sure whether they plotted the crime of his death, except that he, who is said to have speared him [Abbo], is reported to have said in a quarrel with our people that he would consider it nothing if his lance were to stick in his belly."[40]

Aimoinus evidently found significant the coincidence of Anezan's obstinate words and the beginning of the riot. The role of women in the riot suggests that the monks had the sympathy of their compatriots in the town. There is no evidence for the exact relationship between these women and the monks. The townspeople, including the women, may merely have supported the Gascon monks, who were undoubtedly their kinsmen. On the

---

39. Ibid.: "Tum ille perfidus solo nomine monachus ad eos qui se circumstabant infit. Nunc inquiens dicetur meo monitu hoc esse ortum scandalum. Cui quidam ex his qui aderant, Si ait id metuis nobiscum ad hos sedandos progredere motus."

40. Ibid.: "Denique malignorum factio qui illis quos ipse sanctus pater ad eundem miserat locum iniurias irrogaverant in id iam conspiraverat, ut ex qualibet occasione commoto tumultu, tanta famulos ipsius, cedis contumelia afficeret quatinus nec ipse nec quilibet alter eos ulterius adire auderet. Quod vero mortis illius machinati sint dolos, non vere scitur, nisi quia is qui eum percussisse dicitur in iurgio nostris dixisse fertur pro nichilo se ducere si lancea ventrem eius transforaret."

The Making of a Martyr   247

other hand, Abbo's persistent concern with clerical and monastic celibacy makes attractive the hypothesis that some of these women, at least, may have been the wives or concubines of the monks.[41] Aimoinus's account, furthermore, implies that tensions at La Réole had a strong ethnic component. The riot itself began barbarously with the "shouting of the women, according to the custom of this people when a riot is stirred up."[42] Amoinus's image of battle-crazed barbarian women is reminiscent of the account the classical Roman historian Tacitus gives of the barbarian women cheering on their menfolk in battle. Once the riot started, Aimoinus wrote not of the monks of Fleury and those of La Réole, but of the Franks and the Gascons, and ceased to make any distinction between the Gascon monks and the Gascon villagers.

The rioters eventually made enough noise to attract the abbot's attention. When he heard the noise, Abbo left the computus that he had been dictating and hurried out of the monastery. The rioting had begun on the upper portions of the mountain, and as Abbo hurried up, a spear thrown by one of the Gascons hit him near his left shoulder and lodged between his ribs.[43] He gave no immediate sign of being injured but said, "This one is acting in earnest."[44] He then leaned on the arm of the monk William and staggered into a nearby building with Aimoinus following him. Neither Aimoinus nor the other monks realized at first how seriously Abbo had been wounded.

I see a spot of dried blood on the threshold of the house which the holy man had just entered. When I asked whence it had come, I received this response from the man of God, "It is from me," he said, "I swear to God Almighty." Immediately, my hair stood on end, and horror filled my body and made my voice hoarse. For not yet had anyone noticed that he had

---

41. Head, *Hagiography*, 253.
42. Aimoinus, *VsA*, c. 20: "clamor mulierum iuxta morem gentis illius ubi seditio oritur."
43. Ibid.: "ab uno adverse partis satellite, lancea tam valide vulneratur in levo lacerto ut interiora costarum adactum penetraret ferrum."
44. Ibid.: "Iste ait serio haec facit."

been wounded in the flesh, but we thought that only his clothes had been pierced. Therefore, I speak to him, "Where, my lord," I said, "are you wounded?" Then, when he was raising his arm so that he might lay bare the wound, suddenly from the inner recesses a wave of blood burst forth and was caught by the sleeve of his outer tunic.[45]

Within a few minutes a disagreement between the northern monks and the southerners had degenerated into a riot that left the abbot of one of the most important monasteries in northern France mortally wounded.

Despite Abbo's wounds, Aimoinus reported that the abbot remained more calm and cheerful than any of his companions. He gently mocked them for their obvious fear at his bleeding wound, asking them, "What would you do, brother, if you yourself had been wounded?"[46] Meanwhile, the disturbance outside continued unabated, so Abbo sent Aimoinus out to quell the riot. This proved to be a difficult task. The crowd surrounded the house in which Abbo lay dying, tore the door from its hinges, and entered the building. Once inside they wounded a monk named Adelard, who had been crying over Abbo's now lifeless body, and also the custodian of the horses, perhaps in retaliation for the initial dispute over stabling. Adelard died the next day, Tuesday, but the horse master lingered until the feast of St. Andrew on 30 November. When the rioters learned that they had killed the abbot himself, however, they quickly dispersed.[47]

With the death of Abbo the situation at La Réole changed

---

45. Ibid.: "Conspicio super limen domus, quam vir sanctus ingressus iam erat, partem coagulati sanguinis. Interrogansque de quo foret hoc, a dei homine responsum accepi, de me, inquit, est, testor deum [omnipotentem]. [Quia] continuo mihi [in aere] stetere come, horrorque infusus corpori [nimius] raucisonam reddidit vocem. Nondum enim quispiam animadverterat eum in carne esse vulneratum. Sed tantum indumenta estimabamus fuisse perforata. Itaque aio ad eum, qua nam in parte, inquam, tibi domino meo illatum vulnus est? Tum eo elevante brachium ut plagam detegeret repente ab intimis recessiblus unda sanguinis prorumpens manica laxioris pellicie excipitur." Words in brackets appear only in Montpellier, Faculté de médecine 68.
46. Ibid.: "Quid tu inquiens ageres [frater] si ipse vulneratus esses?" Word in brackets appears only in Montpellier, Faculté de médecine 68.
47. Ibid.

dramatically. An eerie quiet settled over the village. By the next day no women could be found in the buildings outside the monastery, undoubtedly out of fear of retribution for their actions in inciting the riot. This reinforces the idea that these women were living in the monastery and not just sympathetic villagers. The monks of Fleury, however, discovered several supporters of their own among the local nobility. A minor noble, Willelmus, son of Oriolus, had arrived at the monastery in the days before Abbo's death, returning to his home a short distance away after visiting with the abbot. He returned to La Réole immediately when he had heard of the riot and the murder of the abbot, remaining with the monks, as their protector, while they tended their wounded at La Réole.[48] Eventually, probably after the monks had departed for Fleury, Bernard, the duke of Gascony, took decisive action against Abbo's murderers. According to Adhemar of Chabannes, the perpetrators were captured by the duke and some sentenced to hang, others to burn.[49] These two punishments suggest that the malefactors were charged with different crimes. Burning, in particular, suggests a charge of heresy in addition to murder.

Despite their shock and fear, the monks paid meticulous attention to providing Abbo with a proper burial. In this Willelmus proved invaluable. The monks had been forced to leave Abbo's body in the house, just outside of the monastery, in which he had died. By the time the riot had dispersed, night had fallen and they were afraid to venture outside the confines of the priory to recover it. Willelmus sent his followers to retrieve the body so that the monks could prepare it for burial. The next question facing Abbo's mourners was where to bury him. Eventually, they decided that "because he had been slain innocently and for Truth, which is Christ, he should be placed in the church."[50] This decision, though mentioned only in passing by Aimoinus, was the first

---

48. Ibid.
49. Adémar, *Chronique,* bk. 3, c. 39.
50. Aimoinus, *VsA,* c. 20: "quia innocenter ac pro veritate que Christus est interemptus erat, in ecclesia poneretur."

step in encouraging the cult of Abbo as a saint and martyr. By interring Abbo in the church, the Fleurisians were asserting his holiness and inviting his adoration as a martyr by the faithful.[51] By this time many others from the surrounding region had arrived to meet with the abbot from the north, only to find him dead. "It cannot be told what sorrow or what groan was given out by those who had come from neighboring places to see him, when they saw dead he whom they longed to see living."[52] On Thursday, 16 November, after having honored their deceased abbot by crying and singing Psalms for two nights and a day, the monks entombed him in the crypt of the church, before the altar of St. Benedict.[53]

Once the monks had interred their abbot, they faced a long and arduous journey home, bearing the worst possible news for their brethren at Fleury. On the fourth day after Abbo's burial, the Fleurisians reached the home of Viscount Amalguin, who was to have helped Abbo expel the most recalcitrant of the monks of La Réole from the priory. The catastrophic end to Abbo's attempts at reforming La Réole must have been a cause of great embarrassment to the viscount, who can hardly have refused to aid the monks in their retreat. Amalguin's wife, Rosemberga, was a relative of Aimoinus, which would have given him an additional motive for showing hospitality to the monks. Aimoinus spoke favorably of his relative's care for the injured: "For she persuaded her husband that he should detain the injured, even if they were unwilling. Furthermore, she provided everything necessary not only for the injured, but also for their servants and horses, who were sixteen in number, total. She sought a doctor, and paid him the price for curing the ill."[54] Aimoinus, as a relative, stayed be-

---

51. For fourth-century controversies over the place of burial, see Peter Brown, *The Cult of the Saints* (Chicago: University of Chicago Press, 1981; Phoenix edition 1982), 23–49; for tenth-century beliefs about the significance of dead bodies, see Fichtenau, *Living in the Tenth Century*, 316–17.

52. Aimoinus, *VsA*, c. 20: "Referri nequit, qui luctus quive gemitus ab his qui ad eum visendum e propinquis venerant locis editus sit, cum eum quem viventem cernere concupierant mortuum conspicerent."

53. Ibid.

54. Aimoinus, *VsA*, c. 21: "Nam ipsa viro suo ut vulneratos etiam nolentes reti-

The Making of a Martyr

hind with the injured while the rest of the monks continued on to Fleury.

The return of the monks to Fleury illustrates well the manner in which news spread in the tenth century. The uninjured monks must have traveled quickly, probably at the same pace they had set on the journey south, because they arrived at Fleury shortly before the feast of the Translation of St. Benedict on 4 December, barely two weeks after leaving La Réole.[55] To reach Fleury so soon after Abbo's death, especially with a brief stop with Aimoinus's relatives, the monks must have traveled at least as rapidly on the road home as on their outward journey, precluding the likelihood that a messenger could have been sent ahead to Fleury. The news they brought dismayed the monks of Fleury.

The rest of the northern French monastic community soon learned of the great abbot's death as well; once their representatives arrived at Fleury to celebrate the Translation of St. Benedict with the Fleurisians, word would have spread quickly back to their home monasteries. This was an important feast in the monastic calendar, and the visitors to Fleury included Odilo, the abbot of Cluny. Aimoinus reported that those who arrived at Fleury to celebrate the Translation had expected to find the abbot alive and in residence: "Some of them had been called by him to negotiate certain business, others had come planning to consult him on certain matters concerning their needs."[56] Their shock and disappointment at finding that Abbo had died suddenly, and apparently senselessly, while attempting to reform La Réole, must have been great. The abbots and monks who had come to celebrate St.

---

neret suasit. Retentis autem, ipsa cuncta tribuit necessaria non solum languentibus verum etiam eorum servientibus atque equis, qui omnes xvi erant numbero. Medicum ipsa quesivit eique pro sanandis egris precium pisa prebuit."

55. Ibid.

56. Ibid.: "horum alii ab ipso ob quasdam ordinandas utilitates erant evocati, alii suarum necessitudinum certis ex causis eum consulturi advenerant." This passage implies that Abbo had intended to return to Fleury in time for the celebration. The implication is that the abbot thought that the affair at La Réole could be concluded in a few days, and that he intended his homeward journey to be just as rapid as the outbound trip.

Benedict's translation soon left to bring the news of another abbot's death to their congregations. In case any monastic community had not heard of Abbo's passing, the monks of Fleury sent out an encyclical letter to several monasteries in the region. In it they not only lamented their loss but also presented Abbo as a martyr who had died defending the faith in Gascony.[57]

[57]. "Monachorum Floriacensium epistola encyclica de caede Abbonis abbatis," in *PL* 139:417–18.

9

CONCLUSION

WHEN WE look back at Abbo of Fleury's career from a distance of over a millennium, many factors blur the clear trajectory of a life devoted to Benedictine monasticism. Intervening events have caused us to view his life as a mere precursor to later monastic reform movements and political settlements. Abbo's own life often followed a different course than he might have planned, taking him across the English Channel, into a Church council that seemed more concerned with secular politics than ecclesiastical precedent, and finally—fatally—into a monastic dispute with unfortunate ethnic overtones. Abbo's immediate heirs, the monks of Fleury, have in many ways further obscured his purpose in life. On the one hand, the *Vita* by Aimoinus celebrated Abbo's monastic virtues, but on the other hand, it downplayed the very real difficulties Abbo faced in pursuing his monastic aims early in his abbacy. Abbo's own writings, because they formed the basis of later social interpretations, have further muddied the waters.

Without neglecting Abbo's lifelong goals, however, the historian needs to consider Abbo's legacy, both intended and unintended. Abbo of Fleury played a role in almost every major intellectual and political controversy of his time. From the establishment of the Capetian dynasty to the refinement of papal prerogatives to the revival of rubricated acrostic poetry to the mathematics of Easter tables, few individuals in the tenth century pursued such a wide range of endeavor as Abbo. Despite his numerous achievements (or perhaps because of them) Abbo's overall importance has been difficult to estimate. Although a participant in numerous pivotal movements, he was always the second person to be mentioned. Gerbert of Aurillac overshadowed him in Capetian, Ottonian, and papal politics as well as in mathematical writings. Aelfric's Old English rendering of the life of St. Edmund is perhaps better known and more studied than Abbo's own earlier effort. The monastic reforms of Cluny and Gorze have received far more scholarly attention than those of Fleury. Abbo's advocacy on behalf of Pope Gregory V does not excite the attention of the Ottonians' eleventh-century efforts at papal reform. Ironically, the greatest impediment to a serious study of Abbo's career is also the greatest aid to Abbo's biographers, namely, Aimoinus's *Vita*. Were it not for Aimoinus, many of the details of Abbo's life would remain unknown. The seeming completeness of Aimoinus's narrative, however, has discouraged past biographers from attempting much more than integrating the *Vita* and Abbo's few surviving letters. Meanwhile, specialists in such incongruous fields as the history of science, Capetian dynastic history, and literary history have contented themselves with providing a narrow context for a particular work without giving thought to Abbo's output as a whole. Pierre Riché's recent biography has largely corrected this as far as his intellectual activity, but Riché elected not to pursue Abbo's political side in as much detail.[1]

Any serious study of Abbo's place in tenth-century politics must take into account the role of his memory in French politics. The establishment of Abbo's cult as a martyr was a key element in that posthumous career. Abbo's cult was important to the monks of Fleury for several reasons. The monastery of Fleury, of course, benefited in prestige from the addition of each saint from the

---

1. Riché, *Abbon de Fleury*.

ranks of its abbots and monks. The monks of Fleury had a further motive in promoting Abbo's cult in the desire to establish firmer control over La Réole. By presenting the abbot as a martyr and his murderers as equivalent to the early persecutors of the Christians, the Fleurisians justified their previous actions at La Réole and their continuing attempts to regulate monastic life there. By portraying the participants in the riot as enemies of God, the Fleurisians may have hoped to persuade the people of La Réole to treat Fleury and its representatives with more respect. The establishment of a cult of Abbo at La Réole would potentially bring economic benefit to the community from pilgrims to the village as well as providing a focus for the religious devotion of the villagers, which would tie them more closely with the parent monastery to the north. Within northern France, in addition, the promotion of the cult of Abbo could add to Fleury's prestige and to the strength of the monastic reform movement that he had so diligently supported throughout his lifetime. Finally, one cannot discount the purely religious motives of the pious monks, who wished to see their beloved abbot recognized for his holiness and bravery in the face of death.

Aimoinus used traditional classical and Christian literary formulae to make the case for Abbo's sanctity and hence to link his temporal accomplishments on behalf of Fleury with divine will. Following the pattern of classical and medieval biographies, Aimoinus devoted the opening chapters of the *Vita* to the saintly abbot's parentage, education, and early life before beginning a thematic survey of Abbo's political activities, scholarly accomplishments, and evidence of his sanctity.[2] The bulk of the *Vita*, six

---

2. Aimoinus, *VsA*, cc. 1–6; A. J. Gossage, "Plutarch," in *Latin Biography*, ed. T. A. Dorey (New York: Basic, 1967), 57; G. P. Townend, "Suetonius and His Influence," in Dorey, *Latin Biography*, 82; Régis Boyer, "An Attempt to Define the Typology of Medieval Hagiography," in *Hagiography and Medieval Literature: A Symposium*, Odense, 17–19 November 1980, ed. Hans Bekker-Nielsen, Peter Foote, Jorgen Hojgaard Jorgensen, and Tore Nyburg (Odense, Denmark: Odense University Press, 1981), 27–36, especially 33. The quintessential example of medieval biography is Einhard's *Life of Charlemagne*, which has appeared in many editions and translations, including Einhard and Not-

out of twenty-one chapters, is devoted to Abbo's passion—his last journey and martyrdom.[3] Aimoinus described in detail only one miracle performed during the abbot's lifetime, the curing of a leper, which echoed Christ's curing of a leper in the Gospels.[4] In the biblical account, a leper was made clean by touching Jesus, who insisted that the man tell no one. The miracle at Fleury involved a leper who had dreamed that to be cured he was to wash himself in holy water in which Abbo had first washed his own hands. Though skeptical, Abbo complied with the leper's request, and the man was duly cleansed of his disease. Like Jesus in the Gospels, Abbo admonished the leper to tell no one of this miracle. Aimoinus explicitly drew comparisons between Abbo's miraculous healing of a leper and Christ's. Abbo's other miracles are less obvious to the modern reader. The deaths of men who had attacked Abbo's entourage on the road to Tours fall into the category of vengeance miracles,[5] a category of miracle familiar to anyone who had studied the *Miracula sancti Benedicti,* the ongoing effort of four Fleurisian monks to chronicle Benedict's active protection of the monks from those who would deprive them of their privileges.[6] Abbo also showed his faith and the efficacy of his prayers several times in the *Vita,* most notably while waiting for the weather to clear on the English Channel.[7] In this way Aimoinus's account followed the early medieval hagiographical tradition of showing "that supernatural power worked in him according to accepted patterns of sanctity."[8]

---

ker, *Two Lives of Charlemagne,* trans. Lewis Thorpe (Harmondsworth, England: Penguin Books, 1969).

3. Aimoinus, *VsA,* cc. 16–21.

4. Ibid., c. 14. Aimoinus described two other miraculous events in the *VsA,* but only in passing: his prayers saved him from shipwreck (c. 5), and he narrowly escaped falling into the Dordogne River while on the way to La Réole (c. 19). Christ's curing of the leper appears in all three synoptic Gospels: Mt 8:1–4; Mk 1:40–45; Lk 5:12–16.

5. Aimoinus, *VsA,* c. 8. For vengeance miracles, see Ward, *Miracles and the Medieval Mind,* 47–49.

6. *MsB.*

7. Aimoinus, *VsA,* c. 4.

8. Ward, *Miracles and the Medieval Mind,* 168. The reason for such close adherence to established patterns was, according to Ward, in order to distinguish Christian miracles, which showed the pattern of God's power, from pagan magic. Note Aimoinus's

Aimoinus continued in the hagiographical and martyrological tradition of imitation of Christ by drawing comparisons between Abbo's martyrdom and the Passion of Christ.[9] Just as the week preceding Christ's death is the most detailed section of the synoptic Gospels, so the week preceding Abbo's death is the most detailed section of his *Vita*. Likewise, just as Christ saw signs of his impending doom that the apostles were incapable of comprehending, so, too, in Aimoinus's account Abbo was the only one of the party from Fleury who really understood the gravity of the situation, though he, like Christ before him, did not attempt to avoid his fate. Finally, the lance wound which caused blood to gush forth from Abbo's side is reminiscent of the posthumous lance wound from which Jesus bled water and blood in John 19:34. Aimoinus's use of the imagery and narrative pattern of the Gospels in describing Abbo's death supported Abbo's claim to martyrdom.

A more immediate model for Aimoinus in composing his tribute to Abbo may have been the growing hagiographical literature surrounding reforming abbots. Jean Leclercq's study of the texts relating to the life and cult of Maiolus of Cluny indicates that their authors stressed several monastic virtues, including a devotion to academic study, personal poverty, and humility, virtues that Aimoinus associated with Abbo despite Abbo's necessary involvement in worldly politics.[10] From the earlier generation of monastic reformers, Aimoinus could have referred to the life of the reformer of Fleury, Odo of Cluny, whom his biographer, John of Salerno, praised for his monastic virtues, including not only patience and poverty but his concern for the clothing and food of his monks and for the spread of monastic reform.[11] Farther afield, Aimoinus could have drawn on the lives of the English saints Dunstan, Oswald, and Æthelwold, though access to the texts as well as the very different circumstances of the English reform make this less likely.

---

preface to the *VsA*, in which he contrasted Abbo's miracles, which were few in number but genuine, with the magic that evil people perform.

9. Ward, *Miracles and the Medieval Mind*, 167, noted similarities between the death of Stephen, the first martyr, and that of Jesus.

10. Leclercq, "Saint Majolus," 207–26.   11. Rosenwein, *Rhinoceros Bound*, 85.

Shortly after completing the *Vita sancti Abbonis,* Aimoinus appended a short collection of miracles performed at Abbo's tomb to his original work. The collection of miracles was an important step in establishing the cult of a saint. Although the procedure for authenticating sanctity had not yet become highly bureaucratized in the early eleventh century, the foundations of the later process for canonization, including a detailed examination of the evidence for sanctity and the production of miracles, had already been laid.[12] If the monks of Fleury hoped to encourage Abbo's cult, however, a record of his miracles was absolutely essential. Three of the miracles recorded by Aimoinus involved cures—of a fever in one case, of blindness in the other two.[13] In another miracle a candle lit by Abbo's tomb remained lit for two nights and a day, while an identical one by the altar of St. Peter was consumed in only a few hours.[14] Miracles of mercy, especially cures, were among the most common sorts of miracles in the Middle Ages.[15] The most interesting of Abbo's miracles, however, was the punishment that was inflicted upon one of the women who had started the riot at La Réole. In Aimoinus's words: "And then on the second day after the death of that holy man, one of those women who had incited the riot with their shouting became deranged and, without a stitch of clothing on her, ran around the church. After this, she was struck with leprosy and expelled from the society of men, and was not cleansed until the end of her life."[16] This miracle of vengeance underscored the role of women in inciting the riot and suggested that the problems at La Réole originated in the town rather than within the monastic community, perhaps

---

12. The first papal canonization occurred in 993, though the papacy did not begin routinely canonizing saints until about 1200, according to Ward, *Miracles and the Medieval Mind,* 185.
13. Aimoinus, *Miracula sancti Abbonis,* cc. 1, 4, 5 (appendix to *VsA*).
14. Ibid., c. 3.
15. Ward, *Miracles and the Medieval Mind,* 34–35.
16. Aimoinus, *Miracula sancti Abbonis,* c. 2: "At vero, die secunda obitus ipsius sancti viri una ex mulieribus quae clamore suo seditionem concitaverant, menta capta totoque nuda corpore per ecclesiam rotabatur. Post haec lepra percussa et a consortio hominum expulsa, usque ad finem vitae non est mundata."

Conclusion 259

involving improper contact between women and men who professed to be monks.

The Fleurisians were successful in establishing Abbo's cult, albeit on a small scale. In the short run, there seem to have been no serious problems at La Réole, though this may be due more to the swift and severe punishment meted out by the secular authorities than to fear of the wrath of St. Abbo. Anselme Davril's examination of liturgical documents indicates that commemoration of Abbo's feast day was probably not a regular part of the liturgical year until the twelfth century, when Fleury seems to have reformed its liturgy.[17] Abbo's cult apparently never spread beyond Fleury and La Réole, except for one indication in a martyrology from Winchester.[18] On the other hand, a popular cult of Abbo may have existed at the local level, and the abbot's fate in local memory was almost certainly considerably better than that of St. Herard, of whom Aimoinus said, "The head of this saint is preserved in the monastery of La Réole, the rest of the body buried in a certain cell of his monastery. Of him, who he was or what he did, we have up to now been able to find nothing else in writing except the day of his passing."[19] By the end of the twelfth century La Réole lay within Plantagenet territory in France, and King Richard the Lionhearted of England is supposed to have venerated Abbo's bones before departing on crusade in 1190, as did King Henry III in 1242.[20] This suggests a popular cult, but not a widespread one.

The postmedieval cult of Abbo was equally localized, though perhaps slightly more successful. Abbo's relics were lost soon after the end of the Middle Ages, when Protestants took control of

17. Davril, "Le culte de Saint-Abbon," 154–55.
18. Ibid., 146–47. The presence of Abbo's cult at La Réole is somewhat speculative, since our only source is a reference by Mabillon to its continued observation at both Fleury and La Réole in the eighteenth century (ibid., 158).
19. Aimoinus, *Miracula sancti Abbonis*, c. 1: "cuius sancti caput in monasterio Regulae reliquum corporis in quadam ipsius coenobii cella humatum servatur. De quo, quis fuerit quidve egerit, usque hodie in scriptis nil aliud reperire quivimus quam diem transitus eius."
20. Teisseyre, "Renouveau," 229.

La Réole in 1577. After this, he was commemorated in several scholarly and religious works of the seventeenth and eighteenth centuries.[21] Abbo's cult seems to have disappeared entirely with the onset of the French Revolution. Not until the nineteenth century did the archbishop of Bordeaux, Cardinal Donnet (1836–1882), attempt to restore the cults of saints who had fallen into neglect in his archdiocese. As part of this effort he assigned Jean-Baptiste Pardiac the task of writing a new biography of the saint and working to revive his cult.[22] As a result of Pardiac's efforts, the cult of Abbo continued to be practiced in the diocese of Bordeaux, even after the Vatican II reforms.[23] The refoundation of monastic life at the site Fleury, in the village now called Saint-Benoît-sur-Loire, was accompanied by the composition of another biography on Abbo, this one by Patrice Cousin.[24] In the long run Aimoinus can thus be considered moderately but consistently successful in the establishment of a cult of Abbo for the benefit of Fleury's success as a monastic community.

Aimoinus's other goals require consideration of literary patronage and interactions between monasteries. Given Fleury's interest in cultivating devotion to Abbo as a martyr, it is surprising that the writing of his *Vita* was commissioned not by the new abbot of Fleury, Gauzlin, but by Hervé, the treasurer of Saint-Martin of Tours. Gauzlin had close ties with the Capetians and was even rumored by Adhemar of Chabannes to be the illegitimate son of Hugh Capet, though such a close blood connection is doubtful.[25] There appears to have been some opposition at Fleu-

21. Ibid., 229–30.
22. Ibid., 231. For a discussion of Pardiac's work, see chapter 1. For more on Cardinal Donnet, see *Dictionnaire de biographie française* (Paris: Letouzey et Ané, 1933–), 11:534–35.
23. Teisseyre, "Renouveau," 236.
24. Cousin, *Abbon de Fleury-sur-Loire*.
25. Adémar, *Chronique*, bk. 3, c. 39: "Rex autem Rotbertus pro defuncto ordinavit abbatem Gauzlenum, licet repugnarent monachi, nolentes sibi praeesse filium scorti. Erat enim ipse nobilissimi Francorum principis filius manzer, a puero in monasterio sancti Benedicti nutritus" (Moreover, King Robert appointed Gauzlin as abbot, although the monks resisted, not wishing the son of a whore to preside over them. For he was the son of the most noble prince of the Franks, raised from boyhood in

ry to Gauzlin's accession, despite the support of King Robert, although the monks of Fleury eventually not only accepted his abbacy but wrote a very flattering account of his career at Fleury.[26] Gauzlin may have been a supporter of Arnulf, the late bishop of Orléans (d. 1003), who had initially aided the Capetians in their quest to solidify royal power but who had often shown himself antagonistic to Abbo's efforts on Fleury's behalf. Hervé would have had a very different perspective on the political situation in northern France. King Robert had appointed him treasurer of Saint-Martin of Tours shortly after the year 1000.[27] His family members were supporters of the count of Anjou. In his youth, however, he had aspired to be a monk and had probably studied with Abbo at Fleury; familial pressure apparently led him to pursue a more worldly career within the Church, so he had become a canon of Saint-Martin, a prerequisite for his eventual advancement to the post of treasurer.[28] Several years earlier, Hervé had enlisted the Fleurisian abbot's aid in a dispute between the canons of Saint-Martin and the archbishop of Tours, who had officiated at King Robert's marriage to Bertha of Blois.[29] Hervé, then, may have wished to use Abbo's death as a reminder to King Robert of the Fleurisian abbot's opposition to the king's marriage to

the monastery of Saint Benedict.) Adhemar's testimony on this count is questionable, since he does not appear to be as well informed on affairs to the north as the south. For a discussion of Gauzlin's parentage, see Bautier and Labory, introduction to André, *Vita Gauzlini*, 18–20, where Adhemar's motives for his portrayal of Gauzlin are called into question as well. Bautier and Labory found that it was just within the limits of chronological likelihood that Robert was the person indicated by Adhemar as Gauzlin's father, rather than Hugh Capet, as other commentators on Adhemar have hypothesized.

26. For opposition to Gauzlin, see Adémar de Chabannes, *Chronique*, bk. 3, c. 39, though one should note Adhemar's bias. André, *Vie de Gauzlin*.

27. Bachrach, *Fulk Nerra*, 84, 316n109. As Bachrach noted, by this time King Robert had repudiated Bertha of Blois and married Constance of Arles, a relative of Count Fulk Nerra of Anjou. Hervé, as a relative of one of Fulk's supporters, appears to have been appointed in hopes of strengthening the Capetian-Angevin alliance.

28. Guy Oury, "L'idéal monastique dans la vie canoniale: Le Bienheureux Hervé de Tours († 1022)," *Revue Mabillon* 52, ser. 3, no. 207 (1962): 7–9.

29. Abbo, letter 5. He was not, by the way, successful in his appeal to the abbot for help, though this would not necessarily compromise his desire to advance his own political goals in the name of his former teacher. See Bachrach, *Fulk Nerra*, 84.

Bertha of Blois, something that Hervé's Angevin connections would have opposed for political reasons, and also as a vehicle for promoting strict independence of monastic institutions from episcopal control—neither one of which issues would have been in Gauzlin's interest in his first few years as abbot.[30] Apart from hard-nosed political calculations, Hervé may have simply wanted to promote monastic virtues and to encourage the establishment of a specifically French monastic cult at Fleury, the place where he received his introduction to monastic life. Hervé appears never to have given up his love for monastic simplicity and reflection. Though unable to join a monastic community, he arranged in the final years of his life to live the life of a hermit at one of the possessions of Saint-Martin.[31]

Although Hervé's motives for commissioning a *Vita* of Abbo will never be entirely clear, Aimoinus's finished product clearly reveals several changes that had occurred in northern Francia over the sixteen years of Abbo's abbacy. The *Vita sancti Abbonis* becomes detailed only in the final years of Abbo's life, that is, in the years following the firm establishment of Capetian rule and the probable rapprochement between Fleury and the king. Aimoinus could have had many motives for concentrating on this period. This may have been the period he knew best, after he had advanced enough in his studies and knowledge of the world to be close to the abbot and to comprehend fully the events in which he participated. Furthermore, the *Vita* is in some ways more a work of martyrology, the study of a death, than of hagiography, intent on the events of the life. If Aimoinus's aim had been to establish a cult of Abbo, then the events of his death were far better suited to his purposes and the demands of sanctity than Abbo's life as a political figure. Nevertheless, Aimoinus probably found it convenient, for political rather than for religious reasons, to gloss over the early years of Abbo's abbacy, when Fleury frequently found

---

30. Though Gauzlin eventually came into conflict with Bishop Arnulf's successor, Fulk of Orléans. See Head, *Hagiography*, 255.

31. Oury, "Idéal monastique dans la vie canoniale," 23–25.

itself in conflict with the Capetians, with whom the monastery later formed close bonds. Even when Aimoinus included details from these early years, his account of Abbo's dealings with Hugh and Robert leave out particulars about politics and ideology that must have stood out to a contemporary reader as glaring omissions. For example, though the dispute over Archbishop Arnulf of Reims placed Abbo and Hugh on opposite sides of the debate and was resolved only after much controversy, Aimoinus mentioned only that Abbo brought back Arnulf's pallium from Rome.[32] He made no mention of Hugh's role in the deposition or Abbo's role in Arnulf's defense. In an equally glaring omission, Aimoinus never mentioned Abbo's relationship with Gerbert of Aurillac, who played such a prominent role in the dispute over the see of Reims, both as a claimant to the archbishopric and as a pope who finally recognized Arnulf as archbishop.

Aimoinus's emphasis instead was on the cooperation between Fleury and the early Capetians. In his account, the beginning of Abbo's abbacy was marked by Hugh Capet's confirmation of the election. After passing over the early years of the abbacy almost entirely, Aimoinus quoted extensively from Abbo's *Apologeticus,* which was the abbot's blueprint for more cooperative relations between monks and kings. Ultimately, the *Vita sancti Abbonis* stressed Abbo's attempts at building a peaceful society in which monks formed a morally superior order, nurtured by lay rulers. The most striking difference between the time of Aimoinus's writing and the early years of Abbo's abbacy lay in the position of the Capetian dynasty. By the time of Gauzlin's abbacy (1004–1030), the Capetians had achieved a degree of stability that had not been at all certain in the years immediately following Hugh Capet's coronation in 987. By the early eleventh century, the Carolingian opposition to Capetian rule had all but died out: with the death of Charles of Lorraine no serious challenger to Capetian power remained; his sons did not present a significant threat to Capetian control of

---

32. Aimoinus, *VsA,* c. 12.

264   *Conclusion*

northern France. With the death of Hugh Capet in 996, full royal power passed to Robert, who eventually proved much more willing to support monastic claims than his father had been. By the beginning of the eleventh century, the dynasty had weathered Robert's marital problems, and, by the time of the composition of Aimoinus's *Vita* of Abbo, Robert may even have produced an heir from his marriage to Constance of Arles.[33] Meanwhile, Fleury had continued to grow closer to the royal family. The monks probably found Robert somewhat more supportive than Hugh. Robert has preserved a reputation, at least, of favoring abbots over bishops (unlike Hugh, who favored bishops).[34] Aimoinus's own testimony suggested that Abbo respected Robert's learning enough to direct a piece of scholarly polemic particularly at him.[35] Under Gauzlin's abbacy, another monk of Fleury, Helgaud, composed a *Vita* of Robert, which portrayed the king as an ideal ruler, both just and pious.[36] Whatever had been Fleury's initial attitude toward the Capetians, by Gauzlin's time, Aimoinus, along with the other monks of Fleury, had every motive for softening as much as possible disagreements between abbot and king in the early years of the monarchy.

One of Abbo's most important legacies was his securing of Fleury's papal privilege, granting the monastery and its abbot a wide range of exemptions from local political control and awarding its abbot with the title "first among the abbots of Gaul." Abbo's successor as abbot of Fleury, Gauzlin, gives proof of the lasting value of this privilege in his efforts to defend it from Bishop Fulk of Orléans, who sought to violate its provisions and even threatened to throw the privilege into the fire if it prevented his involvement in the affairs of Fleury. Gauzlin managed to maintain Fleury's independence with the help of the pope.[37] Not surprisingly, Aimoinus described Abbo's meeting with Pope Grego-

---

33. Duby, *Knight*, 77; Pfister, *Robert le Pieux*, 70.
34. See, for example, Hallam, *Capetian France*, 101–3.
35. Aimoinus, *VsA*, c. 9.   36. Helgaud, *Vie de Robert le Pieux*.
37. André, *Vita Gauzlini*, c. 18 (50–59); discussed in Head, *Hagiography*, 255–57.

Conclusion 265

ry V in detail and held up the relationship between the two as a model. Aimoinus could not give Gregory's predecessor, John XV, the same treatment, so he noted only that Abbo failed to see the pope. To bolster the claims of the papal privilege Aimoinus quoted at length Abbo's letter to "Bishop G" in which he lay forth the case for the superiority of the monastic order to other orders and the precedent, going back to Pope Gregory I, for monastic independence. While on the subject of Abbo's relationship with the papacy, Aimoinus also wanted to make sure that the kings, counts, and bishops of Francia remembered that it was the pope, with the abbot of Fleury as an intermediary, who installed Arnulf properly as archbishop of Reims, not the kings.

Another important element in Aimoinus's portrait of Fleury under Abbo's abbacy was his emphasis on monastic ideals and the patronage of St. Benedict, the founder of Western monasticism. In the very first chapter of the *Vita,* Aimoinus recorded that Abbo had entered the monastic life "to serve Christ and St. Benedict," following the procedure laid out in the Rule of St. Benedict.[38] Likewise, the English house of Ramsey owed its desire for a teacher from Fleury to the "love of the holy father Benedict," who, in Aimoinus's account, returned the love of the monks by protecting Abbo from shipwreck on his journey across the Channel.[39] When it came time for Abbo to return, Aimoinus quoted a letter of Oylbold that invoked the affection Benedict had felt toward his monks, despite other passages that hinted at tensions between the two.[40] Benedict recurred elsewhere in the *Vita,* sometimes invoked in letters that Abbo wrote, often as the center of monastic life at the monastery.[41] Fittingly, at the very end

---

38. Aimoinus, *VsA,* c. 1: "genitores memorati beati pueri Abbonis ipsum ad serviendum Christo et sancto patri tradiderunt Benedicto"; and c. 2. For the ceremony used at Fleury in Abbo's day, see chapter 2.

39. Ibid., c. 4: "Eadem nempe natio ad amorem sancti patris Benedicti memoratique loci duabus ex causis maxime accessit." For Abbo's Channel crossing and his stay in England, see chapter 2.

40. Ibid., c. 6.

41. Ibid., cc. 10 (in Abbo's letter to Bernard of Beaulieu), 13 (Abbo's work on the

of his life, Abbo rebuked a monk who had eaten outside of the monastery in a manner reminiscent of St. Benedict in Gregory the Great's dialog, and his own death became known to the monastic community of the kingdom during the celebration of St. Benedict's translation to Fleury.[42]

In keeping with the ideals of monastic harmony promulgated by St. Benedict, Aimoinus consistently de-emphasized the conflicts that must have divided the monastery during Abbo's lifetime, though he could not entirely omit these. Abbo's biographer hinted at dissension within the monastery when he recounted the "envious ones" who opposed spending communal funds to educate Abbo in music, but without mentioning the envious by name.[43] Nor did he discuss the apparent tensions between Abbo and Constantine of Fleury, who eventually left for another monastery, or the machinations of Frederick, a former monk of Fleury, whom Abbo had denounced as the leader of a monastic revolt.[44] Aimoinus omitted all mention of the dispute over Oylbold's election as abbot and only hinted at dissension upon Abbo's election two years later.[45] This has created significant problems for subsequent historians as they have attempted to untangle the identity of the unnamed "usurper" mentioned in Gerbert of Aurillac's all too contentious letters. Finally, Aimoinus was concerned to paint a picture not only of harmony within Fleury but also of harmony among reformed monasteries generally. Problems at Saint-Martin, Micy, and Marmoutier disappear from this account entirely, and even Abbo's final confrontation at La Réole is a struggle

---

year of Benedict's translation to Fleury), and 15 (altar to St. Benedict enriched by Abbo).

42. Ibid., cc. 20–21.

43. Ibid., c. 3.

44. For the career of Constantine of Fleury, see Warren, "Constantine," 285–92. Warren's account of the tensions between Constantine and Abbo is highly speculative, but he convincingly argues that Constantine did not have a completely harmonious relationship with the other members of the congregation of Fleury. For Frederick, see chapter 6.

45. Aimoinus, V&A, cc. 6–7. For the relations between Abbo and Oylbold, see chapters 2 and 3.

with someone who is a "monk in name only" at the head of antireform barbarians, rather than a member of a properly functioning monastic community. Eschewing its internal conflict, Aimoinus celebrated the learning of Fleury and Abbo's contributions to its physical infrastructure.[46]

Although struggle between monks did not fit Aimoinus's agenda, conflicts with certain outside powers served his purpose very well. Abbo's defense of monastic tithes at the Council of Saint-Denis appears in Aimoinus's account as an honorable defense of high principles rather than a squabble over revenue. In Aimoinus's version of the story Abbo and the bishops appear equally attacked, though Abbo clearly was not the target of the mob and was even suspected of having incited it.[47] Likewise, Aimoinus has selectively recorded Abbo's dealings with Bishop Arnulf of Orléans, who died in 1002, two years before Abbo's death. Arnulf appears as Abbo's attacker, although "honorable in all other things," and provides an introduction to Aimoinus's summary of Abbo's *Apologeticus*.[48] This suggests an ambivalence toward a powerful man so well connected among the nobility and episcopate of western Francia that even in death he cannot entirely fulfill the role of villain. In fact, the situation of Fleury relative to the episcopate remained problematic well into the next generation, when Abbot Gauzlin's strife with Bishop Fulk of Orléans reflected Fleury's continuing importance in Capetian ecclesiastical and secular politics.[49]

Any final evaluation of Abbo's legacy requires an evaluation of Aimoinus's legacy as well. Abbo clearly left Fleury in 1004 stronger in many ways than it had been in 988. In his youth Abbo had traveled through western Francia in search of an education he could not acquire at Fleury. By the end of his abbacy, Fleury's library possessed several treatises of his own composition, excellent textbooks for students, and a cadre of competent writers and teachers. Abbo began his abbacy in an uneasy relationship with weak monarchs. Although he opposed royal policy for much of his early

46. Ibid., cc. 12, 13, 15.
47. Ibid., c. 9.
48. Ibid., c. 8.
49. Head, *Hagiography*, 255–70.

abbacy, in the end he reached a mutually beneficial compromise. The kings gained a new respect for reformed monasticism, and Fleury acquired a certain degree of stability. He secured an important papal privilege, and he also laid the theoretical framework for having that privilege respected by the powerful men of the realm. Fleury's independence was not completely guaranteed, however, as demonstrated by the elevation of Gauzlin, a monarchical partisan, as his successor. Nevertheless, Gauzlin's abbacy saw rich endowments and a channeling of Fleury's educational strengths into practical uses, with the composition of works of royal and abbatial biography. While Abbo may not have approved the extent to which Fleury became a royal supporter, Aimoinus appears to have been comfortable with that role, to the point of downplaying any previous conflicts. Abbo might have been better pleased with the emphasis on peace and harmony within the monastery and within the wider world of reformed monasticism. That had always been a goal of his, however contentious his methods might have seemed at the time. Aimoinus's skill in presenting a believable, coherent narrative of Abbo's life was a tribute to the educational and propagandistic training he had received from a master of the genre. In death as in life, Abbo served his monastic community, providing his beloved monks with a suitable narrative of monastic martyrdom to carry them into the next century and beyond.

CHRONOLOGY OF ABBO'S LIFE AND TIMES

c. 930 Reform of Fleury by Odo of Cluny

between 938 and 953 Birth of Abbo

948–963 Abbacy of Wulfald

c. 950 Translation of St. Paul Aurelian to Fleury; translation of the relics of St. Benedict from crypt to upper church at Fleury; reform of St. Père of Chartres by Fleury

958 Return of Oswald from Fleury to England

961 Return of Germanus from Fleury to England

962 Wulfald installed as bishop of Chartres

963–978 Abbacy of Richard

before 970 Abbo's studies at Paris, Reims, and Orléans

970 and 992 Coincidence of Good Friday and Annunciation

c. 972–989 Gerbert a teacher at Reims (intermittent)

974 Fire at Fleury

978–985 Abbacy of Amalbert

c. 985–987 Abbo a teacher at Ramsey

c. 985–987 Abbacy of Oylbold

987–996 Reign of Hugh Capet in association with Robert the Pious

987 or 988–1004 Abbacy of Abbo

Chronology

988   Death of Archbishop Dunstan of Canterbury

January 989   Death of Archbishop Adalbero of Reims

March 989   Consecration of Arnulf as archbishop of Reims

November 989   Betrayal of Reims by Archbishop Arnulf

April 990   Capture and imprisonment of Arnulf of Reims and Charles of Lorraine by Hugh Capet

Summer 991   Siege of Melun

June 991   Council of Saint-Basil

July 991   Consecration of Gerbert as archbishop of Reims

November 991 or 992   Attack on Abbo on road to Tours

992   Death of Archbishop Oswald of York

993   Charter of Fleury regarding Yèvre-le-Chatel

993 or 994   Council of Saint-Denis on tithes

994   Council of Chelles

994   Death of Maiolus

June 995   Council of Mouzon

July 995   Council of Saint-Remi of Reims

995 or 996   Abbo's first journey to Rome

996–999   Pontificate of Gregory V

996   Death of Hugh Capet

996–1031   Independent reign of Robert the Pious

997   Council of Pavia

997   Abbo's second journey to Rome

998   Restoration of Arnulf to the see of Reims

998   Dispute of Saint-Martin of Tours

998   Dispute at Marmoutier

999–1003   Pontificate of Sylvester II (Gerbert of Aurillac)

1003   Flooding at Fleury

Chronology

1004 Dispute of Saint-Père of Chartres

1004 Dispute at Saint-Mesmin of Micy

1004 Dispute at La Réole

13 November 1004 Death of Abbo at La Réole

1004–1030 Abbacy of Gauzlin

c. 1005–1008 Composition of *Vita sancti Abbonis* by Aimoinus of Fleury

BIBLIOGRAPHY

MANUSCRIPT SOURCES

Dijon
Bibliothèque municipale 1118 [contains Aimoinus, *Vita sancti Abbonis*]

London
British Library Add. 10972 [contains Abbo's letters and *Quaestiones grammaticales*]

Montpellier
Faculté de médicine 68 [contains Aimoinus, *Vita sancti Abbonis*]

Paris
Bibliothèque nationale Collection Moreau 16 [contains charter of Saint-Cyprien]
Bibliothèque nationale lat. 2858 [contains encyclical letter on death of Abbo]
Bibliothèque nationale lat. 5543 [contains "Annales Floriacenses"]
Bibliothèque nationale lat. 12606 [contains Aimoinus, *Vita sancti Abbonis*]
Bibliothèque nationale n.a. lat. 469 [contains Abbo's letter to Girald and Vitalis]
Bibliothèque nationale n.a. lat. 2400 [contains Abbo, *Collectio canonum*]
Bibliothèque nationale n.a. lat. 4568 [contains Abbo's letters to Bernand of Beaulieu]

PRIMARY SOURCES

Abbo of Fleury. *Abbonis Floriacensis opera inedita I: Syllogismorum Categoricorum et Hypotheticorum enodatio*. Ed. A. Van de Vyver. In *Rijksuniversiteit te Gent: Werken uitgegeven door de Faculteit van de Letteren en Wijsbegeerte* 140. Bruges, Belgium: De Tempel, 1966.

———. *Abbo Floriacensis, Quaestiones grammaticales / Abbon de Fleury, Questions grammaticales*. Ed. and trans. Anita Guerreau-Jalabert. Auteurs Latins du Moyen Age. Paris: Société d'édition "les Belles lettres," 1982.

———. *Epistolae*. In *PL* 139:419–61.

———. Letter to Oylboldus. In Marco Mostert, "Le séjour d'Abbon de Fleury à Ramsey." *Bibliothèque de l'Ecole de Chartes* 144 (1986): 199–208.
———. *Liber apologeticus.* In *PL* 139:461–72.
———. "Les oeuvres inédits d'Abbon de Fleury." Ed. A. Van de Vyver. *Revue bénédictine* 47 (1935): 123–69.
———. "Acrostic Poem to Otto III." In Scott Gwara, "Three Acrostic Poems by Abbo of Fleury." *Journal of Medieval Latin* 2 (1992): 227.
———. "Two Astronomical Tractates of Abbo of Fleury." Ed. Ron B. Thomson. In *The Light of Nature: Essays in the History and Philosophy of Science Presented to A. C. Crombie,* ed. J. D. North and J. J. Roche. Dordrecht, Netherlands: Martinus Nijhof, 1985.
———. *Vita s. Edmundi.* In *Three Lives of English Saints,* ed. Michael Winterbottom. Toronto Medieval Latin Texts. Toronto: Pontifical Institute of Medieval Studies for the Centre for Medieval Studies, 1972.
Adémar de Chabannes. *Chronique.* Ed. Jules Chavanon. Paris: Alphonse Picard et fils, 1897.
Aimoinus of Fleury. *Vita sancti Abbonis.* Ed. and trans. Robert-Henri Bautier and Gillette Labory. In *L'abbaye de Fleury en l'an mil.* Sources d'histoire médiévale. Paris: Centre national de la recherche scientifique, 2004.
"Alia vita, auctore altero monacho coaevo, ex codice MS Pragensi cum editione Suriana collato." In *AASS* 3. 23 April.
André de Fleury. *Vita Gauzlini, Vie de Gauzlin.* Ed. and trans. Robert-Henri Bautier and Gillette Labory. Paris: Centre national de la recherche scientifique, 1969.
"Annales Floriacenses." In Alexandre Vidier, *L'historiographie à Saint-Benoît-sur-Loire et les miracles de Saint Benoît.* Paris: A. et J. Picard, 1965.
"Annales Floriacenses." In *Scriptores rerum Ingallensium: Annales, chronica et historiae aevi Carolini,* ed. Georgius Heinricus Pertz. MGH SS, vol. 2. Hanover, 1829.
Arnulf of Orléans. *De cartilagine.* In "Le manuscrit des *Annales de Flodoard,* Reg. Lat. 633 du Vatican," ed. Ph. Lauer. *Mélanges, d'archéologie et d'histoire de l'Ecole française de Rome* 18 (1898): 492–95.
Bede. *Ecclesiastical History.* Ed. and trans. J. E. King. Loeb Classical Library. Cambridge, Mass.: Harvard University Press and London: William Heinemann., 1963.
———. *The Life of St. Cuthbert.* Ed and trans. Bertram Colgrave. In *Two Lives of St. Cuthbert.* 1940. Reprint, Cambridge: Cambridge University Press, 1985.
Benedict of Nursia. *RB 1980: The Rule of Benedict in Latin and English with Notes.* Ed. Timothy Fry et al. Collegeville, Minn.: Liturgical Press, 1981.
Bur, Michel, ed. and trans. *Chronique ou livre de fondation du monastère de Mouzon / Chronicon Mosomense seu Liber fundationis monasterii sanctae Mariae O.S.B. apud Mosomum in diocesi Remensi.* Paris: Centre national de la recherche scientifique, 1989.
Byrhtferth. *Byrhtferth's Manual.* Ed and trans. S. J. Crawford. Early English Text Society, o.s. 177. London: Oxford University Press, 1929.
"Cartulaire de l'abbaye de Saint-Cyprien de Poitiers." *Archives historiques de Poitou* 3 (1874).

"Cartulaire de Saint-Jean d'Angély." *Archives historiques de la Saintonge et de l'Aunis* 30 (1901) and 33 (1901).
Certain, Eugène de, ed. *Les miracles de saint Benoît écrits par Adrevald, Aimoin, André, Raoul Tortaire, et Hugues de Sainte Marie, moines de Fleury.*. Paris: Mme. Ve. Jules Renouard, 1858.
"Chartes de l'abbaye de Saint-Maixent." *Archives historiques de Poitou* 16 (1886) and 18 (1888).
Davril, Anselme, ed. *The Monastic Ritual of Fleury (Orléans, Bibliothèque Municipale, MS 123 [101]).* London: Henry Bradshaw Society, 1990.
Delisle, Léopold, ed. *Rouleaux des morts du IXe au XVe siècle.* . Libraire de la Société de l'histoire de France. Paris: Mme. Ve. Jules Renouard, 1866.
"Documents pour l'histoire de l'église de Saint-Hilaire de Poitiers." *Mémoires de la Société des antiquaires de l'Ouest* 14 (1887).
Dümmler, Ernst, ed. *Poetae Latini aevi Carolini.* Vol. 1. MGH Antiquitates. Poetae Latini medii aevi. Hanover, 1881.
Eadmer. *Vita s. Oswaldi.* In *The Historians of the Church of York and its Archbishops,* ed. James Raine. Rolls Series 71. London, 1886.
Einhard and Notker. *Two Lives of Charlemagne.* Trans. Lewis Thorpe. Harmondsworth, England: Penguin, 1969.
Fulbert of Chartres. *The Letters of Fulbert of Chartres.* Ed. and trans. Frederick Behrends. Oxford: Oxford Medieval Texts, 1976.
Gallia Christiana in provincias ecclesiasticas distributa. Paris, 1715–1865.
Gerbert of Aurillac. "Acta Consilii Causeiensis." In *Annales, chronica et historiae aevi Saxonici,* ed. Georgius Heinricus Pertz. MGH SS, vol. 3. Hanover, 1839.
———. "Acta Consilii Remensis ad Sanctum Basolum." In *Annales, chronica et historiae aevi Saxonici,* ed. Georgius Heinricus Pertz. MGH SS, vol. 3. Hanover, 1839.
———. *Die Briefsammlung Gerberts von Reims.* Ed. Fritz Weigle. MGH Die Briefe der Deutschen Kaiserzeit 2. Berlin, 1966.
———. *The Letters of Gerbert with his Papal Privileges as Sylvester II.* Ed. and trans. Harriet Pratt Lattin. New York: Columbia University Press, 1961.
Gregory the Great. *Dialogues, Book II: St. Benedict.* Trans. Myra L. Uhlfelder. Library of Liberal Arts. Indianapolis: Bobbs-Merrill Educational, 1967.
Gregory V. "Litterae de Synodo Papiensi." In *Annales, chronica et historiae aevi Saxonici,* ed. Georgius Heinricus Pertz. MGH SS, vol. 3. Hanover, 1839.
Gregory of Tours. *The History of the Franks.* Trans. Lewis Thorpe. 1974. Reprint, New York: Penguin, 1982.
Hagenus, Hermannus, ed. *Carmina medii aevi maximam partem inedita.* 1877. Reprint, Berne: Georgius Frobenius et soc., 1961.
Helgaud de Fleury. *Vie de Robert le Pieux. [Epitoma Vitae Regis Rotberti Pii.]* Ed. and trans. Robert-Henri Bautier and Gillette Labory. Paris: Centre national de la recherche scientifique, 1965.
"Historia Francorum Senonensis." In *Chronica et annales aevi Salici,* ed. Georgius Heinricus Pertz. MGH SS, vol. 9. Hanover, 1851.
Leo, abbot and papal legate. "Leonis abbatis et legati ad Hugonem et Rotbertum reges epistola." In *Annales, chronica et historiae aevi Saxonici,* ed. Georgius Heinricus Pertz. MGH SS, vol. 3. Hanover, 1839.

Mansi, Johannes Dominicus, ed. *Sacrorum Conciliorum nova et amplissima collectio.* Venice, 1774; facsimile Paris, 1902.
Migne, J.-P., ed. *Patrologiae cursus completus . . . series Latina.* 221 vols. . Paris, 1841–1864.
Porfyrius, Publilius Optatianus. *Publilii Optatiani Porfyrii Carmina.* Ed. Iohannes Polara. 2 vols. Corpus scriptorum Latinorum paravianum. Turin, Italy: Io. Bapt. Paraviae et sociorum, 1973.
Prou, Maurice, and Alexandre Vidier, eds. *Recueil de chartes de l'abbaye de Saint-Benoît-sur-Loire.* Documents: Société historique et archéologique du Gâtinais 5 and 6. Paris: A. Picard et fils, 1900–1907.
Richer. *Histoire de France.* Ed. and trans. Robert Latouche. Les classiques de l'histoire de France au Moyen Age 17. Paris: Société d'édition "les Belles lettres," 1937.
Robertson, A. J., ed. and trans. *Anglo-Saxon Charters.* Cambridge: Cambridge University Press, 1956.
Rodulfus Glaber. *Historiarum libri quinque/The Five Books of the Histories.* Ed. Neithard Bulst. Trans. John France and Paul Reynolds. Oxford: Clarendon, 1989.
Rudolf of Fulda. *The Life of St. Leoba.* Ed. and trans. C. H. Talbot. In *The Anglo-Saxon Missionaries in Germany.* The Makers of Christendom. Ed. Christopher Dawson. London: Sheed and Ward, 1954.
Stubbs, William, ed. *Memorials of Saint Dunstan.* Rolls Series 63. London, 1874.
Syrus. *Vita sancti Maioli.* In *PL* 137:763–65.
Thierry of Fleury [Thierry of Amorbach]. *Consuetunides Floriacenses antiquiores.* Ed. Anselme Davril and Lin Donnat. Corpus consuetudinorum monasticarum 7.3. Sieburg, Germany: Schmitt, 1984.
———. "Le coutumier de Fleury." Ed. and trans. Anselme Davril and Lin Donnat. In *L'abbaye de Fleury en l'an mil.* Sources d'histoire médiévale 32. Paris: Centre national de la recherche scientifique, 2004.
"Vita auctore monacho coevo ex codice MS Prageus: Collato cum variis editionibus." In *AASS* 3. 23 April.

SECONDARY SOURCES

Althoff, Gerd. *Otto III.* Trans. Phyllis G. Jestice. College Park: Pennsylvania State University Press, 2003.
Bachrach, Bernard S. "Robert de Blois, Abbot of Saint-Florent de Saumur and Saint-Mesmin de Micy (985–1011): A Study in Small Power Politics." *Revue bénédictine* 88 (1978): 123–46.
———. "Toward a Reappraisal of William the Great, Duke of Aquitaine (995–1030)." *Journal of Medieval History* 5 (1979): 11–21.
———. "Fulk Nerra's Exploitation of the *Facultates Monachorum* ca. 1000." In *Law, Custom, and the Social Fabric in Medieval Europe: Essays in Honor of Bryce Lyon,* ed. with an appreciation by Bernard S. Bachrach and David Nicholas. Studies in Medieval Culture 28. Medieval Institute Publications. Kalamazoo: Western Michigan University Press, 1990.
———. *Fulk Nerra, a Neo-Roman Consul in the Eleventh Century.* Berkeley and Los Angeles: University of California Press, 1993.

Bibliography

Banchereau, Jules. *L'église de Saint-Benoît-sur-Loire et Germigny-des-Près*. Paris: Henri Laurens, 1947.
Barnes, Timothy D. "Publilius Optatianus Porfyrius." *American Journal of Philology* 96.2 (1975): 173–86.
———. *Constantine and Eusebius*. Cambridge, Mass.: Harvard University Press, 1981.
Barraclough, Geoffrey. *The Medieval Papacy*. Norwich, England: Harcourt Brace and World, 1968.
———. *The Origins of Modern Germany*. New York: W. W. Norton, 1984.
Bartlett, Robert. *Trial by Fire and Water: The Medieval Judicial Ordeal*. Oxford: Clarendon, 1986.
Batany, Jean. "Abbon de Fleury et le théories des structures sociales vers l'an mille." In *Etudes ligériennes d'histoire et d'archéologie médiévales*. Mémoires et exposés présentés à la Semaine d'études médiévales de Saint-Benoît-sur-Loire. 3–10 July 1969. Ed. René Louis. Publication de la Société de fouilles archéologiques et des monuments historiques de l'Yonne. Paris: Clavreuil, 1975.
———. Review of *The Political Theology of Abbo of Fleury*, by Marco Mostert. *Cahiers de la civilisation médiévale* 33.4 (1990): 402–3.
Bautier, Robert-Henri. "Le monastère et les églises de Fleury-sur-Loire sous les abbatiats d'Abbon, de Gauzlin et d'Arnaud (988–1032)." *Mémoires de la Société nationale des antiquaires de France*, ser. 9, vol. 4 (1968): 71–156.
———. "L'hérésie d'Orléans et le mouvement intellectuel au début du XIe siècle: Documents et hypothèses." In *Actes du 95e Congrès national des sociétés savantes*. Comité des travaux historiques et scientifiques. Reims, 1970. Section de philologie et d'histoire jusqu'à 1610. Vol. 1, *Enseignement et vie intellectuelle (IXe–XVIe siècles)*. Paris: Bibliothèque nationale, 1975.
———. "La place de Fleury dans l'historiographie française du IXe au XIIe siecle." In *Etudes ligériennes d'histoire et d'archéologie médiévales*. Mémoires et exposés présentés à la Semaine d'études médiévales de Saint-Benoît-sur-Loire. 3–10 July 1969. Ed. René Louis. Publication de la Société de fouilles archéologiques et des monuments historiques de l'Yonne. Paris: Clavreuil, 1975.
Berland, Jean-Marie. "La présence bénédictine dans le diocèse d'Orléans." *Bulletin de la Société historique, archéologique et artistique du Giennois* 29 (1981): 3–56.
Bezzola, Gian Andri. *Das Ottonische Kaisertum in der französischen Geschichtsschreibung des 10. und beginnenden 11. Jahrhunderts*. Graz, Austria: Hermann Böhlaus, 1956.
Borst, Arno. *The Ordering of Time: From the Ancient Computus to the Modern Computer*. Trans. Andrew Winnard. Chicago: University of Chicago Press, 1993.
Bouchard, Constance B. "The Geographical, Social, and Ecclesiastical Origins of the Bishops of Auxerre and Sens in the Central Middle Ages." *Church History* 46 (1977): 277–95.
———. "Consanguinity and Noble Marriages in the Tenth and Eleventh Centuries." *Speculum* 56.2 (1981): 268–87.
———. "The Origins of the French Nobility: A Reassessment." *American Historical Review* 86.3 (1981): 501–32.

———. *Sword, Miter, and Cloister: Nobility and the Church in Burgundy, 980–1198.* Ithaca, N.Y.: Cornell University Press, 1987.

———. "The Migration of Women's Names in the Upper Nobility, Ninth-Twelfth Centuries." *Medieval Prosopography* 9.2 (1988): 1–19.

———. "Patterns of Women's Names in Royal Lineages, Ninth-Eleventh Centuries." *Medieval Prosopography* 9.1 (1988): 1–32.

——— "Merovingian, Carolingian, and Cluniac Monasticism: Reform and Renewal in Burgundy," *Journal of Ecclesiastical History* 41.3 (1990): 364–88.

Bowman, Jeffrey A. *Shifting Landmarks: Property, Proof, and Dispute in Catalonia around the Year 1000.* Ithaca, N.Y.: Cornell University Press, 2004.

Boyer, Régis. "An Attempt to Define the Typology of Medieval Hagiography." In *Hagiography and Medieval Literature: A Symposium.* Odense, 17–19 November 1980. Ed. Hans Bekker-Nielsen, Peter Foote, Jorgen Hojgaard Jorgensen, and Tore Nyburg. Odense, Denmark: Odense University Press, 1981.

Boyle, Leonard E. "Diplomatics." In *Medieval Studies: An Introduction,* ed. James M. Powell. 2nd ed. Syracuse, N.Y.: Syracuse University Press, 1992.

Braudel, Fernand. *Civilization and Capitalism, 15th–18th Century.* Vol. 1, *The Structures of Everyday Life.* Trans. Siân Reynolds. New York: Harper and Row, 1982.

Bredero, Adrian H. "Cluny et le monachsme carolingien: Continuité et discontinuité." In *Benedictine Culture,* ed. W. Lourdaux and D. Verhelst. Medievalia Lovaniensia, ser. 1, studia 9. Louvain, Belgium: Leuven University Press, 1983.

Brown, Peter. *The Cult of the Saints.* Chicago: University of Chicago Press, 1981; Phoenix edition 1982.

Brundage, James A. *Law, Sex, and Christian Society in Medieval Europe.* Chicago: University of Chicago Press, 1987.

Bullough, D. A. "The Continental Background of the Reform." In *Tenth-Century Studies: Essays in Commemoration of the Millennium of the Council of Winchester and Regularis Concordia,* ed. David Parsons. London: Philimore, 1975.

Certain, Eugène de. "Arnoul, évêque d'Orléans." *Bibliothèque de l'Ecole des chartes,* ser. 3, vol. 4 (1853): 425–63.

Chevalier, Cyr Ulysse. *Repertoire des sources historique du Moyen Age bio-bibliographique.* Paris, 1903–1907.

Collins, Roger. *The Basques.* 2nd ed. Peoples of Europe. Cambridge, Mass.: Blackwell, 1990.

Constable, Giles. *Monastic Tithes: From Their Origins to the Twelfth Century.* Cambridge: Cambridge University Press, 1964.

Coolidge, Robert T. "Adalbero, Bishop of Laon." *Studies in Medieval and Renaissance History* 2 (1965): 1–114.

Courty, A. "Un compatriote méconnu: Aimoin, moine fleurisien, hagiographe et historien des Xe et XIe siècles." *Revue historique et archéologique de Libournais* 23 (1955): 87–96.

Cousin, Patrice. *Abbon de Fleury-sur-Loire: Un savant, un pasteur, un martyr à la fin du Xe siècle.* Paris: P. Letielleux, 1954.

Cowdrey, H. E. J. *The Cluniacs and the Gregorian Reform.* Oxford: Clarendon, 1970.

Darby, H. C. *The Domesday Geography of Eastern England.* 3rd ed. Cambridge: Cambridge University Press, 1971.
———. *The Changing Fenland.* Cambridge: Cambridge University Press, 1983.
Davril, Anselme. "Le culte de saint Abbon au Moyen Age." In *Actes du Colloque du millénaire de la fondation du prieuré de La Réole.* La Réole, 11–12 November 1978. Bordeaux: Société des bibliophiles de Guyenne, 1980.
Davril, Anselme, and Eric Palazzo. *La vie des moines au temps des grands abbayes Xe–XIIe siècles.* Paris: Hachettes, Litératures, 2000.
Dewindt, Anne Reiber, and Edwin Brezette Dewindt. *Ramsey: The Lives of an English Fenland Town, 1200–1600.* Washington, D.C.: The Catholic University of America Press, 2006.
Dictionnaire de biographie française. Paris: Letouzey et Ané, 1933–.
Donnat, Lin. "Recherches sur l'influence de Fleury au Xe siècle." In *Etudes ligériennes d'histoire et d'archéologie médiévales. Mémoires et exposés présentés à la Semaine d'études médiévales de Saint-Benoît-sur-Loire. 3–10 July 1969.* Ed. René Louis. Publication de la Société de fouilles archéologiques et des monuments historiques de l'Yonne. Paris: Clavreuil, 1975.
Duby, Georges. *Rural Economy and Country Life in the Medieval West.* Trans. Cynthia Postan. Columbia: University of South Carolina Press, 1968.
———. *The Three Orders: Feudal Society Imagined.* Trans. Arthur Goldhammer with a foreword by Thomas N. Bisson. Chicago: University of Chicago Press, 1980.
———. *The Knight, the Lady, and the Priest: The Makings of Modern Marriage in Medieval France.* Trans. Barbara Bray. New York: Pantheon, 1983.
Dumville, David N. "St. Cathroé of Metz and the Hagiography of Exoticism." In *Studies in Irish Hagiography: Saints and Scholars,* ed. John Carey, Máire Herbert, and Pádraig O Riain. Dublin: Four Courts, 2001.
Dunbabin, Jean. *France in the Making, 843–1180.* Oxford: Oxford University Press, 1985.
———. "West Francia: The Kingdom." In *The New Cambridge Medieval History,* vol. 3 (c. 900–c. 1024), ed. Timothy Reuter. Cambridge: Cambridge University Press, 1999.
Fanning, Steven. *A Bishop and His World before the Gregorian Reform: Hubert of Angers (1006–1047).* Transactions of the American Philosophical Society 78.1. Philadelphia: American Philosophical Society, 1988.
Farmer, Sharon. *Communities of Saint Martin: Legend and Ritual in Medieval Tours.* Ithaca, N.Y.: Cornell University Press, 1991.
Fawtier, Robert. *The Capetian Kings of France: Monarchy and Nation (987–1328).* Trans. Lionel Butler and R. J. Adam. London: Macmillan, 1960.
Fichtenau, Heinrich. *Living in the Tenth Century: Mentalities and Social Orders.* Trans. Patrick J. Geary. Chicago: University of Chicago Press, 1991.
Fossier, Robert. *Enfance de l'Europe, Xe–XIIe siècle, aspects économiques et sociaux.* Vol. 1, *L'homme et son espace.* 2nd ed. Paris: Presses universitaires de France, 1982.
Gams, Pius Bonifacius. *Series episcoporum ecclesiae Catholicae.* 1873–1886. Reprint, Graz, Austria: Akademische Druck-u. Verlagsanstalt, 1957.

Ganshof, F. L. *Feudalism*. Trans. Philip Grierson. Foreword by F. M. Stenton. London: Longmans, Green, 1952.
Geary, Patrick J. *Furta Sacra: Thefts of Relics in the Central Middle Ages*. Princeton, N.J.: Princeton University Press, 1978.
———. *Aristocracy in Provence: The Rhône Basin at the Dawn of the Carolingian Age*. Philadelphia: University of Pennsylvania Press, 1985.
Giry, Arthur. *Manuel de diplomatique*. Paris, 1894.
Glenn, Jason. *Politics and History in the Tenth Century: The World and Works of Richer of Reims*. New York: Cambridge University Press, 2004.
Godman, Peter. *Poetry of the Carolingian Renaissance*. London: Duckworth, 1985.
Gossage, A. J. "Plutarch." In *Latin Biography*,. ed. T. A. Dorey. New York: Basic, 1967.
Grierson, Philip. "L'origine des comtes d'Amiens, Valois, et Vexin." *Le Moyen Age* ser. 3, 10.1 (1939): 81–105.
Guillot, Olivier. "La papauté, l'église de Reims et les Carolingiens." In *Xeme siècle: Recherches nouvelles*, ed. Pierre Riché, Carol Heitz, and François Heber-Suffrin. Contribution au Colloque Hugues Capet, 987–1987. Cahier VI. Centre de recherches sur l'antiquité tardive et le Haut Moyen Age. Paris: Centre national de la recherche scientifique,, 1987.
———. "Formes, fondements et limites de l'organisation politiques en France au Xe siècle." In *Il secolo di ferro: Mito e realità del secolo X*. 17–19 April 1990. Settimane di Studio del Centro italiano di studi sull'alto medioevo 38. Vol. 1. Spoleto, Italy: Presso la sede del centro, 1991.
Guiter, Henri. "Limites linguistiques dans la région bordelaise." In *Actes du 104e Congrès national des sociétés savantes*. Bordeaux, 1979. Section de philologie et d'histoire. Vol. 2, *Etudes sur la Gascogne*. Paris: Bibliothèque nationale, 1981.
Gwara, Scott. "Three Acrostic Poems by Abbo of Fleury." *Journal of Medieval Latin* 2 (1992): 203–35.
Hallam, Elizabeth. *Capetian France, 987–1328*. London: Longman, 1980.
Head, Thomas. *Hagiography and the Cult of the Saints: The Diocese of Orléans, 800–1200*. Cambridge: Cambridge University Press, 1990.
Herlihy, David. "Three Patterns of Social Mobility in Medieval History." *Journal of Interdisciplinary History* (1973): 623–47.
———. *Medieval Households*. Cambridge, Mass.: Harvard University Press, 1985.
Higounet, Charles. "A propos de la fondation du prieuré de La Réole." In *Actes du Colloque millénaire de la fondation du prieuré de La Réole*. La Réole, 11–12 November 1978. Bordeaux: Société des bibliophiles de Guyenne, 1980.
———. "'Centralité', petites villes et bastides dans l'Aquitaine médiévale." In *Les petites villes du Moyen-Age à nos jours*. Colloque international CESURB, Bordeaux, 25–26 October 1985. Paris: Centre national de la recherche scientifique, 1987.
Hill, David. *An Atlas of Anglo-Saxon England*. Toronto: University of Toronto Press, 1981.
Hubert, Jean. "Les routes du Moyen Age." In *Les routes de France depuis les origines jusqu'à nos jours*. Colloques: Cahiers de civilisation. Paris: Association pour la diffusion de la pensée française, 1959.

Hunt, Noreen. *Cluny under Saint Hugh*. London: Edward Arnold, 1967.
Iogna-Prat, Dominique. *Agni Immaculati: Recherches sur les sources hagiographiques relatives à Saint Maieul de Cluny (954–994)*. Paris: Les Editions du Cref, 1988.
James, Edward. *The Origins of France: From Clovis to the Capetians, 500–1000*. New Studies in Medieval History. Ed. Maurice Keen. London: Macmillan, 1982.
John, Eric. *Orbis Britanniae and Other Studies*. Leicester, England: Leicester University Press, 1966.
Johnson, Penelope D. *Prayer, Patronage, and Power: The Abbey of La Trinité, Vendôme (1032–1187)*. New York: New York University Press, 1981.
Jones, A. H. M., J. R. Martindale, and J. Morris. *Prosopography of the Later Roman Empire*. Vol. 1 (A.D. 260–395). Cambridge: Cambridge University Press, 1971.
Knowles, David. *The Monastic Order in England: A History of Its Development from the Times of St. Dunstan to the Fourth Lateran Council, 943–1216*. Cambridge: Cambridge University Press, 1949.
Koziol, Geoffrey. *Begging Pardon and Favor: Ritual and Political Order in Early Medieval France*. Ithaca, N.Y.: Cornell University Press, 1992.
———. "Political Culture." In *France in the Central Middle Ages, 900–1200*, ed. Marcus Bull. The Short Oxford History of France. Oxford: Oxford University Press, 2002.
Landes, Richard. "Lest the Millennium Be Fulfilled: Apocalyptic Expectations and the Pattern of Western Chronography, 100–800 C.E." In *The Use and Abuse of Eschatology in the Middle Ages*, ed. Werner Verbeke, Daniel Verhelst, and Andres Welkenhuysen. Louvain, Belgium: Leuven University Press, 1988.
———. "The Fear of the Apocalyptic Year 1000: Augustinian Historiography, Medieval and Modern." In *The Apocalyptic Year 1000: Religious Expectation and Social Change, 950–1050*, ed. Richard Landes, Andrew Gow, and David C. Van Meter. Oxford: Oxford University Press, 2003.
———. "Introduction: The *terribles espoirs de 1000* and the Tacit Fears of 2000." In *The Apocalyptic Year 1000: Religious Expectation and Social Change, 950–1050*, ed. Richard Landes, Andrew Gow, and David C. Van Meter. Oxford: Oxford University Press, 2003.
Landes, Richard, Andrew Gow, and David C. Van Meter, eds. *The Apocalyptic Year 1000: Religious Expectation and Social Change, 950–1050*. Oxford: Oxford University Press, 2003.
Lauer, Philippe. "Le manuscrit des *Annales de Flodoard*, Reg. Lat. 633 du Vatican." *Mélanges, d'archéologie et d'histoire de l'Ecole française de Rome* 18 (1898): 491–523.
Lauranson-Rosaz, Christian. "Réseaux aristocratiques et pouvoir monastique dan le Midi aquitain du IXe au XI siècle." In *Actes du premier colloque du CERCOR [Centre européen de recherches sur les congregations et ordres religieux]*. Travaux et recherches 1. Saint-Etienne, France: Publications Université Jean Monnet, 1991.
Leclercq, Jean. "Saint Majolus and Cluny." In *Aspects of Monasticism*, ed. Jean Leclercq. Trans. Mary Dodd. Cistercian Studies Series 7. Kalamazoo, Mich.: Cistercian Publications, 1978.

LeGoff, Jacques. *Time, Work, and Culture in the Middle Ages.* Trans. Arthur Goldhammer. Chicago: Chicago University Press, 1980.
Lemarignier, Jean-François. "L'exemption monastique et les origines de la réforme grégorienne." In *A Cluny: Congrès scientifique, fêtes et cérémonies liturgique en honneur des saints abbés Odon et Odilon.* 9–11 July 1949. Dijon: Bernigaud et Privat, 1950.
———. *Gouvernement royal aux premiers temps capétiens (987–1108).* Paris: A. et J. Picard, 1965.
———. "Political and Monastic Structures in France at the End of the Tenth and the Beginning of the Eleventh Century." Trans. Frederic Cheyette. In *Lordship and Community in Medieval Europe: Selected Readings.* New York: Holt, Reinhart, and Winston, 1968. [Revised translation of "Structures monastiques et structures politiques dans la France de la fin du Xe et des débuts du XIe siècle." In *Il monachesimo nell'alto medioevo: Settimane di Studio del Centro italiano di studi sull'alto medioevo* 4 (Spoleto, 1957).]
Le Patourel, John. *The Norman Empire.* Oxford: Clarendon, 1976.
Le Stum, Christine. "L'*Historia Francorum* d'Aimoin de Fleury: Etude et édition critique." Positions des thèses. Paris: Ecole de Chartes, 1976.
Levitan, W. "Dancing at the End of the Rope: Optatian Porfyry and the Field of Roman Verse." *Transactions of the American Philological Association* 115 (1985): 245–69.
Lewis, Andrew W. *Royal Succession in Capetian France: Studies on Familial Order and the State.* Cambridge, Mass.: Harvard University Press, 1981.
Lewis, Archibald R., and Timothy J. Runyan. *European Naval and Maritime History, 300–1500.* Bloomington: Indiana University Press, 1985.
Lewis, Charlton T., and Charles Short. *A Latin Dictionary.* 1879. Reprint, Oxford: Clarendon, 1966.
Lot, Ferdinand. *Les derniers Carolingiens: Lothaire, Louis V, Charles de Lorraine, 954–991.* Bibliothèque de l'Ecole des hautes études, sciences philologiques et historiques 24. Paris: Emile Bouillon, 1891.
———. *Etudes sur le règne de Hugues Capet et la fin du Xe siècle.* Bibliothèque de l'Ecole des hautes études, sciences historiques et philologiques. Fasc. 147. Paris: Emile Bouillon, 1903.
Lutz, Cora Elizabeth. *Schoolmasters of the Tenth Century.* Hamden, Conn.: Archon, 1977.
Martindale, Jane. "The French Aristocracy in the Early Middle Ages: A Reappraisal." *Past and Present* 75 (May 1977): 5–45.
———. "The Kingdom of Aquitaine and the 'Dissolution of the Carolingian Fisc.'" *Francia* 11 (1983–1984): 131–91.
Mayr-Harting, Henry. *The Venerable Bede, the Rule of Saint Benedict, and Social Class.* Jarrow Lecture. Jarrow, England: Rector of Jarrow, 1976.
McGuire, Brian Patrick. *Friendship and Community: The Monastic Experience, 350–1250.* Kalamazoo, Mich.: Cistercian Publications, 1988.
McKitterick, Rosamund. *The Frankish Kingdoms under the Carolingians, 751–987.* London: Longman, 1983.
Moehs, Teta E. *Gregorius V, 996–999: A Biographical Study.* Päpste und Papsttum. Stuttgart: A. Hiersemann, 1972.

Mostert, Marco. "Le séjour d'Abbon de Fleury à Ramsey." *Bibliothèque de l'Ecole de chartes* 144 (1986): 199–208.

———. *The Political Theology of Abbo of Fleury.* Hilversum, Netherlands: Verloren, 1987.

———. "Die Urkundenfälschungen Abbos von Fleury." In *Fälschungen im Mittelalter: Interntionaler Kongress der Monumenta Germaniae Historica.* Munich, 16–19 September 1986. Vol. 4, *Diplomatische Fälschungen (II).* Hanover: Hahnsche Buchhandlung, 1988.

———. *The Library of Fleury: A Provisional List of Manuscripts.* Middeleeuwse Studies en Bronnen 3. Hilversum, Netherlands: Verloren, 1989.

———. "The Political Ideas of Abbo of Fleury." *Francia* 16.1 (1989): 85–100.

Murray, Alexander. *Reason and Society in the Middle Ages.* Oxford: Clarendon, 1978.

———. *Germanic Kinship Structure.* Studies in Law and Society in Antiquity and the Early Middle Ages. Toronto: Pontifical Institute of Medieval Studies, 1983.

Neumann, J. "Hydrographic and Ship-Hydrodynamic Aspects of the Norman Invasion, AD 1066." *Anglo-Norman Studies* 11 (1988): 222–23.

Newman, William Mendel. *Catalogue des actes de Robert II, Roi de France.* Paris: Recueil Sirey, 1937.

———. *Le domaine royal sous les premiers Capétiens.* Paris: Recueil Sirey, 1937.

Niermeyer, J. F. *Mediae Latinitatis lexicon minus.* Leiden: E. J. Brill, 1984.

Nightingale, John. "Oswald, Fleury, and Continental Reform." In *Saint Oswald of Worcester: Life and Influence,* ed. Nicholas Brooks and Catherine Cubitt. London: Leicester University Press, 1996.

Ourliac, Paul. "Les coutumes du Sud-Ouest de la France." In *Etudes d'histoire du droit médiéval.* Paris: A. et J. Picard, 1979. [Originally published in Spanish in the *Anuario de historia del derecho espanol* 23 (1953): 407–22.]

Ourliac, Paul. "Coutumes et dialectes gascons (note sur la géographie coutumière du Sud-Ouest au Moyen Age)." In *Etudes d'histoire du droit médiéval.* Paris: A. et J. Picard, 1979. [Originally published in *Droits de l'antiquité et sociologie religeuse, Mélanges . . . Henry Lévy-Bruhl,* 1959.]

Oury, Guy. "L'idéal monastique dans la vie canoniale: Le Bienheureux Hervé de Tours († 1022)." *Revue Mabillon* 52, ser. 3, no. 207 (1962): 1–31.

Pardiac, Jean-Baptiste. *Histoire de saint Abbon, abbé de Fleury-sur-Loire, martyr à La Réole en 1004.* Paris, 1872.

Pellégrin, Elisabeth. *Bibliothèques retrouvées: Manuscrits, bibliothèques et bibliophiles du Moyen Age et de la Renaissance, recueil d'études publiées de 1938 à 1985.* Paris: Centre national de la recherche scientifique, 1988.

Pfister, Christian. *Etudes sur le règne de Robert le Pieux (996–1031).* Paris, 1885.

Poly, Jean-Pierre, and Eric Bournazel. *The Feudal Transformation, 900–1200.* Trans. Caroline Higgitt. Europe Past and Present Series. New York: Holmes and Meier, 1991.

Poole, Reginald L. *Studies in Chronology and History.* Ed. A. L. Poole. Oxford: Clarendon, 1934. [Originally published as "The Beginning of the Year in the Middle Ages" in *Proceedings of the British Academy* 10 (1921).]

Pounds, N. J. G. *An Historical Geography of Europe*. Cambridge: Cambridge University Press, 1990.
Raby, F. J. E. *A History of Secular Latin Poetry in the Middle Ages*. 2 vols. 2nd ed. Oxford: Clarendon, 1957.
Riché, Pierre. *Education and Culture in the Barbarian West from the Sixth through Eighth Century*. Trans. John J. Contreni, foreword by Richard E. Sullivan. Columbia: University of South Carolina Press, 1976. [Original French edition, 1962.]
———. *Les écoles et l'enseignement dans l'Occident chrétien de la fin du Ve siècle au milieu du XIe siècle*. Collection historique. Paris: Aubier Montaigne, 1979.
———. "L'enseignement de Gerbert de Reims dans le contexte européen." In *Gerberto: Scienza, storia e mito*. Atti del Gerberti Symposium. Bobbio, 25–27 July 1983. Bobbio, Italy: A. S. B. publicazione annuale, Studio II, 1985.
———. *Daily Life in the World of Charlemagne*. Trans. and intro. by JoAnn McNamara. 1978. Reprint with expanded footnotes, Philadelphia: University of Pennsylvania Press, 1988.
———. *Abbon de Fleury: Un moine savant et combatif (vers 950–1004)*. Turnhout, Belgium: Brepols, 2004.
Rosenwein, Barbara. *Rhinoceros Bound: Cluny in the Tenth Century*. Philadelphia: University of Pennsylvania Press, 1982.
———. *To Be the Neighbor of Saint Peter*. Ithaca, N.Y.: Cornell University Press, 1989.
Rosenwein, Barbara, Thomas Head, and Sharon Farmer. "Monks and Their Enemies: A Comparative Approach." *Speculum* 66.4 (1991): 764–96.
Rosten, Leo. *The Joys of Yiddish*. New York: McGraw-Hill, 1968.
Schimmelpfennig, Bernhard. *The Papacy*. Trans. James Sievert. New York: Columbia University Press, 1992.
Schmitz, Philibert. *Histoire de l'Ordre de Saint Benoît*. Vol. I, *Origines, difusion et constitution jusqu'au XIIe siècle*. 2nd ed. Maredsous and Namur, Belgium: Editions Maredsous, 1948.
Schneidmüller, Bernd. *Karolingische Tradition und frühes französisches Königtum: Untersuchungen zur Herrschaftslegitimation der westfränkisch-französischen Monarchie im 10. Jarhhundert*. Wiesbaden, Germany: Franz Steiner, 1979.
Sénac, Robert-André. "L'évêché de Gascogne et ses évêque (977–1059)." In *Actes du 104e Congrès national des sociétés savantes*. Section de philologie et d'histoire jusqu'à 1610. Vol. 2. Bordeaux, 1979. Paris: CTHS, 1981.
Sergi, Giuseppe. "The Kingodm of Italy." In *The New Cambridge Medieval History*, vol. 3 (c. 900–c. 1024), ed. Timothy Reuter. Cambridge: Cambridge University Press, 1999.
Stafford, Pauline. *The East Anglian Midlands in the Early Middle Ages*. Leicester, England: Leicester University Press, 1985.
Strayer, Joseph L., ed. *Dictionary of the Middle Ages*. New York: Scribner, 1982–1989.
"Studies in Biography II: An Abbot of the Tenth Century." *Month and Catholic Review* (January–April 1874): 163–77, and (May–August 1874): 28–42.
Teisseyre, Charles. "Le renouveau du culte de saint Abbon à La Réole au XIXe siècle." In *Actes du Colloque du millénaire de la fondation du prieuré de La Réole*.

La Réole, 11–12 November 1978. Bordeaux: Société des bibliophiles de Guyenne, 1980.
Thompson, James Westfall. *The Medieval Library*. New York: Hafner, 1965.
Tosi, Michele. "Il governo abbaziale de Gerberto a Bobbio." In *Gerberto: Scienza, storia, e mito*. Atti del Gerbert Symposium, Bobbio, 25–27 July 1983. Bobbio, Italy: A. S. B. publicazione annuale, Studio II, 1985.
Townend, G. P. "Suetonius and His Influence." In *Latin Biography*, ed. T. A. Dorey. New York: Basic, 1967.
Ullmann, Walter. *A Short History of the Papacy in the Middle Ages*. London: Methuen, 1972.
Unger, Richard W. *The Ship and the Medieval Economy, 600–1600*. Montreal: McGill-Queen's University Press, 1980.
Van de Vyver, A., ed. "Les oeuvres inédits d'Abbon de Fleury." *Revue bénédictine* 47 (1935): 123–69.
———, ed. Abbonis *Floriacensis opera inedita I: Syllogismorum Categoricorum et Hypotheticorum enodatio*. In *Rijksuniversiteit te Gent: Werken uitgegeven door de Faculteit van de Letteren en Wijsbegeerte* 140. Bruges, Belgium: De Tempel, 1966.
Vidier, Alexandre. *L'historiographie à Saint-Benoît-sur-Loire et les miracles de saint Benoît*. Paris: A. et J. Picard, 1965.
Van Meter, David C. "Christian of Stavelot on Matthew 24:42 and the Tradition that the World Will End on March 25th." *Recherches de théologie ancienne et médiévale* 63 (1996): 68–92.
Wallis, Faith. "Abbo of Fleury and the Reckoning of Time." Paper presented at the Twenty-fifth International Congress on Medieval Studies, Western Michigan University, Kalamazoo, Mich., 10–13 May 1990.
Ward, Benedicta. *Miracles and the Medieval Mind*. Philadelphia: University of Pennsylvania Press, 1982.
Warren, F. M. "Constantine of Fleury, 985–1014." *Transactions of the Connecticut Academy of Arts and Sciences* 15 (July 1909): 285–92.
Wemple, Suzanne Fonay. *Women in Frankish Society: Marriage and the Cloister, 500–900*. Philadelphia: University of Pennsylvania Press, 1985.
Werner, Karl Ferdinand. "Important Noble Families in the Kingdom of Charlemagne—A Prosopographical Study of the Relationship between King and Nobility in the Early Middle Ages." Trans. Timothy Reuter. In *The Medieval Nobility: Studies on the Ruling Classes of France and Germany from the Sixth to the Twelfth Century*, ed. Timothy Reuter. Europe in the Middle Ages. Selected Studies 14. Amsterdam, Netherlands: North-Holland, 1979. [Originally published as "Bedeutende Adelsfamilien im Reich Karls des Grossen: Ein personengeschichtlicher Beitrag zum Verhältnis von Königtum und Adel im frühen Mittelalter." In *Karl der Große, Lebenswerk und Nachleben 1: Persönlicheit und Geschichte*, ed. H. Beumann. Düsseldorf: Schwann, 1965.]
———. *Histoire de France*. Vol. 1, *Les origines (avant l'an mil)*. Gen. ed. Jean Favier. [Paris]: Fayard, 1984.
———. "Hugues Capet, duc puissant—roi faible, un essai d'explication." In *Xème siècle: Recherches nouvelles*, ed. Pierre Riché, Carol Heitz, and François

Heber-Suffrin. Contribution au Colloque Hugues Capet, 987–1987. Cahier VI. Centre de recherches sur l'antiquité tardive et le Haut Moyen Age. Paris: Centre national de la recherche scientifique, 1987.

Wollasch, Joachim. "Abbo in Aquitanien." In *Neue Forschungen über Cluny und die Cluniacenser,* ed. Gerd Tellenbach. Freiburg: Herder, 1959.

———. "Exkurs I: Zur Verbreitung des Namens Abbo in Aquitanien (bis zum Ende des 10. Jahrhunderts)." In *Neue Forschungen über Cluny und die Cluniacenser,* ed. Gerd Tellenbach. Freiburg: Herder, 1959.

Wormald, Patrick. " Æthelwold and His Continental Counterparts: Contact, Comparison, Contrast." In *Bishop Æthelwold: His Career and Influence,* ed. Barbara Yorke. Woodbridge, England: Boydell, 1988.

INDEX

Aachen, council of, 153n11, 154, 156n18, 165
abacus, 61
Abbo, monk of Saint-Martial of Limoges, 30
Abbo, St., abbot of Fleury: acrostic poetry, 75, 198–201, 226–29, 254; anti-apocalypticism, 11, 52–55, 143, 230; *Apologeticus,* 12, 14n35, 19, 20, 132–43, 150, 151, 155, 161n34, 163, 171n72, 184, 200n27, 204–5, 225, 263, 267; astronomical work, 13, 45, 222; *Collectio canonum,* 21, 91n34, 161–63, 165, 171–72, 184, 200n27, 225; computus, 46, 49, 54–55, 141–42, 225, 229–30, 245, 247; correspondence, 2, 3, 6, 14–15, 17, 27, 49, 66n29, 69n41, 70–71, 74, 91n34, 100–102, 104, 130n13, 132n19, 153, 161n34, 165, 170–71, 175–76, 178–79, 183, 194–97, 198–99, 201–9, 213–15, 218, 222–26, 229n117, 230, 239, 254, 265; cult, 5–6, 8, 250, 254–60, 262; death and burial, 2–5, 9–10, 41, 46n81, 80n83, 148, 238n17, 246–52; dossier of texts, 161, 175n88, 180, 223n98; education 23, 33–36, 43, 46, 51–52, 56, 63–72, 74, 229n117, 255, 266–67; election as abbot, 1–2, 6, 18, 34, 58, 76–80, 83–84, 123, 127n6, 184, 205n48, 221, 263, 266; entry into monastic life, 27, 34–37; family, 24–33, 203, 239; final journey, 2n2, 237–40; *Life of St. Edmund,* 14, 69, 74–75; leading abbot of Gaul, 3, 10, 18, 181–82, 188, 189, 229; martyr, 3–5, 51, 83, 148, 238n17, 250–52, 254–57, 260, 262, 268; millennial commemoration, 9–10; miracles, 5, 6n9, 32, 241, 256, 258; name, 28–30, 37; political thought, 12–13, 19, 22, 137; *Quaestiones Grammaticales,* 13–14, 72; syllogisms, 49–50, 229; teacher, 35, 39, 44, 45, 47, 48n90, 49–51, 60, 63, 72, 101n69, 161, 214, 217–21, 223; travel to Rome, 85, 167–70, 176n91, 178–79, 186–88, 189, 197–98, 203, 223, 231, 263. *See also* London BL Add 10972

abbots, 7, 34, 57, 71, 78, 86, 89, 91–92, 141, 162, 264; at Council of Saint-Basle, 106, 109–17, 122, 124, 140
acrostics, 75, 198–201, 226–29, 254
Adalbero, archbishop of Reims, 48, 59–60, 61n14, 73, 92–98, 101n69, 157, 162–63
Adalbero, bishop of Laon, 98–99, 101n69, 102, 105n80, 113
Adalbert, St., bishop of Prague, 168, 169, 170–71
Adalgar, priest of Reims, 110, 116, 122, 163n41
Adelaide, wife of Hugh Capet, 61n14, 192n7

287

Adelard, monk of Fleury or La Réole, 248
Adémar de Chabanne. *See* Adhemar of Chabannes
Adhemar of Chabannes: *Chronique,* 221, 249, 260, 261n26
Adrevald of Fleury: *Miracula sancti Benedicti,* 170n69
Adso of Montier-en-Der, 45
Advent and heresy, 141–43
advocatia, 146
Ælfric, 254
Æthelwine, ealdorman, 63, 68, 71, 75
Æthelwold, St., bishop of Winchester, 39, 71, 257
African councils, 164
Aimoinus, monk of Fleury: biases and omissions as biographer, 5–7, 26, 34, 49, 60n9, 63–64, 77–80, 82–83, 173n75, 240–41, 253, 262–68; credentials as biographer, 3–4; death, 4n5, 5n8, 220n85, 222; education, 4, 45, 222; ethnic background, 242–43; family, 26, 237, 240–41, 250–51; *Historia Francorum,* 3n4, 222; *Miracula sancti Abbonis,* 5n8, 258–59; *Miracula sancti Benedicti,* 3, 82, 87–88, 170n69, 183n114, 220; *Vita sancti Abbonis,* 2–8, 10, 24–29, 31, 32, 34–35, 37, 41, 43, 44, 46, 49, 50n99, 51–52, 58, 60n9, 63–64, 66n29, 69, 74, 76–80, 82–83, 123, 126–30, 132–33, 136, 145n55, 152, 168–69, 179, 185–86, 188n134, 193, 198–99, 219–20, 229–30, 234n8, 235–43, 245–51, 253, 254–57, 260, 262–68; writings used by historians, 8, 10, 80n84, 82, 254
Albert, abbot of Micy, 15
Alcuin, 43, 199n25
Aldebald, monk of Cluny, 152
Alps, crossing of, 167–68
Amalbert, abbot of Fleury, 37n45, 40–41, 45, 58, 78n78, 80, 86, 220, 235
Amalguin, viscount, 26n10, 236–37, 250
Amiens: bishops of, 91, 105n82; counts of, 145, 196–97. *See also individuals by name*
anathma. *See* excommunication
André, monk of Fleury: *Miracula sancti Benedicti,* 183n114; *Vita sancti Gauzlini,* 148, 219–22
Andrew, St., 203; feast, 248
Anezan, monk of La Réole, 244–46
Angevins. *See* Anjou
Angoulême, 240
Anjou, 32, 88–89; counts of, 74n57, 175–76, 187, 193, 197, 204, 210n58, 215–17, 224, 231, 261–62. *See also counts by name*
"Annales Floriacenses," 80, 212–13, 235n10
Annunciation and heresy, 53–54
antichrist, 52, 160
apocalypticism, 11, 52–56, 141–43, 213, 230
Aquitaine, 26n10, 29, 31n27, 45, 234, 238; dukes of, 242. *See also dukes by name*
Archembald, archbishop of Tours, 154, 174–75
Argenton-sur-Creuse, 238
Arians, 160, 205
arithmetic, 46, 48, 60
Arius, 205
Armagh, 39
armarius, 43, 50
Arnulf, archbishop of Reims: betrayal of Reims, 102, 107–8, 110, 113, 122, 157–58, 190, 192; oath to Hugh Capet, 99–102, 108–9, 113, 123; restoration to archiepiscopal see, 145, 159, 165, 177, 184, 188, 190, 192–96, 211–12, 263, 265; selection as archbishop, 78, 94–96, 98–99, 157, 163; trial at Saint-Basle and deposition, 18, 49, 92, 103–23, 126, 151, 154–55, 158–61, 164–65, 178, 183n118, 184, 202, 206, 212, 217, 223, 263
Arnulf, bishop of Orléans, 18–19, 41, 72–73, 87–88, 91n36, 92, 131, 134, 138, 141, 145–50, 155, 172, 261,

262n30; attack on Abbo, 126–29, 136, 138, 140, 204, 238, 267; *De cartilagine*, 132, 143–44; at Council of Saint-Basle, 105–9, 114–16, 120–21, 123–24
Arnulf, monk of Fleury, 222
Arnulf of Yèvre, nephew of bishop of Orléans, 88, 128, 139, 146–49
astronomy, 15, 44, 46, 48–50, 60, 93, 222, 229–30
Aubeterre, 240–41
Augustine of Hippo, 53, 194
Augustus, emperor, 199–200
Aunis, 31
Autun, 31, 40, 85–86, 98; bishops of, 105. *See also bishops by name*
Autunois. *See* Autun
Auxerre, 89, 106; bishops of, 105. *See also bishops by name*
Aymard, abbot of Cluny, 152

Bachrach, Bernard S., 88, 193
Barraclough, Geoffrey, 201
Basques, 234n8. *See also* Wascones
Batany, Jean, 13
Beaulieu-sur-Dordogne, monastery, 45, 218
Beauvais: bishops of, 91–92, 105n82
Bede, the Venerable, 142
Benedict of Aniane, 70
Benedict of Nursia, St., 40, 57, 70, 139, 184, 218, 240, 250, 265–66; feast of translation, 1, 237, 251–52; miracles, 3, 41, 183, 222, 245, 256; relics, 5, 18, 38, 39, 42–43, 60, 169n66, 170–71, 179, 182–83, 218. *See also* Rule of St. Benedict
Benedict V, pope, 114
Benedict VII, pope, 166n50, 180n107
Beowulf, 67
Bern of Reichenau, 45
Bernard Guillaume, duke of the Gascons, 235, 249
Bernard of Beaulieu, 126n10; abbot of Beaulieu-sur-Dordogne and Solignac, 101n69, 104n77, 218–19;

bishop of Cahors, 218; student and monk at Fleury, 15n36, 35n41, 44–45, 50, 214, 218
Bernard of Segni: "Commentaria in Mattheum," 34n37
Bernier, abbot of Marmoutier, 204–10, 215n72, 217
Bertha of Blois, wife of Odo of Blois and Robert the Pious, 20, 74n57, 173, 175–78, 183n118, 186–87, 188n134, 191–93, 196–97, 204, 215–17, 261–62
bishops, 33–34, 38, 94, 114, 136–37, 143, 153–58, 163–65, 168–69, 177, 183, 190, 192, 197, 224–25, 265, 267; at Council of Saint-Basle, 98n59, 100, 101n69, 102–13, 115–24, 140, 161, 191, 212; at Council of Saint-Denis, 129–34; and Hugh Capet, 73, 86, 91–92, 125–26, 138–40, 145, 264; and monasteries, 2, 4, 7, 11, 16, 56, 70–71, 86–89, 138–41, 156, 162, 184, 214
Blésois. *See* Blois
Blois: counts of, 74n57, 89, 148, 174, 176, 187n131, 191, 197, 204, 209–10, 213, 215–17, 224, 231; pagus, 40, 85. *See also counts by name*
Blois-Chartres. *See* Blois; Chartres
Bobbio, monastery, 48n91
Boethius, 48, 50
Boniface, Carolingian poet, 199n25
Boniface VII, pope, 114
Bonnée, priory of Fleury, 86
Bordeaux, 239, 260. *See also archbishops by name*
Bouchard, Constance B., 173
Bouchard, count of Vendôme, 120–21, 187n131
Bourges, 238; archbishops of, 91–92, 105. *See also archbishops by name*
Brittany, 38
Brogne, monastery, 60, 89
Bruno. *See* Gregory V
Bruno, bishop of Langres, 89, 98n59, 105n80, 108, 113, 116
Burgundy, 32, 34, 153; dukes of, 26

Byrhtferth, English teacher: 48n90, 49, 50n99, 69n41, 72, 230n122

Cadroe, St. *See* Cathroé
Cahors, bishopric, 45, 218
Calais, 64
canon law, 112, 157, 172, 185
Candidus: "Vita Eigilis abbatis Fuldensis," 34
canonization, 152, 258
canon tables, 14, 223
Canterbury, 75, 202. *See also archbishops by name*
Canute, king of England, 71
Capetian dynasty: and bishops, 18, 73, 78, 86–87, 105, 107, 119, 126, 138, 154, 157, 175, 191; consolidation of power, 12, 16–18, 20–21, 84, 132, 137, 155, 177, 192, 253–54, 262–64; and counts of Anjou, 175–76, 187n133, 210n58, 215–16, 231, 261n27; and counts of Blois, 129n9, 197, 210n58, 215–16, 231; marriages, 74n57, 125, 191–92, 197; and monasteries, 6–7, 12, 16–22, 77–78, 82–83, 89–91, 147–48, 173n75, 176, 185n122, 204, 261–64, 267; origins, 17, 26, 83, 89–90; and Ottonians, 156–57, 254; and papacy, 11, 190; royal authority, 1n1, 7, 20–21, 241n48; territory, 16, 77–78, 105, 107, 133, 137, 148, 156, 158n26. *See also rulers by name*
Carolingian dynasty: and bishops, 98n59; marriage alliances, 191–92; and monasteries, 11, 16–17, 60, 84, 90–91, 185n122; prestige, 191–92, 242–43; royal authority, 20–21, 83, 137, 151, 201; rulers of West Francia, 1n1, 16–18, 20, 75n63, 78, 83–84, 96, 190, 263. *See also Carolingian rulers by name*
Carolingian renaissance, 21, 199, 226, 228
Cathroé, St., abbot of Waulsort, 39, 65
celibacy, 14, 224–26, 247

central-place theory (Christaller), 233–34
Chalcedon, Council of (451), 136–37, 142
Châlons-sur-Marne, 104n79; bishops of, 91, 177
Charlemagne, 199; descendants, 1n1, 15, 87n16; military campaigns, 242–43; and monasteries, 181, 234n6
Charles of Lorraine: 16–18, 26, 73, 84, 94–99, 101n69, 102–3, 108–9, 113, 124, 125, 157, 172, 177, 190, 193, 263
Charles the Bald, king of West Francia, 1n1
Charroux, 240
Chartres, 38, 96, 103, 140, 174, 213–15. *See also counts and bishops by name*
Chasseneuille, Carolingian palace, 242
chastity, 4, 70, 138, 225
Châteauneuf of Tours, 174
Châtillon-sur-Loire, priory of Fleury, 86
Chelles: Council of, 153, 155–56; royal court, 175n87
chirograph, 99–100
Christian of Stavelot, 53–54
Christianus, cleric of Fleury, 27–29, 31–32
Cluny, monastery, 14n35, 17, 34n37, 85, 87, 89, 152–53, 167, 182, 187n132, 204, 205, 210, 214, 223, 254. *See also abbots and monks by name*
Compiègne, 37
computus, 46, 49, 54, 142, 229–30, 245, 247, 254
consanguinity, 25n6, 173, 191
Constance of Arles, wife of Robert the Pious, 74n57, 215–16, 261n27, 264
Constantine the Great, emperor, 198–99, 226–28
Constantine, monk of Fleury: dean and abbot of Saint-Mesmin of Micy, 62n15, 215–16, 220–21; abbot of Nouaillé, 62n15, 221; student and teacher at Fleury, 45, 51–52, 60,

127n6, 220–21, 266; student and correspondent of Gerbert of Aurillac, 49, 51, 60–62, 92–93, 95
Coolidge, Robert, 99, 102
councils and synods, 2, 12, 49, 109–12, 114, 123, 124, 135–37, 141, 155, 161n34, 162, 163n40, 164, 180–81, 184, 206, 225, 253. *See also individual councils and synods*
Cousin, Patrice, 9, 238–39, 260
Crescentius family, 164–65, 168, 170, 178–79, 200
Crowland Abbey, 68
customary law, 233. *See also* canon law; divine law; Roman law
custos infantum, 35–36, 44, 50

Dagobert, archbishop of Bourges, 105, 121, 154
Davril, Anselme, 259
Denis, St.: shrine in Paris, 169n66
dialectic, 45–46
Dionysian era, 45, 55, 230
divine law, 107, 185
Domesday Book, 67
Donatus, grammarian, 43
Donnet, François-Auguste-Ferdinand, cardinal and archbishop of Bordeaux, 8, 260
Dordogne River, 240–41, 243, 256n4
Dover, 66
Droth River, 241
Duby, Georges, 12, 25, 137, 173, 191
duke of the Franks, 17, 73, 83, 90, 181–82. *See also dukes by name*
Dunbabin, Jean, 20–21
Dunstan, St., archbishop of Canterbury, 71, 74–75, 81, 200n26, 227, 229, 257

East Anglia, 66
Easter, 46, 53–54, 80n83, 126n4, 129, 254
Ebo, archbishop of Reims, 164
Ebrard, abbot of Saint-Julien of Tours, 59

Edgar, king of England, 67, 71–72
Edmund, king of England, 14, 74–75, 254
education, 23–24, 34–36, 43–47, 51, 56, 67, 95, 142, 229n117, 255, 267–68
Elisiernus, *custos* of Saint-Benoît de Sault, 32
Elisiernus, monk and benefactor of Fleury, 32
Elisiernus, monk of Fleury, 32
England, 39, 259; and Abbo, 50n99, 51n102, 69–72, 74–75, 81, 84, 95, 142, 178, 229; Channel crossing to, 65–66, 256, 265; diet, 69, 84, 178n100; and monastic reform, 38–39, 60, 63–64, 69–70
Ennodius, 227
Ermengard, wife of Teotard, 28
Ermengard, mother of Abbo, 25, 28, 29, 31–32
excommunication, 109–10, 115, 122, 129, 131, 139–40, 150, 154–55, 174, 178, 183, 187, 192–94, 196

Farmer, Sharon, 209
Fawtier, Robert, 21
fenland (East Anglia), 67–68
Ferrières, monastery, 187
fires, 29n18, 41–43, 208, 213
fishing, 67–69, 86, 213
Fleury, monastery, 1–8, 11, 15, 24, 27, 31–32, 41, 49, 57, 60, 63, 66, 70, 74, 85, 118, 153, 169, 213, 242, 244–45, 247, 251–52, 253, 258–62; abbots of, 1, 37–38, 40, 44–45, 58, 64, 72, 85, 148, 219, 235, 261, 264, 268; and Capetians, 6–7, 16–19, 21, 77–78, 80–81, 82–84, 87, 89–92, 123, 147–50, 151, 173n75, 176, 181–82, 189, 262–64, 268; charters and cartulary, 28–29, 32, 38, 40, 41n65, 55, 74, 85–86, 90, 146–49, 181–85, 188, 206–7; churches, 33, 35, 40, 42; commemoration of the dead, 30–31; election of abbots, 40, 58–62, 76–80, 87, 181, 183, 268; factions within, 1, 6, 46, 49,

Fleury (cont.)
58–64, 72–73, 75n63, 76–79, 84, 95, 127n6, 205n48, 206, 215, 221, 266–67; immunities and privileges, 10, 37, 40, 74, 77, 83, 90, 126, 166–68, 178, 180–81, 185–86, 192, 203–4, 264; international character, 38–39, 56, 63, 65, 69, 75, 142, 169, 171, 265; leading monastery of Gaul, 3, 10, 18–19, 179n104, 181–84, 188, 189, 229; library and scriptorium, 14, 202, 228, 230, 267; and monastic reform, 17–18, 23, 38–39, 41, 60, 63, 87, 89–90, 152, 181–83, 254, 257, 268; monastic ritual *(consuetudines)*, 35–36, 44, 51; origins, 17; and papacy, 151, 166–68, 170–71, 176–77, 180–81, 264–65; possessions, 2, 40, 72–73, 84–86, 90, 128, 132, 139, 146–50, 181, 196; priories, 2, 5–6, 28, 85–86, 232, 234–37, 239–40, 255; relations with bishops of Orléans, 18–19, 87–89, 107, 126, 128, 144, 145n55, 146–49, 151, 189, 215, 267; relics, 1, 5, 18, 38, 39, 42–43, 60, 169n66, 170–71, 179, 182–83, 203, 218, 251, 266; schools, 2, 23, 33–36, 44–47, 50–52, 56, 60, 217–18; scholarship, 44–45, 51, 63, 91, 189, 217–22, 228–31, 268. *See also* Saint-Benoît-sur-Loire

floods, 41, 212–13
forgery of charters, 41n65, 178, 180–81, 184
Fortunatus, Carolingian poet, 227
Francs, hometown of Aimoinus, 240, 243
Franks, ethnic group, 232, 234n8, 242–43, 246–47
Frederick, monk of Fleury, 6, 127n6, 205–6, 215, 266
freedom, 23–27, 30–31
Frotgerius, St., 73
Fulbert of Chartres, 108, 213–14
Fulk, bishop of Amiens, 145n56
Fulk, bishop of Orléans, 262n30, 264, 267
Fulk Nerra, count of Anjou, 20, 88, 153n11, 174, 176, 186–87, 190, 193–94, 196–97, 261n27

G, correspondent of Abbo, 14n35, 162n35, 207, 223–24, 265
Gargano Massif, 218
Garonne River, 86, 232, 234n8, 241–42
Gascony, 2, 5, 7, 41, 85, 232–37, 239–43, 245–47, 252
Gâtinais, 40, 85, 196
Gaul, 3, 10, 18, 104–5, 107, 131, 179, 181–82, 186, 188, 189, 221, 229, 234, 264
Gauzbert, abbot of Saint-Julien of Tours, 130n13, 204–7, 210n58, 223–24
Gauzfred, treasurer of Fleury, 43
Gauzlin, abbot of Fleury, 6, 43, 45, 82–83, 148, 173n75, 183n14, 219–22, 223n98, 260–64, 267–68
Geoffrey, count of Gâtinais, 196
Geoffrey, count of Verdun, 157, 158
geometry, 46, 48
Gerald, monk of Fleury, 45, 222, 229n117, 230
Gerard, abbot of Brogne, 89
Gerbert of Aurillac (Pope Sylvester II), 10, 24; archbishop of Ravenna, 211; archbishop of Reims, 122–24, 131, 162–63, 196, 263; and Capetians, 73, 78, 92, 162–63, 174, 254; correspondence, 48n91, 51, 59–62, 92–95, 106, 131, 139n41, 159, 216, 221; at Council of Saint-Basle, 6, 49, 103–4, 106, 109–12, 114–15, 117–19, 121, 140, 151, 155, 157–59, 161, 164, 166, 211, 263; and dissent at Fleury, 49, 59–62, 72–73, 76–79, 93, 95, 266; education, 47–48; origins 47; and Ottonians, 48, 199, 211, 254; Pope Sylvester II, 6, 33, 46–47, 211–13; removal from Reims, 155–59, 161–65, 176–77, 192–93; and riot at Saint-Denis, 131–32, 150; secretary to archbishop of Reims, 48, 59–60, 93; teacher at Reims, 46, 48–50, 59–60, 92, 95, 106, 254

Index

Gerbert of Reims. *See* Gerbert of Aurillac
Germanus, monk of Fleury, abbot of Westbury-on-Trym, 39, 63, 69
Germigny-dès-Prés, 228
Gerranus of Reims, 46
Ghent, 89
Gibuin, nephew of bishop of Châlons-sur-Marne, 177
Gien-le-Vieil, priory of Fleury, 86
Girald, lord of Aubeterre, 26, 241
Gislebert, abbot of Saint-Cyprien of Poitiers, 27, 29, 239–40
Glastonbury, 71n49
Glenn, Jason, 45
gluttony, 5, 69
Gnato, 205
Gnatonites, 205
Gotesman, bishop of Amiens, 98n59, 105n80, 116, 198, 211
Gombaud, monk of Fleury, 27–29, 31–32
Good Friday: end of the world on, 52–54
Gorze, monastery, 254
grammar, 43, 45–47, 72
Gregory I, the Great, pope, 161n34, 180–81, 184, 186, 194, 206, 225, 240, 245, 265–66
Gregory IV, pope, 166n50, 180
Gregory V, pope: and Abbo, 14, 19, 27, 171, 178–88, 189, 193–97, 200–203, 206, 211–12, 264–65; affair of archbishop of Reims, 118, 177, 184, 186, 188, 195–96; Church councils, 174, 177–78, 191–92; and Crescenti, 170, 179, 200; and marriage of Robert the Pious, 20, 186–87, 191–93, 195; and Ottonians, 170, 198, 200–201, 254; papal privilege for Fleury, 10, 178–85, 206
Grenoble, council attemped at, 154
Guerreau-Jalabert, Anita, 13
Guigo of Chartreuse: "Vita Hugonis Gatianopolitani," 34n37
Guillaume Sanche, duke of the Gascons, 28, 234–35

Gumbald, bishop of Bordeaux and of Gascony, 28, 234
Guy, bishop of Soissons, 98n59, 105n80, 116, 145n56
Gwara, Scott, 201

hagiography, 2–5, 7, 152n6, 238n17, 256–57, 262
Harold, king of England, 65
Hatto, bishop of Vich, 48
Head, Thomas, 149
Heccard, count of the Burgundians, 86
Helgaud, monk of Fleury, 190, 219, 221n91, 264
Herard, St., 259
Herbert, bishop of Auxerre, 98n59, 105–6
Herbert, count of Vermandois, 113
Herbert, lord of Sully, 40–41
heresy, 5–6, 13, 53, 142–43, 207, 209n57, 249
Hervé, bishop of Beauvais, 92, 105n80
Hervé, treasurer of Saint-Martin of Tours, 2, 4, 175–76, 204, 218, 260–62
Higounet, Charles, 233
Hisembertus, monk of Fleury, 222
Horace, 208
Horologium stellare monasticum, 44
horses, 96, 113, 167, 237–39, 244, 248, 250
Hugh, abbot of Cluny, 33
Hugh Capet, king of West Francia, 61n14, 82, 260, 264; and Abbo, 16, 18–19, 76–81, 84, 86–87, 92, 123, 132, 138, 145–46, 148–49, 161–62, 171–73, 263; and archbishopric of Reims, 18, 92, 94–96, 98, 102–4, 108–9, 113, 119–20, 123–24, 145, 148, 154n13, 157–60, 163–65, 172, 191, 263; and bishops, 72–73, 86–87, 89–92, 102–5, 107, 123, 126, 132–33, 136, 138, 145, 147, 149, 156n18, 172, 191, 264; and Carolingians, 18, 73, 78, 84, 95–100, 102, 109; charters, 55, 73–74, 75, 77,

Hugh Capet (cont.)
  90, 146–47, 149, 166; and counts of Anjou, 174; and counts of Blois, 148, 174; duke of the Franks, 73; dynastic strategy, 16, 77; election and coronation, 15–16, 73, 78, 83–84, 92, 96–97, 263; and monasteries, 73, 76–80, 84, 89–92, 145, 147–49, 153, 166, 263; and Ottonians, 61n14; and papacy, 11, 102, 112–13, 158, 163–65, 172; royal power, 105, 113, 124, 147
Hugh of Aquitaine, 44
Hugh the Great, duke of the Franks, 78, 83, 90–91, 181–82
Humbold, petitioner to the pope, 203
Huntingdon, 67

Ildegard, 27–29, 203
Ile-de-France, 16, 83, 148
Ile de la Cité, 129
Ingelheim, Council of, 167n53, 169n63
Ireland, 39, 65
Isembardus, monk of Fleury, 222
Isle River, 240
Italy, 48n88, 153, 155n17, 169–71, 176, 180, 182, 189, 197–98, 200–202, 211, 218
Ivo of Chartres, 34n37

Jarrow, monastery. See Wearmouth-Jarrow
Jean, master of school of Auxerre, 106–7
Jerome, St., 53, 194
Jerusalem, 101n69, 104n77, 218
John, monk of Saints Bonifacius and Alexius, 158
John of Salerno, 257
John Philagathus, 179
John VIII, pope, 166, 180–81, 200
John XII, pope, 114
John XIV, pope, 114
John XV, pope, 113–14, 123, 126, 154n13, 156, 159–60, 166, 167n53, 168–70, 197–98, 265

John XVI, antipope. See John Philagathus
John XVIII, pope, 15
Josephus Scottus, Carolingian poet, 199n25
Julius Caesar, 135

knights, 26, 34n37
Koziol, Geoffrey, 118–20

law. See canon law; customary law; divine law; Roman law
La Réole, priory of Fleury, 85–86, 238, 243–44, 251, 159; charters, 28, 31n29, 31n29, 41n65, 234n7, 235; cult of Abbo, 5–6, 8, 255, 259–60; death of Abbo 2, 4, 5, 248–49, 258; Franks, 242–43, 247; Gascons, 242–43, 247; location, 41, 85–86, 232–34, 237, 240–43, 159; monastic discipline, 5–6, 41, 86, 232, 234–37, 244, 246, 250–51, 255, 258–59, 266–67
Laetus, father of Abbo, 25, 28, 30, 31
Laetus, monk of Saint-Mesmin, 30
Lantfred, monk of Fleury, 45
Laon, 38–39, 98–99, 69n101, 102; bishops of Laon, 39, 91, 105n82; royal court, 77
lay abbots, 89, 204
lay advocates of monasteries, 146, 236
Leclercq, Jean, 257
LeGoff, Jacques, 12, 137
Lemarignier, Jean-François, 11–12, 21–22, 223n98
Leo, abbot and papal legate, 156–61, 163–66, 167n53, 168–71, 177–79, 183, 185–86, 195
Leo VII, pope, 90, 166, 180–82
Leodebodus, abbot of Saint-Aignan of Orléans, 85
leper, cure of, 32, 256
Lérins, monastery: 153
Letald, monk of Micy, 45, 140n43, 141, 145n55
Levitan, William, 227–28
liberal arts, 44–46, 52, 72

Liège: bishops of, 157
Limoges, 30, 45, 238
Lincoln, 67
logic. *See* dialectic
Loire River, 1, 14, 19, 38, 41, 61n14, 69, 78, 84–86, 126, 153, 203, 204n40, 209, 212–13, 217, 228, 234, 238, 243
London BL Add 10972, 14–15
Lorraine, 97, 157, 159
Lot, Ferdinand, 11, 77, 106, 109, 155, 184
Lothar, king of West Francia, 25n6, 37, 40, 55, 58, 73, 94, 97, 108, 181
Lotharingia, 53, 55, 117
Louis, son of Charles of Lorraine, 172n74
Louis the Pious, king and emperor, 25n6, 29n20, 70, 181, 242
Louis IV, Carolingian king, 192
Louis V, king of West Francia, 15, 55, 73, 80n83, 83, 94, 97
Lyon, 105

Mabbo, bishop of Saint-Pol-de-Léon, 38
Mâcon, 105n82, 187n132
Magenard, monk of Saint-Père of Chartres, 213–15, 217
magic, 141, 256n8
Mainz, 54, 168
Maiolus, St., abbot of Cluny, 33, 59, 77n74, 151–53, 167, 223, 257
Marcian, emperor, 136
Marmoutier, monastery, 88–89, 153, 204–5, 207–10, 215, 217, 266
marriage, 20, 24, 25n6, 26, 97, 126, 172–78, 183, 186–88, 190–93, 196–97, 204, 216–17, 225, 261, 264
Martianus Capella, 219
Martin of Tours, St.: feast of, 127, 204, 240, 244; shrine in Tours, 169n66, 174
martyrology, 4, 259, 262
mathematics, 47–48, 151, 254. *See also* arithmetic; geometry
Maurus, St., 73, 169n66

Melun, 146, 148, 150
Merovingians, 17, 90
Metz, 39
Meuse River, 39, 156; Gascon stream named for, 242
Micy. *See* Saint-Mesmin
Milanus, monk of Fleury, 45
millenarianism. *See* apocalypticism
Milo, bishop of Macon, 98n59, 105
Moehs, Teta E., 201
Momolus, St., 234n6
monophysite heresy, 142
monarchy, 12, 13, 17–19, 22, 26, 72, 75, 77, 83, 89n28, 102, 116, 119, 125n1, 137–38, 151, 172, 191, 193, 264, 268
monasticism: discipline, 14, 60, 80, 231, 232, 244; disputes, 6, 49, 244–45, 253, 266; reform, 4, 17, 19, 21–22, 23, 38, 56, 60, 63–64, 70, 71, 86–88, 92, 95, 125–26, 151–53, 155–56, 167, 181, 185, 188, 225, 226, 253–55, 257, 268; rights 2, 4, 11, 14–16, 124, 126, 151, 172, 224–25, 230, 236; rule, 2, 19, 36, 214, 264–65; virtues, 4, 57, 152n6, 253, 257, 262. *See also monasteries by name*
Monte Cassino, monastery, 1, 182
Monte Sant-Angelo, 218
Month and Catholic Review, 8
Morini, 64n23
Moselle River: Gascon stream named for, 242
Mostert, Marco, 13, 19, 50, 74, 137–38, 141n48, 161
Moulins, 223
Mouzon: Council of (995), 156–57, 159, 161n34, 163; monastery, 60, 156–57
Münster: bishops of, 156–57
music, 46, 48, 51, 56, 61, 67, 221, 266

Nanteuil, monastery, 240
Narbonne, 207n53
Nene River, 68
nobility, 26–27, 30–31, 33, 34, 82, 86, 87–89, 108, 119

Normans: conquest of England, 65; invasions of Francia, 234
Notker, bishop of Liège, 159
Notre-Dame, church of Fleury, 1, 40, 42
Nouaillé, 62n15, 221
Noyon: bishops of, 92, 105n82. *See also bishops by name*

oaths, 14n35, 99–102, 104, 108–9, 113, 123, 140n43
Occitan, 243
Oda, bishop of Ramsbury and archbishop of Canterbury, 39, 63
Oddo, monk of Fleury, 222
Odilo, St., abbot of Cluny, 2, 33, 153, 223, 239, 251
Odo, bishop of Chartres, 129, 140, 150
Odo, bishop of Senlis, 105n80
Odo I, count of Blois and Chartres, 146–48, 153n11, 173, 213
Odo II, count of Blois, 210n58
Odo, king of West Francia, 83
Odo, St., abbot of Cluny, 90, 152, 181–82, 257
Odolric of Saint-Martial of Limoges, 45
1000. *See* millennium
ordeal, 206–7, 209
Oriolus, 249
Orléanais. *See* Orléans
Orléans, 24, 27, 29, 31–32, 40, 46, 62, 66–67, 69, 72–73, 78, 85–86, 89–90, 95, 105n82, 123, 133, 136n31, 148, 168, 215, 221; bishops of, 7, 73, 87–89, 105, 107, 128, 145n55, 151, 182n112, 215. *See also individual bishops of Orléans by name*
Osgar, monk, 39
Oswald, archbishop of York, 39, 63, 68, 71, 75, 81, 257
Otto I, Holy Roman Emperor, 48
Otto III, Holy Roman Emperor, 62, 170, 176, 178, 190, 198–201, 211, 226, 228–29

Ottonians, 97, 156, 169, 201, 254
Ourliac, Paul, 233
Oylbold, abbot of Fleury, 6, 15, 26n10, 41, 58, 61–64, 70, 72–78, 81, 86, 93, 235, 265–66

pallium, 186, 188, 190, 193, 195, 263
papacy: and Abbo, 15, 20, 22, 151, 156, 166, 169, 171, 178–79, 183n119, 188, 194–95, 197, 202, 223, 253–54, 265; and bishops, 123, 155, 169, 183; and Capetians, 11, 161, 155, 172, 174, 177, 183, 186, 188, 191, 193, 196–97, 212; criticized, 114–15, 155, 164, 198; and Italian politics, 155n17, 164–65, 168, 170, 179, 190, 197–98, 211; and monasteries, 22, 156, 166–67, 182, 185, 187, 192; and Ottonians, 190, 202, 211, 254; papal prerogatives, 22, 106, 114–15, 122, 124, 136n32, 155–56, 167, 159, 162, 164–65, 171, 184–85, 194–95, 197–98, 211–12, 226, 230, 253. *See also popes by name*
Paray-le-Monial, monastery, 153
Pardiac, Jean-Baptiste, 8–9, 260
Paris, 19, 45–46, 52–55, 58, 129, 131–33, 153, 169n66; bishops, 91
patronage of religious institutions, 16–17, 20, 24, 28, 32, 84, 91, 123, 148, 151, 260, 265
Paul Aurelian, St.: relics, 38
Pavia, Council of (997), 174, 177–78, 191, 192n6
Pepin I, king of the Franks, 87n16, 166, 203
Périgueux, 238
Perrecy-les-Forges, priory of Fleury, 86
Peter, candidate for *presul* of Tours, 174
Peterborough Abbey, 68
Pfister, Christian, 11
pilgrimage, 6, 47, 101n69, 104n77, 167, 169, 171, 218–19, 238, 255
Pithiviers, 146
Plantagenets, 259
Plato, 160

Pliny: *Natural History,* 50n97
poetry, 48, 93, 198–99, 218, 222–23, 226–29, 254
Poitiers, 2, 27, 31, 32, 85, 145, 238–40
Poitou. *See* Poitiers
Porfyrius, Publilius Optantianus, 198–99, 226–29
Porphyry of Tyre, 48
principalities, 20–21, 105n82
Priscan, grammarian, 43
prosopography, 29
pseudo-Isidorian decretals, 117
Pyrenees, 234n8, 242

Raby, F. J. E., 227
Radulf, king of West Francia, 83
Ragenfred, bishop of Chartres, 38
Ramsbury, 63n17
Ramsey, 63, 66–69, 72, 75, 142, 265
Raoul, king of West Francia. *See* Radulf
Ratbold, bishop of Noyon, 92, 105n80, 117
Raynerius, in household of Arnulf of Reims, 116
Regino of Prüm, 225n103
Regularis Concordia, 71
Reims, 85, 118; archbishops of, 60, 84, 89, 91–93, 95–96, 98, 102–5, 107, 123–24, 156, 163, 171–72, 176–78, 186, 188, 190–93, 196, 211, 263; capture, 18, 95, 102, 104, 107, 109–10, 113, 122, 157–58, 177; Council of Saint-Remi (995), 158–60, 161n35, 163, 165n47, 167; monasteries, 59, 89, 100; school, 45–46, 48–50, 59–62, 92, 95–96, 100, 106. *See also archbishops by name*
Remigius, St.: feast of, 61
Rémois. *See* Reims
Renard, abbot of Saint-Pierre-le-Vif, 106
renovatio imperii Romanorum, 201
rhetoric, 45–46, 48, 62, 72
Ri, unidentified monk of Fleury, 202n33

Richard, abbot of Fleury, 37, 40–43, 45, 53–54, 62, 86, 218n77, 235
Richard I, the Lionhearted, king of England, 259
Riché, Pierre, 10, 45, 254
Richer of Reims, 45, 47, 96, 103–4, 112, 121
Riculf, English monk, 64
roads. *See* travel
Robert, abbot of Micy and of Saint-Florent of Saumur, 215–17
Robert I, the Strong, king of West Francia, 26, 83–84
Robert II, the Pious, king of West Francia: and Abbo, 7, 11, 18–20, 81, 132n19, 133, 138, 145–46, 162, 173, 176–78, 193, 263; biography by Helgaud of Fleury, 91, 219, 264; and bishops, 99, 119–20, 124, 132, 138, 145, 153–54, 157, 177, 186, 191–95, 212, 264; and charters, 147; co-ruler with Hugh Capet, 16, 84, 90; counts of Anjou, 174, 176, 187n31, 193–94, 215, 217, 261–62; and counts of Blois, 173–74, 204, 209, 215–17, 261–62; and Gauzlin, 6, 221n91, 260–61; independent reign, 20, 172, 221, 264; marriages, 74n57, 125, 172–74, 177–78, 186, 188n34, 191–93, 215–17, 261–62, 264; and monasteries, 81, 146, 209, 260–61, 264; and papacy, 158, 160, 165, 174, 177–78, 186, 190–92, 195; royal power, 172, 239
Robert, lord of Buzaçais: 176
Robertians, 17, 83–84, 90, 97
Rodulfus Glaber, 173n76
Romald, in charters of Fleury, 41
Roman Empire, 199
Roman law, 161n34, 233
Roman Republic, 135
Rome, 48, 85, 201; Abbo's travels to, 167–70, 177, 186–87, 189–90, 197, 203, 223, 231; attempted council, 154; Council of (998), 192; politics, 1642–65, 168, 177–79, 190, 197–98, 201. *See also* papacy

Romulf of Sens, abbot, 106–7
Rosemberga, wife of Viscount Amalguin, 26, 237, 250
royal court, 37, 76–77, 132, 145, 171, 175
Rozala Suzanna, wife of Robert the Pious, 74n57, 125, 154, 172
Rule of St. Benedict, 34, 36, 44, 57, 64, 70, 76, 80n82, 86n118, 149, 182, 214n67, 244–45, 265–66

Saint-Aignan, monastery, 85
Saint-Basle, Council of, 6, 18, 49, 136–38, 141, 148, 151, 154–57, 168, 179, 190–91, 206, 211, 212, 214; location, 103–4, 120; papal response, 159–66, 170, 184; summary, 103–24
Saint-Bénigne, monastery, 89
Saint-Benoît-de-Retour, priory of Fleury in Orléans, 85
Saint-Benoît-du-Sault, monastery, 32, 239
Saint-Benoît-sur-Loire, modern monastery, 9, 260. See also Fleury
Saint-Bertin, monastery, 38
Saint-Crépin, monastery, 145
Saint-Cyprien, monastery, 27, 31, 239
Saint-Denis, Council of, 18–19, 49, 126n4, 129–41, 144–45, 150–51, 153–55, 162, 214, 223–24, 267
Saint-Denis, monastery, 129, 132–33
Saint-Evre, monastery, 38
Saint-Florent, monastery, 216
Saint-Gérald, monastery, 47
Saint-Germaine, monastery, 89
Saint-Hillaire, monastery, 31n29
Saint-Jean of Angély, monastery, 31n29
Saint-Julien, monastery, 59, 88–89, 153, 204, 223
Saint-Maixent, monastery, 31n29
Saint-Martial, monastery, 30, 45
Saint-Martin, monastery, 4, 88–89, 174–75, 204, 238, 261–62, 266; dean, 204; treasurer, 2, 174–75, 204, 218, 260–61
Saint-Mesmin, monastery, 15, 30, 51, 62n15, 76n68, 93n41, 140n43, 213, 215–17, 220–21, 266
Saintonge, 31
Saint-Père, monastery, 38, 213–14, 217
Saint-Pierre, church of Fleury, 33, 35, 42
Saint-Pierre-le-Vif, monastery, 106
Saint-Remi, Council of (995). See Reims
Saint-Remi, monastery (Reims), 60, 89
Saint-Remi, monastery (Sens), 106
Saints Bonifacius and Alexius, monastery, 169n66
Saint-Thierry, monastery, 60
Saint-Vincent, monastery, 38–39
Sanche Guillaume, duke of the Gascons, 235
Santi Alessio e Bonifacio. See Saints Bonifacius and Alexius
Saracens, 167–68
Saumur, 216
Scotland, 39
Seguin, archbishop of Sens, 60, 73, 78, 81, 92, 98n59, 105–7, 109, 110n106, 116, 124, 129, 131, 140–41, 150, 154
Senlis: bishops of, 92, 105n82; Council of, 109, 111. See also bishops by name
Sens, 106; archbishops of, 34n37, 91, 105n82, 107, 187. See also archbishops by name
simony, 133n22, 139, 157, 218
Slavs, 200–201
social class, 23–26, 31, 33–34, 56–57
Soissons: bishops of, 91, 105n82. See also bishops by name
Solignac, monastery, 45, 101n69, 218
Souvigny, 233
Spain, 47, 242–43
Spoleto, 179–80, 184, 187, 189, 198, 203
Squirs, original name of La Réole, 234
Stubbs, William, 227
Sully, 40
syllogisms, 49–50, 229
Sylvester II, pope. See Gerbert of Aurillac

synods. *See* councils
Syrus, monk of Cluny, 152

Tacitus, 247
technopaegnia, 198. *See also* acrostics
Teotard, husband of Ermengard, 28
Teotilo, archbishop of Tours, 89
Terence, 160
Theodulf of Orléans, 199, 226–28
Theophanu, wife of Otto III, 61n14, 93
Thibault, count of Chartres, 213–15
Thierry of Amorbach, 44n75, 45, 60
Thierry of Fleury. *See* Thierry of Amorbach
Thomson, Ron, 13
Thorney Abbey, 68
tironian notes, 80n83
tithes, 19, 49, 130–34, 139, 141, 143, 150, 224–25, 267
Toledo, Council of (656), 117
Toul, 38
Touraine. *See* Tours
Tours, 2, 4, 59, 78n75, 85, 88–89, 127, 140, 153, 176, 183, 203–4, 214, 218, 223–24, 238–40, 256, 260–61; archbishops of, 154, 174–75, 210, 218. *See also archbishops by name*
travel, 37–38, 64–66, 167, 178, 235, 237–41
treason, 108, 112, 119, 122, 190
Trier, archbishopric, 94, 157
Trinity, 141–43
tripartite society, 12–13, 19, 137–39, 189

usurper abbot of Fleury: 59–62, 73, 77–79, 177, 266

Valois: counts of, 196–87. *See also counts by name*
Van der Vyver, A., 13, 50
Vatican II, 260
Verberie, 37

Verdun: bishops of, 93, 157
Vergil, 160, 199
Verzy. *See* Saint-Basle
Vexin: counts of, 196–97. *See also counts by name*
vicaria, 146
Victorinus, 48
Vikings, 16, 64n23, 83. *See also* Normans
Vita Ludovici, 234n8
Vitalis, monk of Fleury, 45, 222, 229n117, 230

Walter, bishop of Autun, 105n80, 109
Walter, count of Amiens, Vexin, and Valois, 145
Walter of Gâtinais, 196–97
Walter, treasurer of Saint-Martin of Tours, 174
Wasconia, 234n8, 242–43. *See also* Basques; Gascony
Waulsort, monastery, 39
Wearmouth-Jarrow, monastery, 57
West Francia, 1n1
Westbury-on-Trym, monastery, 39, 63
Whittlesey Mere, 67
Wilderod, bishop of Strasbourg, 159
Willelmus, son of Oriolus, 249
William, duke of Aquitaine, 239–40
William, duke of Normandy, 65
William, monk of Fleury or La Réole, 247
William Tailleferre, count of Toulouse, 218
Winchester, 71n46, 259
Winterbottom, Michael, 14
Wissant, 64
women, 23–24, 26, 97, 101, 137n35, 203, 225n102, 233n3, 245–47, 249, 258–59
Wulfald, abbot of Fleury and bishop of Chartres, 36–40

Yèvre, *castrum* and villa, 88, 129, 139, 146–50

www.ingramcontent.com/pod-product-compliance
Lightning Source LLC
Chambersburg PA
CBHW031407290426
44110CB00011B/298